THE INVESTMENT FRONTIER

THE INVESTMENT FRONTIER

*New York Businessmen
and the Economic Development
of the Old Northwest*

JOHN DENIS HAEGER

State University of New York Press
ALBANY

Published by
State University of New York Press, Albany

© 1981 State University of New York

For information, address State University of New York
Press, State University Plaza, Albany, N.Y., 12246.

Library of Congress Cataloging in Publication Data
Haeger, John D.
  The investment frontier.

  Bibliography: p. 293
  Includes index.
  1. West (U.S.)—Economic conditions—19th century.
2. Investments—West (U.S.)—History—19th century.
3. Bronson, Arthur. 4. Butler, Charles, 1802-1897.
5. Capitalists and financiers—New York (State)—
History—19th century. 6 Capitalists and financiers—
West (U.S.)—History—19th century. I. Title.
HC107.A17H33   330.978'02   81-741
ISBN 0-87395-530-7   AACR2
ISBN 0-87395-531-5 (pbk.)

To Cecily

Contents

Illustrations and Tables

Preface

Too often historical literature has overemphasized the importance of geographic location, soil fertility, farmers' quick adaptation to surplus production, and the booster spirit of frontier entrepreneurs in explaining the economic development of the American West. Certainly each of the above factors, both alone and in concert, were important to economic expansion, but I contend that eastern capitalists, operating from the country's financial centers at New York City and Boston and from a score of smaller cities, provided the capital and financial expertise which were essential to frontier economic development and to the integration of the West into the nation's economy. In order to test these assumptions, this book analyzes the business careers of New York City financiers involved in the Old Northwest's urban and agricultural expansion during the frontier period from approximately 1830 to 1845.[1]

Three financiers serve as principal examples: Isaac Bronson, Arthur Bronson, and Charles Butler. Isaac Bronson was the patriarch of a remarkable family which, in the early nineteenth century, was just taking its place among New York City's financial aristocracy. Isaac Bronson had accumulated a fortune through shrewd speculation in government securities and land purchases in western New York. More important, he articulated a conservative philosophy of banking and economic development which provided a theoretical base for the family's business operations, particularly those of his son, Arthur Bronson, who oversaw the family's western land interests in the 1830s. Charles Butler, on the other hand, was born into a political family. His older brother, Benjamin, was a close friend of Martin Van Buren, and consequently Charles Butler also associated with members of Van Buren's political circle. As a young man in the 1820s, Butler practiced law on the frontier of western New York

State. Even though he eventually worked his way into the ranks of New York City's economic and social elite, his years on the frontier imbued him with the booster spirit and with an investment mentality different from that of his close friend and frequent business partner, Arthur Bronson.

The New Yorkers exerted their greatest influence on the West of the 1830s, an area usually designated as the Old Northwest, encompassing the modern day states of Ohio, Michigan, Illinois, Indiana, and Wisconsin. From the end of the War of 1812 until 1832, this region was a curious blend of civilization and wilderness. At one extreme, southern Ohio was settled and possessed a relatively balanced economy. To a lesser extent, this was also true of southern Illinois and Indiana. But with the exception of the outpost of Detroit, Michigan was still a wilderness as were northern Illinois and Wisconsin. Chicago and Milwaukee were only meeting places for the occasional exchange of furs between Indians and whites. Yet settlement slowly pushed westward. The Erie Canal opened the agricultural hinterland of western New York by 1825 and encouraged, within a few years, the movement of people further West by lake steamboats or over barely passable roads linking Buffalo with Cleveland and Detroit. By 1830, the pace of economic change had increased substantially. The southern cotton trade and the continued growth of agricultural surpluses in the East yielded good profits which stimulated further urban and agricultural development along the East Coast and in the interior, particularly in the New York City region. These developments led eastern businessmen to establish banks and trusts companies in order to create more credit and to support new investments. Meanwhile eastern capitalists, farmers, and urban dwellers were driven further West in the search for new opportunities. All these groups, therefore, participated in one of America's most spectacular booms in the years from 1832 to 1837.

During this economic boom, the entire region bordering the Great Lakes was transformed. Chicago grew from a fur trade village and military post of 250 in 1832 to a city of 4,470 citizens with numerous financial, educational, and religious institutions in 1840.[2] Nearly every state embarked on railroad and canal projects to link the surplus-producing agricultural hinterlands with burgeoning cities and outside markets. The boom came to an abrupt halt in 1838, though, and the entire region was plunged into a long and difficult depression. When the Old Northwest emerged from the depression in the mid-1840s, its financial leaders were sobered by the realities of economic loss, but they possessed a growing population, healthy markets for agricultural products, effective transportation links with the East and South, and stable urban centers such as Chicago, Milwaukee, and Detroit. By 1845, then, the Old Northwest had clearly passed through the frontier stage.

A number of problems confront the historian attempting to assess the eastern financier's impact on the West. The economy of the Jacksonian era was unorganized, and individuals, rather than institutions, often directed the movement of funds into various enterprises. As a result, historians lack statistical data on the movement of capital which would reveal the easterners' total investments in western banks, agricultural lands and city lots. Economic historians therefore must depend on the manuscript records of individual entrepreneurs in order to build generalizations.[3] Eastern businessmen of this period further complicated the historian's task because they preferred anonymity to publicity when conducting economic exchanges and particularly when influencing governmental and financial institutions. Eastern capitalists adopted a variety of strategies for concealing their presence in the West. Original land entries were made by their western agents to avoid charges of absentee ownership and onerous tax levies. Stock subscriptions to western banks and transportation companies as well as expenditures for improvements to their land were arranged through western citizens for similar reasons. They lobbied in territorial, state, and national legislative bodies for favorable laws relating to public lands and commerce, usually through subtle pressure on a sympathetic senator or representative.

Because the Bronsons and Charles Butler were hidden from public view, historical studies accorded more attention to their western agents, such as Lucius Lyon, Micajah T. Williams, and Charles Trowbridge.[4] In a 1969 article on land speculation in the Wisconsin Territory, for example, Paul Gates acknowledged that Arthur Bronson had been the largest single land purchaser in 1835 and 1836, yet Gates did not investigate Bronson's influence on the territory. Instead he commented that

> Too much emphasis should not be placed upon eastern capital investments in western land. One of the outstanding facts about the western land business is that westerners, men of initiative, imagination, and shrewdness, and perhaps some capital, early took the lead in buying and selling lands, representing others in the management of their property, laying out towns, subdividing property, renting town lots, houses, farms and exploiting mineral lands.[5]

Conceptual approaches to frontier history also hindered an accurate appraisal of the eastern financier's influence. Beginning with Frederick Jackson Turner's essay "The Significance of the Frontier in American History," historical scholarship concentrated on the farmer and his role in agricultural expansion.[6] Eastern capitalists usually entered the story as villians whose greed prevented farmers from securing their rightful claims to America's landed wealth. For years, historians, writing from a "western" perspective, reproduced the attitudes of frontier residents and stressed the deleterious effects of speculation on economic growth. They convinced themselves that land speculation was both unprincipled and unprofitable and that western economies had prospered in the hands of the untutored but idealistic pioneers. Eventually Allan and Margaret Bogue and later Robert Swierenga assembled sufficient quantitative data to prove that land speculation was not only profitable but also had contributed to the settlement of the West.[7] New research, then, challenged the old assumptions and opened the possibility of a reassessment of both the motives and the economic impact of eastern speculators. In a recent study of the historiography of American land history, Robert Swierenga concluded that "the Progressive school of land historiography, inspired by Turner, is now only a faint whisper . . . . For better or for worse, revisionism is now firmly entrenched . . . .[8]

Despite the revisionist work on land speculation, historians have not advanced any sweeping reinterpretation of the relationship between eastern capitalists and westward expansion. Part of the reason is that historians have been investigating new themes which unintentionally have pushed the eastern financier into the background. In 1959, for example, Richard C. Wade shifted our perspective on the westward movement when he challenged America's idealization of the country's rural character and the farmer's primary role in economic growth in his book *The Urban Frontier: The Rise of Western Cities, 1790-1830*. Wade demonstrated that cities had been in the forefront of expansion or, at the very least, had developed in conjunction with the adjacent countryside.[9] Deprived of the farmer as a cultural hero, historians rushed to create a new champion, the town dweller or "urban frontiersman" who trekked West to establish cities. He was the local promoter who pushed the virtues of his city by boosting its location, by chartering railroads, by establishing banks, and by importing the culture of the East. Daniel Drake of Cincinnati, William B. Ogden of Chicago, Byron Kilbourn of Milwaukee, and James Duane Doty of Green Bay were just a few of these new frontier heroes.[10]

The idea for this book actually emerged from my earlier studies on city promotion along Lake Michigan's western shore.[11] In every city under scrutiny, the western promoter was indeed an important figure, yet invariably he began his career as the agent for an eastern capitalist. There was always an eastern connection for the obvious reason that the city building required large amounts of capital. Towns depended upon outside money for their platting, the leveling of streets, and the construction of buildings. William B. Ogden, for example, often has been cited as the personification of the western promoter who, because of his skill and entrepreneurial daring, facilitated Chicago's emergence as a trade and transportation center. Yet historians curiously have neglected to investigate Ogden's ties to eastern capitalists which included Arthur Bronson and Charles Butler, Ogden's brother-in-law.[12]

In recent years, historians have completed more sophisticated methodological and theoretical studies of the nation's economy, studies which have made remarkable contributions to our knowledge of the antebellum economy. Yet these works also have undervalued entrepreneurial contributions to economic growth. Economic and geographic historians, for example, constructed elaborate models which measured the relative importance of different factors such as transportation innovations, interregional trade patterns, and location in facilitating the nation's and the West's development. These quantitative historians depended heavily on aggregate data; and, with the absence of collective biographies of business leaders, they were unable to measure the impact of eastern businessmen on the regional or national economy.[13]

Similarly, social historians have analyzed the internal structure of western towns in an effort to determine the most important factors in a city's economic growth. Robert Dykstra's brilliant study *The Cattle Towns* described the conflicts which divided local business communities as well as the inter-town competition which shaped the struggle for economic survival. Stuart Blumin's investigation of Kingston, New York, and Don Doyle's book on Jacksonville, Illinois, stressed the formation of a community ideology which sustained the town's common economic goals. Each of these studies, however, examined only a part of the town's history because each concentrated on local events and personalities[14] Yet western cities were not isolated geographic units struggling to survive against nature and the scarcity of leadership and capital. In fact, Chicago and Jacksonville in the 1830s were within the reach of New Yorkers who journeyed West in search of investments. Eastern financiers came West often, knew many towns and their local leadership, and established strong personal as well as financial ties. No western community's history, then, is really complete without some description of its relationship with nonresident capitalists and with the complex financial world beyond its boundaries.

Historians, of course, have studied the western town apart from its eastern connections and separated the analysis of land speculation from urban promotion in order to understand the complexities of the subject; yet this separation neglects important interrelationships between East and West and among the various economic activities. By analyzing the careers of individual eastern capitalists, this study is perhaps more broadly focused and in some ways closer to historical reality than more topically oriented works. Eastern financiers perceived neither geographic nor economic boundaries in their search for investments and profits;

indeed, diversification was the most salient characteristic of the Bronsons' and Butler's investments. Arthur Bronson, for example, invested in New York City banks, New York State iron works, Ohio banks, Chicago and Detroit real estate, and agricultural lands in the Wisconsin Territory, Illinois, Michigan, Ohio, and Indiana. He was simultaneously an urban promoter, land speculator, Wall Street banker, and manufacturer. The New Yorkers also realized that the security of their investments depended upon the actions of legislative bodies in various states and at the federal level. Consequently they lobbied for favorable laws relating to taxes, mortgages, banks, and public lands. Despite the diversification of their financial interests, the easterners, nevertheless, possessed an organic view of the nation's economy. They understood the linkages among land, banking, and urban investments in both the East and the West; and, at the same time, they considered the nation's economic welfare and individual profits to be interdependent goals of their business ventures.

This book, therefore, has three major purposes. The most basic goal is to demonstrate the eastern capitalists' effect on the economic development of the West. Yet I have defined this goal broadly in order to include the New Yorkers' investments in farm lands, town lots, banks, and transportation improvements as well as to detail their influence on western businessmen and institutions. At the same time, several chapters explore their political and economic affairs on the East Coast since these matters dramatically affected the scope of their western investments. My second purpose is to show that historians' generalizations about nonresident investors or eastern speculators assume a common type and business method when, in fact, easterners possessed varying economic goals and utilized different business strategies. In particular, I distinguish between the promoter, as typified by Charles Butler, and the conservative speculator, typified by Arthur Bronson. Finally I have assumed a philosophical stance in writing economic history: individuals affected the pace and course of American economic development. The central characters in this book were not responsible for any wrenching change in the economic affairs of the nation, yet their business careers had a substantial effect upon many western towns, banking institutions and state and federal laws. For this reason alone, their story deserves to be told. Yet, as I attempt to show in the book's conclusion, their careers were not unique but rather exemplified common patterns of business activity. The Bronsons, Charles Butler, and countless other eastern financiers, therefore, were important factors in directing the nation's economy in the early nineteenth century.[15]

Acknowledgments

This book has resulted from the efforts of many people. The staffs of historical libraries across the country responded to my inquiries, tracked down obscure references, and made every effort to facilitate my research into their manuscript collections on my hurried summer visits. A partial list of these institutions includes the: Library of Congress; New York Historical Society; New York Public Library; Columbia University Library; New York State Library; Albany Institute of History and Art; Baker Library, Harvard University; Bridgeport, Connecticut, Public Library; Connecticut State Library; Western Reserve Historical Society; Ohio Historical Society; Bentley Historical Library, Michigan Historical Collections; William L. Clements Library, University of Michigan; Chicago Historical Society; Newberry Library; State Historical Society of Wisconsin; Illinois State Historical Library; Huntington Library; and the Park Library, Central Michigan University.

Several people and institutions merit special mention: Archie Motley of the Chicago Historical Society suggested many valuable research leads; the Baker Library at Harvard University granted me a Kress Fellowship to investigate the history of trust companies; John Cumming and William Miles of the Clarke Historical Library at Central Michigan University helped in the collection of primary sources and, over many years, shared in my enthusiasm for regional history; the Central Michigan University Creative Endeavors Committee provided funds for my frequent research trips and the University's Research Professor Program awarded me a semester's leave of absence to complete the manuscript's final draft; and Richard Williams, Secretary of the Economic History Association, has allowed me to use material in Chapters 1 and 2 which originally appeared in the *Journal of Economic History:* 39 (March 1979): 259-273.

This book also benefited from the comments and criticisms of others. The late Fritz Redlich urged me to explore the role of trust companies. Bronson Griscom entrusted me with his family's manuscript records, thereby enlarging the scope of this work. Robert Gallman offered valuable criticism of my research on antebellum banking. Several colleagues at Central Michigan University, especially David Macleod and Dennis Thavenet, read selected chapters and suggested substantive and editorial changes. Cecily Dickinson Haeger read and reread every chapter and her considerable editorial skils are reflected on nearly every page. For this, and many more important reasons, this book is dedicated to her.

1. The Bronson Family

Few historical studies have described the backgrounds of eastern capitalists who invested in the Old Northwest during the 1830s. Historians, therefore, know very little about the financier's business philosophies and the broader economic goals which determined their techniques of investment. The purpose of this chapter is to provide an introduction to the Bronson family, which until recently was almost unknown to historians despite an extensive collection of family papers at the New York Public Library. Like many families of great wealth, the Bronsons were a talented group who shared a variety of business interests. Isaac Bronson dominates this chapter because he built the family's original fortune through careful land investments and an extensive mortgage loan business in western New York. This success quickly pushed him into the ranks of New York City's financial aristocracy. At the same time, Isaac Bronson became an important theorist and practitioner of commercial banking, a philosophy which he imparted to his son, Arthur. The latter part of this chapter describes the early career of Arthur Bronson since he assumed the task of directing the family's business interests in the 1830s, particularly its investments in western lands. Despite their active business careers, however, both Isaac and Arthur Bronson were economic conservatives who were often at odds with the expansionist economic philosophy of the era.

After nearly 100 years in America as moderately successful farmers, the Bronson family, led by Isaac Bronson, moved into the restricted world of great wealth in less than a generation. Isaac Bronson was born in 1760 in Middlebury, Connecticut, but he left farm life in order to study medicine. During the Revolutionary War, he served as a junior surgeon in a Connecticut regiment commanded by Colonel Elisha Sheldon. When Ameri-

1

Fig. 1. Portrait of Isaac Bronson by John Trumbull (Courtesy of Mrs. Bronson Griscom)

can merchants expanded their trade routes after the war, Bronson made several European voyages and at least one trip to the Far East for the purpose of trade.[1] After some success in these ventures, Bronson settled for a short period in Philadelphia, and there he speculated in the buying and selling of national and state securities. In 1793, he moved to New York City where he continued stock trading. Again his efforts met with success. An indicator of Bronson's increasing wealth was his purchase of a summer home near Fairfield, Connecticut, in 1796.[2] At that time, he abandoned speculation in government securities and placed his surplus funds in more conservative investments such as land mortgages and bank stock. The New Yorker was equally adept in these endeavors, and from 1800 until his death in 1838, he was one of New York City's wealthiest citizens.

Isaac Bronson moved to the top of the economic and social ladder in a single generation, a pattern uncharacteristic of the nineteenth century. Edward Pessen recently estimated the size of Bronson's fortune in 1828 at $250,000 placing him among the ten wealthiest New Yorkers. In 1845, his estate, then administered by his son, was one of fifty-five listed in a category of over $250,000. Moses Beach, in his famous pamphlet on New York City's aristocracy, guessed that the Bronson estate was worth $1,500,000. In addition, Beach separately listed the holdings of Bronson's two sons, Arthur and Frederic, at $500,000 and $250,000 respectively.[3] These are acceptable estimates based on tax assessments in New York City, but they do not consider the fact that the Bronson family owned land throughout the Old Northwest, the South, and the East. They also held stock in several banks, transportation companies, and public improvement companies. Moreover, any number of projects were listed under the names of other family members, thus frustrating any accurate calculation of the actual size of their fortune. By the 1820s, though, Isaac Bronson had provided his children with a solid entree into the economic and social aristocracy of nineteenth century America. Once they became members of the financial elite, Isaac's children proved very adept at maintaining that position.

The Bronson family epitomized the lifestyle of the American aristocracy. Isaac Bronson married Anna Olcott of Stafford, Connecticut, and they had ten children. The financier instilled within each child a regard for the necessity of a good education and a proper marriage. Befitting their social position, the Bronson children were educated at private academies typical of the New England countryside in the early nineteenth century.[4] Academy training was followed by any number of alternatives. Isaac's third son, Frederic, went on to college, graduating from Harvard in 1824 and becoming a lawyer. Oliver Bronson, the first son, was sent to France to study medicine; and Arthur apparently shunned higher education and entered business with his father.[5]

The marriages of Isaac Bronson's children also characterized the family's aristocratic lifestyle as each child sought a partner from a comparable social and economic postion. For example, James B. Murray, who married Isaac's eldest daughter, Maria, in 1814, came from a similar background. His father, John Murray, emigrated to the colonies from Norfolk, England, and settled in Providence, Rhode Island, where he worked for merchants involved in overseas trade. Later he established his own mercantile houses in Alexandria, Virginia, and New York City, but he eventually closed the Virginia firm and permanently settled in New York City. As the son of a wealthy merchant, James Murray attended select schools. After a severe illness disrupted his plans to attend college, he entered his father's counting house and embarked on a career as a merchant capitalist.[6] When James Murray married Maria Bronson, he already possessed substantial wealth and political influence. As a full partner in his father's business, he had come to know James Madison, James Monroe, and Martin Van Buren. In the 1820s, Murray withdrew from mercantile activities and concentrated on land and bank investments. For a brief period in the 1830s, he was the president of the Morris Canal and Banking Company, an important agency in financing western internal improvements.[7] Along with his personal investments, Murray was also a frequent partner in the business operations of the Bronson family. His marriage to Maria Bronson, then, had joined two families in the pursuit of economic power.

Other Bronson children followed similar marriage patterns. Caroline Bronson married Dr. Marinus Willett of New York City, son of a famous New York merchant and former mayor of the city. Frederic Bronson married Charlotte Brinckerhoff of an equally rich and prestigious family. This wedding also brought together the landed interests of the Bronson and Robert Troup families. Robert Troup had been an agent of the Pulteney Estates in western New York in the late eighteenth and early nineteenth century. After his death, his granddaughter Charlotte Brinckerhoff Bronson was one of two surviving heirs. By the late 1840s, Frederic Bronson administered most of the remaining Troup estate. Arthur Bronson was the only child who supposedly married below his class. According to gossip at the time, Isaac Bronson was displeased by Arthur's marriage to Anna Eliza Bailey, the daughter of a former military officer and New York state politician.[8]

Isaac Bronson's political connections were extensive. He knew and advised important officials during the early nineteenth century including Oliver Wolcott and Alexander Hamilton. In the period before 1815, he moved in Federalist circles since their political influence was important to a New England businessman at the time. When the political winds shifted in the 1820s so did the political connections of the Bronson family. By the early 1830s, the Bronsons had access to top national and state Democratic officials. In New York State, for example, Isaac Bronson was related by marriage to Thomas Olcott, who was first the cashier and later president of the Mechanics and Farmers Bank of Albany, the financial arm of the Albany Regency, Martin Van Buren's political organization in New York State.[9] The family's business concerns, though, were above party identification. Despite their own conservative views, the Bronsons' interests in land, banking, and commerce necessitated their working with politicians of every hue on state and on national levels. Over the years, father and sons worked both sides of the political street.

The Bronsons also exhibited the trappings of the wealthy. Like other affluent New York City families, they had residences in New York City and in the country. In 1796, Isaac Bronson had purchased the home of Timothy Dwight, on Greenfield Hill, near Fairfield, Connecticut. Isaac and his sons divided their time between the country estate and New York City. As the years passed, it became a compound as other family members built homes there. Servants abounded, both white and black, as did a variety of workmen. The Bronsons' correspondence was filled with letters from laborers seeking instructions while the family was in New York City.[10] In the city, the Bronsons lived in the most fashionable neighborhoods. Isaac Bronson's residence was on lower Broadway where his neighbors included Nathaniel Prime and John Watts. His son, Arthur, lived further east on Broadway, in the premier neighborhood of the financial elite. Arthur and Frederic also had separate offices on Wall Street befitting entrepreneurs of their stature.[11]

Wealth also provided a variety of social amenities. Isaac Bronson and his wife had their portraits painted by John Trumbull, a close friend. Frederic regularly traveled to Europe for business and pleasure; in 1838, for example, he and his wife left on a honeymoon trip that lasted for eighteen months. Arthur apparently never undertook a European voyage, but he made regular trips to Florida and Avon, New York, both health resorts for the wealthy. Isaac Bronson once had a coat of arms emblazoned upon his carriage.[12] However, an occasional frivolous gesture, such as the coat of arms, should not detract from the essential seriousness of this family. They were extraordinarily hard workers, with little time for idle pursuits, still building a fortune scarcely a generation old.

Although Isaac Bronson seemed to be very aloof, taking few active roles in society other than those connected with business, his sons were more socially aware of the responsibilities of wealth. Arthur and Frederic moved in the smartest social circles and belonged to prestigious clubs, such as the Union Club. They contributed to charities and served on the boards of a number of social agencies. Arthur was on the board of directors of the American Society for the Diffusion of Useful Knowledge, and in 1843, he served with a municipal reform group in New York City. Throughout his life he regularly contibuted to the American Tract Society for the support of western missionaries.[13] The Bronson family, then, personified the economic elite of the early nineteenth century. They combined the much vaunted, but little understood, ethic of hard work with strict morality, viewing these qualities as the underpinning of a successful society. It is impossible to understand the rationale for their many business decisions without realizing that this code dominated their lives.

Isaac Bronson had attained his position of financial preeminence through his writings on banking theory, his management of the Bridgeport Bank, located in Bridgeport, Connecticut, near his summer home, and his land speculation and money lending in western New York. It is important to describe these activities in order for the reader to understand not only the economic theory that motivated Isaac but also to trace its influence on his son, Arthur, who later assumed responsibility for the family's finances.

At the end of the eighteenth century, Isaac Bronson entered a banking world in its formative stage. The colonial period had few banking institutions because of English restrictions, the shortage of capital, and the agricultural base of the economy. Nevertheless, colonial businessmen, taking advantage of the surplus of land, had organized land banks which treated land as money either to support currency issues or to finance improvements.[14] Merchants in coastal towns, on the other hand, provided credit for commercial exchanges through informal arrangements among themselves, and thus commercial banking institutions did not develop before the American Revolution. But the wildly inflated currencies, disrupted trade patterns, and increases in trade volume which characterized the late eighteenth century created a demand for financial intermediaries. The Bank of North America, established in 1781, was the prototype of later nineteenth–century commercial banks. It was a stock company which possessed enormous financial resources and which could provide the credit needs of merchants in a more complex financial world.[15]

Early nineteenth–century merchants and politicians moved cautiously in meeting the demand for new banks since banks appeared to them to be potentially dangerous to society's political and economic institutions. Possessed of a generalized fear of concentrated financial power, financiers and the public questioned the proper function of banks within an economic system: Should they merely facilitate the needs of existing merchants, or should they use their financial resources to stimulate new businesses? In this debate, Isaac Bronson represented the restrictive or conservative view that banks should provide credit for commercial transactions, issuing notes or bills to facilitate trade. He insisted that banks must be "sound" or liquid: that is, they must be able to pay their liabilities on short notice. To accomplish this goal, banks should lend funds only on short-term, often no longer than sixty days, and then on only the safest security—the actual goods in transit. When the trade goods exchanged hands, the transaction was completed and the bank's notes returned. This form of banking was conservative because it furnished credit to merchants for trade, but provided little help to those producing the goods. To the early merchant-bankers, a bank maintained its credit and reputation by its ability to redeem its notes on short notice. Commercial banking of this type came to represent the "soundness" tradition or the "real bills" doctrine.[16] In the early nineteenth century, Isaac Bronson's name was synonymous with this theory.[17]

Opponents of the "real bills" doctrine believed that banks should perform functions other than just providing credit for trade. Liberal financiers thought that banks should supply the necessary credit to undertake new enterprises in agriculture and manufacturing. In the nineteenth century, such bank loans were designated as "accommodation" loans to imply that the bank was encouraging an economic improvement for which there was uncertain security. Although accommodation loans met the financial requirements of a developing country, they were undeniably dangerous. If a manufacturing firm failed, a farm was unproductive, or a borrower died, a bank had limited resources to sustain such losses. Extensive accommodation loans, then, underwrote periods of rapid economic development, but they also threatened the stability of financial institutions and the economy as a whole.[18]

Even though Isaac Bronson was committed to a strict definition of a commercial bank, he, like most other conservative bankers, modified his principles over the years to answer the demands of an expanding economy. Bronson's progressive, yet slow, response to economic change was evident during his years at the Bridgeport Bank. He was the bank's leading stockholder; from 1806 to 1832 he served as a member of the board of directors and, for four years, as its president.[19] As president, Bronson oversaw the institution's general operations and policies, while leaving its day–to–day affairs to the cashier and the clerks. In the beginning, Bronson enforced the "real bills" doctrine. He saw the bank's role as one of provider of credit for local merchants, and he early adopted an inflexible rule that the bank would lend money—that is, issue bills—for sixty days with no renewals. The loan's security consisted of the trade goods.

All transactions, therefore, were on credit. Bronson believed that if the bank's paper returned every sixty days, the institution could never be overextended. Its profits derived from the charge on the use of the bank's paper.[20] The Bridgeport Bank, therefore, existed for two reasons—to earn a moderate profit for the stockholders and to provide credit for merchants.

Bronson further demonstrated his conservatism when he devised policies for the use of the bank's capital, that is, the specie or securities deposited as payment for bank stock. Many banks routinely used their capital for accommodation loans to businessmen. Bronson, however, believed that such practices were inflationary and risked the bank's resources in speculative enterprises. More important, he feared that the widespread misuse of banking capital would threaten the financing of the nation's trade. Consequently, he argued that a bank should operate only on credit, the issuing of notes, and refrain from capital investments to spur economic development. Bronson was actually one of the first bankers to make a clear distinction between a bank's capital and its credit. In 1816, he took the first step toward implementing this idea when he returned half of the bank's capital to its owners to avoid any further investment operations.[21]

Bronson had resisted the idea of banks assuming investment functions partly because he believed that wealthy financiers met the capital needs of manufacturing and agriculture through their own independent investments. According to Isaac Bronson, this was a far better arrangement because individual financiers could sustain losses on risk-taking ventures without affecting other areas of the economy such as trade. Writing some years later, Arthur Bronson summarized his father's view on the role of capital in a commercial bank: "The possession of capital was of no use except to inspire confidence. This being once fully established . . . the latter was found a great inconvenience—a source of real annoyance, because its investment involved a responsibility which it was thought could be discharged with equal safety and greater advantage by the stockholders, in their individual capacities, to whom it belonged, and through whom it would find its way into the hands of the *producing classes.*"[22]

Economic changes forced Isaac Bronson to modify this theory, which was more appropriate to the less complex society of the eighteenth century. As the economy expanded in the 1820s, more and more farmers demanded credit in order to put land under cultivation; speculators needed funds to buy land and securities; and entrepreneurs needed financing for new manufacturing enterprises. Individual capitalists could not respond efficiently to such heavy demands, and they lacked the organization to bring together the wealthy of Europe and America who desired to invest their capital surpluses. Thus economic changes necessitated that institutions undertake the functions of accumulating and investing capital. The only existing institutions which could fulfill these functions were commercial banks. Despite his earlier belief that banks should only support trade, Bronson relaxed his principles and acknowledged that banks might also invest their capital stock.

Isaac Bronson, nevertheless, remained a financial conservative because he carefully limited the bank's use of its capital stock. In 1821, for example, he allowed the Bridgeport Bank to invest these funds, but he stipulated that they must be placed in secure land mortgages. He steadily refused to lend capital to speculators or manufacturers, or to use it to increase the bank's note circulation. Bronson believed that all such transactions carried with them the high probability of failure and therefore threatened the bank's stability. Bronson thus had acceded to the bank's role in assisting in agricultural development, but other risk-taking ventures he still left to individual capitalists. Such careful policies, he believed, would maintain economic stability and assure public faith in financial institutions.[23]

From his position at the Bridgeport Bank and as a respected member of New York City's financial community, Isaac Bronson spent two decades advocating his ideas of sound banking to state and national leaders. It was a difficult task because he was at odds with the prevailing sentiment for liberal credit policies and financial experimentation. Nevertheless, he influenced state and national policy at several key points during these years.

In 1810, for example, Bronson inaugurated a plan that antedated the Suffolk system in Massachusetts in responding to the problem of country bank notes. Country banks, particularly in New York and Massachusetts, issued notes many times in excess of their specie and beyond their ability to redeem. Because the notes circulated a great distance away from the bank and usually flowed into trade centers such as Boston and New York City, country bankers gambled that only a small portion of the notes would be presented for redemption at any one time. Because of the frequent instability of country banks, though, merchants and bankers in the trading centers lacked confidence in these notes and accepted them only at a discount. Country bank notes, therefore, circulated below par, lacking equal value with the notes of more reputable banks. City bankers tried many devices to control the issues of country banks. Boston bankers were partially successful when they collected the notes of a particular bank, journeyed to its location in the interior, and presented the notes for redemption. If nothing else, the action made the country bankers more circumspect in their note issues.[24]

In an effort to guarantee the par value of country bank notes and to introduce regularity in commercial transactions, Bronson developed a plan to improve relations between country and city banks. Because the Bridgeport Bank financed the trade of local merchants, many of its notes eventually reached New York City, but city banks, uncertain of their value, discounted them. In 1810, therefore, Bronson deposited a portion of the Bridgeport Bank's capital stock in the Mechanics Bank in New York City. The Mechanics Bank then used the specie to redeem the Bridgeport Bank's notes at par.[25] Several years later, the Suffolk Bank of Boston adopted the same policy when it urged country banks to maintain deposits at the Suffolk Bank in order to redeem their notes. If the country banks refused, the Suffolk Bank threatened to collect their notes and to return them for redemption. In this way, the Suffolk Bank (later other city as well as country banks joined the system) regulated the note circulation of New England banks.[26]

The Suffolk system provided a minimum of control over banks and a degree of stability in commercial exchanges, but in the 1820s the number of banks increased so rapidly that financiers and politicians recognized the need for a more systematic regulation in order to protect the public and the economy. The first move came in New York State where thirty banks awaited charter renewals and forty petitions had been received for new charters. In 1828 and 1829, Martin Van Buren, the new governor, and a willing legislature seized this moment to reform the state's banking system. Joshua Forman, a representative from upstate New York, presented the original proposal upon which the Safety Fund legislation was based. The Safety Fund required each bank to put three percent of its capital stock into a state fund. This fund would be used to reimburse the depositors and creditors of any bank which failed. To further ensure the proper operation of banks, the plan included provisions for commissioners to examine periodically each institution.[27]

Bronson accepted the basic idea of the Safety Fund, but he urged the state to consider even more far-reaching reforms. In 1828, Bronson's ideas were presented to Martin Van Buren by James Hamilton, a leading New York City Democrat. Hamilton stressed particularly the New Yorker's distinction between a bank's capital and its credit. If the state were to regulate banks in an efficient manner, Hamilton argued, then it must stipulate that banks invest their capital stock in secure, long-term mortgages and government securities. Moreover, no bank, Hamilton said, should be allowed to issue notes in excess of its capital. In this way, banks could not risk their resources in speculative projects, and thus their capital would always be available to redeem their notes.[28] Isaac Bronson elaborated the same ideas to the Safety Fund's principal legislative architect, Joshua Forman, in a correspondence extending over several months. The extent to which Bronson influenced Forman's final proposal cannot be determined, but certainly Forman listened attentively because he was then under consideration for the position of agent for the Bronsons' 400,000 acres of land in North Carolina.[29] Bronson also lobbied with his nephew, Thomas Olcott, cashier of the Mechanics and Farmers Bank of Albany and a member of Van Buren's inner circle. Finally, he requested a business acquaintance, John Bolton, to speak with members of the state legislature.[30]

The eventual Safety Fund legislation, however, failed to reflect Bronson's most important ideas. Thus, the New Yorker was very critical of the Safety Fund since it did not regulate actual banking practices. Bronson again stressed that banks must not employ their capital stock for loans or to increase circulation. Instead, he asserted that these funds should be invested in long-term securities or mortgages, leaving only a bank's credit for the conduct of business. The Safety Fund, Bronson argued, required all banks to contribute to a fund which protected the public in case of a bank's failure, yet it made no effort to prevent the abuses that led to failure. In Bronson's view, the Safety Fund imposed no limitation on the expansionist policy of most banks which, he thought, would inevitably result in financial chaos.[31]

Perhaps in reaction to his defeat in the Safety Fund discussions, Bronson requested a bank charter which embodied his basic principles from the New York State legislature in 1830. He planned to capitalize the proposed institution at $300,000 and to operate it as a commercial bank. The bank's credit would support its note issue, and its capital would be invested in land mortgages and government securities. Bronson subsequently withdrew the petition, although he returned to this basic idea later in the 1830s.[32]

Bronson blamed Martin Van Buren for the state's failure to pass more effective banking reforms. In Bronson's mind, Van Buren had surrendered to politicians and entrepreneurs anxious to take advantage of financial opportunities in an expanding economy. In one sense, Bronson's criticisms were accurate, for most members of Martin Van Buren's political entourage were advocates of liberal banking practices and were heavily involved in land and city speculations in western New York.[33] They naturally opposed Bronson's conservative ideas because such reforms would have controlled the investment practices of banks and limited the resources available for speculation.

Bronson's attempt to alert the country to the dangers of unrestrained economic expansion received an even more devastating blow when he lost control of the Bridgeport Bank. This bank had been a showcase for conservative principles, operating on the rule that no note or bill would be accepted for more than sixty days and no renewals would be considered. Throughout the 1820s, Bronson, along with his son Arthur, who assisted in the bank's management, had developed a fierce pride in this institution. Its record was enviable. For twenty-five years, 1807-1832, the bank had redeemed all its notes on demand and had lost a paltry $50 on a trade exchange. So secure were the bank's loans that Arthur Bronson maintained that it could have closed its entire business without loss within four months. Moreover throughout these years, the bank returned a steady, annual dividend of six percent to the stockholders.[34]

In the late 1820s, though, the Bridgeport community and the bank's stockholders began to question Bronson's conservative policies. As the economy expanded, the bank was inundated with requests from small manufacturers for seed money to open factories and from capitalists anxious to speculate in land and business ventures. "The customers of our bank," Arthur Bronson later wrote, "partook of the general infection— became clamorous for 'more money'—demanded 'accommodation'— insisted that our town was already retrograding . . . ."[35] Isaac Bronson's influence in the bank waned, and the directors altered the old policies in order to provide more credit to merchants and capitalists. Renewals were granted on commercial paper and the bank's capital stock was lent to speculators. Bronson argued against the lenient credit policies, but his opposition only succeeded in stirring criticism from his colleagues. Arthur Bronson remembered some years later the insults hurled at his father: "He was reproached as being quite behind the age, and as belonging to a school then utterly extinct.[36] Rather than face endless fights over policy, Isaac Bronson finally offered either to buy out the other stockholders or to sell his own shares. The latter course was agreed upon, and in late 1832 he terminated his connection with the Bridgeport Bank. After his failure to stop expansionist policies in the Bridgeport Bank, Bronson was so thoroughly disgusted that he never again held stock in a commercial bank. He probably took some solace in the knowledge that the Bridgeport Bank so overextended its circulation that within four years it was forced to suspend specie payments.[37]

Isaac Bronson was, in essence, a conservative banker caught up in a period of rapid change. His banking philosophy had adapted slowly to the demands of an expanding economy, but there was finally a point beyond which he would not go. While Bronson had acquiesced in the Bridgeport Bank's investing its capital stock in secure real estate mortgages, he could not approve its participation in speculative schemes. Despite his withdrawal from the Bridgeport Bank, neither Isaac Bronson nor his son,

Arthur, abandoned the struggle over banking policy, for both New Yorkers believed that the country was headed toward financial disaster. Succeeding chapters will therefore investigate their efforts to reform the Bank of the United States and to establish a new institution, the trust company, in order to relieve the pressure on commercial banks.

In order to understand the Bronson family's later involvement in banking reforms, it is first necessary to describe briefly their early activities as money lenders and land investors. Isaac Bronson, of course, believed that individual financiers, not banks, should "risk" their capital. Yet Bronson demonstrated a very traditional or conservative bent in his own investments. He was not a land speculator, if by that term one implies that there was a substantial risk of failure. Isaac Bronson was a land investor who carefully evaluated each purchase and who was prepared to wait many years for a moderate profit. The security of land was its principal attraction, for it was tangible and indestructible. The New Yorker, thus, did not purchase stock in manufacturing companies because of the uncertainties in the products and in the market. On the other hand, he operated a large mortgage business because of its relative safety. Usually he lent money to farmers, accepting security in land plus a personal bond. He rarely lent funds in excess of one-third of the property's market value; and, in estimating the property's value, an owner could not include buildings due to the hazard of fire. On most land mortgages, Bronson lent funds for five years at 6 percent annual interest. Bronson's most daring ventures—I use the term loosely—were in lending money to entrepreneurs. In this case, the character and reputation of the borrower were carefully evaluated as well as any land offered as security.[38] In order to diversify his investments, the New Yorker also owned and rented stores, hotels, and houses.[39] Bronson's land interests were so extensive that he owned land or held mortgages in over half the counties of New York State. An 1824 inventory of his New York debtors revealed that 134 people had borrowed funds with a balance of $443,910 remaining to be paid.[40]

Because of the size of his real estate investments, Bronson employed agents in many counties. In 1805, for example, he concluded a contract with his brother, Ethel, who agreed to supervise Bronson's land in Jefferson County, New York. The agents' duties were far-reaching and required them to inspect and value the land, sell parcels to farmers, and maintain account books for mortgage payments. The agents generally were important local capitalists and community leaders. His brother, Ethel, for example, settled in Rutland where he became a judge of the county court, president of the local bank, and served three terms in the state legislature. Yet Isaac Bronson was an active landowner, knowledgeable about each region and most borrowers and firmly in control of each sale or loan.[41]

In the 1820s, the elder Bronson introduced two of his sons, Arthur and Frederic, to the land business. On numerous trips to western and northern New York, both learned the techniques of evaluating land by noting its soil characteristics and accessibility to water and transportation. By the early 1820s, Arthur Bronson had taken over most of his father's land business as Isaac increasingly turned his attention to banking affairs. The younger Bronson corresponded with the agents and often conducted the preliminary negotiations on new purchases or on loans to farmers. By the late 1820s, it was difficult to discern the land investments of the father from those of his sons. Many business ventures were by then family affairs in which each member participated equally.[42]

Because Arthur Bronson controlled the family's western interests in the 1830s, it is important to describe his early financial career. Even though he was under his father's influence, Arthur was somewhat more venturesome as a young businessman. One of his first ventures was to speculate in bank paper. Sharing the risks with a partner, Arthur Bronson bought up the circulating notes of a reputedly unstable bank for three-quarters of their face value. He then presented these notes to the bank for redemption at their full value. Although he made an initial profit, Arthur withdrew from the scheme sensing that the bank could not meet any future demands.[43]

Arthur Bronson followed a similar business strategy when he acquired an interest in the Peru Iron Company, a manufacturing firm employing 284 men and producing bar iron, rail, and chain cable. Peru was a small town in Clinton County, New York, situated approximately ten miles from Lake Champlain, which provided water transportation to the South. The Company also maintained an office and warehouse in New York City in order to sell and store its iron products. Established in 1822 as an individual enterprise, it was incorporated in 1824 with a capital of $200,000.[44] Before purchasing stock, Arthur and his brother-in-law James B. Murray travelled to Peru to inspect the books and facilities. Upon their return to New York City, Bronson joined three men in purchasing a controlling share of the company's stock: Murray; John Hone, the son of New York aristocrat Phillip Hone; and Francis Saltus, a director of the Farmers Fire Insurance and Loan Company. Their capital investment totalled approximately $61,000, which included Arthur's $17,500; James B. Murray's $16,500; John Hone's $18,000; and Francis Saltus' $9,000.[45]

The new directors took immediate action to rebuild the firm. Arthur Bronson was elected president, and his first task was the unpleasant one of removing the company's resident manager at Peru, who was blamed for the lack of productivity. Then Bronson convinced his brother-in-law that he should move to Peru and undertake the firm's rehabilitation. Murray accepted the job not only because of the potential for profit but also because of the opportunity for social experimentation. Like many nineteenth-century manufacturing towns, Peru was totally dependent on the company. Murray planned to build a school and a church to care for the workers' educational and spiritual needs.[46] During his few years as director, Murray had only limited success in increasing the company's business. He purchased steamboats in order to ship the iron, but foreign competition flooded the market with cheaper products. In 1828, Murray and Bronson sold their shares because of the firm's slow progress.[47]

Bronson exhibited none of his father's general hostility toward manufacturing enterprises, and he invested in other firms such as the New York Crown and Cylinder Glass Manufacturing Company and the Rhode Island Coal Company.[48] In each project, though, Arthur Bronson followed a cautious pattern of investment. Most often he purchased stock during the initial stages of a company's development and then sold his stock within two years.[49] The strategy was simple. Bronson provided the seed money which caused the firm's stock to rise in value as public confidence grew. The increase in confidence was based less on new business than on the firm's potential. At that point, often with a modest gain on his stock, Bronson withdrew his money and avoided any further risk. Throughout his life, the younger Bronson often returned to this tactic. He rarely risked capital for long periods in ventures which carried the possibility of heavy loss.

Despite his early involvement in manufacturing enterprises, the younger Bronson's principal interest was land. Even while learning his father's business in western New York, he embarked on his own speculations. One of the earliest and largest purchases occurred in 1825 in the North Carolina counties of Rutherford, Mecklenburg and Buncombe. Located in the western region of the state, this 400,000 acre tract included fertile agricultural land and some mineral deposits.

In 1824, the tract was entangled in a web of legal claims and clouded titles. Bronson realized that a patient effort to unravel this web might reveal a profitable investment, especially since most claimants were anxious to sell. Title to the land dated back to 1791 when a group of capitalists, organized as the Rutherford Land Company, purchased most of the land from the state of North Carolina. This company then sold the tract to a syndicate of businessmen headed by Tench Coxe. Coxe and his partners never developed the land, and Coxe himself went bankrupt in 1802. Rather than lose title to the North Carolina property, however, Coxe had borrowed from several men in order to make the outstanding payments. In 1820, Coxe then sold the land, on time, to a group of New York businessmen headed by Augustus Sackett, even though Coxe's partners and creditors still had claims to the land. Sackett then travelled to North Carolina where he sold individual parcels to farmers who were unaware of the confused title. Having sold the land and received payment, Sackett disappeared, stranding the buyers with defective titles and apparently leaving his New York partners without any recompense.[50]

At this point, Arthur Bronson, James B. Murray, and their New York friends Gould Hoyt and James Thompson decided to invest. After trips to North Carolina in order to inspect the land and check titles and then to Philadelphia to satisfy any remaining claims from the Tench Coxe estate, the New Yorkers purchased all other claims and existing mortgages for a sum of $65,000. In 1825, Jacob Hyatt was appointed the first agent and dispatched to North Carolina to represent the New Yorkers' interest.[51]

Even though there were several changes in the partnership over the years and other members of the Bronson family shared in the investment, Arthur Bronson managed the North Carolina lands from his New York office. The job included corresponding with resident agents, drawing up deeds of sale and mortgages, and making occasional trips for personal inspection. In 1828, Bronson began to promote transportation improvements and manufacturing in order to increase the land's value. At one time, his name was included as a stockholder in the North Carolina Land Mining Company having a capital stock of $1 million dollars.[52] Despite these promotional efforts, Arthur Bronson repeatedly attempted to sell the entire tract at a substantial profit, but these lands remained in the family's possession until at least the 1860s.[53]

The distinguishing characteristic of the Bronson family, then, was its conservative approach to the economy. Arthur Bronson's early career generally reflected his father's business philosophy. The younger Bronson accepted the idea that banks were primarily responsible for moving the nation's trade goods while individual capitalists supported the development of the agricultural sector. Both father and son envisioned a society in which trade and agriculture were the primary economic activities and where change occurred gradually. Their business portfolios were much like those of financiers a hundred years earlier. They concentrated on land investments, yet in order to diversify, they spread their capital over a wide geographic area and invested in bank, transportation, and manufacturing enterprises. Such diversification of interests assured that no single business failure would ever destroy the family's economic position.[54] Conservative business values and a traditional approach, however, should not be confused with resistance to change. The Bronsons were attuned to every new business opportunity and were especially active, though cautious, in moving capital into America's western frontier. At the same time, they were receptive to more efficient and secure means of banking. In 1830, for example, they participated in the establishment of the New York Life Insurance and Trust Company which combined their interest in banking reform with the accumulation of capital for investment in the agricultural sector.

2. The Bronsons, Charles Butler, and the New York Life Insurance and Trust Company

When the New York Life Insurance and Trust Company (NYLTC) opened for business in 1830, it was among the first trust institutions in the United States. The NYLTC was not a bank since it did not issue notes, but rather an investment firm which provided capital for long–term economic development. Conservative financiers such as the Bronsons had developed this institution in order to curb what they considered the unsound practices of commercial banks. The company also reflected the Bronsons' conservative investment philosophy as it pioneered the institutional movement of capital into the western agricultural areas of New York State. No less important to the company's development was Charles Butler of Geneva, New York, who worked as a company agent and as a lobbyist for its interests before the state legislature. The NYLTC, therefore, brought together the Bronsons and Charles Butler as business associates. In 1833, they formed a partnership for the purpose of investing in the Old Northwest, and their first step was to establish another trust company in Ohio.

A trust company was a financial intermediary which invested the funds of its depositors on a long-term basis, a middleman standing between the person desiring to invest and the person in need of money. Before the nineteenth century, the trust had been a means of caring for the old, for the sick and for dependent children who were incapable of managing their own affairs. It was usually a private arrangement in which a family member or close friend agreed to direct or superintend a family's financial affairs when the family lost its prinicpal income producer through illness or death. When trust companies were first proposed, they were merely the institutional equivalents of such private arrangements called into existence by the inability of individuals to perform trust functions in an increasingly complex economic world.[1]

As the economy expanded in the nineteenth century, the need for investment institutions increased as more and more people accumulated surplus capital but lacked the expertise to evaluate financial opportunities in agriculture, trade, and manufacturing both on the East Coast and in the developing West. Initially, private capitalists, commercial banks, and savings banks assumed investment functions, but a further specialization evolved in order to meet the increasing demand for financial resources. Trust companies thus naturally expanded their clientele from orphans and widows to include people who simply wished to escape the responsibility of investing their own savings.[2]

Historians disagree on when the first trust company began operations in the United States. The confusion derives in part from the different services offered by early insurance companies, such as the Pennsylvania Company for Insurance on Lives and Granting Annuities, chartered in 1812, and the Farmers Fire Insurance and Loan Company of New York City, chartered in 1822.[3] Nathaniel Bowditch, however, developed the first extensive trust business at the Massachusetts Hospital Life Insurance Company. Formed in 1823 by leading Boston capitalists, it provided a base of support for the Massachusetts General Hospital. Each year a percentage of the company's profits was used for the hospital's support. Although the company initially had intended to concentrate on life insurance, Bowditch directed it toward a trust business. Having served as a trustee in investing the funds of a church and of several private estates, he realized that adequate profits awaited an institution which specialized in that business. Bowditch also knew of the success enjoyed by the Provident Institution for Savings, a Boston firm which invested the savings of the middle class in secure stocks and mortgages.[4]

Bowditch therefore originated the first modern trust company by investing the accumulated funds of Boston's wealthy families for extended periods of time. He set up a committee of finance which scrutinized requests for loans on farms, personal security and stocks. Mortgage loans were granted only on agricultural lands within Massachusetts. The company had four agents in selected counties who judged the land's productive capacity and the character of the borrower. Despite these efforts to offer agricultural credit, the company did not place the majority of its resources in land. As an institution reflecting the financial interests of Boston's wealthy, its portfolio naturally included stock in surrounding banks, mercantile houses, and textile companies. The company returned annual profits of from 4 to 6 percent, and by 1830 it was so inundated with business that Bowditch limited its clientele to Boston families.[5]

Although utilizing techniques developed by the Massachusetts firm, the

NYLTC, established in 1830, reflected the special interests of its incorporators—New York's financial elite who petitioned the legislature for a charter. New York City bankers dominated the list which included John Mason of the Chemical Bank, John Hone and Lynde Catlin of the Merchant's Bank, Garrit Storm of the Phoenix Bank, Abraham Bloodgood of the City Bank, and Philip Hone of the Bank of America. The directors of the Bank of New York were heavily represented along with merchants and land investors, such as John Jacob Astor and Robert Troup.[6] Isaac Bronson figured prominently in the company's founding. He helped write the institution's charter and assisted William Bard, the company's first president, in securing the state legislature's approval.[7]

The trust company's incorporators were primarily conservative financiers upset by the liberal credit policies of commercial banks and the state's inability or unwillingness to regulate them. They envisioned the trust company as an agency for pooling their capital with that of hundreds of other investors both from within the state and from overseas. The trust company, then, was essentially a savings institution for the wealthy, a characteristic which the incorporators mentioned to the legislature when applying for a charter. The trust company's proponents did not request the power to issue notes because they assumed that the responsibility for note redemption would conflict with the company's primary investment function. The New Yorkers anticipated the trust company's taking over the role of moving capital into long-term investments, thus enabling New York's commercial banks to specialize in financing trade. They further hoped that this specialization in economic institutions would encourage financial stability throughout the country and return comfortable dividends to the stockholders and depositors.[8]

To ensure that the NYLTC would accomplish its purpose, Isaac Bronson and other key incorporators devised a charter that allowed them to select the board of trustees and the stockholders. To control effectively the company's operations, the organizers felt that the board of trustees had to represent the "right" people since the board was charged with appointing officers and formulating policy. When submitting the charter to the legislature, therefore, the New Yorkers named thirty of their number as the first board of trustees, thus avoiding the usual procedure of election by the stockholders. In order to guarantee control by a select few, the charter also stipulated that each trustee hold a minimum of $5000 in stock. The board of trustees also was structured as a self-perpetuating body since terms of office were indeterminate and vacancies were filled by the remaining trustees.[9]

Table 1 is a list of the company's trustees in 1833. It demonstrates the domination of New York City financiers, although several men—

TABLE 1

NEW YORK LIFE INSURANCE AND TRUST COMPANY TRUSTEES,
PLACE OF RESIDENCE, 1833

William Bard	New York City
James Kent	New York City
Thomas J. Oakley	New York City
Gulian C. Verplanck	New York City
John Mason	New York City
James McBride	New York City
John Duer	New York City
Stephen Whitney	New York City
Thomas Suffern	New York City
Nathaniel Prime	New York City
John G. Coster	New York City
John Jacob Astor	New York City
Isaac Bronson	New York City
Nicholas Devereux	Utica
William B. Lawrence	New York City
Jonathan Goodhue	New York City
Samuel Thompson	New York City
Peter Remsen	New York City
John Rathbone, Jr.	New York City
Peter Harmony	New York City
H. C. De Rham	New York City
Erastus Corning	Albany
Isaiah Townsend	Albany
Benjamin Knower	Albany
Benjamin F. Butler	Albany
Stephen Van Rensselaer	Albany
Thomas W. Ludlow	New York City
Peter G. Stuyvesant	New York City

SOURCE: New York State, Senate, *Communication from the Chancellor, Relative to the New York Life Insurance and Trust Company*, Senate Doc. 59, 57th Session, 1834, II: 16.

Benjamin F. Butler, Benjamin Knower, and Erastus Corning—represented the Albany Regency, the dominant faction in state politics. The board included both Whigs and Democrats in order to avoid charges that the company favored a particular political party. The trustees were also upper class and wealthy; of the twenty-two New York trustees, twenty appeared on either Moses Beach's list of wealthy New Yorkers or Edward Pessen's more recent tabulation. Almost all were either merchants or bankers. Those New Yorkers who did not appear on the lists, Thomas Oakley and John Duer, were well-known lawyers. Of the six trustees living outside New York City, all were either very wealthy or, like Benjamin Butler and Benjamin Knower, politically influential.[10]

Such close control was not unusual among the directors of nineteenth century banks. Whether accepting a trust for widows, dependents, or a wealthy customer, the organizers believed that the company's success partially depended on the public's confidence. Such confidence, they argued, resulted from the expertise and performance of the board of trustees. The incorporators, therefore, resisted annual elections of the trustees and directors by the stockholders because that practice would lead to constant changes in personnel and policies. They also believed that personnel changes could cause fluctuations in the company's stock and could affect its investments. A closed corporation, therefore, guaranteed a steady succession of like-minded, honorable and skilled men to guide its affairs. The New York State legislative committee, which studied the company's proposed charter, accepted the incorporators' rationale, explaining that:

> A provision will be found in the bill, similar to those inserted in the several charters, incorporating the savings banks of this state, authorizing the trustees themselves to fill all vacancies occurring by death, resignation, or removal. Your committee consider this provision to be essentially important, and to be the best, if not the only means, which can be adopted to secure a succession of able and upright trustees, and to preserve the company from falling into the impure hands of designing speculators.[11]

The NYLTC was theoretically a public corporation in which anyone might obtain stock; however, a small group, which included Isaac Bronson, manipulated the issue of stock. The charter had stipulated that the trustees would name three people to sell stock at a public sale, specifying only that each trustee had to own a minimum of $5,000. Shortly after the charter passed the legislature, the trustees met and further resolved that each of the 61 incorporators would have first call on 100 shares of stock at $100 per share. Of $1,000,000 in capital stock, then, the original incorporators held the majority, $610,000. The remaining stock, $390,000, was to be sold by three trustees who selected the purchasers by lot from letters of application. Under this system, however, Bronson and the other trustees were still able to control the distribution of additional shares. Many friends and acquaintances of Isaac and Arthur Bronson, for example, applied for stock, but with the understanding that they would transfer the shares to Isaac Bronson. Bronson, then, could distribute the shares to whomever he wished.[12] One of the trustees' principal aims in selecting the stockholders was to form a strong link with foreign capital markets. Baring Brothers, for example, acquired 1500 shares. Over the years, in fact, New York state residents owned a declining percentage of the stock as out of state, presumably foreign, money acquired a substantial interest. In 1831, 84.4 percent of the stock was held by New Yorkers; in 1835, that figure dropped to 61 percent. By 1837, New York residents controlled only 57 percent. Throughout the early years, though, the New York interests dominated the policy-making body, the board of trustees.[13]

TABLE 2
THE NEW YORK LIFE INSURANCE AND TRUST COMPANY STOCKHOLDERS, 1834

Stockholder	Shares	Stockholder	Shares	Stockholder	Shares	Stockholder	Shares
John Jacob Astor	131	Ebenezer Dimon	100	in trust	46	Robert Ray	50
William B. Astor	303	Howard Douglas	13	Thomas W. Ludlow	300	Robert Ray, in trust	
George Atkinson	140	John Duer	50	R. H. Ludlow	10	for Cornelia Ray	50
William Bard	50	John Duer, in trust		Thomas W. Ludlow,		Peter Remsen	100
Maria Banyer	25	for Mary Burnton	12	in trust	400	Peter Remsen, in trust	36
Susan Barclay	20	William Durant	50	Mary Ludlow	110	Beverley Robinson	70
Thomas Barclay	14	John Enrico	60	David Lydig & G. Hoyt, in		M. Robinson, Cashier	100
Baring Brothers & Co.*	1500	Gallatin Brothers	85	trust for D. A. Glover	20	W. W. Russell	94
Joseph Battell	150	C. Clarkson Goodhue	10	James Magee	100	Henry Saunders	60
Samuel Beardsley	25	F. A. Clarkson Goodhue	10	John Mason	100	Mary Sheaff	25
Peter V. Belin	24	Jona. Goodhue	50	Ann Masters	35	Roger M. Sherman	100
Maria Berg, in trust		H. Clarkson Goodhue	10	James McBride	100	Charles St. John	5
for E. Lucas	40	R. Clarkson Goodhue	10	Charles McEvers & Adam		Thomas Suffern	250
William Betts, in trust		W. Clarkson Goodhue	10	Treadwell, in trust	183	Samuel Thomson	50
for F. Frederichen	68	George Griffin	50	Elial Metcalf	7	David Thomlinson	150
William Betts, in trust		Robert Hogan	6	L. A. Millandon	10	D. & C. H. Thomlinson	50
for J. W. Mouritzur	90	David Hosack	100	Cathe. Hays Myers	4	Isaiah Townsend	100
John Borland	100	Gould Hoyt	100	Harriet Myers	4	John Townsend	100
Walter Bowne	50	Washington Irving	67	Julia Myers	3	Charles G. Troup,	
Arthur Bronson	150	John T. Irving	40	Eliza North	100	executor	115
Isaac Bronson	100	William James	310	Thomas J. Oakley	100	John Vanderbilt	26
Wm. G. Bucknor	87	Ann Jay	20	T. L. Ogden & T. W.		Stephen Van Rensselaer	50
Benjamin F. Butler	50	E. P. Johnston	13	Ludlow, in trust		Thomas Van Zandt, ex'r	
Coster L. Carpenter	10	John Johnston	10	for F. M. Thomas	32	& trustee of estate	
Catharine P. Chambers	12	Mary Kemble	35	Delia Perry	9	of W. Van Zandt	77
Hannah Channing	100	James Kent	50	Elizabeth B. Perry	16	Daniel C. Verplanck	101
David L. Clarkson	27	Thomas Knox	20	Oliver H. Perry	4	G. C. Verplanck	100
John Clarkson	30	Benjamin Knower	88	Seth Perry	50	Robert White, Cashier	62
John G. Coster	50	Edward B. Lawrence	100	Thad's Phelps	30	Harriet Whitney	50
Erastus Corning	70	William B. Lawrence	50	Nathaniel Porter	100	Stephen Whitney	50
J. G. Crookshanks	1	Lewis Lay	50	James Porter	12	J. C. Whitmore	34
E. Croswell	50	Herman LeRoy	15	Hy. & R. G. Rankin, in		Narcissa P. Whittemore	4
H. C. Dekham	100	Peter Lorrillard	150	trust for Marg't Gosman	37		
Nicholas Devereaux	50	Maria & T. W. Ludlow,	50	John Rathbone	50		

SOURCE: New York State, Assembly, *Communication from William Bard . . .*, Assembly Doc. 279, 57th Session, 1834, IV, pp. 1–4.

In addition to controlling the board of trustees and the stockholders, the NYLTC's incorporators wrote a charter which included several provisions that guarded against speculative financial practices and negligent administration. The company intially required that all stock had to be fully paid for within six months, an important precaution when compared to most commercial banks which permitted fractional payments for stock subscriptions. Article 7 specified that the company's capital stock had to be invested in real estate mortgages within the state. Furthermore, all loans on real estate had to be secured with mortgages double in value. The conservatives prided themselves on a clause which gave the state the power to amend or repeal the charter. The charter also required the company to submit an annual report to the state chancellor, who, in turn, could appoint a court official to conduct further investigations. The chancellor was empowered to remove an errant trustee, although the remaining trustees would still select his successor.[14] Bronson and the other trustees, then had created an institution to stand as a bulwark against the loose banking practices of the time. Roger Minot Sherman, a close friend of Isaac Bronson and a company stockholder, summarized the founders' intentions in a congratulatory letter to Isaac Bronson after the charter's adoption:

> It has several provisions, especially those which relate to the security of its capital, and the public supervision of its operations, which, had they been annexed to all monied institutions, would have given safety to the investments of stockholders, preserved a sound currency, prevented fluctuations in the money market, restrained that indulgence to adventurers which had occasioned so much public and individual distress, and would have greatly contributed to the morality, stability and usefulness of banking and commercial transactions.[15]

The NYLTC began operations in the spring of 1830, and from the beginning, the trustees established an administrative system which reflected their cautious approach. William Bard was elected president, and he administered the company on a day–to–day basis with the aid of a secretary, Edward Nicoll, and several clerks. Yet the trustees assumed an active role in the company's management, meeting at the end of each week to review all business transactions. There were also three standing committees, each consisting of from four to six trustees. The committee on finance directed the lending of the company's funds in personal notes and stocks, whereas the committee on investments oversaw the capital placed in real estate mortgages. A third committee handled the special trusts set up for children, guardians and widows. The three committees met jointly on a regular basis to determine the percentages of capital to be placed in bonds, in personal securities, and in real estate. Isaac Bronson was an influential trustee serving on several such committees in the early 1830s.[16]

The founders considered careful administration and trustee control essential because they anticipated that the firm would become one of the state's most powerful financial institutions. The NYLTC never devoted much attention to life insurance and instead concentrated on its extraordinary trust powers: "To accept and execute all such trusts, of every description, as may be committed to them by any person or persons whatsoever . . . ."[17] Although the company's rhetoric before the legislature had stressed its role in providing financial expertise for widows and orphans, most trusts were for the "living" trusts of capitalists seeking safe investments. Supplementing a capital stock of $1,000,000, the company had two other sources of investment capital: deposits of varying length and estates from the chancery of New York State. Of these sources, deposits were the most important additions to the company's investment capital. The NYLTC accepted deposits stipulating only that the sum must be at least $100 and must be deposited for a minimum of two months. Even though interest rates were low, ranging from 3 percent for periods of less than four months to 4½ percent for over a year, the company was swamped with customers. The deposits of New York State residents climbed from $688,142 in 1831 to $2,000,000 in 1834. Some commercial banks also deposited their funds in the trust company. For example, Thomas Olcott, cashier of the Mechanics and Farmers Bank of Albany, deposited $110,000.[18] By 1834, the New York firm also had attracted over $1,000,000 from foreign depositors. In 1835, the trust company managed more than $5,000,000 in deposits in addition to its $1,000,000 in capital stock.[19]

With a $6,000,000 investment fund, the NYLTC had enormous power to effect economic change within the state, yet it operated cautiously. The company's charter, of course, required that the capital stock of $1,000,000 must be placed in mortgages on real estate within New York State, and half of that amount had to be used in New York City and county.[20] Moreover, conservative financiers on the board of trustees insisted on careful investment policies. The trustees therefore concentrated investment in three areas: loans on personal security, loans on mortgages, and loans on the stock of corporations. Table 3 indicates the company's investment pattern. Each year it maintained the capital stock of $1,000,000 in mortgages, and it showed a marked preference for placing deposits and trust funds there as well. Obviously the trustees considered land the safest investment, but in order to diversify, they lent

TABLE 3
NEW YORK LIFE INSURANCE AND TRUST COMPANY'S INVESTMENT PATTERN, 1831-1837

Year	PERSONAL NOTES		STOCK		REAL ESTATE MORTGAGES (Includes $1,000,000 in Capital Stock Plus Deposits)		Total Invested
	Capital	Percentage	Capital	Percentage	Capital	Percentage	
1831	$ 248,146	12.8	$287,745	14.8	$1,408,481	72.4	$1,944,372
1832	800,521	22.7	619,549	17.6	2,101,560	59.7	3,521,630
1833	528,485	12.7	298,504	7.2	3,320,052	80.1	4,147,041
1834	1,216,787	21.8	591,272	10.6	3,777,995	67.6	5,586,054
1835	1,349,924	21.1	590,929	9.2	4,470,745	69.7	6,411,598
1836	652,590	11.3	451,451	7.8	4,684,392	80.9	5,788,433
1837	538,562	8.0	481,268	7.1	5,740,742	84.9	6,760,572

SOURCES: My figures for the above table were taken from two general sources, the *Annual Reports of the New York Life Insurance and Trust Company* and the reports of the Chancellor relative to the Company. These reports were ordinarily bound together and given a general heading and single document number.

1831—New York State, Senate, *Communication from the Chancellor Relative to the New York Life Insurance and Trust Company*, Senate Doc. 112, 55th Session, 1832, II: 7-12.
1832—New York State Assembly, "Answer of the New York Life Insurance and Trust Company," Assembly Doc. 209, 56th Session, 1833, III: 14-20.
1833—New York State, Senate, *Communication from the Chancellor Relative to the New York Life Insurance and Trust Company*, Senate Doc. 59, 57th Session, 1834, II: 3-11.
1834—New York State, Assembly, *Communication from the Chancellor, Relative to the New York Life Insurance and Trust Company*, Assembly Doc. 284, 58th Session, 1835, IV: 3-10.
1835—New York State, Assembly, *Communication from the Chancellor, Relative to the New York Life Insurance and Trust Company*, Assembly Doc. 143, 59th Session, 1836, III: 2-11.
1836—New York State, Assembly, *Communication from the Chancellor, Relative to the New York Life Insurance and Trust Company*, Assembly Doc. 257, 60th Session, 1837, III: 1-10.
1837—New York State, Assembly, *Communication from the Chancellor, Relative to the New York Life Insurance and Trust Company*, Assembly Doc. 353, 61st Session, 1838, VI: 4-12.

funds, taking personal notes and corporate stock as security. Only a small percentage of the company's total capital, however, was lent on corporate stock because the trustees reflected a common fear of many merchants and land investors that manufacturing enterprises were too risky. When accepting stock as security, the company usually valued it below the current market price.[21] Even though the amount lent to individuals on personal security would seem quite speculative since the collateral depended on the borrower's character, the trustees believed that it fit their conservative stance because " . . . the personal security of men of known character and wealth, especially when the loan was made payable within a moderate period, was among the safest and best which the country afforded, and if not quite equal to the security of real estate, approaching very near to it."[22]

Because the board of trustees included merchants and land investors such as Isaac Bronson and John Astor, who had traditionally invested in agricultural lands, the NYLTC was also heavily involved in moving funds into the farming regions of western New York. Table 4 pinpoints the leading counties in 1833, 1835, and 1837 in terms of total mortgage money invested. As previously mentioned, New York County appears on each list because the company's charter required that half of the capital stock had to be placed there. Albany County also received a substantial infusion of funds because it was second headquarters for the company, an embarkation point for the Erie Canal, and an important political center. The remaining counties were in the central and western part of the state, in need of developmental capital and situated astride the Erie Canal or other major transportation arteries. Despite the fact that the trust company lent money in almost every county in the state, in each of the three years cited, the company placed over 65 percent of its mortgage loans and over 50 percent of its total capital in the central and western counties of New York State.

Isaac Bronson and the other members of the board of trustees also developed a system to invest effectively and securely millions of dollars in farm mortgages that institutionalized their private investment techniques. For those historians convinced that land investment was inherently a speculative business, I should state explicitly that the evidence suggests an opposite thesis—that land investors were among the most conservative businessmen. For example, the company appointed agents in various counties to receive applications from farmers in need of funds. The agents then checked the value of land offered as security, investigated the character of the borrower, and searched for evidence of title and outstanding taxes on the land. From there, the application went to the company's legal counsels, John Duer and Beverly Robinson in New York

TABLE 4
NEW YORK LIFE INSURANCE and TRUST COMPANY, FOURTEEN LEADING COUNTIES of MORTGAGE INVESTMENT, 1833, 1835, and 1837

	1833		1835		1837
County	Amount Invested	County	Amount Invested	County	Amount Invested
Albany	$125,019	Albany	$124,492	Albany	$ 132,262
Cayuga	84,192	Cayuga	82,729	Chautauqua	102,108
Chautauqua	70,944	Chautauqua	93,780	Erie	343,162
Erie	278,183	Erie	331,658	Genesee	354,276
Genesee	234,789	Genesee	329,642	Livingston	165,193
Livingston	122,859	Livingston	160,007	Monroe	361,626
Monroe	312,480	Monroe	318,676	New York	1,037,445
New York	596,992	New York	896,617	Niagara	343,847
Niagara	182,252	Niagara	315,902	Oneida	96,630
Onondaga	72,754	Onondaga	78,560	Onondaga	86,438
Ontario	109,756	Ontario	125,017	Ontario	132,412
Orleans	170,995	Orleans	373,742	Orleans	413,360
Tompkins	80,746	Tompkins	92,446	Tompkins	101,721
Wayne	133,948	Wayne	123,682	Wayne	125,503
Total	$2,575,839	Total	$3,446,950	Total	$3,795,983
Percentage of Mortgage Investments	77.5	Percentage of Mortgage Investments	77.1	Percentage of Mortgage Investments	66.1
Percentage of Total Investment Capital	62.1	Percentage of Total Investment Capital	53.7	Percentage of Total Investment Capital	56.1

SOURCES: New York State, Senate Doc. 59, 1834, II: 3-6; New York State, Assembly Doc. 143, 1836, III: 3-6; and New York State, Assembly Doc. 353, 1838, VI: 3-7.

and Benjamin F. Butler in Albany, who further checked for any encumbrances on the title and then drew up the mortgage. Once the counsels had checked the application, it came before a committee of the trustees which either approved, disapproved, or requested additional information.[23]

Because the western agents were so important to the company's operation, they were chosen with great care. The company preferred that agents possess legal training, and knowledge of land values, and that they hold positions of prominence in the local community. Many were former agents of land investors. The company also considered an agent's political preference, selecting both Whigs and Democrats in order to avoid charges of political favoritism. Agents were commonly located in cities and towns near potentially prosperous farming areas. There were, for example, agents in Buffalo, Lockport, Geneva, Utica, and Troy. Lot Clark, who represented the company in Lockport, Niagara County, was a land speculator as well as the principal stockholder of the Lockport Bank. Later in the 1830s, he would join with Arthur Bronson and Charles Butler in founding the Ohio Life Insurance and Trust Company.[24] Frederick Whittlesey, the agent at Rochester, had previously purchased land for Isaac Bronson and in 1839, he became president of the Bank of Monroe. Although Clark was a Democrat, Whittlesey was a Whig. The agent at Geneseo, Livingston County, was Philo Fuller, another former land agent. In the 1830s, he too served as a Whig representative in the legislature. In 1836, he moved to Michigan where he assumed the presidency of a railroad bank controlled by New York capitalists.[25]

No agent was more important than Charles Butler, and a part of Butler's influence was directly related to his early background. Charles Butler was born into a middle–class family in 1802 at the village of Kinderhook Landing on the Hudson River, sixteen miles north of Albany. Charles's father was a merchant with considerable political interest who served both as a state senator and as judge of Columbia County. Charles was educated at an academy in Greenville, New York, and then followed in the footsteps of his older brother, Benjamin, as a clerk in the law office of Martin Van Buren.[26] In 1822, he became deputy clerk of the New York State Senate, a crucial position for a young man contemplating a career in law and politics. After he was admitted to the bar, Charles Butler chose to practice in western New York. His decision to move West likely represented a desire to escape the shadow of his brother, Benjamin, who had become an intimate friend of Martin Van Buren and an important lawyer in Albany. Moreover, Charles Butler looked forward to new financial opportunities in the small boom towns along the path of the Erie Canal.[27]

Butler spent a short period in Lyons before locating permanently in Geneva, New York, in 1825. It was a wise choice for the young lawyer, since Geneva was a prosperous frontier village located in the middle of a fertile farming region and near enough to the Erie Canal to provide an outlet for agricultural produce. At Geneva, he entered the law office of Bowen Whiting, who served as the county's district attorney as well as a state senator. Butler learned quickly since Whiting was often absent on political business in Albany. Occasionally Butler served as assistant district attorney, and in 1826 he conducted the prosecution of the kidnappers of William Morgan, the ex-Mason who had disappeared from a Canandaigua jail after revealing ritual secrets to the public.[28]

Butler combined his legal work with a time-consuming interest in politics. He participated in local political affairs and worked with the Albany Regency, a wing of the state's Democratic party headed by Martin Van Buren. The Regency was the prototype of more modern parties with its tight organizational structure and use of a newspaper, the *Albany Argus*. Butler sent a steady stream of political information to his boyhood friend, Edwin Croswell, editor of the *Albany Argus*. In 1828, he campaigned with Van Buren in his successful bid for the governorship. Butler's loyalty to the party was rewarded on several occasions: he was appointed to a sinecure post as special agent of the state supreme court in 1828, and in 1829 he was nominated for postmaster at Geneva, a position he later refused. In the 1830s he was urged to run for the state senate, but he chose to avoid the public spotlight. Butler favored the backstage of the political world where he could exert more subtle pressures on legislators. His correspondents in the 1820s included Thomas W. Olcott, William L. Marcy, Silas Wright, and Edwin Croswell, a clear indication of Butler's ties to the powers of New York State politics. Later these same men would share in business ventures orchestrated by Charles Butler.[29]

Butler's political and economic interests were curiously intertwined with his religion. As a child, he had apparently inhaled a large dose of the "work ethic" so that his whole life linked economic advancement with religious salvation. Butler brought the same intensity to his religious life that he displayed in law and politics. In the 1820s in western New York, he was the corresponding secretary of the American Sunday School Union and worked with the American Bible Society. He founded the Geneva Atheneum to provide selected reading materials to local citizens, and cooperated in the establishment of Hobart College, a private school with an Episcopal affiliation. In a sense, Butler embodied the stereotype of the era. He was an "expectant" capitalist, prepared to work hard in order to make his fortune and convinced that such efforts would contribute to the country's economic progress and his own religious salvation.[30]

From the moment he moved to Geneva, New York, Butler was a classic "booster," a frontier entrepreneur who seized upon every opportunity to supplement his salary as a frontier lawyer. In 1825, he and Edwin Croswell explored the country west from Geneva to Buffalo in search of profitable investments in farm land and town lots. In the 1820s, he worked for eastern capitalists who purchased land and lent money to farmers. In this capacity he met and worked for Isaac and Arthur Bronson, and he was subsequently employed as an agent for the NYLTC.[31] Because of his political connections and economic skills, Butler was treated differently from most other company agents. His agency encompassed several counties, and he was permitted more discretion than usual in selecting borrowers and in evaluating security. William Bard, the president of the trust company, often corresponded with Butler when considering new policies and administrative procedures.[32] In addition, Butler assisted the company in lobbying before the state legislature at Albany. Occasionally, he went to New York City on trust company business, and in the early 1830s these visits gave him an entree into New York City's social and financial world. At this time he also formed a close personal friendship with Arthur Bronson.[33]

Charles Butler was the company's most articulate spokesman because, as a lawyer in western New York, he was able to perceive the trust company's significance in agricultural development. Until the appearance of the trust company, farmers in western New York had depended on private money lenders, such as John Astor and Isaac Bronson, for capital to buy and improve their land. Yet this system had its limitations. First, individual capitalists felt less secure in lending money when westward expansion produced requests for money from distant regions. Second, these same financiers, in order to protect their funds, had typically lent money in small amounts and at short-term—four to five years. But this procedure, Butler observed, caused real difficulties for the farmer, who had to produce quickly in order to repay the lender. As a result, the cost of the land and the first two or three years of marginal crops forced the farmer to extend the contract (whenever possible) or to accept tenant status on the land. Because of the trust company's corporate status, Butler explained, farmers could borrow money for extended periods (up to twenty years) provided they paid regular interest. Neither the farmer's death nor that of company officials necessarily threatened the contractual relationship. Thus, Butler realized the enormous advantages of the trust company in moving capital into the agricultural sector. Private money lenders could now deposit their capital or purchase stock in the company and avoid the risks, costs, and time spent in investing in western farm land. Because of the company's size and corporate status, moreover, farmers were able to obtain more capital and for longer periods.[34]

Butler's sense of the trust company's transitional role in the land business was especially evident when he dealt with farmers under contract to the Holland Land Company. Since the late eighteenth century, this foreign company had leased and sold land to farmers in western New York, but by the 1820s settlers had several grievances against the company. Many farmers had been unable to obtain land titles because of the chronic shortage of capital on the frontier, and as a result, they were tenants rather than owners of the land. Western residents also believed that the company should pay more taxes for better roads and schools. In the early 1830s, the New York State legislature responded to these complaints and passed a law that forced the Holland Land Company to pay a tax on debts owed to them by western farmers. When the Holland Land Company tightened its collection of debts and passed part of the tax on to the farmers by charging higher interest rates and fees, the farmers' hostility increased and the anti-foreign sentiment of the legislature deepened. The Holland Land Company then decided to sell all its holdings and opened negotiations with the NYLTC.[35]

Situated in western New York where the effects of the capital shortages were most apparent, Charles Butler vociferously urged the NYLTC to purchase the outstanding morgage and tenant contracts of the Holland Land Company. Enabling farmers to acquire title to the land, Butler claimed, would be a secure investment and a boost to the area's economic development. Butler portrayed the change of the farmer from a tenant of the Holland Land Company into a freeholder with a mortgage from the NYLTC in the following way:

> The borrower, who holds the land by contract, has no interest in the fee of the soil. He is a mere tenant at will under the proprietors. The land has appreciated in value by the application of his labor, and by the general appreciation of the soil of the country. He pays the balance and procures a deed, and his situation is changed from that of mere contractor to a freeholder; so that in any event of sickness, misfortune, or death, the fee of his farm is secured to his heirs. By this operation, the relation in which the borrower stands to his property is entirely changed; and there is a corresponding change in all his circumstances.[36]

Throughout the company's early years, Charles Butler and Isaac Bronson also helped in the formulation of the company's cautious investment policies and procedures. The company's basic mortgage, for example, lent capital for only a year but with the understanding that regular renewals would be automatic provided that the security—land or buildings—had not deteriorated. The borrower also had to meet regular interest payments.[37] Whenever interest was due, farmers were permitted, although not required, to make payments on the principal. These policies were beneficial to farmers, who required several years to develop the land and produce a surplus crop. They did so without fear of a sudden call for the loan's principal. Of course, there was little risk to the company since the land, which secured the mortgage, increased in value as it was cultivated. The NYLTC, then, was not interested in speculating in wild land, in pressing for quick payment, or in foreclosing a loan. As long as the capital was invested, it returned interest each year. The company insisted on the prompt payment of interest, but it showed little concern with the return of the principal. If the borrower failed to pay the interest, the NYLTC would move reluctantly to foreclose in order to obtain the loan's security. The company, however, never intended to become a land owner; instead, as Charles Butler stated, "The object was interest, not land."[38]

The policies regulating mortgage loans also demonstrated the company's conservative approach. William Bard, the firm's president, best expressed the company's philosophy as " . . . [We] have a right to look to perfect security, & may be excused if we are more than ordinarily cautious . . . ."[39] The NYLTC used two major criteria in lending money: the character of the borrower and the security of the land. Butler, for example, acquainted himself with the leading men of an area, such as clergymen and justices of the peace, in order to obtain character references on prospective clients. Butler's religious zeal also led him to check into the drinking habits of his customers.[40] The purpose of these careful procedures was, of course, to lessen the risks in lending money. William Bard claimed that the company refused loans to all " . . . but to an individual believed to be sober, industrious, prudent & thriving—Money employed, as it generally will be by Persons of this description, in making more money is safely loaned to them."[41]

More important than the character of the borrower, however, was the value of the land. The NYLTC and its agents often inaccurately pictured themselves as risk-takers who lent money to farmers first putting land under cultivation. Butler's later reminiscences, for example, constantly praised the "developmental" role of the institution. In 1832, William Bard wrote that "I wish for the success of the Company, but I have a higher and nobler wish that it may be the instrument of great good to the State . . . ."[42] Despite such statements for public consumption, the NYLTC did not "speculate" in probable growth; that is, it did not provide "seed" money. Farmers either needed considerable cash of their own or needed to possess land already under cultivation in order to obtain mortgage money because the charter stipulated that the company could loan no more than a half of the appraised value of the property.[43] In essence, clients of the company were neither subsistence farmers nor pioneers. In refusing a request from an agent to grant mortgages to settlers surrounding Lockport, Bard once expressed the opinion of the board of trustees that "first settlers are generally poor & afford little security in their personal responsibility . . . ."[44]

The company was often more scrupulous than required by the charter in selecting borrowers and landed security. Even though the trust company considered a cultivated farm the very best security, it rarely loaned even half of the appraised value. Town and village property was shunned because of the fluctuation of property values there. Usually the company never accepted more than one-third the value of buildings as security and then only if the property was insured and was located in the center of town. Bard's instructions to an agent in 1832 advised that ". . . so far from coveting village loans of anywhere from Buffalo to Utica, I solicit our Agents to avoid them as much as possible. I think property there more fluctuating & uncertain than in the Country, & the Insurance they require adds to the risk. They can not be avoided altogether, but where they are made let the property be valued low & then a small advance on that valuation."[45] Finally the company avoided loans to manufacturing firms because their success seemed uncertain. Agents were not absolutely prevented from submitting such applications, but the company limited loans to only one-fourth or one-fifth the value of the factory's land and buildings.[46]

The board of trustees also established a system to examine periodically the agents and their land valuations, a system similar to that practiced by the Bronsons in their private land business. In 1832, Nicholas Devereux, a member of the board of trustees, conducted the first inspection. Even though he possessed the power to adjust property valuations, Devereux was generally pleased with the company's loans and their beneficial effect on the agricultural development of the state. He adequately summarized the company's investment practices, stating that

> The loans on improved farms are the most numerous, and by far the greater part of the whole amount loaned by the company, is on this description of security . . . . I observed with pleasure that the company's loans were confined as closely as possible to that class of farmers, who, from their habits and character, were likely to make a prudent and profitable use of their money; from whom the regular and punctual payment of interest may be expected; and whose

profits, increased by the advance of a larger capital, will insure the final liquidation of their debts.[47]

Although historians have not subjected the NYLTC to a thorough analysis, the incidence of mortgage defaults and the record of company dividends suggest that the NYLTC followed its cautious policy statements. Preliminary studies of mortgages granted by the company in selected counties of western New York indicated a careful screening of borrowers and an accurate evaluation of the land. In Livingston County, for example, the company invested $346,610 in the 1830s. Of 266 mortgages traced through the 1870s, 94 percent were settled normally. The company apparently undertook foreclosure proceedings in only 7 cases. In its *Annual Reports* through 1838, the firm generally reported an insignificant number of failures on mortgages, considering the $6,000,000 invested.[48] Moreover, the company's dividends from 1831 to 1837 were consistently modest, ranging from 6 to 9 percent. Speculators, who were after a quick profit, were certainly not prime customers of the trust company.[49]

Therefore, the NYLTC was a conservative force in what historians normally consider a highly speculative business. The company reflected the traditional economic values of its trustees, particularly since they anchored its investments in land. The Bronsons' own land business, both before and after the trust company's establishment, operated on the basis of similar policies. The Bronsons, Charles Butler, and the trust company thus abhorred speculation and favored the cautious development of the nation's resources. Butler perhaps best summarized the cautious investor's mentality which imbued the trust company: "Capitalists do not invest their money upon soil which is unproductive, and which does not, in fact, constitute a security, nor to men who are irresponsible, improvident and intemperate. It is only the best men, in regard to character and property, in the community, who can command a loan of money from the honorable and prudent capitalist. This remark applied with strict truth to the Trust Company."[50]

Despite a record of prudent management, the company came under attack in the state legislature for political and financial reasons from 1830 to 1834. Throughout these years, Charles Butler and the company's president, William Bard, attended most legislative sessions to defend the company. Opposition came first from commercial banks which argued that the trust company was in direct competition. Although William Bard replied to the charges of competition by explaining that trust companies catered to long-term investors, he neglected to consider that commercial banks also had entered the field of mortgage loans.[51] More serious challenges came from other entrepreneurs who wanted a trust company charter with equal powers. In December 1832, Bard projected that at the upcoming legislature session "agents and companies will be as thick as blackberries."[52] Yet the company faced its most serious threat from politicians caught up in the general antipathy toward banks in the aftermath of Andrew Jackson's veto of the recharter of the Second Bank of the United States in the summer of 1832. The trust company's enemies attacked its powerful charter and multi-million dollar capital, and some even expressed a fear that it might someday hold title to the majority of land within New York State.[53]

The most serious challenge to the NYLTC arose during the legislative session of 1833-1834. As the economy expanded, many new companies were requesting trust company charters: among them were the Columbian Life Insurance and Trust Company, the American Life Insurance and Trust Company, and the Farmers Fire Insurance and Loan Company. The majority of the legislators distrusted all banks and financial institutions, and thus the legislature rejected most requests for charters.[54] Yet anti-bank members of the legislature noted the inconsistency of denying charter applications while, at the same time, allowing the NYLTC to increase in size and influence. As a result, a legislative committee investigated the powers of the NYLTC. particularly its power to accept unlimited deposits.[55]

When threatened with the possible limitation of the company's deposits, both Butler and Bard actively lobbied in support of the trust company. Bard sought the assistance of company agents by asking them to solicit testimonies from local people about the firm's beneficial effects. At the same time, both Bard and Butler requested the help of the state's leading politicians and financiers. Bard, for example, complained to Thomas Olcott that any legislative action limiting the trust company's deposits would prevent it from lending money for extended periods. The company, Bard explained, would need to maintain a large reserve fund in order to meet depositors' requests for their money.[56] Charles Butler used a similar argument when he wrote that

> There is no such thing as limiting a *Trust Co:* the object of such a company is to receive monies in trust, to dispose of the same on bond & mortgage & so long as they are unrestricted, of course, they will from time to time receive deposits, enough to meet the current demands on them by the depositors . . . . The trust company confers a great blessing on the country as by means of its great credit, it draws capital from all quarters which it loans out all over the country

> *wherever it is wanted:* where it is wanted, there it does good, . . . for
> where capital is abundant, there every branch of industry prospers,
> money breeds money—capital begats capital . . . .[57]

Despite the opposition of Bard and Butler, the legislature passed a bill
that restricted the company to $5 million in deposits and $6 million in
loans. Yet Butler's lobbying effort was not totally wasted. He had learned a
good deal about the political complexities of the bank issue in the state
legislature and about the deficiencies of the NYLTC's charter that had
permitted the state to pass amendments. When he and Arthur Bronson
proposed the establishment of a trust company in Ohio in 1834, they
carefully avoided political entanglements and drafted a charter which
prevented legislative interference.[58]

The NYLTC, therefore, was an important step in the evolution of
financial institutions. Conservative financiers like Isaac Bronson had established trust companies as investment institutions in order to prevent
commercial banks from abandoning their traditional role in financing
trade. Furthermore, the company reflected the need for a specialized
institution to pool capital for a developing economy. The New York firm
was most important in moving funds to the settled, yet semi-frontier,
region of western New York because it reflected the investment mentality
of the merchants and land investors who dominated its board of trustees.
The need for such institutions was demonstrated by the fact that over
twenty-five additional trust companies were established in the 1830s with
the majority located in eastern urban centers.[59]

The Bronsons and Charles Butler, along with many other stockholders
of the NYLTC, were involved in the establishment of other trust companies. In 1835, for example, the Florida Territory incorporated the
Southern Life Insurance and Trust Company, a firm which was definitely
linked to the New Yorkers, with a capital of $2 million. Lot Clark, its
principal promoter, was an agent of the NYLTC and a friend of Bronson
and Butler. It was also rumored that Arthur Bronson held a large block of
stock, and contemporaries often complained that outsiders owned the
southern firm. The Florida institution operated like the New York company by lending money on landed security, although its investments were
more speculative.[60] Similarly the Bronsons had ties to the Alabama Life
Insurance and Trust Company and to a firm in Connecticut.[61] Yet the
extent of their control and the purpose behind their investments cannot
really be determined because neither stock subscription lists nor letters
between the financiers and local officials have been uncovered.

Fortunately the records of one company do exist, the Ohio Life Insurance and Trust Company, and its history further demonstrates the tech-

niques of eastern financiers in mobilizing capital for western investments. Its principal founders were Charles Butler and Arthur Bronson. As an agent of the NYLTC, Butler had learned the techniques of land investment and had improved his political skills while lobbying in Albany. At some point, probably in 1832, he envisioned another trust company in Ohio and broached the idea to his friend, Arthur Bronson. The partnership would be one of mutually complementary talents. Butler was more a political man and enjoyed the careful lobbying that would be required to obtain a charter. Arthur Bronson preferred a quiet role away from the political world so that he could build the company's institutional structure and secure the allegiance of his wealthy friends. The early financial and political experience of Charles Butler and Arthur Bronson, therefore, had been important preludes to their financial involvement in the Old Northwest during the 1830s.

3. Institutional Innovation and Western Investments: The Ohio Life Insurance and Trust Company

In 1832, the American economy was on the brink of a tremendous boom, but in the West, there was a severe shortage of capital to encourage the purchase of farms, to inaugurate new retail businesses, or to facilitate trade. The Ohio Life Insurance and Trust Company (OLTC) was one example of an institution which responded to these needs in an innovative manner. Its early history, like that of its NYLTC counterpart in New York state, challenges the accepted belief that eastern capital was prevented from moving westward because of legal, institutional, and geographic barriers.[1] In fact, eastern financiers, led by Isaac Bronson, Arthur Bronson, and Charles Butler, dominated the company's early years. They wrote the OLTC's charter, acquired legislative approval from the state, selected the officers and stockholders, and raised the capital. The available records permit an analysis of their techniques of promotion as well as an opportunity to investigate their relationship with Ohio politicians and financiers.

The Bronsons, Charles Butler, and their eastern associates wanted to establish a trust company in Ohio for three major reasons. First, on the basis of their participation in the NYLTC which returned a stock dividend of 7 percent in 1833, the New Yorkers thought that a stock interest in an Ohio trust company might be an equally safe and valuable investment. In fact, eastern financiers commonly channeled money into western financial institutions. The Dwight family of Geneva, New York, and Springfield, Massachusetts, for example, held a majority interest in both the Bank of Michigan and the Commercial Bank of Lake Erie. A trust company, with its emphasis on investments in land mortgages, held an additional attraction in that eastern capitalists could indirectly invest in Ohio agricultural lands without employing their own resident agents and assuming personal supervision.[2] Finally, the Bronsons intended for the OLTC to become a showcase of sound banking principles due to its unique structure, which combined the functions of a trust company and of a commercial bank. Through a prudent investment of the company's capital stock in agricultural mortgages and the careful issue of notes for commercial exchanges, the New Yorkers hoped to demonstrate to Jacksonian Democrats, then dismantling the Second Bank of the United States (BUS), that large financial institutions were necessary to a healthy economy.[3]

Butler and the Bronsons were obliged to establish a separate trust company in Ohio, rather than merely to expand the NYLTC or some other New York State institution, because of the existing legal environment. Each state had the power to charter corporations within its own boundaries, the assumption being that such institutions were formed partially for the benefit of the state's citizens. Furthermore, it was unclear at this early stage of corporate development whether a corporation chartered in one state could conduct business in another state, and both New York and Ohio probably would have challenged the expansion of the NYLTC into Ohio. Since the New York trust company had been chartered to facilitate the state's agricultural development and to provide trust management for widows and children, the New York state legislature would have opposed the lending of capital in Ohio. Ohio, on the other hand, would have objected to the presence of a "foreign" corporation and would have penalized it through high taxes. The state already had laws taxing out-of-state insurance companies at a higher rate than domestic firms as well as laws requiring foreign agents to post bonds. Of course, such laws reflected a general suspicion of "foreign" capital, yet they also reflected the state's attempt to secure economic advantage and control. The economic advantage derived from the fact that an in-state corporation attracted outside capital through the sale of stock on which a standard dividend was perhaps six or seven percent. This obviated the need for the state or its citizens to borrow across state lines at higher interest rates. The state also had more control because the legislature approved the charter and could specify investment practices and conduct periodic investigations. It was common practice in trust company charters, for instance, to regulate the percentage of capital invested in agricultural lands and even to specify certain amounts for particular counties.[4] Thus in the 1830s, eastern financiers moved capital westward by obtaining charters or stock control of banks within individual states.

Ohio's receptivity to the trust company in the 1830s resulted from a combination of economic and political circumstances. Although a state since 1803, Ohio had not experienced economic development in a balanced geographic pattern. In the state's south and central portions, there was already substantial agricultural and urban development, particularly along the Ohio River. In fact, Ohio was a major exporter of corn and wheat. In the north bordering on Lake Erie, though, only the first stirrings of economic growth were evident after the completion of the Erie Canal in 1825 had stimulated migration and then settlement. By 1833, Ohio had constructed 400 miles of canals principally to link this new region to the South, and population statistics reflected this growth. Between 1830 and 1840, for example, the state's population increased 62 percent, a percentage nearly twice that of the country's growth rate. The population of Ohio's cities also climbed dramatically, and the figures for Cleveland and Cincinnati reflected the geographic patterns of development in both the northern and the southern areas of the state. Cincinnati's population in 1816 was 6,493; in 1820, 9,642; in 1830, 24,831; and by 1840, the population was 46,338. Cleveland on Lake Erie had a population of only 606 in 1820; 1,076 in 1830; but during the 1830s, Cleveland's population grew to 6,071. In the 1830s, then, the northern lakeports challenged Cincinnati's economic dominance, although they never surpassed the volume of traffic along the Ohio River until the 1850s.[5]

Even though Ohio possessed many of the requirements necessary for economic growth, it lacked one essential—the financial resources needed to support the demands of merchants for exchange, farmers for land purchases, and manufacturers for risk capital. During the 1820s, Ohio had only a few banks as a result of the anti-bank movement generated by the depression in 1819. In 1826, Cincinnati, the West's leading commercial center, possessed only a branch of the BUS, and in the entire state there were only ten banks issuing notes. As the forces for economic expansion grew in the late 1820s and early 1830s, Ohio citizens and particularly the legislature relaxed their hostility toward financial institutions, reviving old banks whose charters had lapsed and chartering several new institutions. In 1829, for example, the lawmakers reestablished the Commercial Bank of Cincinnati, although it took two years to attract stock subscribers, and in 1831, it chartered the Bank of Norwalk with a capital stock of $100,000.[6] Yet these actions were piecemeal and were ineffective in providing the needed resources. In the summer of 1832, Ohioans sensed a new urgency when Andrew Jackson vetoed the recharter of the BUS. Cincinnati was especially affected by Jackson's action, since it would lose its largest bank, the branch of the BUS. One Cincinnati writer commented that "the distress for money here at present, is greater than can well be imagined, and the branch bank is, from necessity in prospect of winding up, curtailing. We have one other bank in the place, and its capital but $500,000."[7]

As Ohioans searched for a permanent solution to capital shortages, the legislature's proposal for a state bank attracted attention because of the absence of movement among private capitalists to fill the void. The plan called for the creation of a state bank with capital borrowed from the East and with the state's credit pledged as security. The bank would establish branches throughout the state in order to meet local community needs. Subsequently, Governor Duncan MacArthur and the incoming governor, Robert Lucas, both advocated this plan in December 1832. Widespread public support seemed assured after an Ohio Senate committee reported that the total bank capital in the state was only $2 million, a mere fraction of the state's minimum requirements.[8]

Although sentiment had appeared to coalesce behind some type of state bank, the legislative session of 1833-1834 revealed the presence of opposing forces. In the first place, several groups of financiers requested charters for private companies and therefore opposed the state bank proposal. In 1833, these forces blocked any action on the state bank proposal in the legislature. At the same time, they secured immediate help for Cincinnati by approving a charter for the Franklin Bank of Cincinnati and by increasing the capitalization of the Commercial Bank of Cincinnati.[9] But the supporters of the state bank were not defeated, and Governor Lucas returned to the legislature in December 1833, with a slightly altered plan and a new issue. Lucas supposedly had strengthened his case by specifying that only Ohio residents could purchase stock. This move activated the westerners' fear of "foreign" capital controlling state institutions. Lucas's supporters argued that eastern capitalists already held a substantial majority of the state's bank stock, and they raised the possiblity of even further economic domination without a state bank.[10] Lucas further asserted that his proposition would save the money which Ohio citizens normally spent for interest payments on borrowed foreign capital. The *Ohio Monitor* estimated a net savings of $300,000 per year because the state would negotiate for loans from the East and from Europe, thereby acquiring a competitive rate of perhaps 4 percent. Without a state bank, the newspaper explained, private banks might secure foreign capital through stock subscriptions, but would pay dividends of 7 to 10 percent.[11]

Throughout the debate over the state bank, the arguments reflected a curious ambivalence of public officials and legislative bodies who were in desperate need of funds, but who were fearful of the political and economic influence which might be exerted by outside entrepreneurs. But it was a false issue often utilized to excite popular sentiment or to hinder an opponent's progress. Few members of the Ohio legislature in 1833 could really have believed that the construction of roads and canals had occurred without foreign capital. The essential debate was not *whether* to attract foreign capital, but how best to accomplish it: either through private banks or through a large state bank.

A resolution of Ohio's banking problem came in the legislative session of 1834. The legislature defeated the state bank bill in a close vote, and it then proceeded to charter ten new banks with a combined capitalization of $4.4 million—$2 million of which was held by a single institution, the OLTC, located in Cincinnati.[12] Despite their rhetoric against foreign capital domination, then, the Ohio legislature, both Whig and Democratic members, had chartered the West's largest financial institution and one in which outside capitalists controlled two-thirds of the stock.

Acquiring a charter for the OLTC was a masterpiece of careful planning and a skillful job of political lobbying. Charles Butler initiated the idea of a trust company in Ohio and then stirred the interest of Isaac and Arthur Bronson. Together they sought the support of other New York capitalists who would assist in raising capital and preparing a charter.[13] Charles Butler, who directed the operation in its early stages, recruited members of the Albany Regency, such as his brother, Benjamin F. Butler, then attorney general of the United States; Martin Van Buren, Vice President of the United States; Thomas W. Olcott, president of the Mechanics and Farmers Bank of Albany; and William L. Marcy, governor of New York. Although their names added luster to the project, many of the politicians played only minor roles. Martin Van Buren, for example, wrote letters of recommendation for Charles Butler to facilitate his lobbying efforts in Ohio.[14] The Ohio venture was not an exclusively Democratic project, however, for Arthur Bronson recruited additional partners primarily from New York City's merchant and banking communities and from stockholders of the NYLTC. All the people most closely connected with the Ohio enterprise were known as the "associates," and they included, for example, Gould Hoyt, John Ward, Jonathan Goodhue, Stephen Whitney, James B. Murray, James King, Benjamin F. Butler, and Lot Clark.[15]

Charles Butler had insisted on a careful selection of the "associates" because he realized that disagreements among the promoters could wreck the enterprise; nevertheless, Lot Clark, the NYLTC's agent at Lockport, New York, briefly threatened to split the New Yorkers. Butler had initially excluded Clark from the inner circle because of his reputation for divisiveness, but Clark had pieced together the plan after a casual conversation with Isaac Bronson in the offices of the NYLTC. No sooner had Clark forced his way into the venture than he challenged Charles Butler's strategy for obtaining a charter in Ohio. Butler intended to request a new charter from the Ohio legislature, whereas Clark felt that they could obtain control of the Franklin Bank of Cincinnati and convert it into a trust company. But when Clark suggested the idea to others, his proposal was shunted aside. It was understood that Charles Butler was directing the efforts to obtain the charter.[16]

Butler also desired to limit the number of partners in order to maintain secrecy. Butler feared that if too many capitalists were involved another group might propose a competing bank in Ohio. In 1833, for example, Butler alerted all the associates to refrain from open discussion in the presence of Henry Dwight. Although a resident of Geneva, New York, Dwight and other members of his family held a controlling interest in the Commercial Bank of Lake Erie. Butler knew that Dwight disliked trust companies and feared that he would consider the OLTC a threat to his interest in the Cleveland bank. "If he [Henry Dwight] should suspect an application," Butler wrote," . . . [he] might embarrass us by infusing jealousy through the channel of his friends in that state connected with the Cleveland Bank."[17]

After securing the allegiance of a small group of easterners willing to promote an institution in Ohio, Arthur Bronson and Charles Butler had to contact Ohio residents who would push the project among their citizens and before the legislature. Understandably, Bronson and Butler could not personally operate in Ohio without evoking charges of an outside economic conspiracy; therefore, the New Yorkers worked through Elisha Whittlesey and Micajah T. Williams. Both men had excellent political connections—the former a leading Whig, the latter a Democrat—and both were skilled in land investment and banking.

Butler and Bronson enlisted Elisha Whittlesey's support for the trust company, probably because of Whittlesey's political influence. After studying law in Danby, Connecticut, Whittlesey had settled in Canfield, Ohio, where he opened a law office. There he formed an advantageous friendship with Simon Perkins, a prominent Whig, president of the Western Reserve Bank, and promoter of Akron. Perkins helped Whittlesey to gain election to the state assembly in 1820. Three years later, Whittlesey was elected to the House of Representatives as a Whig and served eight consecutive terms until 1838. Throughout this period he regularly corresponded with the Bronsons about Ohio affairs and national politics. In the 1830s, Whittlesey was a supporter of Isaac Bronson's banking plans and worked for their adoption in the Congress.[18]

Whittlesey was also an enterprising businessman. He held stock in several banks and speculated in land throughout the state. Utilizing his political connections with Ohio Whigs, such as Alfred Kelley, and with Democrats like Micajah Williams, Whittlesey had purchased land at Port Lawrence, later renamed Toledo—one of several towns vying to become the principal transfer point between Lake Erie and the Wabash and Erie

Canal. His investments were shared there by several easterners, particularly Senator John Clayton of Delaware. To buttress the value of his lands, Whittlesey was also an active proponent of internal improvements, such as railroads and canals. Even though his zeal for land speculation schemes and internal improvements later carried him close to bankruptcy, he seemed an ideal agent early in the decade. Whittlesey had shown an ability to work with both Whigs and Democrats in business enterprises, and he was familiar with state banks and land values.[19]

Micajah T. Williams, however, was the most important Ohio resident connected with the planning of the trust company, and his early career offered obvious advantages to the New Yorkers. After coming to Cincinnati as a youth in 1812, Williams was first elected to the state legislature in 1822 at the age of twenty-eight. He later served as a canal commissioner, a job which included conducting surveys and writing technical reports. In 1823, he went to New York City to raise money for the Ohio Canals, and there he made contacts with the city's financial community. He was also an active Democrat, and his support of Andrew Jackson earned him an appointment as surveyor general of the Northwest Territory in 1831.[20]

Williams was also an energetic businessman. He speculated in farm lands, promoted townsites, and invested in bank stock. In the 1830s, for example, Williams was also a partner in the development of Port Lawrence, Ohio. In 1835, he and Byron Kilbourn established a townsite on the western shore of Lake Michigan that was later to become a part of Milwaukee.[21] Williams diversified his business affairs by investing in the stock of several banks. He assisted in organizing and later became a director of the Clinton Bank of Columbus. At the same time, he helped to establish the Franklin Bank of Cincinnati, handling nearly $200,000 in stock subscriptions for eastern financiers, and he was elected to its board of directors in 1833. Although Williams was a recognized Democrat, he shared stock purchases in the Franklin Bank of Cincinnati with Alfred Kelley, a leading Ohio Whig.[22] When Butler and Bronson were searching for an Ohio citizen to support the trust company, Williams's ability to mix business and politics must have seemed an especially valuable asset.

Historical investigations of Williams's career, however, have overemphasized his enterpreneurial initiative and thus underestimated the importance of his connection to eastern financiers. Harry Scheiber, the author of an excellent article on Micajah Williams, argued that the Ohioan was a relatively unique western businessman who actively sought out eastern capitalists. In fact, Williams was a fairly typical representative of eastern financiers. Although he was an important figure in Ohio politics, land speculation, and banking, he rarely acted alone. Eastern capitalists usually contacted him to act as their intermediary. He neither proposed the charter for the Ohio trust company nor did he raise the capital, yet historians know more about Williams than about the men who employed him but worked behind the scenes, namely, Charles Butler and Arthur Bronson.[23]

Ohio residents probably first learned of the trust company when Micajah Williams went to New York City to meet with Arthur Bronson and other interested New Yorkers. After Williams had indicated his wholehearted support for such a company, discussions centered on the proper strategy for securing a charter in Ohio. Williams naturally insisted that Ohioans should direct all in-state negotiations. Bronson and Butler should cancel plans to visit Ohio in the summer of 1833, Williams argued, because they might stir the suspicion of state politicians and businessmen that the New Yorkers intended a massive stock speculation. If public opinion were aroused, according to Williams, it might jeopordize the acquisition of a charter or at least force the legislature to limit the company's powers. Williams had a very unflattering view of the Ohio legislature and once characterized its members as " . . . men of narrow and illiberal views."[24] The Ohioan also warned that public knowledge might create a rush to buy stock, thus preventing the easterners from carefully selecting the stockholders. Williams claimed that this situation had occurred when he had subscribed to stock in the Franklin Bank of Cincinnati for another eastern syndicate.[25]

The eastern associates disagreed among themselves over the extent to which they should conceal their influence in the Ohio trust company. Arthur Bronson feared the anti-capitalist sentiment in Ohio, and at one point, he urged Butler to abandon the idea of traveling there. The younger Bronson contended that they desired to purchase stock, a goal easily obtained without managing the whole enterprise. Yet Bronson eventually changed his mind after listening to arguments from Thomas Olcott, Lot Clark, and Charles Butler.[26] Although their opinions varied in intensity, Clark, Olcott, and Butler believed that the easterners should not try to conceal their involvement in the trust company because such a policy might wreck the endeavor. Thomas Olcott, therefore, told Williams that opposition to "foreign" capitalists must be discreetly challenged: "That the feelings to which you allude prevails more or less in every community is to be deplored but cannot be concealed & in the matter under consideration as well as in most others the fears of these alarmists had better be quietly allayed than openly resisted and forcefully subdued."[27] Olcott was convinced that citizens' fears would vanish once they understood the purpose of trust companies, and in a long letter to Williams, Olcott suggested several cogent arguments which might be used to gain Ohioans' support. In western New York, Olcott claimed, the

NYLTC had offered farm mortgages at 7 percent and had raised the value of land 20 percent in three years. Olcott's most important argument, however, directly attacked the hostility toward outside capital. "A wise legislature," he said, "will court the introduction of foreign capital into a state by affording it the greatest protection & the most liberal returns for its use."[28] According to Olcott, the rates of interest in Ohio would decline as money became more abundant. He also warned against Ohio residents subscribing to any large block of stock. The OLTC's purpose was to bring foreign capital into the state, Olcott said, and thus it would be foolish to charter the institution if Ohio citizens were to take the stock.

Williams's desire to indulge anti-capitalist sentiment within Ohio also distressed Lot Clark. He urged Williams to attack the problem by presenting the benefits of nonresident capital to Ohio citizens: "A company therefore in any other state in the Union in the hands of ordinary capitalists could not loan anything beyond their capital. Ohio, an interior state new and without surplus capital could do nothing without the aid of capitalists of the City of New York who are known & established . . . ."[29] In more practical terms, Clark reminded Williams that if Ohio capitalists financed the trust company, the stock would sell at only three-fourths of the par value because of the lack of public confidence. Clark also suggested that Williams could subdue the factional jealousies within the state by reminding Ohio politicians and businessmen that the company needed agents in different counties. Such positions, he added, were lucrative and politically advantageous.[30]

Clark, Olcott and Butler, then, expressed the majority position which favored some public knowledge and total eastern control. While they preferred to work without public scrutiny, they realized that complete secrecy was impossible and undesirable. If allowed to build, sentiment against eastern capitalists might eventually destroy the company. The New Yorkers were also uneasy about allowing Ohioans to secure any appreciable amount of stock. The easterners, of course, wanted the profitable stock for themselves and wanted control over the company's operations, yet they were correct in maintaining that such an arrangement also benefited Ohio by moving eastern money into the state. Thomas Olcott explained this point to Micajah Williams: "The more therefore of the stock . . . which you can have taken out of your state, the more extensive and general will be the advantages to your community."[31]

Arthur Bronson and Charles Butler now planned a trip to Ohio in order to lobby for the company and to allay quietly the fears of resident businessmen. Butler assured Bronson that " . . . we can go there & lay the foundations for success without exciting any of the apprehensions or jealousies, which Mr. Williams alludes to."[32] Bronson and Butler set out in August 1833, intending to visit Williams in Cincinnati after traveling through Michigan and northern Illinois to look over possible land purchases. Repeated delays and a sudden illness which struck Arthur Bronson, however, forced them to return to the East without stopping in Ohio.[33]

Charles Butler, though, felt that a trip to Ohio was essential. After a grueling two–month tour of the West in July and August, therefore, he set out again for Cincinnati in October 1833. Accompanied by his brother-in-law, Mahalon Ogden, and with letters of introduction from Thomas Olcott and Martin Van Buren, Butler left his home in Geneva, New York, traveling by wagon to Buffalo where he secured passage on a lake steamer. Forced off Lake Erie by a storm, he then took a stage to Cleveland and another from there to Columbus. At Columbus, Butler spent several days meeting local businessmen and presumably talking about the trust company. He next stopped at Chillicothe where he spoke with the state representative from that district.[34] Butler also tried to find Governor Robert Lucas, stopping first at his farm near Piketon but not overtaking the Governor until after a church service in Portsmouth, Ohio. Certainly the two men discussed the proposed trust company, although Lucas withheld his support since he backed the state bank plan. Governor Lucas, however, gave Butler additional letters of introduction to Cincinnati politicians. Since Cincinnati was the intended location of the trust company, Butler spent nearly two weeks there conversing with its leading politicians and businessmen. For example, he talked with David T. Disney, a Democrat and then president of the Ohio Senate; Jacob Burnet, a Whig and former senator; and John McLean, a Jacksonian Democrat and recent appointee to the Supreme Court. Many of Butler's contacts later became the company's most ardent supporters and members of the first board of trustees.[35.]

Throughout his trip, Butler conscientiously kept a diary in which he noted Ohio's agricultural potential, its transportation improvements, and its influential people. Always with an eye to future investments, he missed few important points. Departing from Ohio in November, Butler was convinced of the OLTC's future success because of Ohio's economic potential. In characteristically booster prose, Butler observed that "I have left the State of Ohio, with deep impressions of its present & future greatness. The capacity of its soil—the character of its population—its commercial and agricultural resources—all . . . indicate at some future & no distant day it must become a star of the first magnitude in the galaxy of the States."[36]

Butler returned to his home by way of New York City and Albany in order to speak further with financiers and politicians. Certainly he must have communicated his enthusiasm for the Ohio enterprise. In New York City, he stayed at the U.S. Hotel where he spoke twice with Martin Van Buren. He also met with William Bard, president of the NYLTC. Finally he journeyed to Albany where he visited with his brother, Benjamin, who was then preparing to depart for Washington to assume his duties as attorney general. When he arrived back in Geneva, Charles Butler must have been pleased with the trip. He had met with Ohio political officials and smoothed the way for the trust company. Moreover, the sentiment against foreign capitalists had not surfaced in Ohio among those people he had visited.[37]

While Charles Butler laid the political groundwork for the trust company, Arthur and Isaac Bronson assumed responsibility for preparing the company's charter. They asked their lawyer and close friend, Roger Sherman of Fairfield, Connecticut, to write the first draft using the NYLTC's charter as a model.[38] At the same time, they requested input from other New York associates. Charles Butler, for example, insisted that the company should be capitalized at $3 million. He remembered the attacks against the NYLTC because it controlled too much capital, and he obviously hoped to obtain a large capitalization before any backlash developed within the Ohio legislature. Butler also felt that a large capitalization would permit the institution to purchase Ohio internal improvement bonds for resale in foreign markets.[39] Thomas Olcott and Lot Clark, on the other hand, were more concerned with the OLTC's possessing the right to charge 7 percent interest on loans, thereby increasing the profits and making it an attractive investment to nonresident capitalists.[40]

Isaac and Arthur Bronson showed a draft charter to the New York City associates in June 1833. The new institution differed in several ways from the NYLTC, but the essential change was that the Ohio trust company possessed the powers of a commercial bank, that is, the power to issue notes and to deal in bills of exchange. Three years earlier, the Bronsons had supported the NYLTC because it divorced capital investment from note issue, but Jackson's veto of the recharter of the BUS had changed their approach. Isaac Bronson was convinced that without the restraining hand of the BUS, commercial banks would expand their note issues and lend their capital, encouraging speculation and inflation. The OLTC, he hoped, would show the nation that a large financial institution could invest its capital stock in land mortgages while simultaneously issuing notes to facilitate trade. For Isaac Bronson and his son, the Ohio institution represented a workable compromise between merchants desiring credit for short-term exchanges and farmers needing long-term capital. The Bronsons also knew that the charter's banking clause would appeal to

Cincinnati residents and members of the Ohio legislature who wanted a bank to replace the Cincinnati branch of the BUS.[41]

The draft of the charter also contained two clauses designed to avoid the problems of legislative interference which had occurred in New York. Even though these provisions were later removed, they were indicative of Arthur Bronson's thinking. The New Yorker inserted a provision stipulating that the OLTC would possess a monopoly for twenty-five years in order to prevent the legislature from chartering competing institutions. Another clause stated that the charter was to last until the institution voluntarily closed its doors. Although the Bronsons later removed these clauses, they still obtained an extraordinarily strong charter from the Ohio legislature, which gave the company freedom from legislative amendments or repeal until 1870, except in specific cases of negligent management.[42]

The New York partners also added a provision which facilitated their control and anonymity. Whereas the charter of the NYLTC had included the names of the first board of trustees, the bill for the Ohio firm named thirty-five incorporators, all residents of Ohio, but provided that a board of trustees would be elected later. Arthur Bronson pointed out that this provision would enable " . . . the first board to be chosen by the stockholders—so arranged that a limited number may be non-residents."[43] Thus there was no hint in the charter that eastern capitalists intended to obtain stock control. Moreover, the pervasive influence of the Bronsons, Charles Butler, and the New York associates remained unknown except to Micajah Williams, Elisha Whittlesey, and their confidants.

Even though Micajah Williams guided the charter through the Ohio legislature, he had little freedom to act on his own. On two trips to New York City in April and October 1833, Williams received instructions concerning political strategy.[44] His dependence upon the Bronsons was particularly evident during December 1833, and January 1834, when the legislature discussed the trust company bill. Williams reported to Arthur Bronson that certain legislators objected to Section 23, which dealt with the company's power to issue bills and notes. Fearing a negative vote in the legislature, Williams suggested that the company should surrender the power to issue notes; then, without obtaining special legislative approval, the trust company could use bills of exchange or certificates of deposit as notes. Arthur Bronson rejected this strategy because the company would be assuming a power which the legislature had expressly denied. To attempt such a sleight of hand, Bronson said, would simply invite legislative reprisals. Arthur Bronson suggested several alternative compromises, but he cautioned Williams that it was terribly difficult to draft new clauses without proper reflection. Consequently Williams retained the original wording and faced a vote on the issue. An amendment denying all banking powers to the company was proposed in the House of Representatives, but it was defeated as were other attempts to limit the firm's powers.[45]

In February 1834, the OLTC received a charter which was one of the strongest granted to a financial institution in the 1830s. The OLTC was capitalized at $2 million, granted banking powers until 1843, and allowed to have one-fourth of its trustees from out-of-state. The state had set no termination date on the charter, and it had surrendered any right to amend or repeal the charter for thirty-five years.[46]

The Ohio legislature had granted such a powerful charter because of the political and economic situation in Ohio at that particular moment. The legislature had reacted to the perceived need for financial institutions in the aftermath of Jackson's veto of the recharter of the BUS and the subsequent removal of federal deposits. At this same time, the legislature had approved nine additional bank charters. Butler and Bronson were also responsible for the strong charter due to their careful preparations in the East and in Ohio. Arthur Bronson, perhaps, best expressed the feelings of the eastern associates in February 1834, in writing to Micajah T. Williams: "The Charter which you have obtained is conceded on all hands to be a strong and valuable grant, and if confided *to the right kind of men,* under a system of regulation well defined and approved at the outset, no doubt is entertained in the ultimate success of the Institution—of the benefit it will confer on the citizens of your State,—as well as the advantage to be derived by the stockholders."[47]

The next step in Arthur Bronson's plan was to obtain the "right kind of men" as stockholders.[48] Even though the charter stipulated a procedure for securing public subscriptions to the stock which required a set day and time for people to request stock, Bronson engineered a behind–the–scenes distribution to New York's financial elite and political allies. As in the case of the NYLTC and many other banks in the early ninteenth century, financiers did not really believe in an "open" distribution of stock to the public. By selecting the stockholders, the Bronsons and other associates hoped to ensure that the company operated according to the conservative financial principles of its charter while returning a respectable dividend to its founders. Bronson's first step, then, was to duplicate the OLTC's charter and to distribute it among the associates. Next he requested Micajah Williams to come to New York to meet with the eastern partners before policies were set for the stock subscriptions. In March 1834, Williams and the New Yorkers agreed that the eastern investors would control approximately three-fourths of the company's stock, $1,500,000, or 15,000 shares at $100 per share. Ohio residents were to hold the remaining 5,000 shares with a value of $500,000.[49]

Considering that there were twenty-three original associates, Arthur Bronson needed to recruit many additional capitalists in order to distribute $1,500,000 of stock. Ordinarily this would have been an easy task, except that the associates wanted to carefully screen prospective stockholders because the stockholders eventually selected the board of trustees and the company's officers. Arthur Bronson first contacted all the associates to fill their stock requests. Frederick Bronson, Arthur's younger brother, visited the New York offices of Prime, Ward, and King, and they subscribed for 1000 shares. Similarly Gould Hoyt took 2,000 shares. By late May 1834, the Bronsons had parceled out 10,000 of the 15,000 available shares. Even with 5,000 shares remaining to be sold, Frederic Bronson indicated no intention to relax the standards of selection: "The residue of the stock not yet subscribed for can be disposed of without difficulty should it be indiscriminately offered to the public, but the gentlemen who have already subscribed think it would be more for the interest of the Company that the stock should be given to those who would probably take it as a permanent investment & not for speculation."[50]

To secure additional stockholders, the Bronsons took several steps. A general letter describing the OLTC was sent to selected eastern financiers. The Bronsons also wrote to political officials, such as Secretary of War Lewis Cass, to offer him an opportunity to purchase stock.[51] The Bronsons saw benefit in courting Cass because of his close ties to Jackson's administration. Cass also was influential in the Michigan Territory where he had served as territorial governor and where Arthur Bronson owned thousands of acres of land. In some cases, Arthur Bronson assisted potential stockholders by lending them the funds for the stock purchase. Charles Butler, for example, obtained fifty shares after borrowing the purchase money from Arthur Bronson.[52] By June 1834, the Bronsons had completed the distribution of stock in the East.

Table 5 is a list of the OLTC's eastern stockholders, and it reveals the effectiveness of the Bronsons' screening process. New York City's elite merchants and financiers, such as Peter Harmony, Isaac Carrow, Gould Hoyt, Goodhue and Company, and George Griswold, dominated the list. Moreover, Arthur Bronson had enlisted representatives of foreign and domestic investment firms such as Prime, Ward and King; John Ward and Company; and Nevins, Townsend and Company. The Bronsons thus had mobilized over $1,500,000 of eastern money for investment in the West in addition to linking the state of Ohio to foreign and domestic capital markets. The Bronson family held 1,050 shares, a sure indication of their intention to oversee the company's management. Despite his efforts in acquiring the charter, however, Charles Butler held only 50 shares. Most likely Butler's limited interest resulted from a chronic shortage of money due to his penchant for investing in diverse promotional schemes.[53]

TABLE 5

EASTERN STOCKHOLDERS OF THE OHIO LIFE INSURANCE AND TRUST COMPANY, 1834

Stockholder	Shares	Stockholder	Shares
Anderson, Henry James	300	Lydig, D.	200
Battell, I., Jr.	200	Marshall, Charles	80
Beekman, Henry	100	McCracken, J. L.	150
J. D. Beers & Co.	100	McIntyre, A.	50
Belden, H.	50	Mead, Walter	50
Belden, Henry	50	Monroe, James	100
Berney, Robert	200	Mott, Valentine	50
Bowne, Walter	1,000	Mott, William	50
James Boyd & Co.	100	Murray, James	100
Bronson, Arthur	300	Nevins and Townsend	150
Bronson, Frederic	150	Oakley, Thomas	100
Bronson, Isaac	500	Abraham Ogden & Co.	100
Bronson, Oliver	100	Ogden, David	50
Butler, Benjamin	50	Olcott, Thomas	100
Butler, Charles	50	Osborne, Thomas B.	50
Carrow, Isaac	500	Paine, Elijah	50
Clark, Lot	250	Phelps, Thad	50
Clarkson, David	200	Power, Tyrone	50
Coster & Carpenter	200	Prime, Ward & King	1,000
Cruger, John	50	Rankin, Henry	100
Denison, C.	50	Redmond, William	200
Depau, Francis	150	Renalds, Thomas A.	100
DeRham, H. C.	250	Sedgwick, Robert	100
Dimon, Ebenezer	150	Sheaf, M.	120
Duer, John	200	Sherman, Roger	100
Gibbes, Thomas S.	100	Short, William	200
D. A. Glover & Co.	100	Spofford, Tileston & Co.	50
Glover, John	100	Stephens, Benjamin	250
Goodhue & Co.	200	Stephens, John	150
Goodhue, Iona	50	Suydam, John	150
Griffin, Francis	50	Talamadge, N.	50
Griswold, George	200	Tallmadge, James	100
Harmony, Peter	200	Throop, E.	500
Hoyt, Gould	2,000	Tibbits, Elisha	250
Jay, Peter	100	Tomlinson, D.	200
Jones, George	50	Tracy, Frederick	100
J. L. & S. Joseph & Co.	100	Waddington, J.	100
Lawrence, William B.	100	Ward, Henry	200
Leroy & Perry	100	John Ward & Co.	200
Lord, Rufus	200	Willett, Marinus	50
Lorillard, Peter	300	Total Shares	15,000

SOURCE: List of Stockholders to the Ohio Life Insurance and Trust Company, 23 July 1834, BP, 203. Since this list was a handwritten record of stock pledges, the final amounts given to individuals might have varied somewhat. It is also possible that the list includes a few Ohio citizens since the Bronsons might have distributed occasional shares to western citizens. The percentage of stock controlled by out-of-state residents, however, did not vary. See *The Second Annual Report of the Ohio Life Insurance and Trust Company* (Cincinnati: Looker, Ramsay & Co., 1836), p. 19.

The distribution of the 5,000 shares of stock in Ohio was apparently no more open than it had been in the East. Arthur Bronson had urged Williams to recruit the "right" Ohioans. Williams followed that advice and secured stockholders that represented a cross section of Ohio's political and financial elite. Whig stockholders, for example, included Elisha Whittlesey, Simon Perkins, Alfred Kelley, and Jacob Burnet while Micajah Willaims, John H. Groesbeck and David T. Disney represented the Democrats.[54] Especially significant in terms of eastern influence was the fact that Elisha Whittlesey and Micajah Williams depended on loans from eastern capitalists in order to purchase their stock. Williams borrowed $5000 for 50 shares from a group of the "associates" and Whittlesey split his shares with Jesup Wakeman of the Bridgeport Bank.[55]

All the stock was sold, then, before the actual, legal opening of the stock subscription books in Ohio. This fact necessitated complicated transfer arrangements between the New Yorkers and the Ohio partners. While awaiting the legal opening of stockholder books in Cincinnati, the Bronsons deposited the monies in the NYLTC. When the books did open in late July 1834, Arthur Bronson merely sent the money and names of the stockholders to Micajah T. Williams and Jacob Burnet, the two commissioners charged with receiving public subscriptions.[56] Of course, no stock remained for the general public. On the appointed day, the commissioners just entered the names of the subscribers from previously prepared lists. Later, when the company came under attack from political enemies within the state, a fairly accurate protrayal of the stock subscription process appeared in the *Cincinnati Advertiser:*

> On the day appointed for opening the books, there were a number of citizens attended at the hour and place appointed and desired to subscribe and pay their installments, and were told that the stock was all subscribed for and that none could be had, and instead of their Secretary opening the books for subscriptions he opened to enter a number of names which he took from lists in his own possession and would not suffer any one to subscribe. Here, now, is proof of what rich men may do, and what they are capable of doing.[57]

The Bronsons also influenced the membership of the OLTC's board of trustees, the twenty-member principal policy-making body. The charter required that the trustees must be stockholders holding fifty or more shares and that three-quarters of the trustees must be residents of Ohio. Since the New York associates had carefully parceled out the stock, the task of electing trustees was less difficult. After a slate of candidates previously had been agreed to by Williams and Bronson, an election was held in Cincinnati in the fall of 1834. The Bronsons had little difficulty electing their "people" since they had obtained sufficient proxies from the eastern stockholders.[58]

The membership of the board of trustees reflected the Bronson's concern for securing respected financiers and community leaders who would engender public confidence in the institution. The New York City trustees were all wealthy merchants and bankers: Arthur Bronson, James G. King, Isaac Carrow, Walter Bowne, and Gould Hoyt. Of the Cincinnati trustees, the most prominent were Simon Perkins, Elisha Whittlesey, Alfred Kelley, Jacob Burnet, David T. Disney, and Micajah Williams. Not only were these respected businessmen, but they also represented different political views. Whereas Perkins, Burnet, Whittlesey and Kelley were leading Whigs, Williams and Disney were prominent Democrats. The Bronsons wanted a bipartisan board of directors in order to reduce the possibility of political considerations affecting business. Isaac Bronson once wrote to Elisha Whittlesey that "Corporations should be of no party—they derive their power from all the people, and should use it for the benefit of all."[59]

Two steps remained before the company could begin operations—the election of officers and the approval of bylaws, that is, the formal rules of operation. Both these steps were to be taken at a formal meeting of the trustees in Cincinnati in November 1834, but the eastern stockholders completed most details beforehand. The most important office was the company's president, and considerable discussion arose among the Ohio trustees as to whether Elisha Whittlesey or Micajah Williams was the best candidate. Many worried that Williams was too political and would embroil the institution in endless controversies. On the other hand, the Cincinnati trustees, who dominated the board, resisted Whittlesey because he was not a city resident.[60] In fact, there should have been little doubt about Williams's election. From the beginning, he had been the principal representative of the easterners, and as early as May 1834, they asked him to assume the institution's presidency. To avoid an internal dispute, the easterners offered Whittlesey the post of secretary, which he refused in order to keep his seat in Congress.[61] Perhaps the best indication of the New Yorkers' domination of the enterprise was that all the final arrangements were made at a meeting in early November in New York City at which Arthur Bronson spoke for the eastern trustees and M. T. Williams, Simon Perkins, Alfred Kelley, and Jacob Burnet represented the Ohio interests. Leaving New York City, the Ohio trustees carried a list of the company's officers arranged by the New Yorkers and a set of bylaws written by the easterners to be formally adopted at the Cincinnati meeting. The details completed, the company opened for business in January 1835.[62]

Since the eastern associates, led by the Bronsons, prepared the OLTC's charter and bylaws, the operating rules and the administrative structure of the OLTC reflected its close ties to Isaac Bronson's banking theories and to the NYLTC's practices. The company was organized into two administrative divisions, reflecting its dual purpose—a trust department and a banking department. The trust department was responsible for supervising the trust and life insurance business and was charged with investing the company's capital stock and deposits of less than one year (Deposits over one year were transferred to the banking department). There were three standing committees, each consisting of three trustees. The committee on trusts rarely met since the trust and life insurance business was very small. In contrast, the finance committee invested deposits of less than twelve months which totaled $134,960 in 1835 and over $250,000 in 1836. Usually it lent these funds to individuals, while accepting corporate stock, particularly its own stock, as security for the loans. The committee on investments was the most important of the three since it placed the firm's $2,000,000 capital stock in real estate mortgages. It operated in an identical fashion to the NYLTC. The company appointed agents in thirty-six counties who evaluated the character of loan applicants, assessed the value of the land offered as security, and prepared an abstract of its title. Company lawyers then reviewed the whole application before the committee on investments took final action.[63]

Like the NYLTC, the Ohio firm's trust department was very cautious in lending money on real estate. Although the trust company hoped to assist the state's agricultural development, its main customers were established farmers rather than pioneers. The charter bound the company to an operating rule practiced by the Bronsons in their own land business and by the NYLTC: the land taken as security must be double the loan's value. Moreover, the company generally lent funds on land already under cultivation and exercised great care when accepting city property because its value fluctuated. A survey of the company's agents in 1836 revealed that approximately three-fourths of the capital was lent to farmers for improvements on existing farms or to purchase additional acreage. The remaining funds went to merchants and artisans, probably for business expansion, in return for real estate security. Within a year after its establishment, the company had invested $1,858,099 in 64 of the state's 74 counties. Over 2,138 people had received loans averaging $869, and they, in return, pledged landed security totaling $4,338,117.

Since the company was interested primarily in the permanent investment of its capital stock, mortgage contracts generally were for unspecified periods. So long as the mortgagor met his semiannual interest payment and maintained the value of the security, the trust company did not pressure its debtors for the repayment of the principal. For the company's protection, however, the bylaws permitted the company to call in any loan after giving two years notice. A court—appointed inspector who reviewed the company's performance in 1836 praised its conservative management of the capital stock. A further indication of the firm's care in selecting its debtors was the fact that nearly one-fifth of the original capital had been repaid voluntarily by 1840, despite the onset of a depression in 1837.[64]

The trust department, therefore, provided needed economic services to Ohio's agricultural sector. Eastern capital was drawn into the state through stock sales, and farmers subsequently borrowed these funds at 7 percent interest. Institutional loans also guaranteed that the farmers would have use of the money for an extended period, unlike the abbreviated contracts of four to five years which were typical of private lenders and even some commercial banks. In the words of one effusive, though accurate, agent:

> It [the trust company] is the first time in the history of this State, that the farmer has been enabled by a *Banking Institution* to obtain money upon that permanency of credit which has justified its employment. The ordinary operations of banking, afford facilities only to him who can calculate upon a speedy return from his investment. No individual can look abroad upon the farming interests of our State, without being satisfied of the permanent beneficial results of capital vested in the hands of the prudent and practical farmer.[65]

The OLTC's banking department was perhaps its most distinctive feature. Although intending to meet the credit needs of Ohio's mercantile community, the Bronsons still included numerous safeguards in the company's charter and bylaws to guard against what they perceived as the central defect of commercial banks: the expansion of note issues without sufficient security. First, the company's capital stock of $2 million was invested in real estate mortgages as the principal support for the banking department. Second, all funds deposited with the company for more than a year were credited to the banking department to back up the note issue. Third, the charter stipulated that the note circulation could never exceed $1 million or twice the amount of money deposited with the company for over a year. Furthermore, the charter only granted the power of note issue until 1843 and specified that any suspension of specie payments longer than thirty days resulted in the forfeiture of the charter. Finally, the Bronsons included the basic principal of strict commercial banking in the standing rules of the banking department: "No note, bill, or other obligation . . . which has more than one hundred days to run, shall be discounted; and on all paper discounted, payment shall be exacted at maturity; and no discount shall be made with any understanding, express or implied, of any connection between the payment of one note, or bill, and the discount of another.[66]

In the first year of its operation, the OLTC fulfilled the eastern associates' expectations. It became an important institution for drawing eastern money into Ohio through stock subscriptions and deposits. In 1835, its $2,000,000 capital stock was augmented by $810,570 in long-term deposits. The largest depositors were the Bank of the United States, $400,000, and the Phoenix Bank of New York City, $200,000. In 1836, deposits increased to $1,689,000, giving the company total financial resources of $3,689,000. With its large investment potential, the OLTC quickly became an important source of agricultural and mercantile credit while returning a good annual dividend of 8 percent to the stockholders. The Bronsons received periodic reports from resident trustees, like Elisha Whittlesey and Simon Perkins, on the company's careful administration, and they probably read with pleasure the company's first annual report and the court appointed inspector's favorable review. Yet there were unsettling signs of trouble even then; because of the OLTC's location in Cincinnati, Williams faced enormous pressure to expand the note issue and to ease conservative investment policies. But that struggle was still in the future. In 1835 and 1836, the eastern associates and the western management of the OLTC viewed with pride this institution which might serve as an example of sound banking to the entire country.[67]

The early history of the OLTC, then, exemplified key elements in the process by which eastern capital reached the West. In spite of inadequate communications, an immature financial system, and conflicting state laws, the New Yorkers were able to move capital through an innovative institutional structure. Easterners, like the Bronsons and Charles Butler, had to control the company during its first years, given the sophisticated charter and bylaws and the amount of its capitalization. Western capitalists, such as Micajah Williams, did not contest eastern direction; in fact, Williams and other Ohioans assumed that the Bronsons would determine the company's structure and select most of the stockholders. Yet this theme can be overdone, for eastern influence was limited in several ways. The company's officers and three-quarters of the board of trustees were residents of Ohio, and thus business was conducted in Cincinnati without the participation of eastern trustees. In fact, company rules required only six trustees for a quorum to decide most company policies. In the future, then, it was unavoidable that westerners would take over the company's management and that the influence of eastern financiers would correspondingly decline, even though they continued to hold the majority of stock.[68]

4. A Journey to the Old Northwest, 1833

In addition to their involvement with the trust companies, Charles Butler and Arthur Bronson were similar to other Jacksonians in their fascination with the West. This interest led the New Yorkers to the states and territories of the Old Northwest in the summer of 1833, nearly a year before the arrival of most farmers, in order to inspect townsites, search for fertile agricultural lands, and interview prospective agents. Despite nearly twenty years of American control that extended from 1815 to 1833, however, neither the military nor the fur traders had transformed this wilderness into farms and towns. Thus the easterners' trip was especially significant because it represented the initial migration of capital and entrepreneurial skill into the region. This chapter analyzes the easterners' trip in order to demonstrate the care with which they selected investments and to reveal the reasoning behind their financial decisions regarding the economic development of the Old Northwest. The journey itself represents a somewhat incongruous image and strikes at sterotypes of the absentee speculator, since the frontier has always been considered the domain of hardy pioneers—the fur traders, the farmers, and urban boosters—and certainly not an accommodating environment for a Wall Street capitalist and his affluent friend from Geneva, New York.

The United States only had assumed control of the areas bordering the Great Lakes after the War of 1812, when the main thrust of the nation's economic growth was still to the South along the great interior rivers, such as the Ohio and the Mississippi. Consequently, agricultural and urban development had taken place in southern Ohio, Illinois, and Indiana, but settlement had yet to extend north along the shores of Lakes Erie, St. Clair, Huron and Michigan. In northern Ohio along Lake Erie, for example, Cleveland was only a small village of perhaps 150 people.

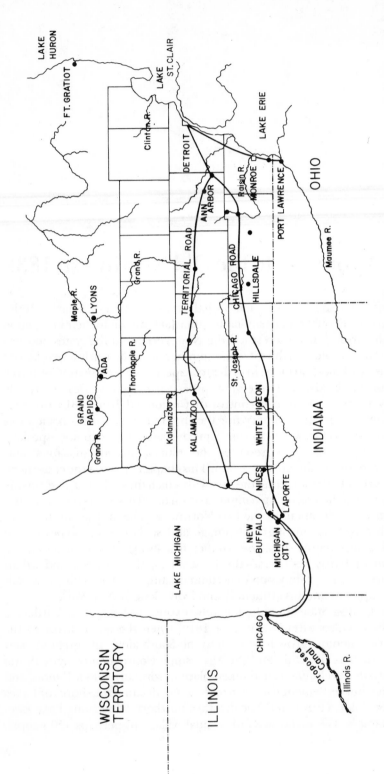

Fig. 2. Michigan and Northern Illinois in 1836 [This map is based on maps appearing in Robert J. Parks, *Democracy's Railroads: Public Enterprise in Jacksonian Michigan*. (Port Washington, New York: Kennikat Press, 1972), pp. 35, 51, and 132; and S. Augustus Mitchell, *Map of the States of Ohio, Indiana and Illinois With the Settled Part of Michigan* (Philadelphia: S. Augustus Mitchell, 1832 and 1838.]

Further West, Detroit was a more substantial outpost because of its early settlement as part of France's North American empire, yet persistent economic problems slowed its growth after the War of 1812. Detroit's residents were isolated because lake travel was infrequent; moreover, the city lacked a thriving commerce and a substantial agricultural hinterland. Its inhabitants, especially the French, were more interested in the fur trade than in the relatively sedentary occupations of merchant and farmer.[1]

West of Detroit, civilization had made only an occasional intrusion into the wilderness. In 1815, therefore, travelers avoided the unsettled areas of southern Michigan and took boats northward from Detroit on Lakes St. Clair and Huron. Mackinac was a strategic point as it guarded the passage between Lakes Huron and Michigan. Green Bay was the only substantial settlement on either the eastern or western shore of Lake Michigan. It had 250 inhabitants, most of whom were of English and French extraction and still loyal to the British government. Further south, Milwaukee, (then unnamed) was an occasional rendezvous point between the fur traders and the Indians. Wherever rivers flowed into the lakes, such as at present-day Kewaunee, Manitowoc, Sheboygan and Grand Haven, the sites were marked for trade but were unaffected by permanent settlements. Chicago had been the location of Fort Dearborn before the War, but its inhabitants had fled in the face of Indian attack during the War. Prairie du Chien, a small fur trading and mining settlement, was located across the territory on the Mississippi River marking the frontier's outer edge.[2] Strategic towns, then ringed the Northwest, but these were only frontier outposts and not harbingers of an emerging agricultural or commercial society.

After the War of 1812, though, the federal government had taken the first steps in the settlement process. Responding to the advice of frontier officials, the government began building forts in 1816 to guard strategic communication arteries. The forts were intended to prevent British participation in the fur trade and to curtail their contact with the Indians and fur traders at interior posts such as Green Bay. They were placed at the juncture of important routes of travel, such as Fort Shelby (Detroit), Fort Gratiot (Port Huron), Fort Mackinac (Mackinac), Fort Brady (Saulte Ste. Marie), Fort Howard (Green Bay), and Fort Dearborn (Chicago). Over the years, the military was also invaluable in the exploration of the country's interior, the collection of scientific data, and the construction of roads.[3]

Military policy was linked to the government's Indian policy. At most military posts, the federal government established Indian agencies whose agents were responsible for pacifying, educating, and, in general, introducing the Indians to Anglo-Saxon culture. Indian agents also regulated the fur trade since it was the principal contact between Indian and white cultures. Eventually Indian policy concentrated on the acquisition of Indian lands and the removal of whole tribes to areas further West in anticipation of agricultural settlement.[4] From 1815 to 1833, therefore, military and Indian policies had prepared the way for settlement even if they had not directly brought about economic expansion.

Throughout these years, the fur trade was the region's principal economic activity. John Astor's American Fur Company dominated the trade with its headquarters at Mackinac and a string of posts at central locations like Chicago, Detroit, Green Bay, and Prairie du Chien.[5] The Indians were an essential part of the trade since they obtained the furs and then sold them for liquor, beads, hardware, and clothes. The fur trade was a profitable enterprise for only a brief period, approximately from 1816 to 1832. When the Indians sold their land to the federal government and moved West, the American Fur Company lost its cheap labor supply, and the fur trade business was transformed. Many individuals continued to trap animals and sell pelts to local merchants, but by 1833 the fur trade was no longer an important economic activity in the emerging frontier society. The fur trade, moreover, had not generated any appreciable economic development in the Old Northwest.[6] It was an extractive business which stifled "spin-off" enterprises that would have led to urban and commercial expansion. The population of the leading trade centers, for example, had not increased significantly in twenty years. In addition, the fur trade generally bankrupted it participants. At Green Bay, Chicago, and Prairie du Chien, the leading traders were forced to surrender their land claims to the American Fur Company in order to pay off existing debts. The fur trade, thus, had been a stage of frontier development with few ties to the later settlement period.[7]

In 1832, several factors indicated that the Old Northwest was on the verge of great changes. There were already pockets of settlement far in advance of later population movements. Detroit and its surrounding hinterland were relatively settled, and across southern Michigan and northern Indiana occasional farms and villages dotted the landscape. These settlements, however, were the vanguard, and their number declined the further west one traveled. In 1830, for example, Michigan's western counties of Berrien and Van Buren had 325 and 5 people respectively.[8] Yet these western counties soon would fill with farmers and townspeople, for the federal government had purchased most of the Indian lands in the path of settlement. Some lands were even surveyed and readied for sale.[9] The defeat of the Sac and Fox Indians in the Blackhawk War of 1832 dispelled any lingering fears that Indians blocked access to the Old Northwest. Finally, favorable economic conditions in the East coalesced with hundreds of more subtle personal factors to start the great western migration of the 1830s.

Arthur Bronson and Charles Butler were among the leaders of this movement. The two men first discussed a western trip in 1832 during one of Charles Butler's frequent visits to New York City on business for the NYLTC. Already involved in a trust company in New York City and planning for another in Ohio, the easterners were conscious of the fact that the Old Northwest was the next frontier of investment. The Blackhawk War in 1832 had alerted them to the region and to the availability of land. Throughout the winter and into the spring of 1833, Bronson and Butler gathered information about the western territories. Arthur Bronson spoke with General Winfield Scott, a family friend, who had commanded American troops at the conclusion of the Blackhawk War. Scott had traveled through a large portion of northern Illinois and southern Wisconsin in his elusive pursuit of military action, and he advised Arthur Bronson that Chicago stood at a critical location for trade in the new country.[10] Additional information about Chicago was secured from Daniel Jackson, a New York City merchant, who supplied goods for the western Indian trade. Through Jackson, Arthur Bronson was introduced to Robert A. Kinzie, a former Indian agent, fort sutler, and member of the best-known and most important family in early Chicago. John Kinzie, Sr. had been an employee of the American Fur Company and later an Indian agent at Chicago. After his death in 1828, his sons, John and Robert, followed their father's career as fur traders and Indian agents.[11] From Robert Kinzie, Bronson secured information on the territory surrounding Chicago plus an offer from Kinzie to sell portions of the family's holdings in Chicago. Bronson tentatively agreed to the purchase for $5,500 contingent on his personal inspection during the summer of 1833.[12]

Assisted by maps and descriptions of the Old Northwest found in John Farmer's *The Emigrant's Guide,* Butler and Bronson set out for the West in late June 1833.[13] Butler left from Geneva, New York, with his wife and a few friends and met Arthur Bronson at Rochester, New York, on June 28. At Niagara Falls, they spent a relaxing day with their friends before the two men headed south to Buffalo where they boarded a steamboat bound for Detroit. On board, Butler passed the tedious hours by keeping a diary and writing letters home, and these sources revealed his somewhat parochial and nativistic attitudes. Unimpressed by his fellow passengers, who were mainly Swiss emigrants, for example, Butler referred to them as " . . . naturally filthy and stupid, and hardly one removed from the natives."[14] At Cleveland, the steamboat stopped for a brief period, and here Blackhawk, chief of the Fox and Sac, boarded the ship for the trip to

Detroit. Although this was not the first time that Butler had encountered an Indian, his comments reflected a deep prejudice. It was ironic that Butler and Bronson came to Detroit in the same steamboat that carried Blackhawk, who had just completed negotiations with the federal government that required his people to move further West.[15]

On landing at Detroit on July 4, Bronson's and Butler's first reactions were unfavorable; their feeling resulted from the crowd which gathered to see Blackhawk and which engulfed the travelers as they left the ship. After a few days, however, the city seemed more hospitable. Part of Detroit's attractiveness was due to its transitional character. Even though it possessed many characteristics of a frontier outpost—a transient population and a primitive economy—Detroit was also sufficiently settled to offer the amenities of urban life such as a hotel and the pretensions of a society. Smaller settlements—Pontiac, Mt. Clemens, and Ann Arbor—surrounded Detroit adding to the country's settled appearance.[16] Detroit's strategic location for commerce particularly impressed Butler, and he wrote that "This place is destined to become a very great city and now its location is unequalled by that of any other place in the union; it has a great back country to contribute to its wealth, & prosperity; the whole territory comprising as fertile a tract of land as can be found in any part of the United States contributes to the business and trade of Detroit . . . ."[17]

Although the New Yorkers had intended to remain in Detroit only a few days before departing for the potentially more rewarding opportunities at Chicago, they extended their stay to explore the city's investment possibilities. Bronson and Butler contacted resident businessmen and explored with them the purchase of city lots and farm land. Information came easily because Butler and Bronson were celebrities in Detroit society. The city's economic elite entertained them, leading Butler to remark "we have had at least four or five parties on our account, & we feel that we should clear out soon to save our credit & relieve the city."[18] Although their extended stay in Detroit was a pleasurable experience, it was also a business trip. Butler kept a record of everyone they met and noted their economic and political position within the territory. His diary included the names of the city's principal politicians and businessmen: Elon Farnsworth, Charles Trowbridge, Oliver Newberry, Major Thomas Forsyth, Thomas Sheldon, and Governor John Porter. From these initial meetings, Bronson and Butler later selected two land agents for the Detroit area, Charles Trowbridge and Elon Farnsworth.[19]

Besides establishing economic and social relationships in Detroit, Butler and Bronson visited other towns and inspected farm lands in the area. On July 9, they rode approximately thirty miles into the interior to look over agricultural lands, and on July 12, they secured passage on a steamboat bound for Fort Gratiot on Lake Huron.[20] Although several small settlements existed along the St. Clair River, few settlers had come as far north as Fort Gratiot even though a military road had been completed from Detroit in late 1832.[21] Although planning only an overnight trip, the party was stranded eighty miles from Detroit at the juncture of the Black and St. Clair rivers when the boat's rudder broke. While waiting for repairs to be completed, they explored the region in the vicinity of Fort Gratiot. Charles Butler, who would later plat a village at this site, noted the region's characteristics:

> We occupied the afternoon in a visit to the Fort, and a ramble along the shore of Lake Huron. The scenery is beautiful beyond description; but it was like a great ocean, of blue water in the midst of a solitary desert; the fort is the only settlement (except for a little settlement beginning at the Black Creek) in all the country . . . . At Black River there is a small settlement of perhaps 8 or 10, log & frame houses all connected with a very extensive steam mill which has lately been put in operation there . . . .[22]

Lacking suitable equipment for further exploration and bored with the prospect of spending several days at Fort Gratiot, the group abandoned their vessel and crowded into a schooner hauling lumber to Detroit. Thirty-five miles into the voyage, a storm forced the small craft to seek shelter off the lake. After an overnight stay in a small cabin on shore, the travelers resumed their voyage, even though the rain and high winds continued. That evening, they again sought shelter. Butler found some consolation in the incongruity of their predicament: two refined and wealthy easterners trapped in a small boat on a lake in the West. In writing to his wife, Butler described their difficulties: "You would have been amused to have seen us in our forlorn plight; wet and jamed [sic] together in this little cabin & hungry & cold. We were glad to take up with the captain's fare, a bit of pork & sour bread. It relished very well, I assure you. Mr. Bronson ate of it with avidity."[23] The storm finally broke, enabling the New Yorkers to arrive back in Detroit on Wednesday, July 17.

Having decided to leave for Chicago the following week, Butler and Bronson filled their final days in Detroit with business meetings and social events. They had an additional interview with Governor Porter and attended an evening party where they conversed with the explorer and Indian agent Henry Rowe Schoolcraft. Later they met with Chicagoan John Kinzie, who had stopped at Detroit. Discussions with Kinzie most likely centered on the property which he had for sale in Chicago. They also talked with the former governor, Lewis Cass, who was then Secretary of War. The conversation covered a number of topics including politics and investment opportunities. Cass was an invaluable source of information since he had led exploring expeditions throughout the Old Northwest. Cass also owned valuable lands near Detroit which would surely become part of the city when it expanded. Bronson and Butler discussed the possible purchase of this parcel.[24] Finally they met Lucius Lyon, Michigan's territorial delegate and a former land surveyor, who owned a considerable amount of real estate in Michigan's interior which he desired to sell to the New Yorkers. Lyon impressed both men, and later he was employed as Arthur Bronson's land agent.[25]

Thus Bronson and Butler made good use of the three–week stay at Detroit. They met most of the territory's leading political and economic leaders. They also acquired an in-depth knowledge of the region's most favorable investment possibilities. In mid-July 1833, Butler expressed the New Yorkers' excitement over Detroit: "While Buffalo and Cleveland have engrossed speculators, Detroit's a place ten thousand times more important than either, [and] has escaped—simply because it is in a territory, there is however the germ of speculation existing here, & an intimation would develop it. Mr. Bronson and myself have come here at a fortunate time."[26] Rather than lose the advantage of their early arrival and excellent contacts, Bronson and Butler changed previous plans to delay all land purchases until they had completed the journey. On July 19, Butler instructed his law partner in Geneva, New York, to call in any outstanding debts and to convert all his assets to cash. "I shall desire to sell," Butler wrote with characteristic zeal, "all that I own in the world (except my house) including bank stock . . . to invest it & all my earnings into property here."[27] Butler and Bronson, then, formed a partnership with Detroiters Elon Farnsworth and Charles Trowbridge for the purchase of city lots and surrounding farm lands.[28]

With their business nearly completed, they then prepared for the overland trek to Chicago. For two easterners, a three-hundred-mile horseback ride across southern Michigan was an arduous undertaking. To ease the difficulties, they purchased several horses, outfitted a wagon with provisions, and acquired the appropriate dress—hats, leggings, and saddlebags.[29] Butler, nevertheless, was uneasy about the trip even though Detroiters "talk of a ride to Chicago as we talk of a visit to Buffalo, and I suppose when we get to Chicago that the people there will advise us to go to the Rocky Mountains."[30] Yet the scores of emigrants who daily poured into Detroit on their way West partially allayed Butler's fears. He wrote that "I met with people from all sections here; the Americans are literally a stirring, & travelling people; they want to see every nook & corner of the country. Everybody is going to Chicago, & we shall doubtless meet with hundreds on the same pilgrimage with ourselves tho with very different objects."[31]

In 1833, there were two overland routes to Chicago. The territory had authorized the building of a road in 1829, and even though it was not officially completed, many travelers used it in the early 1830s. The Territorial Road ran southwest from Detroit to Ypsilanti, then turned north and west through the modern-day cities of Ann Arbor, Jackson, Battle Creek, and Kalamazoo. Then it turned southwest through Van Buren County to St. Joseph on Lake Michigan. But in 1833, the Chicago Road was the preferred route because it ran through more settled territory. It had been designed as a military thoroughfare connecting the military posts at Detroit and Chicago. The Chicago Road ran west from Detroit to Ypsilanti, then veered south and west to Tecumseh passing through the lower tier of counties west to Coldwater and White Pigeon, and south around Lake Michigan to Chicago.[32] Even though Bronson and Butler selected this route, they took periodic side trips both north and south of the road.

The New Yorkers left Detroit on July 24 accompanied by Gholson Kercheval, a sub-Indian agent at Chicago, who acted as guide. They quickly rode through southeastern Michigan passing the small villages of Saline, Clinton, and Jonesville. Although they described the terrain as pleasant, neither man was impressed with the topography as it compared to regions of western New York.[33] Upon entering Branch County, however, the New Yorkers first sighted the prairie region of southern Michigan, and they slowed the journey's pace in order to investigate the possibility of purchasing land. After passing the smaller prairies of Coldwater and Sturgis, they approached a large prairie surrounding the village of White Pigeon. Butler remarked that

> White Pigeon is a pleasant little village . . . situated in the center of an extensive & beautiful prairie 6 or 7000 acres: What is a prairie? It looks like the great ocean, for there is nothing to obstruct or intercept the view except here & there a house; a perfectly level plain without a tree or bush or stone; encircled in the background with the dense & noble forest which looks like the frame of the picture.[34]

At White Pigeon, the financiers stopped for three days to explore the area more thoroughly. White Pigeon was a small town of approximately 600 inhabitants and the temporary site of a federal land office. The surrounding region had attracted many farmers because of its fertile lands and its accessibility from the Chicago Road. Approximately 3000 people each lived in St. Joseph and Cass Counties.[35] While Charles Butler ventured south into Indiana, Arthur Bronson explored the area to the north. He rode twenty-five or thirty miles into Kalamazoo County and onto the Big Prairie Ronde, the largest of Michigan's prairies encompassing 130,000 acres. Most likely, Bronson's route was dictated by previous conversations with Lucius Lyon, who owned land at two settlements in this region. Lyon held many lots at Kalamazoo where he had settled in 1832. He also had platted the village of Schoolcraft on the prairie lands to the south. At Schoolcraft, Bronson paused to meet several residents including Lyman Daniels, a lawyer from Canandaigua, New York, who settled there in 1832 and later became one of Bronson's land agents.[36]

After returning to White Pigeon from separate trips to inspect prairie lands, the two men resumed their journey to Chicago. They continued to ride through prairie lands and oak openings. Crossing the St. Joseph's River, they entered upon Beardsley's Prairie which Butler described as the most beautiful they had seen because of its hilly terrain. After passing through Niles, the road dipped south into Indiana. Even though Indiana had been a state since 1816, the northwestern section was only sparsely settled because the early emigrants had traveled over the National Road from Kentucky and Tennessee and settled the southern part of the state. Moreover, pioneers had not moved beyond the state's midpoint due to unfavorable publicity concerning the wet lowlands in the North.[37] Bronson and Butler, nevertheless, were particularly interested in the prairie located in LaPorte County. Butler reported that it was called the Door Prairie because " . . . the forest in the center of the prairie contracts to a point, leaving a passage just wide enough for the road to pass through it, which, whether travelling east or west, at a distance appears like a door or passage cut through for the accommodation of the road."[38] Aside from its beauty, the New Yorkers were attracted by reports of low prices for prairie lands averaging approximately $300 for 80 acres.

Leaving LaPorte, they headed northwest to Michigan City which was then less a reality than a dream of its promoter, Major Isaac Elston of Crawfordsville, Indiana.[39] Elston had purchased land bordering on Lake Michigan in hopes that it would become Indiana's only port for the shipment of produce to the East. In addition to platting Michigan City, Elston had organized a company to construct a railroad from Lafayette, Indiana, to Michigan City. Butler and Bronson were skeptical of Elston's project since Michigan City was little more than a desolate stretch of "sand and barren land." The accommodations at what Elston called the "City Hotel" elicited the following comments from Butler:

A small log house, with a single room, which answered the purpose of drawing room, sitting room, eating room & sleeping room; in this room some 11 or 12 persons lodged in beds & on the floor including of course our host & his wife: the fact that we have become accustomed & familiarized to scenes, & things which we never dreamed of before leaving home, & which we then should have revolted at; but necessity know of no laws, & we have been obliged to accommodate ourselves to the customs of the country . . . .[40]

After leaving Michigan City, the two men traveled parallel to the shore of Lake Michigan toward their final destination, Chicago. The New Yorkers' first glimpse of the frontier community came on August 2; and despite a long and tiring ride, Butler noted that "At 7 o clock arrived on the prairie surrounding Chicago & had sight of the city: the sun was fast setting & presented one of the most beautiful sights imaginable; it was like a sunset on the boundless ocean: the vast & interminable prairie west and south from Chicago is very much like the ocean hardly a bush or tree to obstruct the view as far as the eye can reach . . . ."[41]

When Bronson and Butler reached their destination in August 1833, Chicago was on the brink of great change. The city had been platted in 1830 after the state of Illinois had received a federal grant to construct a canal linking the Illinois River and Lake Michigan and had designated Chicago as the northern terminus of the proposed waterway. Yet neither the town nor the canal had attracted any substantial interest until 1833 when national and regional forces stirred the movement of settlers and capitalists. Population growth reflected this change. In 1832, Chicago's population did not exceed 250; by the summer of 1833 the population was 500, most having arrived within the preceding two months; and by 1834 the city had 1800 inhabitants.[42]

Chicago's bustling character immediately attracted Butler's and Bronson's interest. They were amazed by the number of emigrants daily pouring into the town forcing most everyone to live in tents or in unfinished houses. Besides the emigrants, Indians arrived each day and camped on the town's edge in preparation for the negotiation of the Chicago Treaty in September, 1833.[43] Charles Butler noted that his own accommodations were in a tavern which " . . . presents a fair sample of the state of things in Chicago. It is new and unfinished. The partition walls not lathed & plastered & of course free communication between all the rooms. Mr. B (Bronson) and I are accommodated with a *private room*."[44]

Remaining at Chicago for a week, Bronson and Butler obtained information on town lots and farm lands from the leading citizens. They depended most heavily on government officials—Indian agents, military personnel, and land officials—who dominated Chicago's society at the time. Thomas J. Owen, for example, was the Indian agent. Through his influence, the New Yorkers learned of many valuable parcels soon to be purchased by the federal government. Bronson and Butler also had several conversations and attended dinners with the officers at Fort

Dearborn. Military officers had explored the country's interior and possessed valuable information on agricultural lands. Some military officers
had purchased lots in Chicago which they wished to sell. Bronson and
Butler eventually purchased land on Chicago's North Side from Captain
David Hunter, who had been stationed at Fort Dearborn.[45]

As the New Yorkers surveyed the Chicago region, they became convinced of its future importance as a trade center. In their minds, its
principal advantages were the plentiful prairie extending south and west,
the on-going construction of a harbor, and the possibility of a canal
linking the Illinois River and Lake Michigan. Bronson and Butler were
also encouraged because they were the first easterners to investigate the
site's investment potential. Consequently, they established formal connections with several Chicago citizens to act in their behalf in the purchase of
land. They also promised to assist Chicagoans in reviving the Illinois and
Michigan Canal project, which had been dormant for several years because the state lacked the funds for construction. As they prepared to start
home, Butler expressed his enthusiasm for Chicago's future:

> I am astonished to find myself here in this distant point . . . . If I
> were a young man & unmarried I would settle down at Chicago: It
> presents one of the finest fields in America for industry & enterprise
> and in a few years we shall think no more of going to Chicago than
> we now think of going to Buffalo. There will be a line of steamboats,
> stages, & railroads the entire distance from Albany to St. Louis on
> the Mississippi, Chicago being an important and commanding point
> on this great thoroughfare.[46]

Although Butler and Bronson had desired to visit Green Bay and
Mackinac, they were unable to obtain steamboat passage; thus, they
decided to part company on the return trip, permitting each to inspect
different locations. Charles Butler headed around Lake Michigan passing
again through LaPorte and then stopping at South Bend. While in Indiana, he made further arrangements for the purchase of prairie lands.
From South Bend, he then went to White Pigeon where he awaited the
arrival of Arthur Bronson who had left Chicago in the company of Lucius
Lyon with the intention of inspecting areas north of the Chicago Road.
After meeting in White Pigeon, the financiers again decided to travel
separately. Butler obtained stage passage on a direct route to Detroit
while Bronson meandered more slowly across the country with Lucius
Lyon as his guide.[47] They planned to meet again in Detroit before setting
out for Ohio and talks with Micajah T. Williams about the Ohio Life
Insurance and Trust Company. But Arthur Bronson was stricken with a

flare-up of a chronic lung disease, and both men decided to return home.[48]

The importance of this journey cannot be overestimated. Butler and Bronson were vanguards of the new frontiersmen, "the pioneers of capital", who came West to evaluate possible areas for investment. They were not the only easterners who came West but they were among the first. The journey also demonstrated the care with which eastern capitalists chose western investments. In his diary, Butler, for example, noted the characteristics of the soil, the availability of water, and the current price of the land.[49] Both men also looked carefully at town lots marking those villages most likely to prosper. They realized the interdependence of town and farm, and their comments about the advantages of an urban location were accompanied by observations on the surrounding hinterland. Both men showed a remarkably comprehensive view of the necessary ingredients for economic development. They regularly inquired about the availability of or the potential for canals and railroads. At the same time, they met and evaluated a score of western citizens selecting some to serve as agents and remembering others as contacts for future economic and political needs.

Finally, both men possessed an ability to envision the West's potential within the nation's economy, and thus they did not delay purchases. The New Yorkers signed a formal partnership in late 1833 in which they agreed to share land purchases in those areas which they had visited on the summer trip. Although the exact terms of the contract were unclear, Butler definitely borrowed his share of the purchase monies from Arthur Bronson, obligating himself to repay that sum before any division of the profits.[50] In late 1833 and early 1834, the New Yorkers bought town lots in Chicago, Detroit, Grand Rapids, and Niles as well as agricultural lands throughout the Michigan Territory, Indiana, and Illinois. Later, each man pursued other land investments outside the partnership.

Bronson and Butler, however, were not alone in their western land interests; and from 1833 to 1836, they were only two of thousands who participated in one of this country's most spectacular land booms. In 1830, for example, the federal government had sold only 1,929,733 acres of public land; in 1833 that figure was 3,856,277; in 1835 sales had soared to 12,564,478; and they peaked in 1836 at 20,074,840.[51] Everyone speculated—doctors, lawyers, farmers, politicians, and city dwellers—because land was one of the few productive investments open to all holders of surplus capital. Different needs and expectations motivated the endless variety of speculators. For some, land purchases held out the possibility of great wealth, while many others sought only modest gains. In the West, for example, fur traders and military officers sold their claims to farmers and speculators for small advances and then moved on. Squatters also accepted money for claims or for partially cultivated farms, and then moved further West. Even those settlers who were primarily farmers speculated in land. They purchased extra acreage for possible expansion or for sales at a higher price to the next wave of settlers. Town dwellers in 1834 and 1835 were similar to their agricultural counterparts; they purchased the lot upon which their house or store was located, but then added the lot next door or down the street hoping it would rise in value when the city expanded. Most westerners, of course, desired to increase their own wealth, yet they also sensed that land purchases contributed to the region's economic development.[52]

The potential for profit and the excitement of participation in the westward movement also enticed eastern citizens to acquire western lands. Many investors were probably small businessmen or craftsmen who bought a few lots or a quarter section of wild lands in a distant state or territory. Wealthier easterners, either as individuals or organized as partnerships with a capital of from $500 to $200,000, employed agents to travel west and purchase land at sales or from second owners. William Thompson traveled west in 1836 as the agent of several Albany businessmen and politicians, including Thomas Olcott and Benjamin Knower. Dixwell Lathrop traveled extensively throughout Ohio, Illinois, and Michigan searching out lands for John A. Rockwell of Norwalk, Connecticut.[53] Some easterners came West to see the territories for themselves, although their journeys typically came two years after Bronson and Butler's trip. Levi Beardsley from Cherry Valley, New York, for example, boarded a steamboat in Detroit and then traveled along the western shore of Lake Michigan stopping at Chicago, Milwaukee, and Green Bay in order to buy town lots. In 1835, James B. Murray, Arthur Bronson's brother-in-law, undertook his own tour of the West only to bump into Boston friends in St. Joseph, Michigan, then no more than a promoter's dream.[54] At times, there may have been more eastern land investors rummaging about the western states and territories than there were real settlers.

Before one can properly understand the role of these eastern capitalists in facilitating the West's economic development, the image of the eastern speculator in most historical literature and in the popular consciousness must be challenged. The idea that most speculators cheated farmers out of just claims, that promoters platted paper cities to bilk an unsuspecting public, and that monopolists held land off the market and delayed settlement can no longer be accepted as historically accurate. In recent years, historians and economists employing sophisticated statistical analysis have challenged these older views which assumed the superiority of the farmer's claim to the public domain. It must be stressed that the purchase of land either for farming or for investment was a legitimate and functional part of the nineteenth century economy.[55] Having set aside arguments about the morality of land speculation, then we can study more thoroughly the methods, motives, and consequences of eastern investments in western lands.

Future chapters, therefore, will explore the western investments of Arthur Bronson and Charles Butler. Since they pursued independent business opportunities in the West after their initial partnership, their careers reflected the two dominant types of eastern investment in the West: the conservative speculator and the classic promoter. Arthur Bronson, who probably purchased more land than any other eastern financier in the 1830s, was a conservative speculator who selected each parcel with great care. His conservative policies contrast sharply with existing stereotypes of the nonresident landholder. Charles Butler, on the other hand, was the classic promoter. He always sought the big profit, the "main chance," and willingly accepted the greater risk of failure. Without a personal fortune to support his purchases, Butler formed land companies and partnerships in order to accumulate funds for the large-scale development of agricultural lands, townsites, and transportation improvements. Despite their contrasting business styles, however, both New Yorkers were important elements in the economic development of the Old Northwest.

5. The Conservative Speculator: Arthur Bronson and the Western Land Business, 1833-1836

A distinguishing characteristic of writings on land speculation is that historians know too little about the business methods and investment philosophies of eastern capitalists who purchased western lands. Due to the number and diversity of people speculating and the large volume of land sold, several historians have conveyed the impression that a lack of organization, exacerbated by a buying mood approaching frenzy, permeated the land boom of the 1830s.[1] Yet underneath that flurry of business activity there were eastern businessmen with comprehensive investment plans, who purchased lands and encouraged supporting activities such as banking in order to stimulate the West's economic growth and to secure themselves a substantial profit. Arthur Bronson typified these land investors.

A major stumbling block in any analysis of land speculation is the word itself. For many years, historians automatically associated the term *speculation* with the wild, unplanned purchase and sale of land which produced high prices and deprived farmers of their just claims to the soil. In rebuttal, economist Douglas North justifiably criticized historians for their refusal to accept speculation as a functioning part of the land market and for their inability to acknowledge its beneficial economic effects. North defined speculation in the following manner: "When anyone buys an asset with a resale or rental value, he is indulging in speculation. Buying that asset, he forgoes buying other assets, all offering prospective income streams that he takes into account. He is guessing about the future value of that asset."[2]

North's definition needs further elaboration, however, if historians are to understand the business methods and goals of land speculators and their effect on urban and agricultural development. Speculation, while impossible to define precisely, should be viewed as an economic activity which included, at one extreme, land purchases which involved great risk and the possibility of large profit and, at the other extreme, land purchases of limited risk and smaller but more certain profits. The degree of speculation was obviously affected by the goals and strategies of the speculator. The classic image of the speculator is an individual who purchased land and held it for resale at a very high price without making improvements. Although this practice was common enough throughout American history, there were many speculators who purchased lands and accepted substantial risks in attempting to improve the land or the surrounding region in order to increase the possibility of profit. The word *investor* might more accurately identify this type of capitalist, but no definition can reflect all the variations in the operations of nineteenth-century businessmen. They adopted different investment strategies depending on the region of the country, the quality of the land, and the economic conditions of the time (to mention only a few of the variables); consequently, they might have been considered high-risk speculators in one transaction but conservative investors in another. In general, though, I argue that eastern financiers like Arthur Bronson and Charles Butler directly and indirectly increased the economic viability of western agricultural and urban communities, and thus their business activity often qualified as "investment" rather than "mere speculation."

The purpose of this chapter is to analyze the business strategies and goals of Arthur Bronson, a conservative speculator who successfully reduced the risks of land speculation, secured large profits, and contributed to the development of local communities. Bronson's land business went through two distinct stages from 1833 to 1836. Ahead of the migration of most western farmers and city dwellers, Bronson concentrated on the purchase and development of city lots while land prices were still moderate in 1833 and 1834.[3] Bronson's urban speculations at Detroit, Grand Rapids, Chicago, and Cassville demonstrated his changing strategies in response to local conditions and to fluctuations in the land market. By 1835, Bronson became so concerned with inflation in the price of city lots and the potential for an equally quick deflation that he pulled out in order to concentrate on the acquisition of farm lands. At the same time he opened a mortgage loan business charging interest rates of from 7 to 10 percent and accepting land as security. The substantially reduced risks and the prospect of only moderate profits indicated that Bronson had switched to more conservative investment policies.

To understand the financial strategies of Arthur Bronson, we must realize that his western land purchases were part of a much larger whole, for the family also had interests in banks, land, mining, and manufacturing in more than a dozen states and several territories, including Virginia, North Carolina, Florida Territory, Missouri, and New York.[4] In New York State, for example, Arthur Bronson oversaw land agents in at least half of the state's counties. Arthur and his brother Frederic participated in promotional ventures such as the Olean Land and Hydraulic Company, a company formed to sell real estate in the village of Olean, New York. They also cooperated in establishing New Brighton, a townsite on Staten Island. Furthermore, both Isaac and Arthur Bronson were widely-known private bankers, and promoters consequently besieged them with requests to assist in new manufacturing enterprises and land deals. Occasionally even state and territorial governments requested cash loans for operating expenses.[5] Like many financiers of the early nineteenth century, then, Arthur Bronson never concentrated on only a single business enterprise.

Arthur Bronson managed his western investments through carefully selected agents who were located in the key cities throughout the modern-day states of Michigan, Illinois, Indiana, and Wisconsin. This administrative system was necessary because institutions such as land agencies, land companies, and banks had yet to be established on the frontier. Most agents were given regional responsiblities: that is, they purchased land and supervised its later sale in a specific area. The reasons for an agent-centered organization were simple: Bronson could trust the westerner's knowledge concerning land values if the agent was familiar with the region. Moreover, Bronson limited agents to a particular state or territory because each governmental unit had its own laws relating to contracts, land titles, taxes and interest rates.[6]

Bronson also separated his land agents geographically in order to simplify the record-keeping for land purchases and to lessen the risks that one unprofitable investment would affect others. The family's entire financial portfolio operated on the belief that diversity brought economic security, and each investment throughout the country was therefore viewed as a separate account. Yet the land business often required Bronson to work with state governments and the federal bureaucracy, and thus he had a few agents with broader responsibilities. Lucius Lyon of Michigan, for example, served in Congress and informed Bronson of both state and national legislation related to land and banking. He also assisted in resolving periodic disputes with the General Land Office in Washington, D.C.

Since the western agents generally purchased and sold the land, Bronson's selection and control of these men was essential to his business. After deciding to invest in Detroit and its vicinity in the summer of 1833, for example, Bronson immediately began the search for a reliable agent.

He selected two Detroiters, Elon Farnsworth and Charles Trowbridge. Both men were typical Bronson employees: young, knowledgeable about land, skilled in legal or financial matters, and respected members of the local community. Charles Butler once referred to the two Detroiters as "two of the safest and soundest gentlemen in the city."[7]

Charles C. Trowbridge was a native of New York State who had come to the Michigan Territory in 1819 at the age of nineteen as an aid to a United States Marshall. Trowbridge was immediately befriended by Governor Lewis Cass, and in 1820 Trowbridge accompanied Cass on an exploring expedition to the upper Mississippi River. He later moved into the ranks of Detroit's economic and social elite, and in 1825 he accepted a position as cashier of the Bank of Michigan, then controlled by the Dwight family of Geneva, New York, and Springfield, Massachusetts.[8] Trowbridge met Arthur Bronson briefly in New York City in 1832, and Bronson renewed the acquaintance on his arrival in Detroit in 1833. In 1834, he had sufficient trust in Trowbridge's economic abilities to urge on him the position of secretary of the Ohio Life Insurance and Trust Company. Trowbridge refused the offer, preferring instead the seemingly unlimited opportunities available in Detroit, a city which elected him mayor in 1834.[9] Trowbridge thus possessed obvious talents that Bronson sought in western agents: economic expertise, political influence, and excellent standing in the community.

Elon Farnsworth's skills complemented those of Charles Trowbridge. Farnsworth was a native of Vermont where he had graduated from Middlebury College and later studied law. When he came to Detroit in 1822 at the age of twenty-three, Farnsworth entered the law practice of Solomon Sibley and Andrew Whiting. In 1825, he was admitted to practice before the territory's supreme court, and he subsequently appeared in more than seventy-five cases before the court between 1825 and 1836. His legal career merged with politics when he was elected to the territory's legislative council in 1834. In 1836, he was appointed as the state's first chancellor, a legal post directing the Court of Chancery.[10]

Recognizing that Trowbridge and Farnsworth possessed the necessary skills for successful investment, Bronson established a partnership with the Detroiters in which he and Butler agreed to share profits and losses on land investments initially totaling $20,000 and possibly increasing to $50,000. Bronson supplied all the capital while Trowbridge and Farnsworth assumed responsibility for the land's purchase, management, and eventual sale. In return, they were to receive a one-third share of the profits after reimbursing Arthur Bronson for their share of the capital at 7 percent interest. Butler and Bronson agreed to split equally their two-thirds share of the profits, although Butler first had to repay Bronson for his share of the investment capital. The contract was to continue for five years, at which time the profits and any remaining lands would be divided among the partners. Oral agreements probably limited the land purchases to Detroit and its immediate vicinity, the areas with which Trowbridge and Farnsworth were most familiar.[11]

Several provisions of Bronson's contract demonstrated his control of the business and his agents. He first drew up the contract based on the family's extensive experience with agents in New York State, and he supplied all the capital. Second, he stipulated that the contract would last only for five years, a provision indicative of his intention not to hold land off the market, a strategy usually attributed to speculators. Instead, Bronson wanted all lands sold quickly to protect him from the unpredictable fluctuations in the price of land and from the possibility that the partners might disagree on the proper time for closing the venture. Bronson further guaranteed his equity in all lands purchased by stipulating that deeds carry his name. This clause was not surprising since all the other partners were indebted to Bronson for their share of the capital.[12] To assure that his agents followed these instructions, Bronson required semiannual reports that accounted for all purchases and sales. Finally, Bronson insisted that the westerners work exclusively for his interest, a clause that avoided any possibility of a conflict of interest which might arise if agents invested for several capitalists concurrently.[13]

Conscious of the dangers inherent in land speculation, Arthur Bronson also attempted, although not always successfully, to regulate the Detroiters' business practices. In a stream of detailed letters, the New Yorker set down guidelines for the selection of land. He cautioned against hasty purchases and urged that agricultural selections should be based on an analysis of soil type, access to water, and the availability of transportation. Since Bronson executed all final deeds and purchase agreements in New York City, Trowbridge and Farnsworth could not ignore his advice. Bronson further controlled most agents through the Bank of Michigan where he established credit and deposited funds for land purchases. Bronson typically set limits on the amount of money which any of the agents might obtain in order to curtail their ability to make expenditures without his approval.[14]

Bronson also determined the general investment strategy for each region in the Old Northwest. In the Detroit area, he invested funds in three principal locations: Detroit lots, property adjacent to the city in the path of expansion, and agricultural lands in the immediate hinterland. This diverse pattern was calculated to spread out the risks of speculation. At the same time, Bronson concentrated a majority of his funds in town lots because they carried the potential for greater profit. Indeed, Detroit was a boom town when Bronson arrived in 1833; its population had risen from 1,517 in 1828 to 2,222 in 1830, and 4,968 in 1834.[15]

But increasing population also had stimulated Detroit's land market and had caused an intense investment in city lots as speculators attempted to promote different areas of the city as the principal business district. Bronson accordingly adopted several policies to reduce the dangers of city speculation. He first carefully selected a few areas of the city where he concentrated lot purchases: on Jefferson Avenue and Shelby Street, the corner of Fort and Cass Streets, and on Woodward Avenue. The purchases were "safe" because they were either in or adjacent to the town's existing business district. Bronson, moreover, had not clustered his lots in a single block in order to reduce the cost of improvements.[16] If a capitalist owned a complete block, it was then necessary for him to construct all the buildings in order to attract retail and wholesale merchants; consequently, the amount of capital expended and the risks taken correspondingly increased. It was safer, the New Yorker believed, to purchase single lots in selected locations where the erection of a building would add to an already established neighborhood. Bronson periodically agreed to erect buildings on his lots, but only when the sale or rental of the structure could be expected to return construction costs plus a profit of at least 7 percent. When the New Yorker did purchase an entirely undeveloped section within the city or land immediately on the outskirts, he resisted Trowbridge and Farnsworth's requests to undertake grandiose building schemes and insisted on waiting for the growth of the surrounding region before committing additional funds.[17] Bronson, therefore, was not a "promoter" of Detroit who was willing to invest large amounts of money in order to build a business or residential district with the hope of huge profits in the future. Instead, he chose the more prudent course and purchased isolated lots where an occasional improvement aimed at increasing the property's value offered the prospect of more immediate profit.

Bronson also demonstrated this conservative approach to city investments in his refusal to participate in potentially profitable yet highly speculative ventures. In 1833, for example, Bronson had noticed that Detroit's expansion along the waterfront was blocked by "ribbon" farms—undeveloped agricultural lands extending back from the riverfront which were longitudinal in shape as a result of the original French titles. Former Governor Lewis Cass owned one of the most valuable of these farms, and in the summer of 1833, Bronson and Butler discussed the purchase of this land in their first meeting with Cass at Detroit.[18] The financiers made a formal offer to Cass, but he rejected it, conscious that a delay of several months or a year would increase the property's value.

Trowbridge and Farnsworth continued negotiations over the next year until Arthur Bronson prohibited any further discussions. Bronson characteristically decided that the asking price was so inflated that it would be very difficult to realize even a moderate profit after making the necessary improvements. Butler and Trowbridge, on the other hand, later joined with other capitalists in the purchase of the Cass farm for nearly $100,000. Their hopes of developing the land as part of the city failed because the extensive cost of improvement left too small a profit margin, particularly after the onset of the 1837 depression.[19]

Despite his concern with rising land values and the excessive costs of developing property, Bronson did assist the western agents when he believed that internal improvements might increase real estate values. For instance, he helped the Detroiters in their efforts to build a railroad from Detroit across the lower peninsula to Lake Michigan. The territorial legislature had granted a charter for the Detroit and St. Joseph Railroad in 1832, but there were delays in raising the capital and in acquiring a land grant from the federal government.[20] When it came time to acquire stockholders, Arthur and Frederic Bronson personally introduced Charles Trowbridge to their New York friends and testified to the railroad's potential. Moreover, the Bronsons and Charles Butler subscribed for shares of stock. Of course, the support of the railroad reflected a judgment that this improvement would solidify Detroit's economic position and increase land values along the railroad's route.[21]

Only a year and a half after the partnership had been established and $30,000 had been invested, Arthur Bronson differed with his partner, Charles Butler, and his agents, Charles Trowbridge and Elon Farnsworth, over business strategies. Butler, Trowbridge, and Farnsworth were boosters who wished to purchase more land, particularly in Detroit, in the belief that values would continue to escalate. In May, 1834, Farnsworth expressed this optimism: "Our city has never been more brisk than this Spring, and the immigration thus far has been greater than in any former year. It was computed that we [received] 2000 immigrants, in 36 hours last week. It really seems to use the phraseology of the historian of the crusades as if the whole east was loosened from it foundations and precipitating itself upon the West."[22] Charles Butler and Charles Trowbridge voiced similar judgments throughout the boom years. In late September 1833, for instance, Butler observed that he was " . . . more and more convinced of the excellence of our investments in the city of Detroit, [and] as to those in the interior there can be no doubt."[23] In 1834, he told Bronson that Detroit lots could be sold for a 100 percent advance. Perhaps Trowbridge best expressed the westerners' almost total trust in an expanding land market and rising land values when he wrote that :

The investment of money in the lands of Michigan is in my opinion one of the most certain sources of wealth the world offers . . . . I have not known a single failure in this business, even where the agent was not a man of enterprise and cool judgment . . . . There is nothing visionary in this, the business is almost reduced to a certainty . . . . Land judiciously selected may be fairly expected to rise one hundred per cent per annum.[24]

Arthur Bronson, on the other hand, was apprehensive. When land values doubled and tripled, he worried over the inflation and urged his agents to sell rather than wait on additional increases. Furthermore, Bronson had one eye riveted on the eastern money markets and national banking policies which, he believed, threatened the economy's stability. By late 1834, he decided that Detroit land values were too inflated to justify further risks; he therefore decided to close the partnership with Trowbridge and Farnsworth, thus accepting a modest gain in preference to the possibility of heavy losses in a potential deflationary period.

After several months of negotiation, Bronson withdrew from the partnership in November, 1835, selling his share to Charles Butler. Butler again borrowed the money from Bronson, the new contract stipulating that Bronson had to be reimbursed before the partners could split any future profits. Despite this sale, Bronson still had a substantial interest in the Detroit area; he owned thousands of acres of agricultural land and isolated town lots purchased under other contracts, and he held mortgages on town lots and farm lands as security for the eventual repayment of the debts of Trowbridge, Farnsworth, and Butler.[25] In other words, Bronson had reduced his risks in Detroit; he was no longer responsible for improvements to most city property, but instead he had lent money to the urban promoters taking land as security and receiving annual interest payments.

The closing of the partnership revealed a crucial difference in investment strategy between Arthur Bronson and Charles Butler and between Arthur Bronson and his western agents. Bronson was certain that the inflation of the economy eventually would cause credit restrictions and a recession, and he consequently desired only the safest investments.[26] While Bronson pulled back his most speculative commitments in 1835, Trowbridge, Farnsworth, and Butler increased their landholdings convinced that even greater profits were in the future. These men must have thought that Arthur Bronson was an overly cautious penny-pincher in 1835 and 1836; they would think differently in 1840.

Outside Detroit and vicinity, Lucius Lyon managed the bulk of Bronson's investments. Like Trowbridge and Farnsworth, he was an important frontier entrepreneur with all the land agent's requisite skills when he first met Bronson and Butler in the summer of 1833. Born on a farm near Shelburne, Vermont, Lyon had abandoned the agricultural life for a job assisting a civil engineer in Burlington, Vermont. He had come to Detroit in the early 1820s and gained employment as a land surveyor. For ten years a deputy surveyor, Lyon traversed the Old Northwest acquiring an unmatched knowledge of advantageous locations for farms and town-sites. He also made good use of this knowledge by purchasing real estate at the minimum government price throughout the Michigan Territory in partnership with other western citizens. Finally, Lyon was an important territorial politician; he served as Michigan's territorial delegate from 1833 to 1836, and after Michigan achieved statehood, he returned to Washington as one of the state's first senators.[27]

Because of his unique position and talents, Lyon became the Bronson family's most important western agent. Arthur Bronson concluded several different contracts with Lyon giving him the right to invest in Michigan, Illinois, and Wisconsin; supervisory responsibilities over other agents; an investment capital of over $75,000; and permission to draw up to $10,000 from Bronson's account at the Bank of Michigan. Lyon was to receive half of the profits on their joint investments after reimbursing the Bronson family for his share of the purchase money at 7 percent interest. In return, Lyon was to manage the property without charging the partnership for travel expenses or legal fees. The contract was to last for five years, at which time there would be a general accounting and a division of the profits. Because of the amount of money entrusted to Lyon, Arthur Bronson insisted on semiannual reports and Lyon's exclusive services as an agent.[28] Over the years their business arrangement ripened into a close friendship. Lyon often stayed at Bronson's New York City home on various trips to and from the nation's capital.[29]

Arthur Bronson followed somewhat the same investment pattern with Lucius Lyon as he had with Trowbridge and Farnsworth. From 1833 to 1835, the New Yorker concentrated his capital in city lots, while purchasing some agricultural lands surrounding the towns, and then sold out when it appeared that land prices bore no relation to real value. This pattern was evident in three towns: Grand Rapids, Ada, and Lyons. Bronson, however, also changed his tactics to fit local conditions. Since this area of western Michigan was virtually unsettled, Bronson shared a major responsiblity for the original promotion of each town; yet at each site he stressed the cautious approach to urban development.

Although historians have credited local residents, such as Lucius Lyon and Louis Campau, with the development of Grand Rapids, neither of these men possessed the necessary capital nor the financial expertise to build a city alone. In fact, during the first years, they probably drove away

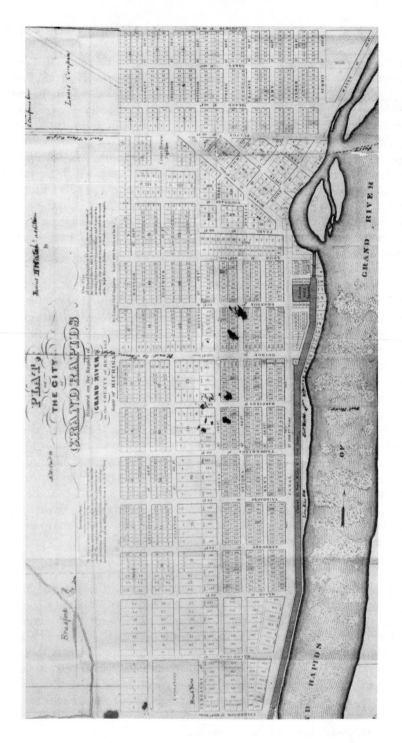

Fig. 3. Plat of Grand Rapids, c. 1833 (Courtesy of the Clarke Historical Library, Central Michigan University)

potential investors with foolish competition over the town's location. Campau, who had operated a fur trade post in the region since 1826, was the first to realize the possibilities of the Grand River location in the early 1830s, and he purchased seventy-two acres from the federal government for a paltry ninety dollars. Lucius Lyon was equally impressed by the region after conducting government surveys, and he bought the northern part of Campau's tract plus additional land to the south.[30] In November, 1833, Campau officially platted his land into a town which he called Grand Rapids. After Campau had established his plat, Lyon had maps drawn of essentially the same land, plus additional parcels to the north and the south, and called his townsite, Kent. For a brief period, Lyon and Campau engaged in an inane competition which included the refusal of either promoter to lay out streets which connected their contiguous parcels.[31]

Arthur Bronson, however, exercised a moderating influence on the promoters. In late 1833, Lyon had sold Bronson a large share of his plat for just $400 in order to secure his assistance in developing the site. Bronson immediately urged Lyon to avoid a wasteful competition by either buying out Campau's interest or cooperating with him. Subsequently, the struggle between the two sites lessened even though they were not officially united as the city of Grand Rapids until 1838.[32] Bronson also contributed funds for new buildings and for the construction of a canal around the rapids to improve the navigation of the river. Yet Bronson and Lyon struggled over the pace and financing of such improvements. Lyon wanted to build a mill as well as steamboats to ferry passengers and goods while Bronson counseled delay until all improvements could be properly financed. The New Yorker further hoped to apportion the costs equally among all the interested capitalists at the site, and at one point he suggested the formation of a joint stock company for that purpose.[33] Bronson outlined his position on improvements to Lucius Lyon in 1835:

> I have noticed your observations of the importance of investing in improvements on our land at Grand River Rapids . . . . I am willing to unite with the joint owners, and advance my proportion of monies for the object specified, it being understood that your interest and mine will receive their full share of benefits derived from such investments; it would not be worthwhile for us to invest monies to advance the value of lands in which you and myself have no concern. As you are better acquainted, with localities than I am, I leave this to your management, and also the character of improvements . . . . Briefly I wish the present owners to understand that I will concur in

any arrangement of the kind, which a majority of interest shall determine on.[34]

Bronson and Lyon never reached agreement on the proper techniques for promoting Grand Rapids, and in December, 1835, Bronson sold his share back to Lyon for $20,000, a profit of approximately $16,000 after considering his expenditures for street and building construction.[35] Since Lyon lacked the necessary capital, Bronson sold the land on time accepting Lyon's personal bond and the lands as security in return for Lyon's periodic payment of interest and principal. Bronson again had extricated himself from the responsibilities of city promotion because he was so afraid of overcommitting funds for long periods to what he considered a fundamentally risky venture. Bronson, moreover, had grown wary of local promoters who were unable to agree on common objectives.[36]

In 1833, Bronson and Lyon were also partners in the promotion of Ada, a town located east of Grand Rapids at the juncture of the Thornapple and Grand Rivers, and of Lyons—in 1834 called Arthursburg—which was situated at the confluence of the Maple and Grand Rivers. Bronson and Lyon hoped that the townsites would become county seats. While Lyon worked toward that objective in Michigan, Bronson prepared lithographic maps and wrote a brief description of the sites for inclusion in John Farmer's *The Emigrant's Guide*. At the same time, Lyon used money acquired from Bronson and a few lot sales to clear the land and build houses. Despite these efforts, Bronson again sold his interest to Lyon when he decided that the townsites were too far north of the state's settled areas. Rather than risk more capital, then, Bronson settled for a tidy profit, double his original investment.[37]

In the process of selling his town property in 1835 and 1836, Bronson shared his analysis of the land market and national economic trends with his agent, Lucius Lyon. The price of town lots were beyond all relation to their real value, Bronson explained, and thus represented mere "speculation" which threatened the security of all investments possessing a real "growth" potential. Bronson clearly did not consider himself a speculator; rather, he viewed land as an investment which returned a steady income. Bronson, of course, having the benefit of his father's years of experience in western New York, sensed that property values would inevitably fall. In 1836, therefore, he instructed Lyon that "There are now in operation a combination of circumstances which a most unprecedented and peculiar state of things has brought about that renders it highly important for our mutual interests in my judgment, to embrace by disposing of all property which partakes of a *speculative character*, such for example as city, town, & village property, and such other real estate the value of which depends on contingencies."[38]

Lucius Lyon obviously disagreed with Bronson's assessment of the land market. Not only did he purchase Bronson's share of Grand Rapids, Lyon, and Ada on long-term mortgage contracts, but he also poured all available funds into improvements at the sites. At Grand Rapids, for example, Lyon continued construction of the canal by employing twelve men throughout the winter. In 1836, Lyon and other local promoters built a hotel, established a newspaper, and prepared charters for a bank and a bridge company. Lyon's spirits were high as settlers moved into the town. In 1835, Grand Rapids had only 50 inhabitants, but in early 1837 the population was approximately 1,200. Lyon also acquired a new source of eastern capital, Charles Carroll of Groveland, New York, whose family possessed a substantial fortune derived from land speculation in the eighteenth century. Like many westerners, Lyon was exhilarated by the visible growth of towns and farms surrounding him. John Almy, Lyon's own agent at Grand Rapids, best expressed the westerners' optimism: "There are now several persons in the place who have come for the express purpose of purchasing and also to become citizens—let me but see one year more and I will show what can be done in the way of building a city."[39] Bronson's decision to sell while Lucius Lyon continued to buy, in short, represented the difference in judgment between the investor and the promoter.

Bronson exhibited this same pattern in smaller ventures in southern Michigan and northern Indiana. In association with Cogswell Green of Niles, Michigan, for example, Bronson purchased hundreds of acres of farm land in addition to lots in New Buffalo, St. Joseph, and Michigan City, all aspiring lakeports on Lake Michigan's eastern shore. In each case, Bronson sold his urban land in 1835 and 1836.[40] The New Yorker also owned lots in Lafayette, Indiana, where his agent was Jacob Walker. By 1835, Bronson again decided that land values were too inflationary, and he sold out to Walker. The resident agent, however, was more than willing to buy Bronson's share on the assumption that values would increase. In requesting additional money to buy urban lots in 1835, Walker reflected the westerners' booster mentality when he wrote that if "I was master of $5000 I am conscious that I could make a handsome western fortune in five years in buying and selling real estate."[41]

One distinctive aspect of Bronson's land business was the even distribution of his investments throughout the Old Northwest; his interests in Illinois and the Wisconsin Territory, therefore, were no less important than those in Michigan and Indiana. As Bronson moved into northern Illinois and the Wisconsin Territory, though, he increasingly assumed more of the burdens of urban promotion because these areas were far less populated and, as yet, had attracted few other eastern financiers. Bronson, moreover, adopted this somewhat more precarious business strategy in the belief that it would be at least two years before speculators

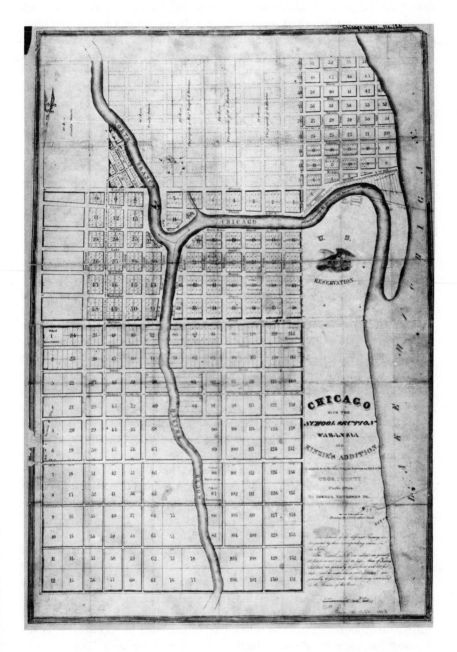

Fig. 4. Plat of Chicago, 1834 (Courtesy of the Chicago Historical Society)

drove up the price of land and threatened the stability of land values. Yet Bronson still approached such efforts with extreme caution: he conducted a meticulous evaluation of each area's potential before investing, carefully selected agents over whom he exercised close supervision, and bought agricultural lands within the shadow of the towns in order to diversify his interests. These were tactics that the New Yorker would employ with great success in Chicago.

When Arthur Bronson and Charles Butler visited Chicago in the summer of 1833, the settlement had a population of only 350, yet both New Yorkers looked beyond the small population at Chicago's numerous prerequisites for urban growth. First, the federal government had acquired and surveyed the majority of lands in Chicago's immediate hinterland in preparation for the influx of emigrants, and a final Indian treaty at Chicago was scheduled to purchase the remaining lands in September, 1833. Second, Chicago had already received an appropriation from the federal government to improve its harbor which would facilitate the movement of people and goods into the city. Most important was Chicago's strategic location near a possible link between the Illinois River and Lake Michigan which could bring together the southern trade with New Orleans and the eastern commerce destined to come over the Great Lakes. The state of Illinois already had received a land grant from the federal government in 1827 to assist in the construction of a canal and, as a first step toward the development of the city, had surveyed and platted the city of Chicago. Yet the project had generated little additional enthusiasm from investors in the early 1830s because northern Illinois was still a wilderness. But when Bronson and Butler arrived in Chicago, they knew that urban and agricultural pioneers were only a step or two behind and that the possibility of a canal gave Chicago a substantial advantage over the other townsites along the lake shore. In 1833, Charles Butler observed that "In Chicago, as it is we see the elements, the nucleus of a great city, its location is peculiar and very eligible; it is at the head of navigation in the West and on the great western thoroughfare, to the Valley of the Mississippi . . . ."[42]

Ahead of other capitalists in journeying West, Bronson seized the opportunity to purchase lands in Chicago. The New Yorker first directed his attention toward land designated as the "Kinzie Addition." After Chicago had been surveyed in 1830, the heirs of John Kinzie, an early nineteenth-century fur trader, had acquired land north of the Chicago River but immediately adjacent to the original town. Kinzie's two sons, John and Robert, attempted to sell part of the tract to speculators. After Arthur Bronson talked with Robert Kinzie in New York City in April, 1833, they signed a tentative agreement giving Arthur Bronson and Charles Butler an option to purchase a quarter interest in the parcel for

$5,500, but Bronson refused to sign a final contract until he could conduct a personal inspection during his summer visit.[43]

Bronson decided against the Kinzie purchase, demonstrating again his timidity in embarking on urban speculations. After a personal inspection, he and Charles Butler agreed that the price was too high for unplatted and undeveloped land. Bronson was also apprehensive because there were already several local owners. In his view, too many resident share-holders complicated the decision-making required for successful pro-motion.[44] Finally, both financiers had discovered other parcels in the same area which eventually would give them full control of 80 acres on the North Side of the Chicago River.

After turning down Kinzie's offer, Bronson wrote to Captain David Hunter, an army officer formerly stationed at Fort Dearborn, who had acquired a substantial amount of property at Chicago. He owned an 80 acre tract adjoining the Kinzie Addition and Block Number 1 in the original plat. This block was especially valuable because one tier of lots fronted on the Chicago River. Even though he desired to sell, Hunter worried that Bronson might leave the parcel undeveloped and thus frustrate the efforts of his Chicago friends who hoped to develop the North Side of the Chicago River. Although Bronson's arguments in reply were calculated to convince Hunter to lower his price, his arguments, nevertheless, reflected the investment principles which guided his ac-tions. The New Yorker assured Hunter that he intended to establish commercial and residential neighborhoods, but he claimed that no pro-moter could accomplish that objective unless the land's initial cost was moderate. Otherwise, Bronson claimed that he would have neither suffi-cient capital nor a profit incentive to improve the property and to sell lots at affordable prices to merchants and homeowners. Bronson summarized his promotional philosophy in the following general statement:

> I am not nor have I ever been disposed to engage in those specula-tions which are based on the cupidity and avarice of the speculators who give an unnatural value to property by 'blowing up a bubble' and then throwing their responsibilities upon their too enthusiastic and credulous competitors, and therefore if I should make any arrangement at all in this matter, I shall expect so to make my purchase as to realize a fair profit in this and for the risque [*sic*] and difficulty of the undertaking by pursuing that plan which shall administer both to the general advantage of the country, and the partial interests of the proprietors.[45]

In November, 1834, Arthur Bronson purchased the Hunter property for $20,000, but he allowed several other financiers to purchase an in-terest. Bronson often attracted other eastern shareholders to his larger promotional ventures in order to spread the risk as well as to secure additional money for future improvements. Bronson first offered an interest and responsibility for the property's management to Charles Trowbridge and Elon Farnsworth, but they refused. At the last moment, Charles Butler also backed out, having already expended his available funds in Michigan, Ohio, and in smaller purchases at Chicago. But Lucius Lyon accepted a share as did other eastern financiers, including Lot Clark, a participant in the New York and Ohio trust companies.[46]

The Hunter tract was only part of Bronson's landholdings on Chicago's North Side. In August, 1833, he had acquired a partial share in an adjacent forty acre parcel owned by John Temple. Temple had settled in Chicago in July 1833, with the intention of practicing medicine but he immediately succumbed to the prevailing land fever and plunged into land speculation. Bronson established an agency relationship with Temple on the pattern used in Detroit and Grand Rapids. The agreement benefited both men. In return for a half interest in Temple's land and Temple's on–site supervision, Bronson supplied the money and financial expertise necessary for development.[47]

Bronson furthered his control of land on Chicago's North Side when he appointed Walter Newberry as his chief Chicago agent. In 1833, Newberry resided in Detroit where he and his brother Oliver had interests in lake shipping and a retail store. At the same time, they had speculated in lands throughout the Old Northwest and had acquired title to forty acres adjacent to Bronson's Chicago property. Bronson's appointment of Newberry as his agent was a logical move, for in so doing he united their mutual interests on Chicago's North Side. Bronson also felt secure in tendering the offer to Newberry because he was a close friend of Lucius Lyon.[48]

With a share in over 120 acres on Chicago's North Side, Bronson hoped to make this area the town's principal business district. Yet he faced a real handicap in the race for commercial dominance because the Chicago River divided the town into two sections, the North and the South, and because overland traffic naturally stopped first on the South Side. Crossing to the North Side where Bronson held property required passage on a ferry or crossing a small bridge.[49] Nevertheless, Bronson maintained a correspondence with John Kinzie, the other major landholder on the North Side, and together they discussed and provided for the most needed improvements such as residential buildings, a tavern, and a hotel. Bronson also cooperated with Kinzie in platting the addition and in the preparation of lithographic maps. Moreover, he assisted in obtaining the services of a newspaper editor and a press; as a result John Calhoun established the *Chicago Democrat* in late 1833.[50]

Bronson often intruded into local political and economic affairs in order to stimulate large-scale improvements which might be beneficial to the region and to his own investments. He assisted Chicagoans in selling, stock for the unsuccessful Chicago and Vincennes Railroad.[51] More important, he was a major force in pushing the Illinois and Michigan Canal toward completion. When he and Charles Butler had arrived in Chicago in 1833, several local citizens—Gurdon Hubbard, John Kinzie, Richard J. Hamilton, and John Temple—had enlisted the New Yorkers' aid in attempting to revive the state's interest in a canal. Consequently, a public meeting was called on August 7, at which Bronson, Butler, Lyon, and the leading men of Chicago agreed to draft resolutions for submission to the Governor demanding the construction of a railroad or canal by a private company. The Chicagoans turned the actual preparation of the resolutions over to Bronson and Butler for the obvious reasons that they possessed the legal skills and financial expertise to produce a coherent proposal and direct the formation of a private company.[52]

Arthur Bronson and Charles Butler immediately worked on tentative resolutions even as they continued their western trip in August, 1833. Within two weeks, they communicated their initial thoughts to Lucius Lyon revealing their willingness, under certain conditions, to undertake responsibility for the canal. Both men assumed that the state was unable to manage such a large project. The lack of capital and the absence of sound financial institutions, they argued, " . . . present almost insuperable difficulty in the way of constructing great works of internal improvements which require large expenditures of money."[53] The New Yorkers, therefore, proposed that the state allow a private company, capitalized at $1 million, to construct the canal. They also recommended that the state should transfer its federal land grant for canal construction to the private firm, a move which they hoped would convince foreign capitalists that the proposed company was financially stable. Bronson and Butler also agreed to organize the company and to raise the necessary $1 million because, as they stated, "We have been on the ground personally and we are therefore in a situation to act understandingly, and to secure a capital interest with our friends, which would hardly be done, without the aid of those who have enjoyed the opportunity which we have, and who also enjoy the confidence of capitalists."[54]

The New Yorkers had hurried the preparation of these proposals in the hope of expediting action: they were subsequently sent to Lucius Lyon, who had returned with them to Chicago. There, another meeting of Chicago citizens accepted Bronson's plan. With the support of Chicagoans, Bronson and Butler began work on a formal charter for the Illinois and Michigan Railroad and Canal Company which was to be submitted to the Illinois legislature when it met in late 1834. At the same time, Bronson discussed the idea with other eastern financiers while Chicago citizens lobbied for the project throughout the state. In order to attract public support, Arthur Bronson wrote an article for a New York newspaper praising the economic soundness of a canal or railroad, but he never published it, knowing that some Illinois residents might raise the issue of foreign capitalists controlling the state's economic growth. Instead he sent similar articles on the proposed company to newspapers in Vandalia and Chicago where they were published under the names of Bronson's agents there.[55]

But in the summer of 1834 Bronson and Butler's plans for a private company broke down. After reviewing the charter for a railroad or a canal, Chicago citizens began to disagree on the most advantageous course of development. John Kinzie and Gurdon Hubbard favored a railroad, while Richard J. Hamilton and Thomas J. V. Owen wanted a canal. To further complicate matters, other eastern capitalists with heavy investments in Chicago real estate forced themselves into the project. Edward and Samuel Russell from Middletown, Connecticut, who invested through Chicagoan Gurdon Hubbard, wanted to share in each step of the planning.[56] Such personality problems alone would have worried Arthur Bronson, but then conditions worsened when Chicago's newspapers publicized the infighting among the capitalists, took sides in the dispute between the canal and railroad advocates, and raised the old cry of domination by eastern capitalists. An editorial in the *Chicago Democrat* of November, 1834, for example, urged a state directed and financed project, whether railroad or canal, and alerted their readers "to the fact that a project was underway to build a railroad by a group of eastern speculators centered on Wall Street."[57]

At this point, Bronson again exhibited the traits of the cautious speculator and dropped the canal plan after considering the additional risks. He was no stranger to charges of eastern domination and was fully aware that such allegations could endanger the company's success. Besides being caught between two factions within the Chicago community, Bronson found himself at odds with an agent, John Temple, who was angered over a business disagreement with Bronson and supplied the newspapers with information on the New Yorker's activities, further destroying the harmony necessary for a successful investment.[58] Bronson also sensed a change of mood within the state in favor of quick action on a state-constructed canal. Arthur Bronson decided that if the state was prepared to build the canal, he would withdraw quietly. In December, 1834, he wrote to Lucius Lyon

> Do not mention my name in connection with the Michigan and Illinois Canal or Railroad—the Editor of the *Chicago Democrat* has

published in his paper of 19th an article ascribing a project now on foot in the state for the latter to *Wall Street.* I have this day written to Colonel Hamilton and John H. Kinzie, not to press the charter if the state will undertake either on her own account, our desire being rather to have some communication opened than to do it ourselves.[59]

Despite the collapse of his own plans, Bronson had been a critical force in reviving the moribund canal project. Moreover, he continued to exhibit an active involvement through the purchase of bonds issued by the state for the canal's construction.[60]

At the same time that Bronson worried over the dangers of promoting the Illinois and Michigan Canal, he also considered selling his property on Chicago's North Side because the risks of further expenditures seemed to outweigh any possible gains. Bronson consistently had feared the effect of spiraling land prices on real value, and price movements in Chicago between 1833 and 1835 gave him little comfort. In September, 1833, for example, Lyon reported to Charles Butler that the price of land in Chicago had skyrocketed and that "the purchase of the few lots that Mr. Bronson took contributed a good deal to produce this effect."[61] In 1834, a tract measuring 80 by 180 feet was sold for $3,500 when it had cost only $100 in 1832. The same lot brought $15,000 a year later. By 1835, Chicago had become the rage among town speculators, and all speculators, urban or rural, anxiously awaited the first government sale in the Chicago land district in June, 1835. Although never one to sneer at a healthy profit, Bronson simply did not believe that prices would continue to rise indefinitely, and thus he decided to get out at the opportune moment. Bronson planned to sell his property at the same time as the public sale, when the city would be inundated with speculators.[62]

In May 1835, however, Bronson changed his mind and sold the Hunter property to an eastern firm, the American Land Company, for $100,000—five times the original purchase price. The American Land Company brought together New York City and Boston capitalists for investments in western land, and its principal organizer and president was Bronson's close friend, Charles Butler. Under the terms of the sale, Bronson deeded over the Hunter property to the trustees of the American Land Company, although he maintained a one-fifth interest for the original owners. The sale was particularly beneficial to Bronson and his associates; they obtained a gross profit of 400 percent and stood to gain from the property's future development because Bronson had maintained a one-fifth interest. Yet he had avoided the costs and time necessitated in superintending its further improvement. This arduous task now fell to Charles Butler and the American Land Company. Butler, of course, had gambled that land values would continue to rise and that greater profits could be acquired in the future.[63]

Advantageous as the sale appeared, Walter Newberry, one of Bronson's agents and partners, thought that the proprietors should have waited for an even higher price. The difference of opinion between Bronson and Newberry was reflective of the conservative mentality of Bronson versus the speculative inclination of western agents. Unable to block the sale, Newberry had to accept his $20,000 profit. At the same time, however, Newberry voiced his displeasure with Bronson's action:

> This same Arthur Bronson has been a perfect marplot in everything relating to this . . . . He has had it in his power to make a quarter of a million out of this town had it not been for his timidity. He has had the bird in his hand and all he had to do was shut his fingers. You are no doubt by this time beginning to think that I am hard to satisfy that $20,000 ought to suffice for me in one operation for a few months. I am I assure you well satisfied with it but I can't help censoring a man when he acts like an ass.[64]

In the Wisconsin Territory, Bronson followed the same pattern of investment as he had in Illinois. Although he owned a few lots at Milwaukee, Manitowoc, and Racine,[65] he was primarily involved in the development of Cassville, a small settlement located on the shore of the Mississippi River in the lead mining region of southwestern Wisconsin. As Michigan approached statehood in 1834, Lucius Lyon had convinced Bronson that Cassville would be an excellent site for a capital whenever Wisconsin became a territory. It was a logical choice since the lead mining district was more populated than either Green Bay or the emerging towns on Lake Michigan's western shore. Furthermore, a vast amount of territory west of the Mississippi River was to be part of the Wisconsin Territory, and thus Cassville had the added advantage of a central location within the territory. Cassville, however, never became the territorial capital; instead, it proved to be Bronson's most unsuccessful urban promotion. At least part of the reason was that Bronson abandoned some of his cautious tactics and misjudged the site's potential and the complexities of territorial politics.

Bronson's first mistake at Cassville may well have been in the formation of the partnership of eastern financiers and western citizens to promote the site. At Chicago, Grand Rapids, and Detroit, Bronson had usually been only one of many eastern capitalists all intent on building a prosperous city. Yet there was a narrow base of support at Cassville, for Bronson and his partners were solely responsible for the site. The Bronson family held a 50 percent interest in the townsite, a portion which they shared

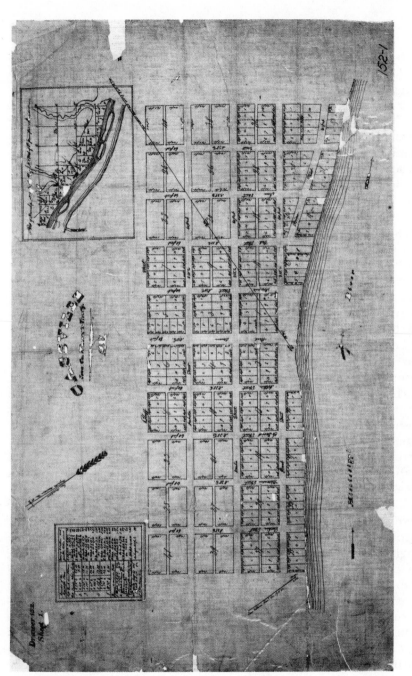

Fig. 5. Plat of Cassville, 1836 (Courtesy of the National Archives, Cartographic Division, RG 77)

with John Ward of Prime, Ward and King, and with Lucius Lyon. Thomas W. Olcott, president of the Mechanics and Farmers Bank of Albany and a frequent partner in Bronson's land investments, and Garrett V. Denniston, an Albany lawyer, held the other 50 percent interest.[66]

The eastern partners at first made a substantial effort to make the site attractive to politicians and settlers. In 1835 and 1836, they sent approximately $35,000 to the resident agent, Lyman Daniels, for building construction and street repairs. Some of this money financed the migration of carpenters and masons from New York City to hurry completion of the buildings to accommodate the possible meeting of a territorial legislature. Bronson simultaneously worked on a lithographic map which marked out each lot and block and named the streets after the town's proprietors: Arthur, Frederic, Prime, Ward, and Denniston Streets. Bronson, Olcott, and Denniston also made a time-consuming, although unsuccessful, effort to seize the stock control of the Bank of Wisconsin in order to move it to Cassville. They lost this battle to other eastern capitalists such as John Jacob Astor and John Martin, who were pushing Green Bay as the site of the territorial capital.[67]

Losing the bank charter was the least of Bronson's worries at Cassville, for in 1835 and 1836 he faced a serious challenge to his legal title. Bronson had originally purchased a part of the plat from a local settler, Richard Ray, who held a preemption claim to the tract. Bronson then had routinely applied to the General Land Office for a patent. But Bronson's ownership was challenged by another local resident, William Weyman, who claimed that he had a half interest in Ray's preemption. When confronted with conflicting claims, the commissioner of the General Land Office and ultimately the President had to decide whether to approve a final patent.

Throughout the spring and summer of 1836, Arthur Bronson tried to resolve the contested legal claim. This effort was not characteristic of Bronson's behavior since he had withdrawn from other investments at the slightest indication of economic or political difficulty. In this case, though, he carried on an extensive correspondence with officials of the General Land Office and even the President. At one point, Bronson went to Washington to present his case before land office officials and the attorney general. A main point in his argument was that local officials tentatively had confirmed his title. With such assurances, Bronson pointed out that he had spent a considerable amount of money in providing facilities for the legislature to meet at Cassville.[68] Attorney General Benjamin F. Butler, however, issued the government's opinion that tentative assurances from the local land office or even the General Land Office did not constitute a legal title. Realizing that his position was tenuous,

Bronson settled with the other parties contesting the preemption. He bought out Weyman's claims, thus establishing his ownership and ending rumors of defective titles harmful to Cassville's image.[69]

Along with the entanglement over the Weyman claim, Bronson experienced numerous problems with his agent, Lyman Daniels. Daniels had piqued Bronson's patience in early 1834 when he had avoided several scheduled meetings. Daniels also failed to submit his semiannual accounts. Bronson once complained that Daniels had not sent him a land title in over a year nor had he accounted for over $20,000 intended for Cassville's improvement. During the crucial months in the summer of 1836, moreover, considerable responsiblity for Cassville's promotion fell to Daniel's young and recently employed assistant, Nelson Dewey.[70]

Cassville's promoters also stumbled in trying to exert political influence on local politicians. In the final meeting of the Michigan Territorial Council at Green Bay in January 1836, the delegates had recommended to Congress the creation of the Wisconsin Territory with a capital at Cassville. Lyon, who was senator-elect from Michigan, tried to strengthen that recommendation by asking George Jones, the territorial delegate-elect from Wisconsin, to insist that Congress name Cassville as the capital in the bill creating the Wisconsin Territory. Bronson even suggested that Jones might be offered a share in the Cassville site. But in March 1836 charges surfaced that Cassville was controlled by eastern financiers, and territorial politicians, fearing the adverse effect of such allegations on the creation of the territory, agreed to a bill which left the selection of a capital to the governor and the people.[71] Undaunted, Lyon offered lots at Cassville to John Horner, the leading candidate to be named secretary of the Wisconsin Territory, and Horner agreed to move to Cassville in order to assist in its promotion. When Horner was subsequently named secretary of the Wisconsin Territory, he immediately opened the territory's executive offices at Cassville in the absence of the newly appointed governor, Henry Dodge, who was in Washington. Lyon and Horner obviously hoped that the temporary location of territorial offices in Cassville would improve its chances of becoming the capital.[72]

In this endeavor, Bronson and his associates were outsmarted. Governor Dodge left the final decision of naming a capital to the first session of the territorial legislature which was to meet in the fall of 1836. This legislative session turned out to be more a congress of real estate promoters than a legislative body. Although the easterners had sent Garrett Denniston and John Horner to lobby for their interests, several other towns had enlisted their own supporters. But Denniston and the others were no match for the promotional skills and political clout of the wily territorial politician James Duane Doty who presented a plan for a capital at Four Lakes—Madison—then a totally undeveloped site. After endless debate, clever compromises, and a little bribery, Doty secured the necessary votes; Cassville was defeated.[73]

Cassville was undeniably a failure, yet Bronson's investment strategy of diversifying his interests throughout the territory and sharing the risks protected him from a serious financial loss. He had, for example, purchased approximately 15,000 acres of agricultural and leadbearing lands in southwestern Wisconsin. He even held land in the Madison region.[74] In addition, the Cassville proprietors could still investigate the possibility of developing the town as a regional trade center or county seat. After the Cassville fiasco, however, Bronson understandably entered into no other city promotions.

It would be inaccurate to conclude from Bronson's urban investments that he simply purchased town lots for quick sale without affecting the region's growth. Even in the brief period of his involvement, Bronson had an impact on the development of Detroit, Grand Rapids, Chicago, and even Cassville. His money helped in the platting of cities, the laying out of streets, and the construction of buildings. There were also secondary benefits, for Bronson directly employed local citizens whose profits from land investment were plowed into the local economy. Bronson and his associates indirectly created a market for laborers to work on canal projects and local building construction. He also provided influential leadership in planning for improvements such as railroads and canals. Yet Bronson was never able to control the enormous energies of local citizens and the forces of the land market which expanded cities and led to new improvements which were far ahead of supporting retail, commercial, agricultural, and institutional developments. Bronson's realization of this fact eventually forced him to shift the emphasis of his land business from urban to agricultural land in 1835 and 1836.

One substantial error of most studies of land speculators is that historians separate urban and agricultural purchases even though investors like Bronson perceived a relation between the two. Bronson had a keen sense of the interdependent nature of town and farm and realized that increases in the real value of urban land ultimately depended on the cultivation of the surrounding agricultural hinterland. Thus, in 1833 and 1834, Bronson purchased thousands of acres of agricultural land, usually in the same general region as his urban promotions. Bronson was no less cautious in handling agricultural property, and his approach again assured his own financial success and contributed to the region's economic development.

The most important ingredients of Bronson's successful investment in agricultural land were the cautious policies which governed the actual purchase of land. First, the New Yorker was extremely careful about the land's initial cost. He instructed his agents to avoid government auction sales where competitive bidding pushed up prices. It was preferable, Bronson reasoned, to wait until after the auction sale and then purchase the many excellent tracts which remained at the minimum price of $1.25 per acre. A survey of 90,000 acres which Bronson purchased in 1835 and 1836 revealed that approximately 95 percent of that land was obtained at the minimum price. Bronson also insisted that parcels should possess distinctive attributes, such as water, trees, prairie lands, or access to roads. On occasion, the New Yorker purchased land at prices ranging from $2 to $5 per acre when it was located along a major improvement, like the Illinois and Michigan Canal, or when it possessed mineral deposits, such as coal or lead. Bronson was particularly alert to land within the shadows of emerging towns. Near Detroit, for example, he bought more than 1,000 acres along the Grand River Road, a major artery running into the city.[75] Not only did Bronson diversify his landholdings throughout the Old Northwest, but also he obtained small, non-contiguous parcels of from 80 to 320 acres in partially-settled townships. This policy, which reflected the same tactics generally employed in his urban investments, had several benefits: it avoided the risks of concentrating capital in a single area, and it took advantage of increases in land values that resulted from productive farms in the neighborhood. As Bronson explained to an agent in 1836: "We would suggest that as the effect of single individuals taking large tracts in a body is to deter actual settlers from coming into this vicinity, we should think it would be well that the locations should be separated and would respectfully suggest whether small farms of from 160 to 320 acres would be more saleable and be more likely to have a rapid advance than larger bodies."[76]

Thus, Bronson's business strategy of diversifying his landholdings challenges the common belief that speculators generally purchased large tracts of land and reserved them from sale in order to profit from increases in land values. According to this argument, farmers were unable to buy the land due to rising costs, and they were consequently forced to work as tenants for an emerging class of landlords. Paul Gates in his studies of land speculation in the Old Northwest twice cited the Bronsons as among the worst absentee landholders on the basis of land office records indicating that they purchased 24,464 acres in the Wisconsin Territory and 7,730 acres in Indiana in 1835 and 1836.[77] Land office records, though, are misleading: they list individual land purchases at a particular date, but they do not reveal the absentee investor's business strategy or the land's eventual disposition. Arthur Bronson's general rule was to sell land within the shortest possible period: a month, six months, certainly not longer than a year. All contracts with his agents were limited to five years with the intention that the land would be quickly sold and the capital used over and over again to buy and sell more land within the five-year period. Bronson was thus satisfied with a moderate gain on prompt exchanges, although he certainly accepted any opportunity for larger profits. He instructed his agents to sell land to farmers whenever possible because their presence in a region raised property values in both city and country and generally contributed to the area's overall economic development.[78]

Perhaps the best example of Bronson's conservative investment philosophy in regard to agricultural land was his attempt to establish trust companies wherever he invested. He believed that trust companies would benefit both eastern capitalists and western farmers while helping to stabilize the western economy. Eastern capitalists would profit from the stock of each trust company, a stock which generally returned a dividend of from 6 to 10 percent. State and territorial economies, on the other hand, would secure approximately $3,000,000 from each trust company through the eastern financiers' subscriptions for stock and deposits. In addition, Bronson designed each trust company so that it would invest its capital stock in farm mortgages, thereby assisting farmers in the development of the land. As Bronson purchased land from the federal government, then, he could sell it to farmers who obtained mortgage money from the trust company. The sooner farmers brought land under cultivation within a given region, the more rapidly Bronson's remaining acreage increased in value.[79]

Finally, Bronson believed that trust companies in Michigan, Indiana, Illinois, and the Wisconsin Territory might halt or at least curtail the speculative practices of western commercial banks which exacerbated the inflation of land values. Between 1833 and 1835, Arthur Bronson was convinced that Jackson's veto of the recharter of the Second Bank of the United States, his removal of government revenues from that bank, and their subsequent deposit in Pet Banks throughout the country was contributing to the nation's runaway inflation. Bronson was particularly concerned about the financial situation in the Michigan Territory because Detroit's commercial banks, the Bank of Michigan and the Farmers and Mechanics Bank, were Pet Banks with the potential for unrestrained credit expansion through note circulation.[80]

Bronson, therefore, wrote a charter for a Michigan Life Insurance and Trust Company and included the two central tenets of conservative banking. The company's capital stock would be invested in secure real estate mortgages, thereby preventing its use in land speculation or in encouraging new businesses for which there was limited security. Second, the trust company would issue only short-term notes, no longer than 120 days, and the total note circulation would not exceed the bank's capital stock. With a trust company in Michigan, then, Bronson hoped to control speculation in land and commerce, to ensure the stability of property values, and to enforce his conservative financial practices on other western banks.[81]

Arthur Bronson, however, never succeeded in establishing trust companies in the Old Northwest. In Michigan, he spent an immense amount of time in late 1834 organizing the Michigan Life Insurance and Trust Company. He wrote the charter, secured capital subscriptions from other eastern financiers like Thomas Olcott and Lot Clark, and convinced his western agents that the trust company would benefit the territory. Yet just before the meeting of the Michigan Territorial Council in 1834, when Elon Farnsworth was to petition for a charter, Michigan's leading politicians backed out, fearing that the trust company's application might incite fears of outside influence and ultimately jeopardize the territory's move toward statehood. Local politicians, like Trowbridge and Lyon, also worried over possible conflicts of interest since they were immersed in the affairs of Detroit's commercial banks which were then requesting the legislature's permission to establish branches.[82] In Illinois, where the legislature moved overwhelmingly in the direction of chartering a state bank, Bronson gave up the idea of the trust company in hopes of acquiring stock control of the state bank. Again, Bronson organized an eastern syndicate and appointed an agent in Illinois to subscribe for stock, but he was outmaneuvered by other capitalists, including Ohioans Micajah Williams and Samuel Wiggins.[83]

Bronson's inability to establish what he considered safe financial institutions and an increase in land prices forced the New Yorker to alter the organization and conduct of his land business in 1835 and 1836. Bronson first abandoned the purchase and development of most urban property. Although he continued to purchase farm lands, Bronson increasingly organized partnerships with other eastern financiers in order to share the risks. Diversity of contracts and of investments were his ruling principles. In late 1834, for example, Bronson joined with Gould Hoyt in a partnership capitalized at $30,000 for the acquisition of Illinois agricultural lands. He also served as a middleman moving the capital of other easterners through his system of agents for a share of the profits. In 1836, he offered to invest up to $500,000 for two European banking houses, Hottinguer and Company of Paris and Hope and Company of Amsterdam. Although the offer was refused, Bronson subsequently invested $50,000 for S. V. Wilder, the American agent of Hottinguer and Company. At the same time, Frederic Bronson received $10,000 to purchase western lands for John Ward of Prime, Ward, and King.

Bronson was to receive a 50 percent share of the profits after Ward recovered his capital plus 7 percent interest. Such contracts had endless variations, yet each carried a minimal risk for the Bronsons. In the contracts with Ward and Wilder, the Bronsons committed no capital, yet they had a possibility of 50 percent of the profits merely for using their agents.[84]

Bronson most clearly exhibited his altered investment policies when he opened a mortgage loan business throughout the Old Northwest in 1835 and 1836. Typically Bronson's agents submitted applications from western farmers which contained a report on the applicant's character, a full legal description of the property offered as security, and an appraisal of its value. Bronson also lent funds to urban residents for business needs or real estate improvements, but he applied more stringent rules when accepting urban property as security because of its uncertain value. Bronson's interest rates ranged between 7 and 10 percent annually on loans which averaged about $1500 each. These interest rates were not usurious, but within the legal rates set by various states at the time. The New Yorker's purpose was to secure a moderate profit with limited risks; in the process, he also provided needed money for farmers and town dwellers.[85]

Two questions remain unanswered in evaluating Bronson's success as a land speculator and his economic effect on the region: how much land did he own and what profit did he make? Unfortunately there are only fragmentary records on which to base even tentative estimates. The use of federal land records are of only limited value in identifying land owners. The Bronsons often entered land in the names of their agents, and even if the land was listed in their name, its actual ownership might have been split with other eastern capitalists, with resident agents, or with farmers. Despite these caveats, there are occasional pieces of information which suggest the size of the Bronson's landholdings and their rate of return. In 1835 and 1836, for example, the New Yorkers were the largest purchasers of public lands in the Territory of Wisconsin—24,464 acres. A fragmentary land book for the same two year period, encompassing purchases in Illinois, Wisconsin, Michigan, and Indiana, indicated that they had bought 90,638 acres with a total capital of $113,298.[86] I would estimate that, in 1835 and 1836, the Bronsons held at least 225,000 acres, a figure which does not take into account that they owned lots in every major urban center in the Old Northwest. It is instructive to compare this figure with Paul Gates' estimate that the American Land Company was probably the largest corporate owner of land in the 1830s with 349,695 acres in eight states, including major investments in the South.[87] If one added the Bronson's 400,000 acres in North Carolina and at least 200,000 acres in

New York State along with their interests in the Old Northwest, they must be considered among the largest antebellum landholders.

Bronson's land business could have served as a primer on how to make money from land. Windfall profits of from 100 to 500 percent were not uncommon, particularly on city property sold in 1835. Bronson once claimed that he had purchased a 70 acre tract near a town for $400 that later sold for $20,000.[88] Yet based on his extensive correspondence with agents, I would *estimate* that Bronson averaged—and was quite satisfied with—a net profit of 20 percent a year on a particular contract after subtracting the agent's share, lawyers fees, travel, and general administrative costs. Given the fact that land prices commonly rose 100 percent per year between 1833 and 1835, Bronson's profit margin is not surprising. The most reliable indication of Bronson's changing desires in regard to profit, however, was his mortgage loan business in which interest rates averaged 7 to 10 percent annually.

Throughout the Old Northwest, then, Arthur Bronson made a substantial profit on land investments. Several factors emerge when attempting to pinpoint the reasons for his success. First, like merchants and businessmen of the eighteenth century, Bronson had a wide range of interests—farm lands, town lots, and bank stock—and in several regions throughout the country. Undoubtedly such diversification of his capital resources guaranteed that a single investment failure would have a limited effect. More important, Bronson's widespread financial interests illustrated his organic view of economic development. He knew that simple ownership of land was unproductive and unprofitable in the long run unless it was accompanied by efforts to build buildings, lay out roads, construct canals, and charter banks. Obviously his efforts were always related to the value of his own property, such as encouraging buildings in downtown Detroit, the canal at Grand Rapids, or the Illinois and Michigan Canal; yet the New Yorker's expertise and capital often helped to generate western proposals. Caution, rather than daring, then, characterized Bronson's approach. He never overcommitted his resources to capital improvements. The New Yorker always insisted on sharing the risks with other capitalists and, except at Cassville, he quickly backed out at the first sign of political or economic difficulty. I suspect that if westerners had listened to Bronson's advice on conservative banking practices, the inflated price of land, and the necessary relationship of economic improvements (such as buildings) to economic need, the West's runaway land boom might have ended with less than catastrophic consequences for most aspiring western businessmen.

Bronson's success was also a result of the fact that he was always the dominant element in the relationships with his western agents. Not only were his agents limited by contract, but also the New Yorker specified the type of investment, the location, and the amount. A constant stream of correspondence moved from East to West as Bronson monitored the westerners' more liberal approach to land and city speculations. Moreover Arthur Bronson or some other member of the family made yearly trips to the West to inspect land purchases and to maintain a personal supervision of their agents. In order to understand the needs of the western economy and to make proper business decisions, Bronson also read numerous western newspapers, reviewed state internal improvement documents, checked appropriate state and national laws affecting land titles, and kept an elaborate account for each agent and each parcel of land purchased. Arthur Bronson, thus, does not fit the image so popular in historical literature of the eastern land speculator subservient to the actions and plans of western agents.[89]

It was perhaps Bronson's basic conservatism, however, that most distinguished his attitudes from those of his western agents, led to his change in investment practices in 1835 and 1836, and protected him from the deflation of land values in 1837. Based on his extensive knowledge of national banking practices and his awareness of the history of previous land booms, Bronson decided that the nation's economy was in trouble and that the value of town property and some agricultural land had inflated beyond its intrinsic worth. He closed several partnerships and sold those lands that appeared too speculative—such as lots at Grand Rapids, Detroit, Chicago, and Lyons. Of course, he held onto some lots and even purchased additional farm land, but more and more he chose to lend money to farmers taking land as security and obtaining an annual interest. Understandably his western agents—Trowbridge, Farnsworth, Kinzie, and Lyon—regarded him with dismay. In the middle of burgeoning western communities and caught up in the booster spirit, they used all their capital and credit to purchase Bronson's share, buy other lands, and undertake internal improvements. These differing judgments about land values reflected the conservative and liberal approaches to western development and later provided some explanation for patterns of financial success and failure among individuals.

6. An Eastern Promoter: Charles Butler and the Economic Development of the Old Northwest, 1835-1837

This chapter describes the western investments of Charles Butler during the years of economic expansion. Butler was a promoter, a risk-taking entrepreneur who sought the "main chance" and who never doubted the West's potential for uninterrupted economic growth. Possessing only modest capital resources in the early 1830s, Butler had shared in Arthur Bronson's investments, but by 1835 he had established a financial base that enabled him to embark upon his own business ventures. The ambitious New Yorker organized or participated in many partnerships and stock companies to buy agricultural land and town lots, and he was an important broker in mobilizing eastern capital for investment in western railroads and banks. Whereas Arthur Bronson withdrew his capital from western townsites in 1835 and 1836, Butler chose that period to undertake massive development projects at Chicago, Illinois; Toledo, Ohio; and Port Huron, Michigan. Butler's career, then, was in stark contrast to that of a conservative investor such as Arthur Bronson.

Charles Butler climbed rapidly in the political and financial world during the early 1830s. He participated in the New York Life Insurance and Trust Company and the Ohio Life Insurance and Trust Company, and few men possessed a better understanding of the role of banks in facilitating economic development. His western investments in partnership with Arthur Bronson returned a substantial profit, and this success probably fired Butler's desire for more extensive undertakings. In addition to his financial expertise, Butler was politically influential. His brother, Benjamin, was the Attorney General of the United States and his Albany friends, like Edwin Croswell, the editor of the *Albany Argus,* provided easy access to Democratic politicians in New York State. Butler also knew Martin Van Buren, and, on one occasion, they shared land

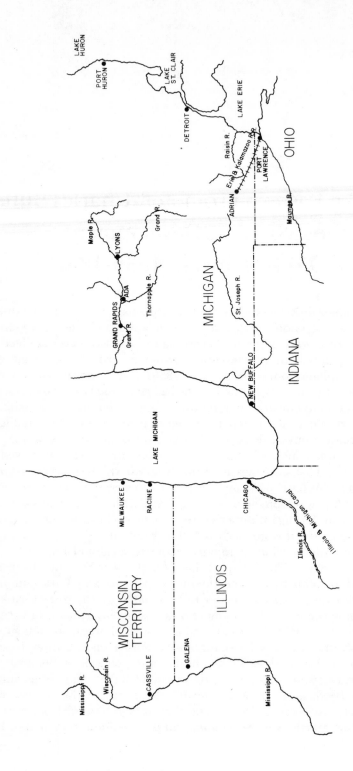

Fig. 6. Michigan, Northern Illinois, and the Wisconsin Territory in 1836 [This map is based on maps appearing in Robert J. Parks, *Democracy's Railroads: Public Enterprise in Jacksonian Michigan* (Port Washington, New York: Kennikat Press, 1972), 35, 51, 132; and S. Augustus Mitchell, *Map of the Settled Part of Michigan* (Philadelphia: S. Augustus Mitchell, 1832 and 1838).]

purchases. Financial institutions and individual capitalists often requested Butler's services as a lobbyist before state legislatures and the Congress because of his political contacts and demonstrated competence in earlier work for the New York and Ohio trust companies.[1]

Because his business affairs increasingly concentrated on the East Coast, Butler left the western New York village of Geneva in 1835 and established his permanent residence in New York City. From there he moved among the country's political and economic centers, such as Albany, Boston, and Washington, D.C., on his numerous land and bank projects. Butler's location in New York City also assisted his upward mobility since he now circulated among the country's political, social, and financial elite. Butler's New York financial connections later enabled him to raise the necessary capital for his business ventures.[2]

Charles Butler was a complex man who personified what Daniel Boorstin in *The Americans, The National Experience* called the new species of American businessman. His booster spirit and the frenetic pace of his professional life resulted both from his drive for wealth and from his religious zeal. For Butler, the financier's life involved a commitment to hard work and a striving for economic gain that went beyond mere personal advancement to include responsiblities to the nation and to his own religious salvation. Butler, thus, was a man of strong, although rather simplistic, religious convictions who followed his calling with relentless dedication. Although constantly traveling from Boston to New York City to Washington, D.C. and making yearly journeys to the West and the South, Butler always kept Sundays free for personal reflection about his ultimate destiny. In numerous diaries and letters written on these trips, he repeatedly described his inner struggle between the drive for worldly success and the fulfillment of some higher goal.[3]

Butler's western trip in 1833 exemplified this amalgam of religion and business. Carrying a letter of introduction to western churchmen from Absalom Peters of the American Home Missionary Society, Butler considered himself a missionary whose economic efforts would somehow produce religious progress. In his diary, Butler commented on the religious condition of the people, the number and type of churches, and the presence of heretical sects alongside his notations on soil quality and land prices. Struck by the primitive conditions in Chicago and the attendant difficulties of religious worship, Butler, with the assistance of Arthur Bronson, later sent a Sunday school library to the frontier village.[4] Butler further demonstrated his blending of religion and economics in the following observation of Chicago in 1833:

This is the most important *point* in the great west for missionary effort; it is a concentrating & diffusing point: it is at the head of navigation & of course a great commercial point. It has a very extensive back country extending to the Mississippi & rich beyond calculation. It is on the great eastern and western thoroughfare. There is at this point a national harbor being constructed & a national fort—an Indian agency—population is already flowing in beyond all conception—people from all quarters the East & West— the North & the South. There should be here a Bible, Tract & Sunday School depository forthwith. A moral influence should be diffused in the beginning to give character to the society which is growing up here.[5]

Butler practiced his religion in many ways. After his move to New York City, he helped to establish the Union Theological Seminary and worked with it for years. From 1870 until his death in 1891, he was president of the board of directors. He was one of the founders of the Mercer Street Presbyterian Church in New York City. The financier also contributed to an array of charities and social causes. He led a move in the 1830s to organize institutions for the mentally ill and to transfer the responsibility for their care from the county to the state. At the same time, he helped to establish the New York Half Orphan Asylum. Finally, he was an active supporter of New York University for over a half century.[6]

Despite his concern with religious and social life in New York City, Butler was first a businessman. The American Land Company, established in 1835, was the largest and most important of his many ventures. Capitalized at $1,000,000, the company under Butler's presidency united capitalists from Boston, New York City, and Albany for land purchases throughout the United States. Five trustees, reflecting the geographic division of the stock, managed the company. They included Charles Butler and Edward Nicoll from New York City; John B. Jones and John W. Sullivan from Boston; and Erastus Corning from Albany.[7] Many of Butler's New York friends and financial associates were among the stockholders: Lot Clark, 100 shares; Thomas Olcott, 175 shares; Edwin Croswell, 200 shares; and John Van Buren, 125 shares. The Bronson family owned 300 shares and on occasion, they assumed leadership positions. Frederic Bronson served one term as a trustee in 1837, and Arthur Bronson audited the company's books for its annual report to the stockholders in the same year.[8]

The American Land Company reflected a gradual shift in the operation of the land business brought about by the expansion of credit on the East Coast and the rapid settlement of the western states. A few years earlier, most eastern capitalists who desired to purchase western lands had to work through local agents but the American Land Company and similar stock companies and extended partnerships which proliferated on the East Coast in 1835 and 1836 simplified this system considerably. Through the purchase of stock in a company, an individual could invest in western lands without spending the time securing his own knowledge of the region. Individuals also avoided the responsibility of selecting their own agents. Corporate status brought an additional benefit in that companies often lobbied at both the state and national level for favorable government land policies. Through a purchase of stock, therefore, the capitalist secured an interest in western lands without any of the administrative problems associated with such a business. At the same time, entrepreneurs like Butler were able to utilize the capital resources of stock companies for more extensive agricultural purchases and the development of townsites.

The American Land Company did not replace the large investors' participation in separate agreements or other companies, but instead it opened up the possiblity of a broader range of investments. Thomas W. Olcott, president of the Mechanics and Farmers Bank of Albany, perhaps typified the investment pattern of company stockholders. In addition to his 175 shares of American Land Company stock, Olcott joined with William L. Marcy, Senator from New York State, and Lot Clark, a banker from Lockport, New York, in a partnership for land purchases in the state's western region. In 1835, Olcott participated in two companies, each designed to develop townsites in western New York. He also held stock in the Michigan State Bank and the Ohio Life Insurance and Trust Company. Simultaneously he bought agricultural lands in these states, and he owned shares in townsites at Monroe, Michigan, and Maumee City, Ohio. Combining his land and bank stock, Olcott probably possessed western investments in excess of $250,000.[9] This pattern of accumulating diverse interests was not unique to Olcott. Joseph Beers, a New York merchant, private banker, and key organizer of the American Land Company held 850 shares of its stock, but at the same time, he organized the New York and Mississippi Land Company to acquire cotton lands in the South.[10] Arthur Bronson and Erastus Corning had equally complex financial portfolios.

Although some financiers sought a stock interest in the American Land Company because of the advantages of reduced personal risk and administrative involvment, Charles Butler as the company's president and one of the largest stockholders—350 shares—had the obligation to utilize its $1,000,000 capital stock. He first appointed agents who resided in the key regions of the Old Northwest and the South. The agency relationships were similar to those used by individual capitalists. Agents assumed responsibility for the purchase, care, and sale of designated properties.

Their expenses were paid from the proceeds of the sale, and most agents shared in the net profits on a percentage basis. For large purchases, the agent could receive as much as one-third of the profits.[11] During the company's first year, Charles Butler directed the investment of $800,000. Of that sum, over 70 percent was used to acquire southern cotton lands, the principal interest of many stockholders. Through its agent, Henry Anderson, the American Land Company spent approximately $350,000 for lands which the federal government originally had allotted to the Chickasaw Indians. Lands suitable for the cultivation of cotton were also purchased in the Florida and Arkansas territories. To maintain close supervision over these large endeavors, Charles Butler regularly traveled to the South to inspect the company's lands and to confer with its agents.[12]

The company also made extensive investments in the Old Northwest. In early 1835, Butler first tried to entice Lucius Lyon away from his contract with the Bronsons in order to supervise the firm's operations. Failing in that attempt, he invested through a series of agents located in each state or territory. In Michigan, the American Land Company's agents included Dr. Eli Hill, Seba Murphy, Alexander Ely, Theodore Romeyn, William Young, and Nathan Kidder. In 1836, the firm spent approximately $53,000 to acquire 25,000 acres in Michigan. In listing its property before a public auction in 1844, the American Land Company indicated that it had accumulated over 41,000 acres in Michigan with additional town lots in Adrian, Monroe, Tecumseh, and Berrien.[13] In Ohio, the company acquired approximately 20,000 acres. Edward Bissell was the chief Ohio agent, and he invested over $55,000 in Toledo and its surrounding region in 1835 and 1836. At the 1844 auction, the company still held 23,339 acres of Ohio agricultural land plus town lots in Toledo. In Illinois, William B. Ogden became the principal agent in 1836, and he managed a major interest on Chicago's North Side and agricultural properties along the route of the Illinois and Michigan Canal.[14] In the Old Northwest, then, Butler had directed the American Land Company's capital into regions that he had first inspected on his western journey of 1833.

It is very difficult to determine accurately the size of the American Land Company's holdings, not only because of the absence of detailed records but also because of the complex investment practices of the stockholders. Butler and Bronson, for example, owned lands unconnected to the American Land Company in similar locations throughout the Old Northwest. These lands were often entered in partnership with businessmen who also held stock in the American Land Company. Because the acquisitions of the American Land Company were often entered in the names of the trustees, it is impossible to know if a particular tract belonged to the individual or to the company. The historian, thus, cannot really distinguish between Butler's, Olcott's, or Bronson's private and corporate investments.[15] The American Land Company, therefore, cannot be studied without simultaneously investigating other investments of its principal stockholders, particularly Charles Butler.

The American Land Company is also difficult to analyze as a business enterprise because of its unsavory reputation among contemporaries and later historians. Early political attacks portrayed it as a voracious octopus grabbing available agricultural land away from farmers. In the election years of 1836 and 1840, Whig newspapers charged that the American Land Company was a group of New York State Democratic politicians organized for the purpose of speculating in public lands. The charge had a superficial relationship to the truth since Charles Butler was the firm's president and his brother, the Attorney General of the United States, was also a stockholder. Moreover, John Van Buren, President Martin Van Buren's son, was a stockholder, which led to the accusation that the President himself speculated in western lands. New York State Whigs, especially Thurlow Weed, delighted in elaborating the seeming contradiction between the Democrats' anti-monopoly stance and their participation in the land company. The *Chicago American,* also a Whig newspaper, pointed out that the Democrats were in direct competition with western farmers for a share of the public domain due to their connection with the land company.[16]

In 1845, William L. Mackenzie kept alive charges that the American Land Company was a creation of the Albany Regency in his vicious book, *The Lives and Opinions of Benj'n Franklin Butler and Jesse Hoyt.* Mackenzie published many letters of Butler and his associates which strongly suggested that they had misused their official positions in order to speculate in the public lands. Yet Mackenzie had distorted the evidence. For example, he advanced the preposterous thesis that all the Democrats' banking and land policies were part of an intricate plot to defraud the people. By ending the Second Bank of the United States and distributing the surplus to selected state or Pet Banks, he charged that the Democrats provided themselves with the necessary credit to buy the lands which they subsequently sold at exorbitant prices to farmers. Mackenzie, though, was something less than an impartial witness. Leader of the unsuccessful Canadian rebellion in 1837, Mackenzie blamed this failure and his brief prison sentence on President Van Buren.[17]

Historians have been no less critical of the company. In *History of the Public Land Law Development,* Paul Gates presented the case against the American Land Company. Although cognizant of the politically inspired nature of the charges against the company, Gates still believed that "The

American Land Company, like so many of the absentee investors insofar as their wild lands were concerned, did nothing to enhance the value except perhaps to advertise their lands, which was more than some speculators did. It did not identify itself with the welfare of the communities where the lands were located and was a 'monopoly' to the local people."[18]

Many of the charges against the American Land Company were inaccurate or half-truths advanced for political reasons. The firm was not a conspiracy of Van Buren Democrats to monopolize the public domain, although there were many Albany and New York State Democrats among its stockholders. The Bronson family, for example, held 300 shares of stock, and their political sympathies were Whig, not Democratic. Similarly, Martin Van Buren was not a stockholder, unless his shares were held by someone else; but even so, such ownership would have been neither illegal nor unusual in the 1830s. The control of the company's stock was actually split among New York City, Albany, and Boston capitalists. In fact, in 1838, the Boston stockholders were sufficiently influential to almost unseat Charles Butler as the company's president.[19] The American Land Company, thus, was a business firm which brought together capitalists—some Democratic, some Whig—to make money. Charles Butler was genuinely puzzled by the attacks against the firm since speculation in public lands was hardly a Democratic vice during the boom years of 1835 and 1836.[20]

Critics of the American Land Company also have assumed that individual and corporate speculation was routinely detrimental to farmers and local communities, but an analysis of the company's business methods and a little logic challenges that view. The company's detractors argued that it held land off the market, thereby preventing that land from being cultivated. Such a stance assumes first that there was a shortage of land, a position that economist Douglas North has shown to be untrue throughout the nineteenth century. Furthermore, the company did not intentionally hold land off the market for long periods. According to the "Articles of Agreement" which established the firm, the American Land Company was to last only for six years, and its trustees were required to sell all lands within that period. The firm thus sought to buy cheaply and sell quickly, thereby accepting a moderate profit and limited risk. Agents were continually urged to sell lands, often within two or three months of the original purchase. The company's 1836 report stated that "the object will be to diminish the risks by sales as speedily as the interests of the shareholders demand, and always to sell, when they can do so, at a fair profit."[21] Even during the height of the speculative boom, the company was satisfied with an annual return of 10 percent on the total invested capital. Admittedly the American Land Company lasted well beyond 1841, but it was not a matter of choice. With the onset of the depression, the company could not sell all its holdings without sustaining catastrophic losses.[22]

Charges concerning the political character of the American Land Company and the detrimental effect of its purchases on a particular region have hindered our understanding of the process of western economic development. Historians must broaden their perspectives and recognize that the American Land Company's purchases in a particular region represented only a small fraction of the investment portfolios of capitalists like Charles Butler, Arthur Bronson, and Thomas Olcott. At Toledo, Ohio; Port Huron, Michigan; and Chicago, Illinois, Butler exhibited the comprehensive promotional interests of many eastern capitalists and the linkage which they saw between agricultural speculation, urban promotion, and transportation improvements.

In 1832, Benjamin F. Stickney, a member of the Port Lawrence Company, was anxious to increase the scale of promotional activities, and he platted an adjacent town, Vistula. Stickney then solicited eastern subscribers to the new town as a means of securing capital for future improvements. Samuel Allen of Lockport, New York, was a major stockholder at Vistula, and although he later sold out, Allen sent a Lockport resident, Edward Bissell, to Vistula to supervise the town's development. Bissell later became the chief conduit for eastern capitalists, his role marking the beginning of a close link between New York and Ohio entrepreneurs.[24]

Port Lawrence and Vistula were not the only townsites competing to become the principal port on Lake Erie. Population increases and the projected Wabash and Erie Canal, which promised to link the Maumee River with the Wabash River and ultimately provide a water route to the Mississippi River, encouraged the platting of numerous towns along the Maumee River, each hoping to be the crossroads of trade between Lake

Promoters had long recognized the potential for establishing a lakeport near the juncture of the Maumee River and Lake Erie. Speculation had begun in the Toledo region in 1817 when local residents platted the town of Port Lawrence. With little population and no agricultural development in northern Ohio along Lake Erie, the town's proprietors sold a mere seventy-nine lots of a projected 500 lots. Despite this early failure, several stockholders managed to retain their interests throughout the 1820s, and they tried again in the early 1830s by forming the Port Lawrence Company. Micajah T. Williams, then Surveyor General of the Northwest Territory and soon to be president of the Ohio Life Insurance and Trust Company, was among the company's predominately Ohio stockholders.[23]

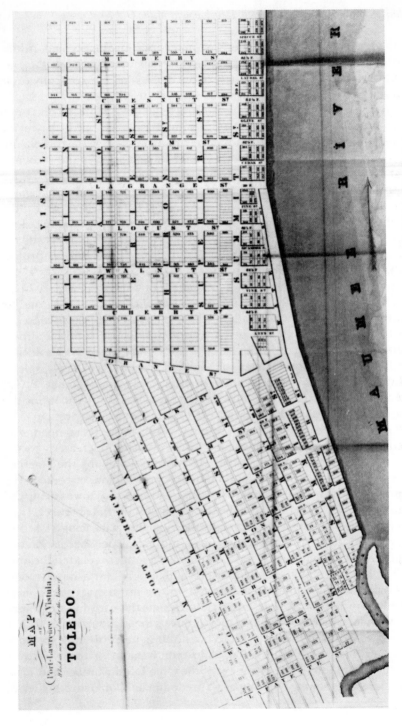

Fig. 7. Map of Toledo, 1834 (Courtesy of the Clarke Historical Library, Central Michigan University)

Erie and the rivers to the South. Isaac Smith and Henry Hicks of New York, who also held shares in both Port Lawrence and Vistula, platted the town of Oregon. A group of Buffalo speculators established the town of Manhattan, although it later disappeared from the map in the intense competition.[25] Despite this competition, however, eastern money concentrated in the development of Port Lawrence and Vistula, especially after the towns were merged into the city of Toledo in 1836.[26]

Charles Butler had been aware of the scramble along the Maumee River since the early 1830s after Micajah Williams first directed his attention to Port Lawrence. He had planned to visit the site during the western trip with Arthur Bronson in 1833, but delays in Chicago and Detroit made that visit impossible. Arthur Bronson later explored the possibility of a purchase at Port Lawrence by sending Elon Farnsworth to inspect the general potential of the townsites on the Maumee river. But in 1834, Farnsworth warned against a purchase because of the area's reputation for disease and because of the intense speculation over which location would become the principal port.[27]

Even though rising land values scared away Arthur Bronson, Charles Butler perceived unlimited opportunities for profits in the Port Lawrence and Vistula regions. The American Land Company, therefore, bought agricultural land in northwestern Ohio through the agency of Edward Bissell. Moreover, it invested $50,000 directly in Port Lawrence and Vistula town lots and in undivided acreage just west of the towns. Charles Butler also acquired town lots and agricultural lands on his own account. At the same time, Butler and the American Land Company bought lands in southeastern Michigan, particularly in and around the village of Adrian. These investments were linked in Butler's mind by the possibility of building a railroad—the Erie and Kalamazoo—from Adrian to Port Lawrence, thus enhancing the advantages of both the urban locations and the agricultural lands between them.[28]

The early history of the Erie and Kalamazoo Railroad further demonstrated the importance of eastern capitalists like Butler to western economic development. Local entrepreneurs from southeastern Michigan first had proposed the Erie and Kalamazoo Railroad to provide transportation for agricultural products. Michigan's Territorial Council granted the company a corporate charter in 1833, with a capital stock of one million dollars to build a railroad from Port Lawrence to Adrian and then west to a point on the Kalamazoo River where the railroad would connect with steamboats from there to Lake Michigan. Situated on a southerly line from Adrian, Port Lawrence was the logical choice for the eastern terminus. Not only did Port Lawrence provide an outlet onto Lake Erie but also it was then considered to be in the Michigan Territory. Family connections also helped to link the two cities. Darius Comstock and his son, Addison, who led in the incorporation of the railroad had come West in the 1820s from Lockport, New York, acquired land in southeastern Michigan, and established Adrian. Darius Comstock's cousin, Stephen B. Comstock, on the other hand, was a leading figure in the promotion of Port Lawrence.[29]

Although western entrepreneurs had easily acquired a charter for the Erie and Kalamazoo, they were unable to obtain sufficient capital until they sought eastern assistance. For over a year, the railroad failed to raise $50,000, the sum which the legislature required before construction could begin. Eventually the railroad obtained the $50,000, but it was expended in completing just the basic surveys and engineering reports.[30] Local directors then sold shares to eastern capitalists, but, in the process, they yielded control of the railroad. In 1835, Charles Butler bought $25,000 of the railroad's stock, and Joel McCollum from Lockport, New York, subscribed for $30,000. Since the railroad's $1,000,000 of stock was subscribed beyond $150,000 in the 1830s, the easterners had stock control. McCollum then became a director of the railroad, and Edward Bissell, the easterners' principal agent, was appointed to supervise the construction.[31]

Eastern financiers also obtained control of the Erie and Kalamazoo Railroad Bank. In 1835, the Michigan Territorial Council had amended the railroad's charter allowing its stockholders to establish a bank at Adrian, Michigan, capitalized at $100,000. The local promoters originally had hoped that the bank's stock would attract investors and that their capital would support the issue of notes both for the payment of laborers and for the purchase of materials. Although a separate legal entity, the railroad's directors were to manage the bank.[32] With a major interest in the railroad, the New Yorkers naturally sought a like influence over the bank. In 1835, therefore, Joel McCollum subscribed for over a half of the available stock, $60,000. Charles Butler personally held $8,000 in stock, but more important, he convinced other easterners, such as Erastus Corning and Levi Beardsley, to acquire stock. The easterners also had indirect control over many local stockholders. Edward Bissell and Darius Comstock, for example, bought $18,000 in bank stock, but the money was borrowed from Corning, Butler, and Beardsley.[33]

With an extensive stock interest, Butler, McCollum, Corning, and Beardsley were unwilling to entrust the bank's management to local businessmen. Consequently, the easterners had set a precondition before they subscribed to the bank's stock: the right to name the bank's president, cashier, and attorney and an agreement that local stockholders would seek a legal separation of the bank's management from that of the railroad. In 1836, Joel McCollum became president of the bank's board of directors. The most important official, however, was the cashier because he controlled its daily operation. Thus the easterners hired a New York resident, Philo C. Fuller, to move West and fill that post. Fuller had been an agent of the New York Life Insurance and Trust Company at Geneseo, New York, and had served in both houses of the New York State legislature.[34]

With the assistance of eastern financiers, then, the Erie and Kalamazoo began construction. Its major section from Toledo to Adrian was completed in 1837. In 1838, a spur line, known as the Palmyra and Jacksonburgh Railroad, was finished to Tecumseh. For a few years, both the bank and the railroad were in excellent financial condition. The bank issued a stock dividend of 5 percent for the 1836 financial year, and the railroad declared a dividend of 30 percent for 1837.[35]

Charles Butler's varied interests in the Toledo region were characteristic of his western investments. In the first place, the New Yorker mixed his private holdings with those of the American Land Company such that the total mobilized capital is impossible to estimate. The salient point, however, is that the New Yorker drew eastern money into the region not just through the land company but also through his extensive contacts with capitalists such as Erastus Corning. Although Butler was not the sole financier involved, his active interest in the railroad and the bank marked him as the central contact between eastern and western financiers. At one point in the 1830s, for example, Butler served as the railroad's agent for purchasing iron, and at another time, he attempted to secure government deposits for the bank.[36] Finally, Butler demonstrated his understanding of the need to develop town and agricultural properties in conjunction with the construction of transportation lines. Either through his own investments or those of the American Land Company, Butler held agricultural land along the railroad's route, lots in Adrian and Toledo, and stock in the principal bank. Whereas Arthur Bronson would have shied away form such grandiose schemes, Butler always possessed enthusiasm and daring for the "great" project. His goal was nothing less than to develop the Toledo region in order to make Toledo a major port on Lake Erie and a key access point for trade goods and people moving west to Michigan and Indiana and south to the Wabash and Erie Canal.

Butler further exhibited his promotional techniques at Huron, a townsite on Lake Huron's western shore. Part of the original plat is today Port Huron, Michigan. The site was strategically situated where the St. Clair River, the Black River and Lake Huron merged; consequently, it had been used for economic and military purposes. Fur traders had bartered there with the Indians, and Detroiters regularly tapped the abundant lumber supply in the surrounding region. The military had established Fort Gratiot there in 1814 to guard access to both the upper lakes of Huron and Michigan and the lower lakes of St. Clair and Erie. The military's presence eventually led to congressional approval in 1827 for the construction of a road from Detroit to the fort. Despite this military and economic activity, Butler found a sparse settlement when he visited in 1833. In addition to the eighty–man contingent at Fort Gratiot, the population consisted of only eight families totaling perhaps fifty people. Local citizens, hoping for a population influx in 1834 and 1835, drew up several city plats both north and south of the Black River, but little economic development resulted until Butler planned a city in the region.[37]

Butler again combined individual and corporate investments at Huron. In 1836, he purchased land north of Fort Gratiot for $125,000. Even though the tract was entered in his name, it was held in trust for the Huron Land Company, a stock firm composed of eastern capitalists, many of whom also held shares in the American Land Company. Joining Butler as the principal stockholders were William Bard and Edward Nicoll, president and cashier of the New York Life Insurance and Trust Company. Other New Yorkers included Benjamin F. Butler, Erastus Corning, Joseph Beers, a Wall Street banker, and Thomas Suffern, a merchant. There were also Boston stockholders, such as John McNeil, former commander at Fort Gratiot, Samuel Hubbard, and John Borland. Butler also acquired land south of Fort Gratiot bordering on the Black River, and the American Land Company bought agricultural lands in the general area.[38]

Butler supervised the site's development. He first warned his eastern partners to avoid visiting the region for fear of alerting their local competitors. Meanwhile, he began a search for a reliable agent, and in the late summer of 1836, he contacted Nicholas Ayrault, a resident of his former hometown, Geneva, New York. Stressing Huron's potential for retail businesses, Butler offered to pay Ayrault's expenses for a journey there and promised him a share in the entire plat. Shortly after his visit, Ayrault agreed to manage Butler's affairs there plus the accounts of the Huron Land Company and the American Land Company.[39]

In 1836, Butler oversaw the writing of two promotional pamphlets on Huron designed to attract settlers and investors. No sources better illustrated the New Yorker's promotional mentality and unbounded enthusiasm for the West. According to Butler, Huron was destined to become a key trade center standing between the trade of the upper lakes—Michigan, Huron and Superior—and the lower lakes—Erie and Ontario. The narrow channels of the Detroit and St. Clair Rivers prevented the free movement of large ships into the upper lakes, Butler explained, and thus Huron would become both a point of trans–shipment and of original shipment between the two tiers of lakes. Given this belief, it is not surprising that Butler's plat consisted of 8,000 lots, sufficient for a city of 40,000 inhabitants.[40]

But the New Yorker had even greater hopes for Huron. He believed that it had the potential to become a gateway city, the principal transfer point for goods and people moving from East to West. At that time, travelers heading for Chicago or destinations further West took lake steamers north on Lake Huron through the straits of Mackinac and then down Lake Michigan's western shore to Chicago. A more difficult overland trek was also possible from Detroit across southern Michigan to Chicago. Yet the publications about Huron suggested a possible alternative route. Butler envisioned a combination of lake and railroad conveyances which would shorten the distance and the time between East and West. Embarking by lake vessel from Oswego on Lake Ontario, for example, the emigrant could travel to the head of Lake Ontario at Hamilton. From Hamilton, a railroad would carry travelers across Canada, stopping at London enroute to Point Edward near Sarnia, Ontario. Sarnia, located directly across the St. Clair River from Huron, was a short trip by ferry. This route, combining lake and railroad travel, avoided the longer, more tedious itinerary from Buffalo on Lake Erie to Detroit and then north to Huron. Readers were assured that the Canadian government had recognized the advantage of diverting travelers into Canada to reach northern Michigan and stops further West. Butler cited numerous reports written by the Canadian government which indicated that plans were underway for a railroad from Hamilton to Sarnia.[41]

The brochures also suggested that Huron would become the principal transfer point for travelers heading further West. In 1837, Michigan was committed to a railroad running across the northern counties linking Lake Huron and Lake Michigan. If Huron were selected as the railroad's eastern terminus, it would guarantee the viability of the townsite and a steady stream of emigrants to the state's northern counties. Yet Butler also projected that the railroad would connect with ferries across Lake Michigan to enter Chicago or Milwaukee, thus obviating the need for the more southerly route across lower Michigan. One pamphlet concluded with the following observations on Huron's potential as a strategic trade and transportation center:

> These considerations of shorter and easier routes of travelling, . . . address themselves to all classes of persons, who are desirous of investing at the West, and especially to emigrants, who must look at the fact, that the State of Michigan by the construction of the Great

Western Rail-Road through Canada will be made the middle ground
for location and settlement between the counties east and west of the
great lakes. The importance of the Great Western Rail-Road . . . to
the State of Michigan . . . cannot be too highly estimated. It will
secure to Michigan, almost exclusively, the whole tide of emigration
from the country lying directly east of it, embracing the State of New
York and the whole of the New England States, the most densely
settled portions of the United States, and from whence she is drawing her best supplies of population. By no other route can this result
so important to her agricultural interests be secured. It may be
added also, that this route is the natural antagonist of southern
routes and interests from which Michigan by reason of her peculiar
position, has everything to fear.[42]

The prospectus for Huron also indicated that a survey and an engineering report had been completed for the construction of a ship canal which
would aid lake navigation. The canal would enable lake vessels to bypass
the rapids between the St. Clair River and Lake Huron. Butler claimed
that ships were unnecessarily delayed while awaiting favorable winds
before passing the rapids. A map attached to the pamphlet showed that
the canal would utilize the Black River to carry ships inland around the
west side of Huron. The canal then would run diagonally through the
town back to Lake Huron. Excerpts from an engineering report assured
readers of the canal's feasibility. The engineering reports bore the unmistakable marks of Butler's influence since the engineer, swept away by his
enthusiasm, projected that the canal might also link up with the railroad
leading west to the Grand River, with the ferry to Milwaukee, and finally
with a railroad across the Wisconsin Territory to Cassville. It is important
to note that the engineer mentioned Cassville, since Butler's friends were
involved in the promotion of that town on the Mississippi River.[43]

No less important than Huron's strategic commercial location was its
internal potential for retail businesses and trade. The literature stressed
the availability of water power while a map marked specific sites for mills
on the town's west side. Moreover, brochures stated that the town already
possessed a population of 500—probably an exaggerated claim—with a
newspaper, a public house, and several stores. The brochures emphasized
the need for mechanics and artisans as well as the availability of agricultural land in the interior at the minimum government price of $1.25
per acre. Despite the somewhat exaggerated claims for the townsite,
Butler's plan was no chimera concocted merely to bilk unsuspecting investors and emigrants. The New Yorker obviously believed that he could
make Huron a thriving commercial center and therefore poured thou-

sands into promotional literature, engineering reports, cartographic work, and building construction.[44]

To a great extent Huron's success depended on the projected railroads west from Huron to Lake Michigan and east from Sarnia to Lake Ontario. Even though Butler was unable to exert any influence in the legislative councils of Upper Canada, he followed the discussions there with great interest.[45] The Canadian government was anxious to support a railroad running on an east-west axis in order to siphon off passengers then going south around the lakes, but there was a debate over the best route. Many Canadians preferred a railroad from Hamilton through London and then south to Detroit. In 1836, nevertheless, the London and Gore Railroad, which already possessed a charter to build from Hamilton to London, obtained legislative approval to extend the road to Point Edward near Sarnia on Lake Huron. The name of the railroad was changed to reflect its new goal—the Great Western Railroad. It was seen as part of the great transportation system passing through Canada linking New York City with Chicago and destinations further West. Besides the railroads saving time and distance, the Legislative Council of Upper Canada observed that it would benefit the province " . . . by the introduction of numerous travellers, who will cross Lake Ontario in steamboats, and then proceed to the western shores of the United States, or, perhaps, numbers of them be attracted by the fertile country through which they will pass, and become permanent settlers in Upper Canada."[46]

Even though the Canadians assumed that Michigan would build a railroad west from Huron to an outlet on Lake Michigan to complete the route of the Great Western Railroad, the Michigan legislature was mired in a protracted debate over the number and the location of canal and railroad projects in early 1837. The Internal Improvements Act, passed March 1837, finally approved a northern railroad, but the act did not specify the route or terminus. The legislation called only for a railroad to be constructed from either Huron or Palmer along the fourth tier of counties to the head of navigation on the Grand River in Kent County or to the shore of Lake Michigan in Ottawa county. Michigan's Board of Commissioners of Internal Improvements were to make the final judgments after completion of preliminary surveys.[47]

Butler, of course, was vitally interested in the location of the railroad's route. Not only was Huron's future at stake, but his other Michigan interests in alliance with Lucius Lyon and Arthur Bronson would benefit from a route which passed through the villages of Lyon, Ada, and Grand Rapids. Even though Butler occasionally exchanged letters with Michigan residents on the subject, he was unable to affect directly the railroad's location. Nevertheless, the existence of settlements at Lyon, Ada, and

Grand Rapids certainly swayed the surveyor's decision to link these existing points with a railroad.[48]

Butler did, however, have an indirect influence on the location of the railroad's eastern terminus. After passage of the Internal Improvements Act, the Board of Commissioners authorized surveys to be conducted from both the competing locations, Huron and Palmer. Public meetings were held at these villages on successive days in December 1837, so that each town could present its arguments for the depot. Palmer, which was located further south along the St. Clair River, argued that it was in an established county with a thriving agricultural hinterland and that it was closer to Detroit. The Board of Commissioners, nevertheless, turned against Palmer in favor of Huron. Their decision was based partly on Huron's strategic location at the foot of Lake Huron and at the rapids of the St. Clair River. But more important than any other consideration was the hoped–for linkage with the railroad being constructed across Canada to Sarnia.[49] The Board of Commissioners must have read Butler's pamphlet on Huron since its final report bore a striking similarity to it. The engineer who completed the surveys, for example, commented on the importance of the northern railroad in language much the same as that contained in the Huron brochure, especially the mention of Cassville on the Mississippi River:

> It appears obvious that the road is to be constructed, not only for the accommodation of the inhabitants in the immediate vicinity of the route and adjacent district, but also as an essential link in the great chain of railroads, finished or in progress, from New York and Boston to the valley of the Mississippi and the far West. It is in fact almost a direct line to pass from Albany on the great thoroughfare through the principal cities of western New York; thence through Canada by the great western railroad to the St. Clair River; and thence through the geographical centre of Michigan by the northern railroad to Lake Michigan; thence to Milwaukee and Cassville, in the centre of the Mineral district on the Mississippi.[50]

Alongside his commitments to the development of Toledo and Huron, Butler embarked on an equally ambitious project in Chicago and its vicinity. From the time of his first visit in 1833, the New Yorker believed that Chicago was destined to become a thriving lakeport. In 1834, he had been unable to share in Arthur Bronson's acquisition of the Hunter property because his capital was pledged to other ventures, but he had worked with Bronson and Chicago citizens in revitalizing the Illinois and Michigan Canal. Before 1835, therefore, Butler had made numerous contacts and had evaluated investments in and around Chicago, a necessary prelude to active involvement.

Like his operations in Toledo and Huron, Butler's Chicago investments were a complicated mix of private and corporate interests. In April 1835, for example, he put together a $50,000 partnership in which he and nine other eastern capitalists each invested $5,000 for land purchases principally in Chicago and along the route of the Illinois and Michigan Canal. The other partners were also members of the American Land Company: Williams Bard, John Ward, Isaac Carrow, John Delafield, J .L. & S. Joseph & Co., Edward A. Nicoll, Beverly Robinson, Thomas B. Olcott, and Nathaniel Bloodgood. Butler supervised the purchase and sale of all lands through two Chicago agents, John Kinzie and Hiram Pearson, who agreed to invest the funds for a share of the profits. To reduce the risks inherent in land speculation, the contract stipulated that all lands were to be sold and the partnership closed by 1841.[51]

Scarcely a month after signing this contract, Butler began negotiations to purchase the Hunter property on Chicago's North Side from Arthur Bronson. Whereas Bronson had decided that Chicago land values were too inflated to ever return steady profits, Butler believed that the inflation proved that Chicago was an ideal location with the potential for rapid development under proper leadership. Consequently, Butler paid $100,000 for over 150 acres or 1000 city lots. The money probably came from the corporate funds of the American Land Company and some combination of Butler's own capital and that of close friends.[52]

Following the typical pattern Butler immediately appointed an agent to supervise the property. Perhaps because the investment was so large, the New Yorker avoided the selection of a resident Chicagoan and instead prevailed on his old friend, William B. Ogden, to accept the job temporarily. As young men, Ogden and Butler had moved in the same social and political circles in Albany. In 1825, Butler had married Ogden's sister, Eliza. Like Butler, Ogden had prospered in the 1820s after taking over his father's mercantile business. He was also politically active, and in the spring of 1835, he was a Democratic senator from Delaware County in the New York State legislature. Ogden had demonstrated that his economic philosophy was compatible with that of Charles Butler when he spearheaded legislation for the financing of the New York and Erie Railroad.[53]

Butler talked Ogden into coming to Chicago for a short period in the spring and summer of 1835 to prepare part of the Hunter property for sale. Butler wished to advertise and sell his lands while many speculators were in Chicago for a government auction sale in June 1835. Ogden was assisted in this work by Frederic Bronson who, after turning over legal title, remained in Chicago as a representative of other eastern shareholders. The two New Yorkers faced an immense task in preparing lots for sale since the tract was largely undeveloped. Spring rains had left

Fig. 8. Portrait of Frederic Bronson (Courtesy of Mrs. Bronson Griscom)

portions of the land under water, and neither street nor lot boundaries had been fixed. In a few months, Ogden conducted new surveys, put through streets, and began construction of a few commercial and residential buildings. Ogden estimated that he spent between $15,000 and $20,000 on improvements that first year.[54]

Butler sent Ogden and Frederic Bronson an overall plan for development based on his generally optimistic appraisal of the future. His enthusiastic letters also were intended to bolster Ogden's gloomy spirits as he prepared the wet and marshy lands for sale. Butler hoped to improve the land in stages, the profits from the first sale being used to develop more lots for the next sale. Consequently Butler withheld from sale all waterfront lots because their value as points of trade and commerce would increase over the years. Looking to the future, the New Yorker projected a minimum profit of $200,000:

> . . . You cannot be too confident in regard to the intrinsic value of property in Chicago—it is really and intrinsically valuable & every day but adds to this value, & confirms public opinion in regard to it—and who can pretend to say what property will be worth in Chicago ten years hence when the canal shall have been constructed & in full operation & when the northern part of Illinois shall be filled with an active, intelligent, moral and industrious population. Chicago is the market for a very extensive country & no place *can* compete with it. It is the head of navigation—the place of trans– shipment . . . .[55]

Butler had gauged correctly the proper timing for his first sale. The government's auction of land in northern Illinois was a spectacular success. From May 28 to September 30, the government accepted preemption claims, auctioned land, and sold it outright to the total value of $459,958. The excitement brought hundreds of farmers and speculators to the city. Land was sold at every street corner as everyone used this opportunity to sell his own parcels. Edward Russell from Middletown, Connecticut, for example, sold hundreds of acres and many town lots through his Chicago agent, Gurdon Hubbard. For a brief moment Chicago went wild in the exchange of property.[56] Land values were fixed to nothing other than the "craziness" of the moment. Arthur Bronson's brother-in-law, James B. Murray, was in Chicago at this time and recorded his impression: "Indeed it appears to me that everything here is scarce and dear except money—and that is plenty to a degree that is absolutely laughable. You see men apparently without a second shirt to their back handling rolls of bills like waste paper, and buying and selling lots for thousands and tens of thousands."[57]

Butler could not help but benefit from Chicago's land market in 1835. Ogden sold roughly one-third of the Hunter tract for $100,000. Thus the initial sales recovered the purchase money, and Butler looked forward to additional profits from future development and sale. One Chicagoan, Walter Newberry, was so astounded by Chicago land prices that he predicted that Butler's North Side property eventually would yield profits of a half million dollars. With seemingly unlimited possiblities for profit, William Ogden decided to make Chicago his permanent home in 1836 and plunged ahead with Butler's scheme for the development of Chicago's North Side.[58]

During the boom years of 1835 and 1836, then, Butler was the epitome of the promoter who was willing to spend money in order to make money. Without a family fortune as a basis, Butler had put together a series of complex financial arrangements to raise capital. These included stock companies, the American Land Company and the Huron Land Company; partnerships, such as that with Hiram Pearson and John Kinzie in Chicago; and numerous individual agreements with eastern business associates. I doubt that any historian could ever determine precisely which corporation or partnership predominated in the ownership of Chicago lots, Ohio agricultural land or the Erie and Kalamazoo Railroad Bank, but clearly Butler's most important fucntion was mobilizing the capital surpluses of the East for investment in western projects. Moreover, Butler's operations were not unusual. In Chicago, Toledo, Detroit, Green Bay, and Huron, other eastern financiers, such as Thomas Olcott and Erastus Corning, moved capital into similar projects. Taken together, the involvement of eastern financiers demonstrated that their capital and financial leadership was central to the West's economic development.

Butler's promotional activities also challenge many popular stereotypes of the absentee speculator. First, neither Butler's partnerships nor the American Land Company intended to hold all land off the market for long periods. Profits were derived from quick sales and were often then reinvested. Second, Butler had a broad conception of economic development. This in part resulted from the tremendous diversity of his holdings throughout the Old Northwest. Besides his large interests at Toledo, Huron, and Chicago, he also owned agricultural lands throughout the region and shares in the promotion of Detroit and Green Bay.[59] He knew that a region's agricultural land and urban property increased in value as the community acquired retail stores, banks, and transportation lines. Thus the New Yorker mobilized the capital and often provided the leadership that fostered building and railroad construction. Perhaps more than most western citizens who were tied economically and personally to a single town, a promoter like Butler could envision the West's place in the national economy and simultaneously invest in towns, railroads, and agricultural land throughout the Old Northwest.

Finally, Butler's career reflected essential differences in investment philosophy and technique from that of the conservative investor such as Arthur Bronson. Butler was most often the initiator of large-scale developments, such as at Chicago and Toledo. He rarely waited for other financiers to share the costs or responsibilities, but instead "promoted" the building of a railroad or the establishment of a bank. Whereas Arthur Bronson avoided concentrations of capital in particular regions, Butler poured thousands into three principal projects: Chicago, Huron, and Toledo. In fact, Butler stressed urban over agricultural investments while Bronson's technique was just the reverse. Butler was also bolder and more optimistic with his eyes riveted on America's future economic development. In 1835 and 1836, he did not believe that his various projects entailed any substantial risks, and he would have rejected the notion that he was a speculator. Although Butler could conceive of an economic slowdown and a single financial failure, his booster spirit and his belief in the long-term economic progress of America prevented his envisioning total financial collapse. It was Arthur Bronson's belief in that possiblity, based on his analysis of past land booms, that had curtailed his investments at the precise moment that Butler began his most daring promotions. Perhaps it was this vision of the country's economic future which separated Butler, the promoter, from Bronson, the investor.

7. Eastern Financiers and the Struggle for Banking Reform, 1832-1843

Too often historians divorce the study of land speculators and western economic development from the broader economic and political issues of the time. The investment policies of Arthur Bronson and Charles Butler, for example, cannot be understood without an analysis of their participation in the chaotic world of Jacksonian financial policy. Not only did the New Yorkers make busines decisions affecting Chicago or Grand Rapids on the basis of economic conditions in the East, but they also attempted to influence directly the shape of government financial policies. Like businessmen throughout American history, Bronson and Butler realized that the stability and profitability of their investments often depended upon the decisions of government officials.

The central economic issues of Jacksonian America revolved around the structure of the banking system, and for Isaac and Arthur Bronson, and to a lesser extent Charles Butler, Jacksonian financial policies, beginning with the destruction of the Second Bank of the United States (BUS) in 1832, had exacerbated the speculative practices of most banks and had led to the excessive issue of credit, price increases, and rampant speculation in public lands. Throughout the 1830s, therefore, the New Yorkers campaigned with financiers holding similar views at the state and national levels in order to reform banking practices. First, they hoped to establish a new national bank which would exert central control over the banking system and slowly inject credit and capital into the economy. At the same time, they tried to maintain control of the Ohio Life Insurance and Trust Company (OLTC), an institution which they had founded in order demonstrate the efficacy of their banking principles. Finally, the Bronsons advocated free banking in New York State and Michigan as another means of gaining acceptance of their banking ideas. Throughout this period, Isaac Bronson was the theorist who drafted the plans while Arthur Bronson corresponded with key bankers and lobbied with state and national politicians. Since he moved easily among Jacksonian Democrats in Washington, Charles Butler often assisted in lobbying for the Bronsons' plans, even though his own business ventures seemed incompatible with a conservative banking system.

Isaac Bronson's theories of banking were already established when the bank issue surfaced in the early 1830s. Throughout the early nineteenth century, he had tried to restrict the function of commercial banks to the financing of trade, that is, providing notes and bills of exchange for the movement of commodities. After 1815, however, the rapid pace of economic development generated a tremendous demand for capital, and Bronson grudgingly acknowledged the necessity for commercial banks to expand their functions by investing their capital (the money received in payment for bank stock) in farm mortgages and government securites. Yet the New Yorker soon discovered that commercial banks were incapable of resisting the pressure for speculative uses of their capital and credit since they increased note circulations, granted renewals on commercial paper, and invested their capital in land schemes. According to Isaac Bronson, these practices threatened to disrupt the whole business system, especially the movement of trade goods, since the money supply was being used for highly speculative business enterprises. Bronson also contended that the continual expansion of bank notes led to higher prices since speculators were willing to pay more for goods. Although Bronson may not have considered all the factors that determined price and trade movements, he was remarkably prescient in predicting the periods of excessive speculation and depression.

In 1830, Isaac and Arthur Bronson had cooperated with other financial conservatives in the establishment of the New York Life Insurance and Trust Company (NYLTC) as a response to the country's chaotic banking system. The trust company was to accumulate the surplus wealth of New York State citizens and invest it in farm mortgages, personal notes, and occasional manufacturing enterprises. In essence, the trust company would provide financial support for economic expansion, although its investments would be selected carefully. The NYLTC, however, did not possess the power to circulate notes, leaving to commercial banks the responsibility for financing the movement of trade goods. In Bronson's view, this specialization of financial institutions would reduce or eventually eliminate the need for commercial banks to venture their capital in speculative enterprises. Consequently, Bronson hoped that America would expand its agricultural and manufacturing potential in an economic climate free of the land speculation and currency inflation which previously had disrupted trade and had caused innumerable personal and business failures.[1]

Because of his concern for the regulation of financial institutions, Isaac Bronson was inevitably led into the quagmire of the national bank issue. Chartered in 1816, the BUS was the centerpiece of the nation's financial system. It possessed enormous resources as the depository of government funds, and it was also the nation's largest commercial bank, issuing notes and bills of exchange to facilitate trade. Nicholas Biddle, who assumed the institution's presidency in 1823, further enlarged the bank's potential for regulating the economy; in other words, Biddle operated the institution as a central bank. For example, Biddle occasionally returned for redemption the notes of state banks which had accumulated in the BUS's many branches. Such action taken against a single bank could force it to curtail its extension of credit, and a general policy of prompt note redemption could slow a temporary inflation throughout the country. At other times, the BUS increased its own circulation or discounts to remedy a shortage of credit in the market. Of course, these functions made the bank extremely powerful, and many people, including Andrew Jackson, considered its monopoly status as a chartered agent of the government an affront to democracy and free enterprise. Moreover, the bank's imperious president, Nicholas Biddle, was extremely jealous of his power and prerogatives, and he easily antagonized the equally vain occupant of the White House. The bank was on a collision course with the administration, and the spark ignited when Nicholas Biddle requested the bank's recharter from Congress in 1832 even though its current charter would not expire until 1836.[2]

Isaac Bronson was a staunch defender of a central bank which possessed the power to regulate state banks and to provide overall direction to the nation's economy. He thus supported Nicholas Biddle's request for a recharter even though he opposed Biddle's use of credit and capital to stimulate economic expansion. Bronson quickly abandoned Biddle, however, when his political contact in the House of Representatives informed him that the administration intended to stop the recharter. Bronson then saw a chance to draw up a national bank plan that reflected his own economic philosophy. Bronson's proposal called for a national bank with a capital stock of $20 million, securely invested in bonds and mortgages triple the value. The bank's circulation could not exceed $20 million, and to assure compliance with that provision, the federal government was to control the issue of notes. Through branches located in the country's chief commercial centers, the bank's credit would be employed in strict commercial banking operations, that is, issuing only short-term notes. The bank would also be a government depository, but clearly this function was not to be intertwined with banking operations. If at any time the bank could not redeem its notes within sixty days, the charter was to be forfeited, the stock sold, and the bank closed.

Bronson believed that such a bank was essential to the nation's economy for several reasons. First, it prevented currency inflation since the government would control the issue of notes and since the bank's capital stock of $20 million would support the notes. Second, the bank would discourage speculation since its notes would be issued for only sixty or ninety days. Third, the bank's capital stock would be invested in land mortgages throughout the nation thereby generating agricultural expansion, unlike the capital of the BUS which was utilized in the institution's day to day operations. Finally, the bank's size and its function as a government depository would allow it to regulate the operations of state banks whose notes would find their way to the national bank's central location.[3]

In early 1832, Isaac Bronson submitted his plan to Congress, but it attracted little attention. Congress was then embroiled in Biddle's request for a recharter and was unwilling seriously to consider competing plans. Nevertheless, Bronson marshaled the family troops in support of his proposal. Arthur Bronson and his brother-in-law, James B. Murray, visited important Democratic politicians in Albany, New York, and then Murray traveled to Washington in order to talk with key national legislators. Few politicians, however, were willing to support Bronson's plan while the recharter question was still before Congress. Churchill C. Cambreleng, a powerful adminstration leader in the House of Representatives, expressed interest but urged Isaac Bronson to wait until after Congress's action on Biddle's request. Cambreleng assured Bronson that the President would never sign a recharter bill no matter what Congress did.[4] But the political situation changed during the summer. Jackson vetoed the recharter bill in July 1832, and shortly thereafter he faced the electorate on the bank issue. When he was reelected by a large majority, Jackson assumed this to be a sign that he should proceed more boldly against the BUS by withdrawing government deposits even before the expiration of its current charter. The administration was suddenly unwilling to consider plans for a new national bank, and Cambreleng was no longer receptive to Isaac Bronson's ideas.[5]

In late 1832, Isaac Bronson sought new political allies for submission of another proposal to Congress. He acquired help from Albert Gallatin, a former Secretary of the Treasury, who agreed to speak with prominent financiers.[6] Bronson also met with a group of New York merchants and bankers in February 1833, to discuss the country's financial condition. At that meeting, a committee was appointed to draw up a plan for a national bank to be located in New York City. The committee consisted of Isaac

Bronson, George Griswold, Daniel Jackson, and John Bolton. The resulting scheme, *Outline of a Plan for a National Bank,* was published in the
summer of 1833. It involved the same basic ideas that Bronson had
proposed a year earlier even though he shared the authorship with other
committee members. In justifying the need for a new bank, the authors
cited the overtrading and speculation which had occurred because banks
had lent their capital and extended their note issues. This plan carried an
explicit statement of commercial banking principles: "The true and legitimate purpose of banking institutions are fulfilled by enabling the merchant who sells his goods on credit to realize the amount of sales, and not
by furnishing capital to trade on, and thereby involving the banks in the
results of such trading."[7]

As Isaac Bronson worked on the new proposal, he had two opportunities
to influence the administration's thinking on the removal of government
deposits from the existing BUS. Arthur Bronson arranged a meeting
between his father and Vice–President–Elect Martin Van Buren in New
York City in February 1833. At this meeting, Bronson warned Van Buren
against the removal of government deposits and stressed the need for a
new national bank.[8] James A. Hamilton, a New York City Democrat and
presidential adviser, subsequently asked Bronson to answer a series of
questions probing the possible effects of removal. Although Bronson
indicated his support of Jackson's veto of the bank's recharter, he insisted
that removal would create havoc throughout the financial system. Bronson
predicted a period of rapid inflation because each state bank, having
received an infusion of government funds, would expand its circulation
in the absence of a central bank to limit this natural tendency.[9]

Whether Jackson ever read this advice is doubtful, for the political
atmosphere in Washington in 1833 grew more hostile to Bronson's views.
In the fall, the Treasury Department issued the removal order and
government funds in the BUS were transferred to select state or "Pet"
banks. At the same time, Nicholas Biddle, providing for the loss of
government funds, contracted the credit of the BUS, sending temporary
shockwaves throughout the economy. The administration interpreted
Biddle's action as a deliberate attempt to create financial disruptions in
order to establish a rationale for the bank's recharter. Jackson was then
more than ever convinced of the dangers inherent in concentrated financial power.[10]

Jackson's action and Nicholas Biddle's response appalled Isaac Bronson
since he expected that state banks would immediately increase their note
circulations, causing more speculation and inflation which, in turn, would
increase land and commodity prices. Consequently, he and Arthur
Bronson renewed their efforts to change the nation's banking policy. In

January 1834, they met at Isaac Bronson's New York City residence with the city's leading financiers, and this group decided to submit once again Bronson's bank plan to Congress. Yet Isaac Bronson harbored no illusions that this would be an easy battle, given the existing political climate. To a congressional supporter, he observed that "when politicians turn bankers, merchants may put on sackcloth."[11] The New Yorker sensed that Congress would not readily consider a change until deteriorating financial conditions forced such action. Moreover, Vice-President Martin Van Buren refused his support because he feared that any request for a new bank might split the anti-Biddle forces in Congress, thereby opening the possibility of Biddle receiving a new charter.[12]

Despite Van Buren's position, Charles Butler used his influence with other New York State Democratic politicians to lobby for Bronson's proposal. In 1834, he wrote to Silas Wright, a powerful Democratic senator and a friend of Martin Van Buren. Butler first assured Wright that he supported the President's removal of government deposits from the BUS and that he opposed its recharter. The BUS had two contradictory goals, Butler explained: to make a profit and to regulate the nation's credit supply for the public good. Butler asserted that the bank had expanded and contracted its circulation for its own profits even though such action had harmed the public. Biddle's contraction of credit throughout the commercial world in order to strengthen his bargaining position with the President and Congress, Butler said, was a vivid example of the excessive and contradictory powers possessed by the BUS.[13]

Despite this indictment of the BUS, Butler still tried to convince Wright that the country required some institution to regulate the note issues of state banks and the commercial exchanges between the states. He unveiled a plan for an "Office of Exchange and Currency," a proposal which was actually Bronson's scheme under another title. The Office of Exchange and Currency would be located in the District of Columbia and would have the power, with the consent of the states, to establish branches in commercial centers such as New York, Boston, Philadelphia, New Orleans and Cincinnati, where it would receive and disburse government funds, deal in bills of exchange, and issue notes. Butler stressed, however, that the Office of Exchange and Currency was substantially different from the BUS because its goal was to regulate currency, not to make a profit for the stockholders.[14]

With the Democrats in control of Congress, the Bronsons asked Butler to present this plan to the legislature. Leaving his home in Geneva, New York, for the upcoming congressional session, Butler stopped at Albany where he spoke with Thomas Olcott, the Albany Regency's leading banker, and gained his support. Butler interrupted his trip again in New York

City and visited with both conservative and liberal financiers. In Washington, he testified before a Senate committee where he supported the President's action on the bank issue but recommended the Office of Exchange and Currency. Butler's most important new bargaining point may well have been that the Office of Exchange and Currency would locate its central office in the District of Columbia. This stipulation was calculated to allay the fears of some Democrats that New York City capitalists were trying to make their city the nation's financial center.[15]

Butler had little chance of success in Congress because the lines of the pro- and anti-bank forces were clearly drawn. Arriving each day an hour early to obtain standing room at the Senate, Butler listened intently to the debates on the bank issue. Henry Clay and John Calhoun, Butler reported, were willing to allow financial distress throughout the nation in order to force a recharter of the BUS. According to Butler, the administration faced a stern test, yet he clearly supported their efforts to argue the moral and legal issues which existed between the " . . . great monied institution and the civil power . . . ."[16] The acrimony of the congressional debates convinced Butler that the Democrats would not support another bank proposal until Biddle's forces were totally defeated. A half-hour visit with Andrew Jackson in which conversation centered on the country's financial condition further strengthened Butler's assessment of the political realities. In late March, he informed Arthur Bronson that he had withdrawn the plan for the Office of Exchange and Currency from further congressional consideration.[17]

For nearly a year, 1834–1835, neither the Bronsons nor Charles Butler was involved in the national bank issue. Butler was content to allow the administration an adequate period of time to stabilize the country's finances; the Bronsons, on the other hand, recognized that the political lines were too taut to allow discussion of a new national bank. Instead, they concentrated their efforts on establishing new trust companies at the state level which perhaps would be of sufficient size to exert control over other banks or, at least, to serve as a model of sound banking principles. For this reason, they established the Ohio Life Insurance and Trust Company, which possessed both the power to invest trust funds and to circulate notes.[18]

In the Bronsons' view, financial conditions did not improve throughout 1834 and 1835. The economy rapidly expanded as credit was available for the massive purchase of public lands in the Old Northwest and in the South. Economic historians disagree on the precise cause of the expansion. Jackson's destruction of the BUS and the establishment of Pet Banks may not have been the sole or even the precipitating factor, since large imports of specie from England and Mexico also generated a credit explosion. Isaac Bronson, nevertheless, had considered all these factors and still believed that the government's financial program had lessened the controls for regulating the boom. A complicating factor in 1836, however, was that the government had accumulated a surplus of funds in the Treasury from public land sales. When the administration began to draft proposals for distributing that surplus to the states, Bronson believed that such action would worsen the condition of an already overheated economy. Consequently, in early 1836, he decided to submit another bank proposal to Congress.[19]

Isaac Bronson proposed a plan for a fiscal agency which would keep and disburse government funds through a series of branches throughout the country and accept commercial paper, such as bills of exchange and bank notes, in payment for public debts. The fiscal agency would regulate currency by periodically returning bank notes and bills of exchange to the issuing bank. The institution was to have a capital stock of $30 million invested in secure bonds and mortgages. One significant departure from earlier plans was that the agency would lack the power to issue notes. Isaac Bronson claimed that it therefore would not require a congressional charter but only a grant of authority to open offices throughout the country. The concept of a fiscal agency, Isaac said, "will render unnecessary any specification of power except such as will be contained in the articles of association; and thus remove that bug-bear—constitutional scruples—and enable the government to preserve at least as much consistency on the subject as they have in most others."[20]

Three salient points should be noted concerning this plan. First, it was very similar to Isaac Bronson's proposals to Congress in 1831 and to the Office of Exchange and Currency suggested in 1834. In other words, the Bronsons were still seeking some form of central control over the economy. Second, the plan incorporated the basic principles of the trust company, particularly that the capital stock would be invested in secure bonds and mortgages. Finally, the Bronsons had deprived the fiscal agency of the power to issue notes in order to mollify anti-bank Democrats still smarting from Biddle's use of the BUS' note circulation for political purposes in 1834.[21]

Isaac Bronson asked Elisha Whittlesey, the Whig senator from Ohio and the Bronsons' confidant on the OLTC's board of trustees, to introduce the proposal in Washington. Whittlesey was surprised that the New Yorkers would even attempt to sway the administration at this time, particularly since Churchill C. Cambreleng, the administration's key leader in the House of Representatives, had just introduced legislation which proposed the distribution of the Treasury's surplus to the states. If passed, there certainly would be little need for Bronson's fiscal agent.[22]

Although disappointed that his program had not reached Congress before Cambreleng's distribution scheme, Isaac still requested Whittlesey quietly to seek the opinions of powerful congressional leaders and members of the administration. Whittlesey's response was not only a caustic evaluation of the country's political leadership but also a signal that the fiscal agency was doomed. Of President Jackson, Whittlesey observed that "he only thinks through (Amos) Kendall . . . and is grossly ignorant of the details and principles of currency and banking . . . ." In any case, Whittlesey said, Jackson "is as the king on his death bed, and all look to his successor. No one cares what Jackson thinks now." Whittlesey, though, left little hope that Martin Van Buren would be favorable to the New Yorker's plan: "Van Buren knows perfectly well the absolute incapacity of the present deposit banks, to carry on the business of the government with safety to themselves, the people, & the government; but he dares not move an inch to the right or left, until after the election . . . ."[23]

Despite Whittlesey's report, the Bronsons embarked on an intensive lobbying campaign. They asked Lucius Lyon, who served as Michigan's Democratic senator, to use his influence with members of Congress.[24] Charles Butler wrote to his brother, the attorney general, and urged him to accept the idea. But Benjamin F. Butler refused, explaining that the administration was still involved in a life and death struggle with Biddle's bank which had acquired a charter from the Pennsylvania legislature after the expiration of its congressional charter. The Attorney General further warned his brother to "avoid all entangling alliances with those persons and classes whose habits, feelings, and principles . . . " were not in favor of popular government.[25]

Although unable to sway his brother, Charles Butler still journeyed to Washington in the company of Arthur Bronson to lobby for the proposal. Arthur Bronson first presented the plan to the President, and then he met with Senator John Calhoun. Calhoun, though, refused his support because he no longer believed that the country needed another national bank.[26] Butler, meanwhile, visited Churchill C. Cambreleng in order to reinforce the message contained in a series of letters which Isaac Bronson had already addressed to him. Isaac Bronson had warned Cambreleng that the country was headed for a depression unless the administration changed its economic policy. Cambreleng, though, told Butler that political considerations prevented any drastic changes.[27] His patience exhausted and frustrated by years of inaction, Isaac Bronson bitterly attacked Cambreleng's statement that politics determined the administration's financial policies:

> . . . Everybody knows already who knows anything that the system must be changed, and that the commercial storm will terminate in

shipwreck if something is not timely done to allay its fury. It is not within the reach of my comprehension to perceive how this plain business like transaction can have anything more to do with party politics, or political questions of any kind, then if it had for its object the extrication of a stagecoach from a slough which had been upset by unskillful drivers.[28]

The Bronsons realized from the beginning that the political climate was unfavorable to action on their proposition. Isaac Bronson believed that Van Buren and the Albany Regency politicians intended to use the Pet Banks and the distribution of the Treasury surplus to insure support in the 1836 election. The Bronsons had gambled that they could back Van Buren into a corner by gaining the support of key Regency politicians surrounding him, but Van Buren proved a worthy adversary. Sensing defeat in April 1836, Isaac Bronson spared few kind words for politicians. He harbored a special dislike for Van Buren claiming that if Biddle had not mismanaged the Bank of the United States ". . . Mr. Van Buren would not now have had the public revenues under his control for the purpose of electioneering and stock jobbing enterprises nor would he have been any nearer the President's chair than I am."[29] When Congress passed an act for the distribution of the government's surplus funds to the states, the Bronsons temporarily suspended their campaign to alter government policy. Most supporters of a national bank now looked for certain financial disaster. The Bronsons, for example, curtailed their land investments and warned their western agents of the approaching financial storm.

Although the Bronsons temporarily withdrew from further effort at the national level, their struggle for banking reform continued in the states. In Michigan they attempted to influence the state's laws related to banking. Before admission into the Union, the Michigan Territory held a constitutional convention from May to June 1835, at which Arthur Bronson's agent, Lucius Lyon, chaired the committee on banking. At Lyon's request, Isaac Bronson sent copies of his various bank proposals and even suggested wording for proposed articles in the Michigan constitution. When Lyon's committee issued a report, it bore the unmistakable imprint of Isaac Bronson. The report criticized the country's banking system claiming that the excessive issue of notes was the chief defect. The report recommended that Michigan should require all banks to issue notes only for sixty or ninety days and that all banks should invest their capital in land mortgages. Lyon's justification for these proposals merely paraphrased Isaac Bronson's ideas:

By retaining, for merchants, the facilities and advantages usually derived from the *credit,* and giving, on good security, to farmers and the producing classes, generally, the loan of the *capital* of such institutions, for such periods as may be required, the different classes of the community will share more equally the advantages of whatever moneyed incorporations may be granted; and at the same time, . . . those institutions will be placed on a more secure and stable foundation.[30]

Like other states during the boom years of 1835 and 1836, Michigan rejected Lyon's proposals and the concept of a conservative banking system.[31] Although disappointed by Michigan's actions, the Bronsons were not defeated. They already had decided to support the free banking concept, particularly in New York State, as another means of reaching their objectives. Free banking meant simply that any group of individuals could establish a bank after meeting a few state requirements designed to protect the public. Until the first free banking laws in Michigan and New York, state legislatures had chartered banks giving them a quasi-monopoly status. Most states also had restraining laws that required a two-thirds vote in the legislature to approve a new bank charter. Such laws effectively limited the number of banks and protected existing institutions.

In New York State, free banking was a complex political movement that attracted support from normally antagonistic political groups. Radical Democrats or Loco-Focos supported free banking because it eliminated the monopolistic position of banks. The Loco-Focos eventually hoped to free society from all banks and paper money even though they realized that free banking might produce a temporary proliferation of banks. New York's Loco-Focos were joined by entrepreneurs anxious to establish banks but stymied by the state's restraining law. If entrepreneurs could secure repeal of this law, they could enter the banking business.[32]

The political forces marshalled against chartered banks gained added strength when conservative financiers like the Bronsons joined the movement in 1835 and 1836. At first glance, the New Yorkers seemed unlikely supporters of a move to increase the number of banks, and in fact, they were never in favor of the open-banking concept. In 1835 and 1836, however, they desired free banking as an alternative means of obtaining a strong central bank. The strategy was simple: frustrated in their efforts in Washington and conscious that neither Jackson nor Van Buren would charter a naional bank or establish a fiscal agency, the New Yorkers decided to request a bank charter from the state legislature. The proposed bank was to be located in New York City and was to be large enough to control the country's commercial exchanges. Yet the Bronsons and their associates were politically astute and realized that the Albany Democrats, in alliance with the state's entrenched banking interests, would never grant such a charter. Their only recourse was to support free banking, thereby ending the requirement for legislative approval.

The Bronsons first attempted to repeal New York State's restraining law in 1836. They joined with other New York City financiers in a letter to the Governor stating their intentions. In late April, they participated in a public meeting in New York City which united Loco Foco and merchant sentiment against the existing chartered banks. The meeting was held at Tammany Hall, and among the hundreds attending were some of New York's leading financiers: Isaac Bronson, James B. Murray, Charles Butler, Philip Hone, Joseph Beers, Jonathan Goodhue, and Jesse Oakley. Those in attendance drew up a memorial requesting repeal of the restraining law and appointed a committee, of which Isaac Bronson was a member, to carry the memorial to Albany. Democratic leaders responded by sending Edwin Croswell to New York City to appease the city's merchants.[33] But neither the Bronsons nor other capitalists were sympathetic to Croswell's mission because they knew that the Regency was politically vulnerable. In February 1837, the legislature took the first steps toward free banking by allowing individuals and associations to receive deposits and make discounts without a charter. The legislature, however, stopped short of completely open banking since a charter was still required in order to issue notes.[34]

Encouraged by this success, Arthur Bronson sent out invitations to leading New York City businessmen for a meeting at his father's home on February 6, 1837, to discuss the organization of a joint stock company which presumably would be established when the legislature passed a more comprehensive free banking act. A small but influential group attended the meeting including Saul Alley, Charles Butler, Boswell Colt, John Ward, Jonathan Goodhue, Jesse Hoyt, James Anderson, Samuel Ward, William Lawrence, John Rathbone, and James King. At the meeting, Arthur Bronson reviewed previous efforts to establish a national bank in New York City and then read the proposal sent to the President in 1836. James King moved to establish a committee with the responsibility for drafting a bank plan modeled on Isaac Bronson's earlier proposals. The financiers appointed Isaac Bronson to chair the committee and selected Charles Butler, Arthur Bronson, William Lawrence, and Henry J. Anderson to serve with him. After adjoining for one week, the group met again on February 13 to consider the committee's plan for the "American Joint Stock Banking Company." Each article of the plan was read, scrutinized, and then approved. The committee was then asked to prepare a final copy, arrange for its printing, and secure nominations for a board of directors. At a third meeting held on February 20, the group discussed the nominations.[35]

The group never met again for reasons that are not entirely clear: the New Yorkers probably had decided to wait on further developments in the New York State legislature, which was moving toward additional reforms in the state's banking laws. Moreover, the financiers might have become preoccupied with other financial matters after New York City banks suspended specie payments in May 1837. Finally, the New Yorkers might have been momentarily distracted with the possiblity of a change in national policy when Martin Van Buren became president in the spring of 1837.

Whatever the reasons for dropping the American Joint Stock Banking Company, the Bronsons and other conservatives still exerted a substantial influence on New York State's Free Banking Act passed in April 1838. Although the Bronsons cannot be linked directly to the final legislation, their ideas permeated the bill. Free banking included more than a cessation of the monopoly privileges accorded to banks. The New York law required that banks deposit stocks, bonds, and mortgages with the state's comptroller in order to back up their note issues. Based on the bank's security deposit, the comptroller then issued the appropriate amount of notes which the bank could put into circulation. If a bank subsequently refused to pay its bills or notes, the comptroller could sell the bank's security at public auction. Such ideas to limit speculative banking practices had been central, although not exclusive, to Isaac and Arthur Bronson's thought for many years. Both the New York and Ohio trust companies, for example, had invested their capital stock in bonds and mortgages, and almost every proposal for a national bank had incorporated the same idea.[36] The Bronsons similarly influenced the nation's first free banking law which was passed in Michigan in 1837. It also incorporated the notion of bank notes secured by real estate mortgages, an idea that Isaac Bronson had first suggested to Lucius Lyon in 1835.[37] Even though some institutions established under free banking laws later became the worst examples of unsound banking, the difficulty was often in the state's administration of the system, not in the law's basic conception.[38]

Although the Bronsons achieved some success in the struggle for banking reform inNew York State, their most important experiment, the Ohio Life Insurance and Trust Company (OLTC), was a bitter disappointment. It had been established not only as an agency for moving eastern capital into the western economy, but also as the prototype for a national bank. Its capital of $2 million was invested in real estate mortgages and served as security for the company's banking operations, which included the power to issue notes. The company's unique powers and its size soon elicited the hostility of the anti-bank faction in Ohio and embroiled the company in a political squabble. The Bronsons knew that successful banking precluded political involvement, yet even in Ohio they could not escape the Jacksonian onslaught.

Robert Lytle, a defeated congressional candidate from Ohio, led the initial assault against the company in 1835. Lytle, a Democrat, had blamed his defeat in the election on another Democrat and president of the OLTC, Micajah T. Williams, who had supposedly prevented Lytle from using the trust company as a campaign issue. Other radical Democrats, particularly Benjamin Tappan, joined the fray and unsuccessfully attempted to repeal the company's charter in the legislative sessions of 1835 and 1836. The company's broad powers and near monopoly status most disturbed its enemies. The *Cincinnati Advertiser,* for example, stressed that the charter could not be amended for thirty-five years and predicted, with some exaggeration, that "by that time it will have so wormed itself into the vitals of the land, that nothing short of revolution can put it down."[39] Fears were also voiced over the trustees' ability to borrow up to $20,000, their power to fill vacancies among themselves, the company's ability to purchase stock in other corporations, and its power to circulate notes.[40] The attackers also dredged up the bogus issue of outside control. Publishing a list of the company's stockholders, the *Western Hemisphere* observed that the "Wall St. Gentry of New York" dominated the institution.[41] The OLTC was thus trapped in an intra-party and mini-bank war. In September 1835, the *Niles Register* dramatized the issue's seriousness: "Every good citizen and true lover of his country was called on to exert his energies to abolish an institution teeming with such alarming privileges; otherwise, the battle we had fought against the United States Bank had been, so far as Ohio and the West were concerned, fought in vain and that in every possible aspect, this institution was more odious than the present bank of the United States."[42]

Throughout the dispute, the eastern associates were powerless to assist. Although the Bronsons followed the matter closely and often corresponded with Micajah Williams and other trustees, they could only offer advice. The one message, reiterated over and over again, was that the westerners should stay out of politics in order to reduce the level of animosity against the company. When a vacancy opened on the board of trustees, for example, the Bronsons insisted that the replacement should be nonpartisan so as to avoid the opposition's notice. Having been through a long struggle on the national level, Isaac Bronson, in particular, had developed a somewhat jaundiced view of the public and politicians.[43]

Although upset by the OLTC's political problems, the Bronsons were even more concerned with the institution's liberal banking practices which operated in violation of its charter and bylaws. Located in Cincinnati, the West's most important trade center, and having replaced a branch of the BUS, the OLTC was understandably besieged by the credit demands of merchants. In 1835, the trustees altered a bylaw which had called for immediate foreclosure when a borrower missed a payment or a note's security decreased in value. The trustees now permitted a two year grace period before initiating foreclosure proceedings. In certain respects, this was not an unreasonable relaxation of the bylaws, since it provided for the unexpected crop failure or the occasional fluctuation in the money market. Yet it was the beginning of a general relaxation of conservative banking principles.[44]

The most serious problem was that the company's directors dealt heavily in "accommodation" paper, that is, loans or bills issued only on the borrower's credit or reputation. The institution regularly granted renewals on notes beyond 100 days, particularly for the movement of agricultural produce to New Orleans and the return of retail merchandise and manufactured products. This trade generally produced a favorable balance for the Ohio institution, which should have resulted in the movement of specie from southern banks to the OLTC. Yet the company rarely called in its accommodation notes or outstanding balances for fear of alienating good customers. The Bronsons, however, believed that accommodation notes were inflationary because they permitted businessmen to speculate in land or commodities, thereby threatening the bank's credit, its other customers, and its investments in real estate mortgages. In referring to the Ohio firm's practices, Isaac once commented, "it may be *politically good policy;* but it is what I should call *practically bad banking.*"[45]

The Bronsons disagreed with the company's management, yet they had no power and little real influence. For those who see conspiracies and undue political influence in the westward movement of capital, the OLTC demonstrated that eastern financiers exercised little control despite holding three-quarters of the stock and five of twenty seats on the board of trustees. It took only six board members to constitute a quorum, and eastern financiers, obviously limited by time and distance, could not attend regular meetings. Local businessmen, susceptible to the pressures of the local community, determined the company's day-to-day policies, and the trust company thus reflected their personal economic philosophies. Micajah T. Williams and many other trustees had expansionist viewpoints, and they were personally entangled in Ohio's economic boom with investments in land, town, and transportation projects.[46] Favorable economic conditions thus continually encouraged the company's officers to liberalize their banking policies. Officials of the Ohio courts who conducted annual investigations in 1836 and 1837, nevertheless, praised the company's prudent management, advancing only a mild criticism about the extended credit. This judgment appeared to be correct; the company declared dividends in 1836 and 1837, and its stock sold above the par value on the New York Stock exchange.[47] Like the economy in general, the OLTC prospered from and contributed to the boom.

The Bronsons, nevertheless, made several attempts to alter company policies. After Micajah Williams had been forced to request an emergency shipment of specie from eastern banks to meet note demands in early 1836, they opened an extended correspondence on the necessity of curtailing the note issue. They asked western trustees friendly to their theories, such as Elisha Whittlesey and Simon Perkins, to visit Cincinnati personally and enforce proper banking practices.[48] As conditions worsened, Isaac Bronson's letters became stronger in their denunciation of the company's inflationary policies. "How is it possible," Isaac Bronson queried Williams, "that men of reflection can venture upon so dangerous an experiment, as an attempt by an advance of their credit to supply others with *capital* when they have none of their own?"[49]

Relations between the Bronsons and Micajah Williams slowly deteriorated. Despite Williams's admittance that some discounts were overextended, he felt that the Bronsons' criticisms were unjustified and unnecessarily personal. He wrote that ". . . differences of opinion as to the prinicples of transacting business . . . may be discussed earnestly, in plain language, but in a spirit of courtesy . . . ."[50] When the eastern trustees requested a complete statement of the company's operations in late 1836, Williams was personally offended.[51] The Bronsons' critical letters also affronted other western trustees. Ohioan Jacob Burnet tried to explain to the New Yorkers that the company had to respond to the needs of Cincinnati's residents and to grasp at the opportunities for large profits. Burnet's position typified the economic philosophy of the liberal western trustee caught up in a period of rapid economic growth.[52]

Despite their efforts, the Bronsons and other conservative trustees were unable to prevent the company's headlong plunge into financial difficulty. Between October 1836, and February 1837, the company increased its circulation from $392,595 to $766,265 and its discounted bills from $1,423,265 to $1,679,588.[53] When New York banks suspended specie payments in May 1837, the OLTC felt immediate pressure to redeem its own notes. Consequently, the OLTC soon followed the example of the New York banks.[54] In the view of Isaac and Arthur Bronson, even the temporary suspension of specie payments was a catastrophe because it represented a moral failure of the trust company to operate according to its contract with the public. Suspension, therefore, was the culmination of the trust company's repeated violations of sound banking principles. In May 1837, Isaac Bronson expressed his frustration with the OLTC:

An experience of more than a half a century convinces me of the utter impracticality of committing to a board of directors, or trustees the discretion of *issuing* credit, without incurring the hazard of *loosing more*, than the prospect of advantage can possibly *compensate* for . . . . I had hopes the principles embraced in the charter, would compel its managers to use its credit with more discretion. I am equally disappointed in the only two instances in which I have been interested . . . .[55]

Arthur and Isaac Bronson, therefore, sold their stock, and Arthur Bronson resigned from the board of trustees in September 1837. The real problem, Arthur Bronson explained to the company's management in his resignation letter, was that the trustees had violated their own rules, especially the basic principle of conservative banking: ". . . No note or bill, or other obligation . . . which has more than a hundred days to run shall be discounted, and on all paper discounted payment shall be made exactly at maturity, and no discount shall be made with any understanding express or implied of any connections between the payment of one note or bill and the discount of another."[56] The continual violation of this rule, the New Yorker said, resulted in the company's "final public dishonor and discredit." Arthur Bronson admitted that the company's abandonment of conservative banking was a great personal disappointment because the institution could have been the "precedent and example for the remodeling of the banking system of the country."[57] The OLTC, then, demonstrated to the New Yorkers that only a central bank could control financial institutions within the states. Their personal experiences in Ohio impelled them to once again seek a national bank.

Martin Van Buren's election to the presidency opened the possibility of a change in government policy. Charles Butler went to Washington in March 1837, where he attended Van Buren's inauguration. He was close enough to the Albany Regency's inner circle to be present at the White House reception after the inaugural ceremonies and later for Jackson's informal departure for the Hermitage. Butler utilized these opportunities to suggest new directions in government policy. He also wrote to Edwin Croswell, an important member of the Albany Regency, that ". . . it is the first and pressing duty of the government to exert its power and influence, so far (as) they may be exerted without prejudice to the public *security*, to afford relief, and to restore *confidence*."[58] He wrote an equally strong appeal to his brother, one of Van Buren's closest advisors, outlining an economic program for the incoming administration. In particular, Charles Butler urged the repeal of the Specie Circular, an executive order issued in July 1836, in order to slow down the economy. It stipulated that only specie would be accepted in payment for public lands. Charles Butler reminded his brother that the Specie Circular was intended to curtail speculation, a goal which had been accomplished. The commercial community has despaired, Butler said, and dramatic action, such as repeal, might restore confidence.[59]

By late 1837, though, Butler spoke less forcefully for the Bronson's banking ideas. As the economy faltered, Butler increasingly worried over his speculative investments in the West, and he probably was unwilling to support a banking system which envisioned further credit restrictions. At the same time, Butler was unable to pay his debts, leading to a temporary quarrel with Arthur Bronson, who was one of his major creditors. Consequently, Butler was of little assistance in the Bronsons' continuing discussions with the Van Buren administration.[60]

Even without Butler's help, the Bronsons revived the plan for a fiscal agency. Arthur Bronson went to Washington to lobby for the scheme, and the elder Bronson cautiously suggested the idea in his correspondence with Van Buren's aides.[61] In April 1837, Isaac Bronson formally proposed the fiscal agency in a long letter to the Secretary of the Treasury, Levi Woodbury. Analyzing the country's financial problems, Bronson argued that the deposit banks, in failing to regulate currency issues, had jeopardized the government's financial resources. The proper solution, according to Isaac Bronson, was quite simple: "All reflecting men . . . now admit that without some controlling power over the issues of state banks there can be no security for our currency."[62] Obviously thinking of his struggle with the OLTC, the New Yorker claimed that state banks not only possessed ignorant managers but they also ". . . have within themselves no limiting principle."[63] Consequently, without the control exercised by an outside agency, state banks issued currency as long as their customers requested it.

Bronson further informed Woodbury that the current situation was critical because of international developments, especially the flow of specie between England and the United States. In the early 1830s, Bronson explained, English financiers had made heavy capital investments in the United States, thus augmenting America's specie reserves. The Bank of England, worried over its own gold reserves, subsequently raised the exchange rates making the export of specie more difficult. This action, combined with the fall of cotton prices and other trade setbacks, Bronson argued, would upset America's balance of trade and would require the export of specie. As a result, American banks would be forced to restrict credit and pay their specie debts leading to the suspension of specie payments and to a serious business contraction. The severity of the economic recession might be lessened, according to Bronson, by the imposition of immediate controls. Although Bronson overemphasized the role of banks in the economy, his stress on specie movements as a precipitating factor in the depression demonstrated a sophisticated understanding of the economy even by the standards of modern economic historians.[64]

The New Yorker's analysis naturally led to his proposal for a fiscal agency which would secure public funds and regulate the currency. Since this agency would not possess the power to issue notes, Isaac said, it would be able to impartially control the issue of all other banks. Because of its size and its ability to deal in commercial paper (bills of exchange) and government transactions, the fiscal agency would function like the BUS. It would collect and then periodically redeem the notes of state banks. The proposal contained no new ideas; the question was whether Washington's mood had changed under Van Buren. Isaac Bronson had no illusions, however, that Van Buren would bring a fresh wind. In fact, he believed that the economic slowdown of early 1837 merely showed

> . . . The inevitable consequence of this political unholy crusade which has been carried on against the established principles of political economy—the laws of commerce, the lessons of experience, and the dictates of the plainest common sense—merely to make a man a President who has not a single qualification for the situation. Tell our friends . . . to *clue up* their sails, as soon as possible, and lie too till the hurricane has spent its force—the worst part of it, by all comparison, has not yet reached either them or us.[65]

Isaac Bronson's warning proved correct. Shortly after Bronson submitted his proposal to the Secretary of the Treasury, the depression's first blow struck when New York City banks suspended specie payments. The Bronsons suddenly sensed a new urgency and summoned the family's lawyer and confidant from Fairfield, Connecticut, Roger Sherman, to help them in petitioning the government. Sherman, of all the Bronsons' friends, was the most conversant with their banking theories. During the summer, Sherman, under the pseudonym of "Franklin," addressed three letters to the Secretary of the Treasury repeating Isaac Bronson's earlier analysis of the country's finances and urging the adoption of a fiscal agent. These letters were then published in order to attract public support.[66]

The Bronsons' wishes were at odds with the intentions of the Van Buren administration. By the summer of 1837, Van Buren had decided to suggest to Congress an independent treasury which would sever any connection between government revenues and banks. Certain elements of the plan must have pleased the Bronsons, for it withdrew government funds from state banks and placed them in more secure government depositories. But Van Buren's independent treasury did not grapple with the problem of "organizing" the nation's economy, and thus state banks still could expand their note issues without regulation. Whenever specie flowed into the country, Isaac Bronson argued, banks would overexpand their circulations and disrupt the nation's economy. He was unable to understand Van Buren's reluctance to regulate bank issues: "In a country where the government & people are amalgamated in one mass of democracy, the plan of having one currency for the government and another for the people, is too aristocratic for my taste."[67]

Van Buren had great difficulty in securing congressional approval for the independent treasury idea. When it was first presented to Congress at a special session in October 1837, the Democrats were split. Nathaniel Tallmadge, a New York senator, and William C. Rives, a senator from Virginia, led the conservative Democrats who felt the plan went too far in abandoning the deposit banks. Van Buren's proposal was subsequently defeated. The Bronsons and their New York associates seized this opportunity to petition Congress for a fiscal agency, but they again were rebuffed. When Isaac Bronson died in May 1838, the movement for a national bank was deprived of its most articulate spokesman and the opposition to Van Buren's scheme was reduced. The Independent Treasury finally was adopted by Congress in 1840; by that time, however, it was a meaningless victory for the President. He faced the electorate a few months later with a divided party and a country in the grip of a depression. His defeat was not unexpected.[68]

For several years after his father's death, Arthur Bronson avoided all connection with banking issues. But in 1841, he consented to write an article for William Gouge's *Journal of Banking* on the history of the Bridgeport Bank when it was under his father's direction. Using the pseudonym of "An Old Fashioned Man," Arthur Bronson explained his father's commercial banking principles: that banks should facilitate the movement of trade goods, that no loan should be allowed to run longer than sixty days, and that a bank's capital should be permanently invested in mortgages and securities. The Bridgeport Bank never had failed to honor its notes, according to Arthur Bronson, until Nicholas Biddle had enlarged the discounts of the BUS. Biddle's action had initiated a wave of speculation in which "Everybody then became a speculator—the farmer left his plough in the furrow—the mechanic abandoned his tools—the manufacturer stopped his spindles—the lawyer laid aside his brief—the doctor dropped his pestle—even the divine quitted the sacred desk, and the *whole nation* was suddenly transformed from a great, moral industrious and frugal people, into an array of gamblers."[69]

Bronson's article was the opening salvo in a final effort to establish a national bank. The lingering depression along with the election of the

Whigs in 1840 seemed to raise a slight possibility of success. Bronson, however, faced a complex political situation after William Henry Harrison died and John Tyler, more a state's rightist than a Whig, succeeded to the presidency. Tyler not only confused the party's political leadership but also had different ideas on the government's financial policy. The Whigs agreed to repeal the Independent Treasury system, but there the party's consensus fell apart. Henry Clay, the Whig's congressional leader, wanted a strong bank of the United States, a proposal which he pushed in Congress in the summer of 1841. President Tyler, though, sent his own plan to Congress which recommended a "national" bank in the District of Columbia but with the states reserving the option of accepting or rejecting its branches. Henry Clay, who chaired a special committee on banking, accepted a few of the President's recommendations, yet it was essentially Clay's proposal that Congress passed and sent to the President. In particular, the bill included a complicated provision which gave the states only minimal control over the branches of the national bank. In August 1841, Tyler vetoed the bill on the grounds that the bank had too much control over the nation's commercial exchanges. Unstated in the veto message, but equally significant, was Tyler's obvious political challenge to Clay's leadership of the Whig party.[70]

The President's cabinet now formulated a bill for a Fiscal Corporation to satisfy both Tyler and Clay. Although the bill emanated from Tyler's own cabinet, it was apparently not shown to the President before submission to Congress. After its passage in September 1841, therefore, Tyler again exercised the veto. At this point, a majority of his cabinet resigned but Tyler was undaunted and submitted yet another proposal calling for a Board of Exchequer to serve as the government's fiscal agent. Yet there was little hope that this plan could survive in a hostile Congress.[71]

At this moment, Arthur Bronson entered the political fray. He intended to draft a proposal which would attract Whig support because it was not identified with either the President or Henry Clay. At the same time, Bronson hoped to entice sufficient Democratic votes to break the congressional logjam. Working with Roger Sherman, Bronson essentially revived the concept of a fiscal agent—a national bank to regulate the currency issue of state banks and to receive and disburse government funds. Assuming substantial Whig support, Bronson also shared his ideas with two powerful Democratic senators from New York State, Silas Wright and Nathaniel Tallmadge. Tallmadge, in particular, was in an influential position as chairman of a special Senate committee which reviewed all bank proposals.[72] Wright and Tallmadge responded cautiously to Bronson's idea, yet both senators thought it possessed sufficient merit to be submitted to Congress.[73]

Arthur Bronson lobbied for the plan as it wound its way through the appropriate congressional committees. For several weeks he stayed in Washington, and even after returning to New York City, he corresponded with committee members in the Senate and House. His efforts were unproductive. The House of Representatives' committee drafted a bill which the New Yorker disliked because it was comprised of too many conflicting interests. He held greater hopes for a Senate bill since Tallmadge, the committee chairman, had allowed him to comment on the bill's early drafts. In February 1842, Tallmadge reported to Bronson that the committee had finally recommended a bill which incorporated most of the New Yorker's ideas, although it carried the President's title and outline.[74]

Neither Roger Sherman nor Arthur Bronson agreed with Tallmadge's assessment or the committee's plan to establish a board called the Exchequer of the United States. Sherman, for example, opposed a provision which allowed government agencies to keep individual deposits and government funds in the same institution. Both financiers eventually urged their Washington acquaintances to vote against the bill, but with the Congress split between the forces of Clay and Tyler, the bill never even came to a vote. Throughout the rest of Tyler's administration, the issue of a central bank was moribund, particularly after the Democrats regained control of Congress in 1842.[75] Bronson finally withdrew from any further involvement at the national level.

Even though frustration and failure marked the Bronsons' and Charles Butler's struggle to alter American banking practices, the effort exhibited an important dimension of their business life. The financiers obviously perceived a relationship between their western investments, the nation's banking system, and the health of the economy. Thus Isaac Bronson, Arthur Bronson, and Charles Butler devoted an extraordinary amount of time to drafting proposals, writing letters, attending meetings, and lobbying in Washington in an effort to influence government policy. These exertions often shaped the form of state and national policies, if only in an indirect fashion. The Bronsons, for example, were important to the passage of free banking legislation, the result of a temporary alliance of radical and conservative political elements. They also worked to secure the widespread adoption of conservative banking practices, such as the investment of capital stock in real estate mortgages, and they developed new institutions, such as the trust company.[76]

The Bronsons and Charles Butler, though, reacted differently to the unfolding economic crisis in the 1830s. The Bronsons consistently predicted the fluctuations in the economy with each shift in government policy. Throughout the 1830s, therefore, they continually presented the government and other financiers with a cogent argument for conservative economic policies which might have tempered the impact of the boom and bust cycle. Although few heeded their analysis, the Bronsons nevertheless altered their own western investments in anticipation of the depression.[77] Despite his closeness to the Bronsons and his support of their banking plans, Charles Butler never believed that the system was fundamentally unsound. Consequently, he poured new capital and credit into his western projects until the depression could no longer be ignored. Arthur Bronson's and Charles Butler's differing views of the American economy in the 1830s partially explains the subsequent history of their western investments.

8. Charles Butler and the Depression in the West

The effects of the depression on eastern capitalists and their western agents and on the growth of the western economy have been difficult to understand because historians have been unable to extricate themselves from the impressions left by farmers, speculators, novelists, and newspapers of the era. Contemporaries blamed the depression on the overblown expectations of eastern and western promoters who produced half-finished railroads and canals, cities with magnificent hotels but no retail businesses or trade potential, and agricultural regions plagued by absentee owners who either charged excessive interest rates for loans or refused to pay taxes for local improvements.[1]

Perhaps because western towns grew so fast and the physical evidence of the depression's effects were highly visible there, contemporary observers used western towns to personify the evils of speculation and the misguided efforts of promoters. In *Home As Found*, published in 1838, James Fenimore Cooper poked fun at the grand delusions of his countrymen through the character of Aristabulus Bragg. It remained, however, for Charles Dickens in *Martin Chuzzlewit* to satirize thoroughly western town speculation. His young English hero, Martin Chuzzlewit, came to America and purchased a share in a western town called Eden. When Chuzzlewit visited the site, he discovered that it consisted of a few shacks and a population decimated by disease.[2] In later reminiscences, speculators themselves often labeled their investments as hysterical and ill-considered. Levi Beardsley, who had invested with Charles Butler at Toledo recalled that

> The whole country seemed to be in motion; and most extravagant anticipations prevailed in regard to the settlement of the country, and rapid growth of towns on the margin of the lakes. Just in

proportion to these high expectations, were the prices of village and city lots enhanced; and as almost everybody desired to purchase, the sellers soon became rich as Nabobs, on paper: but when a change, in 1837, "came o'er the spirit of their dreams," debtors were unable to pay; and creditors who relied on these payments, and on the strength of them had made other engagements—nearly the whole list of creditors and debtors went down with one general crash, and bankruptcy became the fate of most of them.[3]

Contemporary accounts and later reminiscences, however, often distorted the reality of the depression, for these sources concentrated on the most extreme examples of excessive speculation and financial collapse. Historians thus know little about the process by which eastern capitalists and western agents readjusted their investments to cope with the depression. This chapter, therefore, examines Charles Butler's business affairs during the depression years. A classic promoter, overcapitalized in a complex and interrelated series of investments, Butler was not the heartless eastern capitalist so prevalent in the contemporary literature who left the western landscape strewn with partially built towns and debt–ridden agricultural lands. In a struggle which must have been fairly typical among eastern capitalists, Butler fought to salvage his western investments in order to avoid bankruptcy. Even though his relationship to western communities and agents changed during the depression years, he nevertheless remained an important factor in the development of the Toledo, Huron, and Chicago regions.

The depression years were the most difficult of Butler's eventful life. Certainly part of the reason was that he, reflecting the booster mentality so common in the 1830s, depended on a near–impossible rate of economic development. His expectations were understandable when one considers that Butler knew only success from his early days as a young lawyer in Geneva, New York, to his later balancing of complex investments at Huron, Toledo, and Chicago.

Similarly western merchants, territorial governments, land speculators, and farmers came to expect a phenomenal pace of economic growth in the 1830s. Between 1832 and 1837 land values soared, population increased, new businesses opened daily in burgeoning towns, and blueprints for canals and railroads proliferated. Illinois began construction on the Illinois and Michigan Canal, and Michigan was in the process of building three railroads crossing the state as well as canals linking the major waterways. Indiana and Ohio also launched massive programs of internal improvements, and the new territory of Wisconsin was headed in a similar direction. To answer the needs of the booming economy, eastern and western banks increased their circulations and extended credit. Thus neither Butler nor his western counterparts were psychologically or financially prepared for an economic slowdown and depression.

Butler's acknowledgement of the country's economic difficulty and of his own overzealous economic projections was slow and grudging. In October 1836, after Jackson issued the Specie Circular to slow the rate of land speculation, and after severe disturbances shook the New York money market, Butler assured his brother, Benjamin, that "If after two years of uninterrupted and abundant and undeserved prosperity I am not willing to endure a season of severe reaction & pressure & sacrifice, I ought to lose all that has been given. Nothing short of the most severe pressure in the money market of this country will ever bring the people to reflection & moderation."[4]

It is perhaps indicative of Butler's state of mind at the time that he did not consider himself a promoter or speculator. In December 1836, he commented "we have passed through the crisis . . . . The abundant strength and resources of the country have been thoroughly tested—rash and improvident speculations have been checked and rebuked . . . ."[5] By March 1837, Butler's correspondence had changed in tone; he admitted the seriousness of the crisis, yet he still tried to bolster the confidence of his friends. "The sources of wealth in this country are just too deep to permit a long depression," Butler observed, and ". . . I hope for the best and endeavor to encourage and inspire hope in others around me—at any rate nothing is gained by yielding to despondency but a good deal is lost."[6]

Butler's efforts to shield his financial interests from the depression were tentative, at first, yet the escalating financial crisis necessitated increasingly more drastic measures. The essence of Butler's problem was that his financial empire (like that of his western agents) was built on a foundation of credit. To support his investments in banks, railroads, and building projects, Butler had borrowed from several New York banks and private capitalists. At the same time, he had loaned his money to westerners for their stock and land purchases. The continued movement of funds between East and West, then, was primarily dependent upon the periodic sale of western property, which enabled Butler to meet payment on his notes to eastern banks and westerners to meet their obligations to Butler. Therefore, when the financial squeeze began, Butler urged his agents, such as William Ogden and Charles Trowbridge, to collect outstanding notes and to sell property at reduced prices.[7] But he soon realized that his debtors would be unable to sell enough land to pay their notes because the depression had reduced the amount of capital and credit in circulation throughout the country.

Butler's only recourse was to work out a settlement with his eastern creditors. As a first step, he sought extensions on his notes. Creditors such as Thomas Olcott and Arthur Bronson initially accommodated these requests, and thus they supported the fragile credit arrangements between East and West. When the depression worsened, falling property values combined with the unpaid interest and principal on his obligations again threatened Butler's financial position. He countered by surrendering more and more property to secure his existing notes, and by 1838 he occasionally gave up parcels of land in order to cancel a debt. By late 1838 Butler exhausted his available specie and therefore resorted to the complicated transfer of his debtors to his creditors. For example, Charles Trowbridge and Elon Farnsworth together owed Butler in excess of five thousand dollars secured by mortgages on Detroit property. Butler made the Detroiters' obligation payable to Arthur Bronson who then cancelled a part of Butler's outstanding debt to him. Trowbridge and Farnsworth, of course, were now obligated to Arthur Bronson.[8]

In addition to his unsettling financial problems, Butler was also faced with severe personal problems. His misfortunes began with the death of his second son, Arthur Bronson Butler, in 1835, followed by his wife's serious illness. Tragedy struck again in June 1838, with the death of another son, Charles. Given the economic and psychological strain, it is not surprising that Butler himself was stricken with a serious throat and lung ailment in 1838. At this point, physicians recommended an ocean voyage and a change in climate, and the New Yorker, in the company of family and friends, left for England in July 1838. Although he originally planned to return in two months, he found little relief from his illness in England and went on to France. Eventually, his travels took him to Italy where he stayed throughout the winter of 1839. This sojourn apparently had its beneficial physical and psychic effects, for Butler returned to the United States in June 1839, and immediately plunged into salvaging his financial affairs.[9]

The effort would take all the spirit he could muster, for in the spring of 1839, Butler's creditors were both numerous and angry. At minimum, he owed $8,686 to the New York Life Insurance and Trust Company; $3,000 to his former law partner, Bowen Whiting of Geneva, New York; $19,000 to Joseph Beers, a New York merchant and banker; and $30,000 to the Bronson family.[10] He was also indebted to Thomas W. Olcott's Mechanics and Farmers Bank for $30,000 and to Erastus Corning's Albany City Bank for an equally large sum. To further complicate the situation, Butler's debts affected many other people who were either partners or endorsers on his notes. William B. Ogden had cosigned several notes when purchasing land for the American Land Company, and in 1840 Ogden feared that these notes would ruin both him and Butler. On the notes to Olcott's bank, Martin Van Buren and Benjamin F. Butler were secondarily responsible. Ironically, this fact probably helped Butler because Olcott was anxious to keep President Van Buren's name off the bankruptcy pages of the newspapers.[11]

Butler's extended trip to Europe and his inability to pay his debts naturally threatened his reputation even with his old friend Arthur Bronson. When rumors circulated that Butler teetered on the brink of bankruptcy and that he had settled some debts but not others, Bronson doubted whether his friend ever intended to reimburse the Bronson family. Butler's obligations included a $10,000 note to the estate of Isaac Bronson, a $5,000 note to Oliver Bronson, and a $23,000 defaulted mortgage on which Butler was secondarily responsible. Before other creditors moved against Butler, Bronson instructed a Chicago law firm to obtain a writ attaching Butler's property in Chicago as security for debt payment. Bronson's letter to his Chicago lawyers indicated the strain in his relationship with Butler: "I feel that I have been ill used by Mr. Butler & believe that he is conscious of not having done justice to me. I have however no disposition to injure him in any way . . . . But I am bound in justice *to myself* and to those for whom I act, to protect my & their interest, even if the feelings of others should thereby become hostile and unfriendly to me."[12]

Butler, however, scurried to avoid such legal action, conscious that any hint of bankruptcy would besmirch his reputation and completely ruin his chances for recovery. In 1840, he issued a document publicly acknowledging the outstanding debts which he owed to each of his major creditors. At the same time, he informed the noteholders that he had borrowed a sum of $100,000 from his brother, Benjamin F. Butler, which would be used, beginning in 1843, to repay his debts. In effect, Charles Butler asked his creditors for a three year extension in return for his legal declaration of indebtedness and a guarantee that funds existed for payment. Arthur Bronson, as well as Butler's other creditors, realized that the document represented little additional legal or economic security since neither cash nor property had been exchanged. They, nevertheless, accepted Butler's promise since it was more advantageous to receive late or reduced payments than to force Butler into bankruptcy.[13]

In subsequent years, Butler took other steps to reduce his indebtedness. He often surrendered property, even though of limited market value, in order to liquidate specie debts. In other cases, he would agree to make periodic payments in exchange for an immediate reduction in the debt's principal. Occasionally, Butler allowed his creditors to take the security pledged for specie debts. For example, Butler was secondarily responsible for a $23,000 mortgage secured by Chicago city lots. So long as the original debtors and Butler were unable to pay, the property could neither be sold nor developed. Butler, therefore, assisted in the foreclosure of the mortgage so that the title could be transferred to the mortgagee, Arthur Bronson. Butler, of course, hoped that Bronson would develop the property, and thus help to stabilize property values in Chicago. After difficult years in 1840 and 1841, then, Butler had reached an accommodation with his creditors, such as Thomas Olcott and Arthur Bronson.[14] Even though he continued to pay on his debts into the 1850s, Butler had avoided bankruptcy and had maintained his reputation as a financier, albeit less wealthy, less optimistic, and less willing to risk everything on the "big" project.

Throughout the period during which Butler sought a settlement with his creditors, the progress of his western investments was sharply curtailed. As creditors pressed him for payment he in turn, called in the notes of his western debtors. The whole credit structure thus linked East to West and connected the projects at Huron, Toledo, and Chicago. When one debt was called for collection, it automatically created a chain reaction in Butler's other investments. The depression years, therefore, forced the New Yorker and his western associates to reassess potential profits and possible outcomes. Throughout this painful reassessment, Butler remained at the center of the decision-making process, and his efforts were often critical in lessening the depresion's impact on western communities.

The American Land Company was at the center of the New Yorker's investment portfolio, and all his other interests were loosely organized around it. Formed in 1835, the stockholders had planned to invest $1 million dollars in land, hold it for six years, and then sell, dividing the profits among the shareholders. In addition to its major interest in southern cotton land, the company purchased thousands of acres in Ohio and Michigan along the line of the Erie and Kalamazoo Railroad, in St. Clair County near Huron, and in Illinois adjacent to Chicago. Despite the company's optimistic projections of profits, the lengthening shadow of the depression made sales very difficult. The company had not intended to monopolize thousands of acres of land in the Old Northwest, but the depression had trapped it with lands purchased at inflated prices in 1835 and 1836. The trustees were understandably reluctant, at first, to sell at the deflated prices in 1837 and 1838.

As the president of the American Land Company, Butler led the struggle to avert financial disaster. Throughout the late 1830s and early 1840s, he continued to make inspection trips both south and west on the company's behalf while he sought every opportunity for sales.[15] In December 1844, Butler led the trustees, despite serious internal bickering, in the first attempt to unload its vast holdings and recover a fraction of the original investment. The company auctioned its lands in the Old Northwest, allowing the company's shareholders to purchase lands with their stock. This sale had several effects. First, stockholders gained private ownership of the land enabling them to sell privately or to improve it. Second, the company divested itself of unproductive investments with the ultimate goal of liquidation. Finally, the sale should have encouraged western settlement because enormous tracts of land came on the market at the prevailing price. Despite the fact that there is no way to determine how much land reverted to private hands, the sale was at least indicative of the company's preference to sell rather than hold on to its western lands.[16] But the 1844 sale did not signal the firm's recovery; it was never again profitable even though Butler directed its operations until the final liquidation in the 1870s.[17]

Butler's complex financial interests in the Toledo region were perhaps the most difficult to adjust to the changing financial conditions. Besides managing the American Land Company's holdings, he owned Toledo lots and adjacent farm lands. The New Yorker also controlled stock in the Erie and Kalamazoo Railroad in addition to managing the interests of other eastern stockholders. To assist in the railroad's construction, he had engineered the eastern takeover of the Erie and Kalamazoo Railroad Bank. The financier maintained an active voice in the railroad's management as a director, and the bank's cashier, Philo Fuller, was the representative of eastern capitalists working through Butler. Initially these arrangements at Toledo were quite successful. Land values increased and the railroad completed its major line to Adrian, Michigan. The railroad's directors were so elated that they apparently ignored unsettled financial conditions and declared dividends in both 1836 and 1837.[18]

But temporary successes only masked serious problems. The railroad was actually in financial trouble in 1836, but for political and economic reasons unrelated to the depression. The Michigan Territory had chartered the railroad when Toledo was still part of that territory. After Michigan applied for admission into the Union, Ohio blocked congressional action on the grounds that the boundary lines were incorrect and that actually lands on Lake Erie and the Maumee River, including Toledo, belonged to Ohio. The argument dragged on through 1836, inciting local and state pride and claims of economic advantage for whomever gained the outlet on Lake Erie. Eventually the dispute was settled when Ohio gained Toledo and a contested strip of land along its northwestern border and Michigan received land in the present-day Upper Peninsula. With the compromise accepted, Michigan was admitted into the Union in 1837.[19]

The boundary settlement had a disastrous effect on the Erie and Kalamazoo Railroad because it now ran between two political units. This should not have affected its traffic, but it did. Michigan citizens complained that the Erie and Kalamazoo Railroad was a foreign corporation, draining the state of valuable products and tax revenues through Toledo, Ohio. In 1838, Michigan's Board of Internal Improvements, hoping to capture this trade, routed the projected southern railroad from Monroe on Lake Erie through Adrian to New Buffalo on Lake Michigan to compete with the Erie and Kalamazoo Railroad. By 1839, Adrian, Michigan, could boast of two railroads even though there was probably never a town with less need. The Erie and Kalamazoo Railroad reported a meager profit of $15,804 in 1839. This was also the last year its figures were in the plus column.[20] At the same time, Michigan residents began to sell their railroad stock allowing Ohioans to acquire a substantial majority. When Ohioans came to dominate the board of directors in 1839, they moved the railroad's offices from Adrian to Toledo.[21]

With the jurisdictional controversy and the depression cutting into the railroad's traffic, Butler attempted to stabilize his Toledo interests by reducing the bank's commitments and slowing the railroad's construction. Since the railroad bank had advanced the funds for equipment and stock subscriptions, Butler urged Philo Fuller, the cashier, to limit its circulation. At the same time, he instructed Fuller to stop any further loans to resident businessmen, thereby curtailing their expansionist program. Finally, Fuller was urged to collect outstanding debts or, at least, to obtain additional property as security.[22]

The New Yorker was especially concerned with the financial affairs of Edward Bissell, the railroad's principal western leader. Bissell had originally purchased a large stock interest in the railroad with a loan, which Butler endorsed, from Erastus Corning's Albany City Bank. Bissell had agreed to transfer his railroad stock to the bank as collateral for the note, but he subsequently sold several shares to a third party. Moreover, Bissell had secured additional loans from the railroad bank. Bissell, like other western businessmen at Toledo, was so certain of the railroad's success that he never worried over his extensive indebtedness. Yet Butler, already feeling the shortage of capital, realized that he must make the decisive move to limit these financial activities. His instructions to Fuller on the Bissell matter revealed his strategy as well as his influence over the bank:

> Mr. Bissell ought not to have applied to the Bank for one farthing. He assures me that he will make the Bank perfectly secure if they are not already, now will you see to it that you have this security. Do not intimate that you have any advice from me on the subject. You must now hold on till you weather the storm—take every pain to cover the weak point and to strengthen your securities—do not increase your discounts one farthing except to add to your security—keep your

counsel, and . . . people will take for granted that you are as well off
and as strong, as any of your neighbors . . . .[23]

The bank's restrictive policies opened a quarrel between western citizens, who dominated the railroad, and eastern capitalists, who controlled
the bank, on the advisability of limiting the railroad's expansion. The
western businessmen won the initial skirmishes. After Fuller had called in
loans and limited the bank's circulation, the railroad's directors exercised
their legal option to control the bank. According to the bank's original
charter, the railroad's directors were to manage it. They had surrendered
this right, under a gentlemen's agreement, when the easterners had first
subcribed for stock. But at a meeting of railroad stockholders in May
1838, Edward Bissell led the railroad's directors in reasserting partial
control over the bank by selecting its officers. Throughout 1838, Bissell
ran both the railroad and the bank as he desired. Butler and other eastern
financiers, particularly Erastus Corning, did not contest his control in the
hope that Bissell intended to secure his loans and assume complete stock
control of the railroad.[24]

When Bissell made no such effort, the relationship between the western
residents and the eastern financiers deteriorated. Even though Butler was
in Europe, Erastus Corning, William E. Jones, secretary of the American
Land Company, and William B. Ogden, Butler's Chicago agent, tried to
protect eastern interests in the bank and the railroad. Ogden made
several trips to Toledo in an effort to settle Bissell's outstanding loans.
Unsuccessful in negotiations with Bissell, Ogden next tried to regain
control of the bank at a stockholder's meeting, but Bissell was a step ahead
of his creditors. At the meeting in April 1839, he successfully moved to
rejoin the bank and the railroad under a single management despite
Ogden's objections.[25]

Returning from Europe in June 1839, Butler immediately confronted
the crises at Toledo. Ogden had reported to him that "Bissell's case is
totally hopeless and it is in truth no charity to lengthen his existence
pecuniarily—the sooner he gets to the end now the better for him."[26]
With this advice, Butler put together a slate of candidates for railroad
directors who were known for their conservative financial views. He then
wrote other eastern stockholders in Buffalo, New York City, and Albany
and obtained their proxies for the stockholder's meeting in September
1839. The slate of candidates included the names of western residents
friendly to Charles Butler—Philo Fuller, William B. Ogden, George
Crane, Richard Mott—and eastern representatives—Henry Hicks, J.
Stringham, and Butler himself. Unable to attend the meeting, Butler gave
his power of attorney and the following instructions to William Ogden:

"the general object you will understand perfectly, which is to put the management of the railroad in safe and responsible hands, & to protect it against the action of the bank, to do which you will understand the Power of Attorney is intended to be ample and broad enough, to enable you to apply for an injunction or any other process if necessary."[27]

At the crucial meeting in September 1839, Bissell outmaneuvered Ogden and Butler. The existing board of directors, which Bissell controlled, adopted a rule allowing stockholders to vote even if their shares were mortgaged as security to someone else. In effect, it allowed Bissell to vote the 546 shares normally accredited to Charles Butler. With the support of other western stockholders, then, Bissell personally controlled 914 shares. As a result, he dominated the new board of directors leaving Butler with no voice in the railroad's management.[28]

Butler now sought the haven of the courts. In October 1839, the court agreed to put the railroad into receivership—court control—during the resolution of the conflict. This action forced Bissell to negotiate with his eastern creditors, and by the summer of 1840, Bissell had acknowledged his debts to Butler. Because Bissell was unable to raise the funds necessary to settle his debts, Butler foreclosed many outstanding mortgages and sold the property at a public auction in 1843. The sum derived from the sale never fully compensated Butler, who also stood as the endorser on Bissell's notes to Corning.[29] The Bissell case, of course, had affected Butler's own financial position. As his debtors were unwilling or unable to meet their obligations, Butler, in turn, could not obtain funds to pay his creditors.

Despite his difficulties with Edward Bissell, Butler did not abandon the railroad. He maintained a large stock interest until 1856, and he continuously served as a director, except for a brief hiatus in 1853.[30] Even though the railroad was moved in and out of receivership in the early 1840s as different parties sued for delinquent payments, Butler's contacts in the eastern money markets eventually helped the railroad to recoup some of its losses through a merger with the Michigan Southern Railroad.[31]

In the 1840s, eastern financiers had employed Butler to help in acquiring control of the Michigan Central and the Michigan Southern railroads. Michigan had begun construction of these railroads through the issue of bonds, but the depression prevented the state from paying its bondholders and from raising additional capital to complete construction. Consequently, the state desired to sell its railroads as a means of reducing its indebtedness and of securing capitalists willing to complete the railroads. Butler first helped a syndicate of capitalists from Boston and New York in purchasing the Michigan Central Railroad in 1846. He next assisted eastern financiers connected with the Erie and Kalamazoo Railroad who sought to purchase the Michigan Southern Railroad. This group intended to merge the two railroads and run a direct line from Toledo to Chicago. Butler obviously favored this plan since it might increase the value of his Erie and Kalamazoo Railroad stock. Consequently, he lobbied for this proposal before the Michigan legislature and with his influential political friends.[32] Having just sold the Michigan Central to eastern capitalists, however, the Michigan legislature was in a nativistic mood, and it turned down this offer in favor of one from local capitalists based in Detroit and Monroe.[33] The decision to keep foreign capital from totally dominating the state's transportation system and to maintain the Michigan Southern's terminus within the state at Monroe reflected an understandable upsurge of state pride.

Butler's plan was not dead, however, because local financiers, with limited capital resources, could not save the uncompleted and heavily indebted Southern Railroad. In 1847, therefore, George Bliss of Springfield, Massachusetts, and Washington Hunt of Lockport, New York, bought the controlling share of the Michigan Southern. In 1848, they acquired the entire capital stock of the Erie and Kalamazoo Railroad and then leased it to the Michigan Southern.[34] Finally the plan that Butler had worked toward since 1845 was a reality; Toledo was now the terminus of the Michigan Southern. In 1851, he again appeared as an advocate of the Michigan Southern when it fought the Michigan Central to be first into Chicago. In 1852, the Michigan Southern won the competition, and Butler, along with other important railroad capitalists, rode the Southern's first train into Chicago.[35]

Despite the problems encountered in the Toledo region during the depression, eastern capitalists, notably Charles Butler, did not abandon their city lots, agricultural lands, railroad and bank interests. Their decision was hardly charitable, but rather a practical action designed to protect their financial interests. It was perhaps inevitable that easterners would clash with some western businessmen who disagreed with efforts to stop improvements or slow the pace of economic development. Butler's fight with Edward Bissell, the local head of the Erie and Kalamazoo Railroad, represented a classic confrontation between the conservative course pursued by the eastern creditors and the desire of western debtors to delay the depression's effect on themselves and their communities. Such struggles were not uncommon during the depression years in the West, and they later formed the substance of bitter attacks against outside capitalists. As in the case of the American Land Company, however, Butler's leadership maintained the viability of the railroad and the bank until the original investors sold their stock in the late 1840s.

Butler's city promotion at present–day Port Huron, Michigan, paralleled his experiences at Toledo. In 1836, he had formed the Huron Land Company to promote a city at the narrow point between Lakes St. Clair and Huron. He not only projected that the city would be a natural trade break between the upper and lower lakes, but also envisioned a transportation network running from Buffalo across Canada to Sarnia, then hooking up with a projected northern railroad across Michigan to Grand Rapids. Butler further envisioned a ferry crossing Lake Michigan to Milwaukee and a railroad from there to Cassville on the Mississippi River. Huron seemed on its way to becoming a burgeoning city with the publication of an elaborate pamphlet on the town, the Canadian government's projected railroad to Sarnia, and in 1838 Michigan's selection of Huron as the eastern terminus of the northern railroad.

Huron's financial structure, though, was unstable from the beginning. Butler embarked on this plan in 1836, at a time when more conservative investors warned him of an impending financial recession. By early 1837, Butler already had problems raising capital for needed improvements. The Huron Land Company had financed the town at first with the capital derived from the stockholders' subscriptions. But the stockholders understood that eventually the company's directors would call for additional capital. Yet Butler was unable to raise enough money to allow the resident agent, Nicholas Ayrault, to construct his own housing for the winter of 1837. Instead, Butler urged him to move into the deserted buildings at Fort Gratiot.[36] In February 1838, Butler brought Ayrault back to the East Coast to help in publicizing Huron's desperate need for capital. Ayrault met with Butler and other stockholders in New York City and stopped in Albany for a visit with Erastus Corning. But Ayrault had little success in raising money since the depression left most eastern financiers with no extra capital.[37]

Even though Butler was in Europe in 1838, other proprietors attempted to save the site, and Butler's friend and the secretary of the American Land Company, William E. Jones, directed the efforts. Meeting at William Bard's home in New York City, the easterners decided to send two members to Huron on an inspection tour. Shortly thereafter they dispatched representatives to Washington with orders to lobby for a harbor appropriation at Huron, but the federal government refused. Repeated calls on stockholders for funds were also unsuccessful. After returning from Europe, Butler informed Ayrault that the proprietors would no longer spend money for improvements. To exacerbate matters, the depresson had stopped construction on Michigan's proposed northern railroad, and the Canadian line to Sarnia forfeited its charter in the early 1840s.[38] Huron, too, had fallen victim to the depression.

Having acknowledged the failure of his grand design for Huron, Butler still attempted to salvage the site. In 1840, he estimated the value of all the land there, which included 1000 city lots and 5,000 acres of farm land. Each shareholder of the Huron Company was then given individual title to lands in proportion to his stock interest. Next the Huron Company vacated a portion of their plat realizing that they had projected a town many times too large. The more northerly area later became the village of Fort Gratiot and that to the south, Port Huron.[39] Even though some capitalists allowed their lots to sit encumbered by mortgages, Butler continued to advance the town's interest. As late as 1844, for example, he and Erastus Corning were still pouring money into a local hotel in order to keep it operating.[40]

Huron was Butler's most serious financial blunder and the best example of his runaway promotional enthusiasm. Unlike Chicago or Toledo, Huron possessed few existing economic advantages, such as location or population. In 1836 and 1837, moreover, it was north of the principal population areas of Michigan. To expect to change the normal routes of travel from the southern route using the lakes to a northern route across Canada and northern Michigan was conceptually possible but practically impossible. Butler had also miscalculated the optimal location and size of the town. He projected a site for 40,000 people primarily situated north of Fort Gratiot and away from the Black River. Settlement, though, centered near the Black River because the river facilitated access to the interior.[41] Nevertheless, Butler's sense of the region's strategic importance was not totally inaccurate. Eventually a city of more modest proportions grew up there, built on the foundations laid by its first promoters.

While Butler assumed an influential role in the recovery efforts at Huron and Toledo, local business leaders were more important at Chicago. Butler had first invested there and in the adjacent agricultural region under a $50,000 contract with Chicagoans John Kinzie and Hiram Pearson. Subsequently he acquired the Hunter property, a tract of approximately 150 acres on the Chicago River's North Side. Butler intended to develop the North Side into the city's principal business district. His brother-in-law, William B. Ogden, located permanently in the city in 1836 to supervise the urban promotion as well as the American Land Company's purchases of agricultural lands in Illinois and in the Wisconsin Territory.

The depression's onset in 1837 began the now–familiar chain of events. Butler was unable to secure capital from his debtors, many of whom were residents and businessmen on the North Side and were overextended in their financial affairs. Without capital, Butler could no longer contribute to the necessary improvements, and eventually he surrendered much of his Chicago property in order to satisfy his creditors. In 1840, William Ogden described the situation: "The embarrassments of the whole community seem to me to increase firmly and business in this quarter decreases astonishingly. We shall never get to the bottom, I fear, until all this rascally old speculation debt is wiped off & let the Bankruptcy law come wiping the whole ground . . . . Charles's affairs, I fear, are desperate & the Bankruptcy law his only relief. He probably carries me & many others with him."[42]

Ogden's predictions were unnecessarily gloomy, for Butler survived the depression years in Chicago, and William B. Ogden was one of the principal reasons. Unlike the situation at Toledo where Edward Bissell challenged the easterner's leadership, Ogden worked closely with Butler and Arthur Bronson to soften the depression's impact. In fact, Ogden's career represented a subtle shift of power and leadership away from the eastern capitalist to the western agent. Unlike earlier years when Bronson and Butler had influenced the pace of improvements and controlled the expenditure of capital in the absence of a cohesive local business community, Ogden now came to control such economic decisions. This was an important transition because it represented the maturation of the community's business institutions and leaders.

Ogden's emergence as a western financial leader, though, was intimately linked to his eastern connections. Originally he came West at the request of Charles Butler to prepare the Hunter property for sale, but the excitement of Chicago in 1835 and the community's seemingly golden future persuaded Ogden to make it his permanent home in 1836. He was first employed as the chief agent for the American Land Company in the Old Northwest. In this capacity he checked land titles, paid taxes, and negotiated land sales. He made new purchases along the route of the Illinois and Michigan Canal and in the Wisconsin Territory, and he conducted periodic inspections of company properties in other areas of the country. In the late 1830s Ogden traveled south to check on the company's cotton lands, and he often represented Butler on business connected with the Erie and Kalamazoo Railroad.[43]

Like other agents of Charles Butler, Ogden also became a community leader. In April 1837, he ran for mayor against the representative of the "old" settlers, John H. Kinzie. The Whig newspaper attempted to exploit the obvious fact that Ogden was a newcomer, a representative of an out-state corporation and a Democrat. It suggested that Chicagoans

> Must have a permanent resident, not a transient speculator—a man whose interest in his own, not that of a *foreign company*—a man who has long resided among us, not a citizen of yesterday—a man

who spends his time among us, not one who journeys hither and thither, now to New York and now to Arkansas, as may suit the convenience of the American Land Company . . . . Let the people of Chicago answer at the *Polls* whether they will have one of their own sons to rule over them, or whether they will consent to be governed by an off-shoot of the Albany Regency . . . whose only object in coming here is to make money out of us, and then return home and spend it.[44]

The divisive charges that Ogden was a carpetbagger were to no avail; he won the election and assumed the mayor's chair scarcely a year after establishing permanent residence. Certainly Charles Butler must have felt greater security about his Illinois and Chicago investments knowing that Ogden occupied a strategic political position in the local community.

But William B. Ogden was his own man. Even though he began as the American Land Company's agent, each year he increased his financial independence and stature within the community. A significant step in this direction occurred in 1838 when Ogden opened his own land agency. Its importance was solidified when William E. Jones, the former secretary of the American Land Company, joined the agency in the early 1840s. Its name was then changed to reflect its geographical scope, the Northwestern Land Agency. Ogden's firm was not unique, for many similar companies were established in the principal western cities in the late 1830s and early 1840s. Such firms reflected the growing economic stability and independence of western communities. Eastern capitalists no longer depended on an extensive system of one to one contacts with western agents located in a score of different cities. Land agencies located in key cities could now provide all the needed services.[45] More important, perhaps, western citizens who directed these agencies came to assume crucial positions in the development of the regional economy.[46]

Ogden, for example, was essential to the advancement of the North Side of Chicago, particularly, since Butler was preoccupied with his financial affairs at Toledo and Huron. Ogden thus made the decisions about needed improvements. For instance, he lowered lot prices to attract new businesses, hoping that they would subsequently raise the value of the surrounding lands. Whenever possible, he required lot purchasers to erect buildings, and he continually enticed absentee owners, including Arthur Bronson, to construct buildings by offering his services in collecting rents.[47] Ogden's aim, of course, was to strengthen property values on the North Side, thereby benefiting himself and the other owners.

Although few improvement projects were totally planned or executed without the assistance of eastern financiers, Ogden was the initiator in

Fig. 9. Portrait of William Butler Ogden (Courtesy of Chicago Historical Society)

securing adequate transportation. In 1836, for example, he and Walter Newberry organized a steamboat company capitalized at $200,000, intending to build the boats on the North Side and thus add to its commercial attractiveness. Both Chicagoans subscribed $5,000 to the company's stock and then made appeals to eastern financiers, particularly Arthur Bronson and Charles Butler.[48]

Ogden and Newberry also led in the fight to secure a bridge uniting the North and South Sides of the city, a project crucial to property values on the North Side. In 1838 and 1839, the warehouses and forwarding businesses, such as Hubbard and Company and Newberry and Dole, were on the North Side. Yet there was only one bridge, at Dearborn Street, to move agricultural produce from the south, and in 1839 that bridge was destroyed because it hindered river traffic. There were a few ferries, but they were inefficient in moving people and heavily-laden wagons across the river. Ogden first tried to raise funds for a new bridge through private solicitations.[49] Failing in that effort, he talked the city council into issuing bonds for bridge construction. Ogden then sold the idea to the absentee property holders. In corresponding with Arthur Bronson, Ogden warned him that "the facilities for crossing our River, however, must be greatly increased or business property on the North Side will yet suffer great depression."[50]

Ogden and Newberry also agitated for the construction of the Galena and Chicago Union Railroad. Local citizens T. W. Smith and Ebenezer Peck had originated the project in 1836, but they were unable to raise the necessary capital. Ogden and Newberry revived the idea in the late 1830s in order to provide the city's North Side with a link to the agricultural interior. Arthur Bronson and Charles Butler assisted in the planning and in the attempt to raise money, but unlike improvements undertaken four years earlier, Ogden and Newberry were now the principal promoters.[51]

Despite the efforts of Ogden, property on the North Side stagnated during the depression for several reasons. First, the property was not favorably located to become the city's principal business district. Farmers bringing produce to market entered the city from the south, and thus the South Side was naturally situated to become the business area.[52] If the North Side were to compete for commercial superiority, then its promoters had to build bridges and construct new stores and homes. But these projects were slowed and sometimes halted by the lack of capital and the increasing burden of debt. Because Butler was besieged by his creditors, he was unable to contribute to improvements at Chicago. At the same time, Butler had to press his own debtors for payment, many of whom were North Side businessmen. As a result, the North Side declined in commercial importance, even though it still served as one of the city's most fashionable residential neighborhoods. Only in later years, when population and business expansion pushed commercial development across the Chicago River, did the North Side fulfill the promoters' original expectations.[53]

Charles Butler's experiences during the depression perhaps mirrored the struggles of many eastern promoters. Accepting without question the premise that America would grow and prosper, he had invested all his capital and pledged his credit for land, stock purchases, and building construction at Chicago, Huron, and Toledo. When the depression struck, Butler was overextended and unable to sustain his numerous projects. Yet he believed that financiers stood morally responsible for their debts, and he realized that his financial career depended on reducing his losses wherever possible. Thus he directed the American Land Company in efforts to liquidate its landholdings in the West. At the same time, he exerted strong, often unpopular, leadership in western communities as he pressed his debtors for payment and reduced their mutually unreasonable expectations for profits. Even though none of his western projects succeeded in the ambitious manner originally envisioned, Butler, along with many other eastern financiers and resident businessmen, continued to participate in the decision–making that determined the direction of economic development in the Huron, Toledo, and Chicago regions.

9. Arthur Bronson and the Depression in the West

During the depression Arthur Bronson was in a fundamentally different position from Charles Butler. First, the Bronson family possessed a fortune beyond the reach of an economic slowdown. Second, the Bronsons had prepared for the sharp deflation. Isaac Bronson had been through other boom and bust cycles, and he had advised his son, Arthur, to reduce investments in speculative city lots and to concentrate his excess capital either in a mortgage loan business or in the purchase of agricultural land. Third, Arthur Bronson was the creditor in all of his business relationships, never the debtor. Not only did he own thousands of acres of farm land, but he also held the mortgages of many farmers and urban residents. Bronson, moreover, had the power to affect dramatically the West's economic development since his debtors included several of the region's leading entrepreneurs—Lucius Lyon, Charles Trowbridge, Elon Farnsworth, and John Kinzie.

Given Bronson's position as a creditor, it was perhaps unavoidable that the depression of 1837 would generate economic difficulty and personal animosity between Bronson and many western citizens as each sought to protect his own business interests. Western land agents, for example, desperately searched for a means to delay or remove debts incurred during the boom years, yet Arthur Bronson stood as a stark reminder of their financial mistakes and as a barrier to a new start. Bronson's Detroit agent in the 1840s referred to him as ". . . the closest, most penurious rich man in New York . . . ."[1] Western farmers and village residents were generally hostile toward eastern investors during the depression's worst years and blamed them for the thousands of defaulted mortgages, the high interest rates, and the increasing incidence of tenant farming. Arthur Bronson, thus, was often the target of the westerner's frustration.

A Michigan agent reported in 1843 that "There are many persons in this village who have imbibed a groundless and foolish prejudice against you, because by honest industry and perseverance, you have been more successful in life than themselves. They think that you are dealing harshly with them, simply because you have mortgages and claims on their houses and lands. Plainly speaking, they would cheat you if they could."[2]

Was Bronson guilty of the charges directed toward nonresident investors during the depression? Did he routinely throw farmers off the land or force city residents into the courts to squeeze out every penny, unconcerned with the fate of individuals and communities? To what extent were Bronson's debtors responsible for the financial hardships which befell them during the depression? This chapter analyzes Bronson's land business during the depression in order to answer these questions. Since he worked through a number of agents who shared in the profits and losses of his investments, Bronson's relationship with these men must be the starting point of the investigation. In almost every case, the depression bankrupted his agents, resulting in long and often bitter disputes over a final settlement. But Bronson neither caused the westerners' financial collapse nor exacerbated their hardships; in fact, Bronson warned each of his western agents of the impending financial collapse. Yet they ignored him and plunged ahead with land purchases.[3] Throughout the depression, nevertheless, Bronson adopted business policies which sought to minimize his own losses and which reluctantly recognized the westerners' need for extended time payments and additional credit. Bronson stuck with his western investments and often made new monies available to farmers and city dwellers, conscious that he would benefit most from patient efforts to stabilize land values.

Arthur Bronson's relationship with his western agents was typified in the case of Detroiters Charles Trowbridge and Elon Farnsworth. In 1833, they had contracted to invest approximately $50,000 for Butler and Bronson over a five-year period with the understanding that the Detroiters would not accumulate profits until they reimbursed Bronson for their share of the original capital. In 1835, Bronson, alarmed by escalating property values in Detroit and its vicinity, sold his share of the partnership to Butler. Subsequently, Butler, Farnsworth, and Trowbridge purchased additional lands under the partnership, and each also began several more speculative enterprises. Trowbridge and Farnsworth erected buildings on many Detroit lots hoping to gain rental income. Trowbridge organized a syndicate of capitalists to purchase the Cass farm, a potentially valuable tract which stood in the way of the city's expansion. Over the next several years, this syndicate poured capital into improving the land in preparation for its sale but when the depression slowed emigration and limited specie, the whole scheme collapsed stranding the promoters with commitments to pay for the improvements but without any possibility of selling the lots. Trowbridge was also involved in the promotion of Allegan, a townsite in the western part of the state, and he purchased extensive tracts of wild lands.[4] Both Detroiters were convinced that all of the projects would make a profit and were therefore unconcerned with the tremendous financial obligations which they had assumed. In fact, in 1836, Trowbridge was so confident of success that he resigned as the cashier of the Bank of Michigan so that he might live and work in the style of the nineteenth century gentlemen-capitalist.[5] No doubt he saw himself as the West's equivalent of Arthur Bronson.

Trowbridge and Farnsworth were unprepared for the depression in 1837. They had spent all their capital and pledged themselves to pay, periodically, the principal and interest on a score of mortgage contracts. When credit tightened at the depression's onset, they were trapped in a chain reaction as each creditor attempted to call in outstanding loans and to sell unproductive property. Charles Butler, their principal creditor, who in turn owed numerous individuals, pressed Trowbridge and Farnsworth for payment. The Detroiters similarly asked their debtors for a settlement. No one, however, could raise sufficient specie because property sales brought only a fraction of prices received just a year earlier. Butler temporarily resolved his problems by making Trowbridge and Farnsworth's debt payable directly to his creditor, Arthur Bronson. In 1842, this debt was $5,000 plus interest secured by a mortgage on property and buildings in Detroit.[6] But Arthur Bronson was not the Detroiters' only creditor, for they owed approximately $25,000 to other eastern financiers. They had obtained, for example, a loan of $8,000, secured by a second mortgage on Detroit property, from Thomas Olcott of the Mechanics and Farmers Bank of Albany.[7]

Contrary to the general impression left by reports of the depression period, none of Trowbridge's and Farnsworth's creditors immediately moved in to foreclose on these obligations. Although the debts had been due since 1836, the Detroiters were still negotiating with Bronson and Olcott over a settlement as late as 1842. Both easterners were content to delay the payment of the principal so long as the westerners met their interest payments and provided sufficient collateral. Even when interest payments became irregular or stopped altogether, Bronson and Olcott, at first, merely demanded additional security or secondary endorsers for the notes.[8]

Eastern capitalists followed such policies not out of charity to the western agents—although there were elements of that apparent—but out of dissatisfaction with the alternatives. Neither Bronson nor Olcott wished to force the debtors into court in order to foreclose the mortgage because such action meant accepting the property as payment for the debt or selling the property at auction to the highest bidder. To accept the property as total payment for the debt inevitably meant a substantial cash loss. Property values in the West had declined to ridiculously low levels, making property a poor exchange for a cash debt. Bronson, moreover, already held enough property, none of which could be sold at a profit. The creditor could sell the property at auction, yet such distress sales in a region short of specie resulted in low prices. An auction sale of the landed security would not net the loan's actual value. The eastern capitalists also knew that time and expense were involved in the utilization of the courts to foreclose a mortgage and conduct an auction sale. If at all possible, therefore, the capitalist preferred to grant the debtor extended time so long as the possibility of eventual payment existed. Finally, Bronson also must have thought in a broader context; his investments—which included western farms, city property, and bank stock—could not improve if the West's leading businessmen went bankrupt. Bronson protected his own financial interests, therefore, by supporting his debtors until the financial storm passed.

Western agents, however, often resisted such policies on the part of their eastern creditors. The Detroiters did not relish the prospect of paying yearly interest and facing the eventual repayment of the debt's principal. They realized that debts accumulated during the boom period could never be settled at their face value without extreme financial hardship. Trowbridge and Farnsworth first hoped, but did not seriously expect, that Bronson and Olcott would simply grant a moratorium or even wipe the slate clean. When the easterners refused these requests, Trowbridge and Farnsworth understandably tried to bargain with their creditors in order to reduce or avoid part of the debt, thus forcing the creditors to absorb a share of the losses caused by the depression. The Detroiters first offered the property which secured their notes in exchange for the cancellation of the specie debts. The Detroiters would, in a sense, declare bankruptcy without the legal stigma of a public declaration, a stigma which any businessman wished to avoid.[9] Having proposed such a plan to Thomas Olcott, Trowbridge dramatized his financial condition and his desire to avoid the courts:

> Mr. Farnsworth and myself have some vacant lots in this city and some wild lands which we should be glad to substitute for that you now hold, but neither of us owns a dollar's worth of productive property not already encumbered to its value. We are both very poor and wholly unable to pay the interest on our debt. I have already given up my dwelling house which I built 17 years ago, to a creditor,

and I do earnestly hope that you will see the propriety of accepting our proposal and thus aiding us so far in the desperate struggle we are making to get free. It is hard at best, but it will be harder still to be driven to that last resort of an honorable man—the U.S. District Court—Do spare us from this if you can.[10]

Throughout the 1840s, Bronson and other easterners struggled with the two Detroiters over the terms of a final settlement. During these negotiations, tempers flared and mutual respect deteriorated into hostility and mistrust on both sides. Trowbridge and Farnsworth, for example, insisted that they were unable to make interest payments and that the easterners would have to accept property in satisfaction for the debts. At one point, Trowbridge blamed all his financial problems on his original contract with Bronson and appealed to the New Yorker's charity rather than his pocketbook: "Having no profession, it is even worse with me than with Mr. Farnsworth. As I am situated I can enter into no business—and with my ability and desire to be employed, I am wasting my energies and fretting out my existence. You have never known poverty—have never been in the poor debtor class. You can therefore form no idea of my feeling."[11]

Although Trowbridge and Farnsworth continually described their financial condition as one step from penury, these characterizations were exaggerated and Bronson knew it. In actual fact, both Detroiters remained at the center of Michigan's economic and political life. Trowbridge unsuccessfully ran for governor in 1837 and returned later to the presidency of the Bank of Michigan in a futile effort to save it from bankruptcy. In 1845, he was the president of the Michigan State Bank, and later he became an important railroad executive.[12] Farnsworth continued to serve as the state's chancellor, ran for governor in 1839, and in 1842 was appointed attorney general. Later he too became a railroad executive, serving on the board of the Michigan Central for twenty years. He was also president of the Detroit Savings Bank in later years.[13] Finally, it should be remembered that the Detroiters were also creditors and expended considerable effort during the depression pressing their own debtors for payment.

Bronson refused to consider the westerners' appeals because he perceived them as a device to avoid payment. Even though the Detroiters came to view him as the enemy, Bronson saw no reason why he should suffer the financial loss caused by Trowbridge's and Farnsworth's land speculation schemes. In 1843 and 1844, therefore, Bronson traveled West to force a partial settlement. Bronson accepted the fact that he could never obtain the debt's face value since specie and property values had declined during the depression. Yet Bronson was also unwilling to accept property to cancel a specie debt since that property had little value in the marketplace. Bronson thus compromised; he accepted some property along with a cash payment to reduce the outstanding principal. He continued, however, to collect interest on the remaining balance until the whole debt was retired in the late 1840s.[14] This settlement did not make Bronson the villain and the westerners the vanquished or vice versa. Unquestionably, Bronson struck a hard bargain which protected his interest, yet *he was the creditor*. Admittedly the Detroiters lost part of their landed wealth, yet *they were the debtors*. Neither party emerged unscathed. Bronson reduced the debt's principal, accepted property as partial reimbursement, and granted a long period for repayment. In many ways, it was Bronson's indulgence that enabled Trowbridge and Farnsworth to remain effective political and financial leaders in Detroit.

Lucius Lyon experienced a fate similar to that of Farnsworth and Trowbridge. Lyon signed contracts in 1834 to invest up to $75,000 for the Bronson family in lands throughout the Old Northwest. At the same time, he sold valuable lands at Grand Rapids, Lyons, and Ada to Arthur Bronson in order to secure his financial support for improvments. Lyon also shared in the promotion of Chicago, and he purchased thousands of acres of agricultural land throughout the western states. In 1836, he boasted that his land investments exceeded $200,000 in value.[15] Confident of continued success, Lyon did not hesitate to purchase Bronson's share at Grand Rapids, Lyons, and Ada when the New Yorker decided to sell out. Lyon subsequently embarked on building construction and on a canal at Grand Rapids.[16] Yet Bronson warned him that credit and specie contractions would come and that conservative investment policies would be advisable. In June 1836, Bronson wrote to Lyon that

> The crisis in respect to speculative property it appears to me cannot be far distant. Communities, self-organized companies acting through agents wild and inexperienced, and multitudes of individuals from the East, North and South are now swarming the West, presenting an opportunity for making sales, which calm and prudent men should not permit to pass by unimproved. I hope you will feel the force of these remarks, and in making sales require such payment and security as shall secure their fulfillment.[17]

Lyon ignored these warnings, and by the summer of 1837 his landed empire began to crumble. Lyon's fortune existed only on paper because most transactions had been based on credit. Debtors owed Lyon for city lots in Grand Rapids and for farms throughout the state which they had purchased with small down payments and promises of regular installments over the next five or six years. Lyon, in turn, had purchased additional properties on time for which he gave personal bonds, mortgages, and the promise of periodic payments. In the heady years of the boom, Lyon also had pledged his property and credit so that his friends might borrow capital. Finally, Lyon had poured any surplus capital into improvements at Grand Rapids, Kalamazoo, and Lyons.[18] Lyon, therefore, lacked specie to meet his creditors' demands in 1838 and 1839.

Lyon's principal creditor was Arthur Bronson, who represented himself as well as his father's estate. Although the total indebtedness was difficult to calculate, Lyon was clearly responsible for two principal cash obligations secured by land mortgages. The first derived from the 1834 contract in which Isaac Bronson had employed Lyon to purchase western lands. Lyon was to share in the profits accumulated from sales after first contributing his share of the purchase money. In April 1837, Lyon owed nearly $49,500 on this contract.[19] The second major debt resulted from Lyon's purchase of Bronson's share in the Grand Rapids property in 1835. In 1839, Lyon still owed the full principal of $20,000 plus interest accumulating at an annual rate of 7 percent. Arthur Bronson was content with the collection of the yearly interest on both debts in the late 1830s, but eventually Lyon was unable to make even interest payments.[20]

Lyon's difficulties were compounded by the fact that he was unable to oversee carefully his financial affairs due to his service as Michigan's senator in 1837 and 1838. When he lost a bid for reelection in 1838, Lyon returned to Grand Rapids and attempted to save some of his business investments. Hearing of Lyon's defeat, Bronson told him that "it is the most fortunate thing that could befall you. I hope you will not, for your own sake, ever again return to *political life*. It is an unprofitable miserable calling."[21]

After Lyon returned to Grand Rapids, he tried mining salt in order to produce a steady income, but his financial position steadily worsened. When Lyon was no longer able to pay interest or offer additional security, he lost much of his real estate to Bronson and other creditors. In 1839, Bronson concluded a partial settlement which required Lyon to surrender all his rights to lands purchased under their joint contract. Later Arthur Bronson foreclosed on a mortgage held jointly by Lyon and other Kalamazoo residents on a hotel there.[22] Subsequently, Lyon also lost most of his valuable agricultural land including farms on the Prairie Ronde in the southern part of the state, a farm at the mouth of the Grand and Maple rivers, and another at the mouth of the Thorn Apple river, plus 25,000 acres of wild land. In early 1842, Lyon described his rather bleak circumstances: "I have been struggling against increasing debt and embarrassment for the last five years, while my property has been growing every day less valuable, till at last it will not sell for enough to pay the mortgages with which it is encumbered."[23]

With each passing year, the previously close friendship of Arthur Bronson and Lucius Lyon broke apart. Although the Bronsons were not Lyon's only creditors or the cause of his difficulties, Lyon believed that they shared a major part of the blame: "I have to be sure been helped down the hill a good deal by being endorser and surety for my friends, but my dealings with the Bronsons injured me more than anything else. It will require ten years of diligent attention to business and the strictest economy on my part to enable me to pay my debts. I have been hard at work since 1839 to effect this object, but make slow progress."[24]

Given the fact that Lyon wrote the above statement even before he had discharged all his debts to Arthur Bronson, the remaining negotiations were certain to be difficult. The debts which resulted from Lyon's purchase of Bronson's share in the Grand Rapids speculation were still outstanding. In 1843, Arthur Bronson traveled West to conclude a settlement, but Lyon at first refused to see him. Bronson warned him that the development of Grand Rapids could not continue while lots were encumbered by delinquent mortgages. People would not purchase these lots, Arthur explained, until the seller could deliver a clear title. Lyon finally consented to a meeting at Detroit, but negotiations still were not completed when Arthur Bronson died in November 1844.[25] Lyon then attempted to force a settlement in the confusion following Arthur's death. Claiming that Arthur Bronson had cheated him in 1833 and 1835, Lyon offered to make a cash payment of $5,000 to clear his $12,000 debt. Frederic Bronson, who now directed the family's business affairs, refused to accept Lyon's terms, and when threatened with a court fight, Frederic testily replied to Lyon that "There is an intimation in your letter that if I should proceed to the forecloseure of that mortgage without examining the subject with you it might cause a very expensive and troublesome litigation which might last for ten years. The expenses and delay of obtaining justice is no argument why justice should not be obtained, nor does it throw any light on the merits of the controversy."[26]

In 1845, Frederic Bronson and Lyon renewed a friendly correspondence; yet the mortgage issue remained until well into the 1850s and complicated Grand Rapids' land titles. As a result, the eastern capitalist was assumed to be the villain who merely held mortgage rights with no thought of advancing the city's welfare. At the same time, Lyon remained a respected community member. He served another term in Congress in 1843, and in 1845 he became a surveyor general for the midwestern states.[27]

Yet Arthur Bronson was not the villain in this case. Lyon had been far too reckless in spending his capital resources on land and city promotions.

Arthur Bronson certainly did not exhibit an excess of charitable zeal, yet he reacted as one might expect. He insisted that Lyon abide by the terms of his two bonds and mortgages, although Bronson agreed to delay the return of the principal so long as the interest was paid. When Lyon was no longer willing or able to remit the interest, Arthur Bronson required additional security, and finally he reduced the debt's principal. Bronson, nevertheless, insisted on at least a partial reimbursement. It is not surprising that their friendship dissolved under such financial pressures and that their correspondence was punctuated with charges of capitalistic piracy on the one hand and laziness and dishonesty on the other. Historians need not enter into this quarrel; rather it seems fair to observe that both Arthur Bronson and Lucius Lyon were products of their financial class, their geographic regions, and their unstated economic philosophies. Neither was shyster nor deadbeat, but both were participants in an economic system struggling to regain stability.

Bronson was also engaged in a fight with Cogswell Green, his agent in southwestern Michigan. The New Yorker had employed Green to invest $10,000 in farm lands and town lots. In 1836, Bronson sold his interest, yet Green continued to invest on his own. Bronson reluctantly agreed to finance these purchases through a loan of $3,000 at 7 percent annual interest, yet the financier was so concerned with fluctuating property values that he required landed security appraised at triple the loan's value. When the depression hit, Green was unable to meet the terms of his contracts with Arthur Bronson. In 1841, after several years of increasingly nasty letters from the New Yorker about overdue payments, Green sued in the Michigan courts to be released from one mortgage arguing that Arthur Bronson had violated the state's usury laws.[28] Once again, the eastern capitalist and his western agent had ended their business relationship in mutual distrust and in the courts.

The case itself revealed the conflicting motivations of the creditor and debtor before and during the depression. Green freely admitted that he had signed the contract with Bronson, an act illustrating the western agent's poor judgment at a time (1836) when success seemed certain. The westerner, who was besieged by creditors in 1838 and 1839, obviously sought the court's aid in avoiding a debt then close to foreclosure. With several attempted settlements and court delays, the dispute was still not resolved in 1845. Such delays benefited Green since he was able to postpone the payment of both principal and interest.

Bronson was no less intent than Green in protecting his financial interests. In 1836, he struck as safe and "hard" a bargain as the law allowed and Green would accept. Conscious of the deteriorating financial conditions, he naturally lent money on terms reflecting the added risks. In this particular contract, he lent $3,000 for which he required security consisting of land mortgages valued at $9,000. Moreover, Bronson charged the maximum legal interest rate of 7 percent yearly, and he made it payable in New York City so that the debtor also bore the cost of exchange rates between West and East. When Green was unable to pay the interest, he accused Bronson of usury since the effective interest rate was perhaps 9 percent considering the cost of the exchange. Bronson, of course, responded to protect his property and reputation. He had maintained copies of all contracts, relevant laws, and correspondence so that he was able to present written evidence refuting Green's allegations.[29] In fact, I suspect that Bronson won most cases against his debtors because he possessed a thorough knowledge of the law: a law which he rarely violated but which he certainly utilized to his every advantage.

This court case and many others like it unfairly contributed to the unsavory reputation of eastern capitalists. Bronson, of course, pressed his debtors for what he considered legitimate claims; Green's position was also understandable as he sought to use the courts to delay payment and shift the depression's burden onto Bronson. Although Bronson and Green had each perceived the other as a villain, neither was regarded as such by his friends and peers. Green, for example, served as president of the village of Niles in 1844.[30] In effect, the depression created a stark conflict of interest between the debtor and the creditor. There was perhaps no way that obligations could have been satisfactorily settled without imperiling old friendships and business relationships. Unfortunately, most historians have viewed this dynamic struggle through the debtor's eyes, and they have not acknowledged the creditor's equally valid concerns during a time of economic insolvency.[31]

Bronson faced similar problems with his Illinois agents. Before the depression, Chicago had been the center of Bronson's Illinois land business. From there, his agents purchased mineral and farming lands in addition to city and town lots throughout the state. The agents were responsible for selling the land, for paying taxes on unsold properties, and for the collection of interest on mortgages. The depression substantially changed this business; there were few additional land purchases and seemingly endless appeals for specie loans and extensions of time to make mortgage payments.[32] Many of his agents found themselves unable to pay their own debts, especially those deriving from contracts with the New Yorker. Stephen Forbes, for example, had purchased land outside Chicago under an agreement in which he had to reimburse Bronson for a share of the purchase money. Forbes defaulted in 1837, but Bronson agreed to extend the contract until 1843. When Forbes was still unable to pay, Bronson foreclosed the bond accepting the land in lieu of specie.[33]

Archibald Clybourne suffered the same fate. He purchased land for the Bronsons in the Chicago region along the line of the Illinois and Michigan Canal and at Milwaukee. Clybourne shared in these investments, and he was also responsible for a percentage of the investment capital. When the Chicagoan could not meet his obligation in 1838, Bronson extended the due date after obtaining additional security. Later Clybourne could not make interest payments and, as a substitute, he superintended Bronson's properties without charge and provided the New Yorker with free beef from his meatpacking business. In 1844, Clybourne finally gave up any further attempts to save his interest in the land. Without bitterness, he agreed to the property's sale and allowed the proceeds from the sale to retire his debt.[34]

Bronson's most difficult financial decisions in Illinois derived from his entanglement with Charles Butler and the promotion of Chicago's North Side. Bronson, of course, had sold his principal interest in that area to Butler in 1835 partly because he sensed that it was too speculative. He still, however, owned lots on the North Side and lent money to city residents. When Butler ran into financial difficulty in 1838, Bronson accepted his Chicago lots and the mortgages of many other Chicagoans as security for Butler's notes.[35] Bronson thus was left with the unwelcome and unexpected responsibility for the North Side's future promotion.

Bronson assisted the Chicago community in many ways that helped to stabilize property values and improve its business potential. The New Yorker lent money to city residents through William B. Ogden's land agency. (Ogden had assumed the supervision of Bronson's land business after his independent agents had encountered financial difficulties in the late 1830s.) Bronson's interest rates fluctuated between ten and twelve percent, the maximum rate allowed by law but a common fee charged by brokers at a time of unstable property values. Bronson's debtors at this time included many of Chicago's most important citizens such as Archibald Clybourne, John Dean Caton, Hiram Pearson, Robert A. Kinzie, John Kinzie, Gurdon Hubbard, Richard J. Hamilton, and Alexander Fullerton.[36]

Bronson also participated in city improvements; he provided money for bridge and building construction and actively supported steamboat and railroad projects. In 1837 and 1838, for example, he worked with Ogden and Walter Newberry on a plan to widen the Chicago River in order to aid navigation and, more important, to make the lots fronting the Chicago River on the North Side more attractive to businesses.[37]

Yet Bronson was less willing to support the North Side's development when the depression continued into the early 1840s. Many factors prompted his decision. He was especially fearful of the expense involved in future improvements after the financial collapse of Charles Butler and his associates who previously had shared the costs. In addition, Bronson knew that the North Side was no longer the prime business location since most commercial traffic entered the city from the south.[38] Finally, the depression carried on so long that many Chicagoans were unable to pay Bronson the interest on their outstanding debts. Bronson found it necessary, then, to make realistic business decisions on what and who could be supported. These decisions did not endear him to the city's business community, and they often had a deleterious effect on the North Side's economic viability.

Bronson's relationship with Gurdon Hubbard vividly exemplified his changing financial policies. Although starting out as a fur trader in the 1820s, Hubbard became an important frontier businessman during the boom years. Hubbard owned land on Chicago's North Side, where he built a warehouse for the storage of goods. Subsequently he established a forwarding and commission business for the shipment of grain and beef to the East. Hubbard and his partners also purchased shares in several ships that traveled the lakes. He further extended his portfolio by speculating in land—an interest which eventually bankrupted him. Beginning in 1833, he invested for Edward and Samuel Russell of Middletown, Connecticut. Later he organized his own land agency, and typical of the westerner's unfettered enthusiasm, Hubbard wanted to handle only eastern clients capitalized in excess of $200,000. Hubbard also became one of three proprietors of Racine, a town on the shore of Lake Michigan in the Wisconsin Territory.[39] To finance these ventures, the Chicagoan depended on borrowed capital and on a constantly increasing volume of business.

When the money supply tightened in 1838, Hubbard's financial empire collapsed. Among his many creditors were Arthur Bronson and Charles Butler. Hubbard had borrowed $9,000 from Charles Butler on collateral consisting of his city lots and the warehouse. In 1838, Butler, in order to settle his own obligations, transferred Hubbard's bond to Bronson. Hubbard later informed Bronson that he was unable to make interest payments.[40] Bronson, nevertheless, did not foreclose the note since Hubbard's business contributed to the North Side's commercial well-being. Bronson extended the debt for several years, effectively subsidizing Hubbard's operations and protecting the commercial viability of the North Side. Bronson was always cognizant of William Ogden's advice that "property now on the North Side for business purposes is so dependent upon correct movements & efforts that I feel anxious to have this house (Hubbard's forwarding business) fully sustained for a year or two to come. I hope some arrangement to that end mutually advantageous may be hit upon."[41]

In 1840, Bronson changed his policy in regard to Gurdon Hubbard in order to protect his own financial interests. At this time, he decided that Hubbard could not recover his financial position, that the North Side would continue to lose its commercial attractiveness, and that the depression would not end soon. Bronson also feared that Hubbard would satisfy his other creditors before repaying him. After several years of pressing Hubbard for a settlement, Bronson finally threatened to sue the Chicagoan for more than $10,000. As a result, Hubbard agreed to relinquish title to his warehouse and lots on the North Side, although he retained the right to lease the warehouse. A codicil to this agreement guaranteed that Hubbard could repurchase the property for $10,000, if and when his financial condition improved.[42]

Even though the arrangement seemed reasonable, it created hostility between the two men. When Hubbard could not raise the capital to repurchase the warehouse, he dismantled the building, carrying off a salt house and a dock. Hubbard justified these actions believing that the New Yorker had cheated him out of valuable property because he foreclosed the mortgage.[43] In later years, Hubbard recalled the depresion years as a time when many Chicagoans lost everything while the city". . . was ridiculed by eastern people & her citizens abused, called a set of defrauders, our city a swamp full of deadly malary [sic], a death hole . . . ."[44] In Hubbard's mind, therefore, eastern capitalists like Bronson were responsible for the city's economic difficulties. To balance Hubbard's somewhat biased views, it should be pointed out that he was never indigent. He survived the depression, and although he had lost some property, he remained a respected pioneer and business leader.[45]

Bronson's association with John Kinzie further demonstrated the conflicts between eastern capitalists and western citizens. The Kinzie family had lived in Chicago since before the War of 1812. In the 1820s, John Kinzie had been an Indian agent and fur trader, but in the 1830s he became a merchant and land speculator in the frontier village. In 1835, he joined with Hiram Pearson in the investment of more than $50,000 for a syndicate of eastern capitalists that included Butler, John Ward, Thomas Olcott and William Bard. Encouraged by the town's prospects and anxious to increase the business potential of the North Side where he owned land, Kinzie united with Hubbard and others in 1836 to build the Lake House Hotel at the corners of Kinzie, Rush, and Michigan Street. The partnership changed over time, and by the late 1830s Kinzie owned a substantial part of the hotel on his own.[46]

For a brief period, the Lake House was known as the city's best hotel, but then it fell victim the the depression and Kinzie's debts.[47] As a result of his several land speculation schemes and business endeavors, Kinzie had many creditors of whom Arthur Bronson was the most important. In the late 1830s, Bronson lent Kinzie over $10,000 and accepted the Lake House and other Chicago lots as collateral. Even though Kinzie was unable to pay even the interest on the note in 1840, Bronson granted an extension while Kinzie searched for other remedies. At first, the Chicagoan unsuccessfully tried to sell the hotel, hoping to use the proceeds to satisfy his creditors. The hotel's value, moreover, had rapidly deteriorated because Kinzie and the other owners had no money to maintain the property. Consequently, the Lake House lost clientele to other hotels. Knowing that the Chicagoan could not recover financially and that the hotel's value would continue to decline with further delays, Bronson foreclosed Kinzie's mortgage in 1842.[48]

After Bronson acquired the hotel, he faced a difficult decision which revealed the clash of financial interests between the West and East. North Siders, particularly Walter Newberry, expected Bronson to refurbish the hotel and reopen it for business. Newberry placed the responsibility entirely on Bronson:

> You and your family have probably five fold the interest that I have on the North Side of the River and ten fold more than any other individual. Some sacrifice is necessary at this time to materially promote our mutual interest. From whom ought that sacrifice to be expected? I do not imagine that the Lake House can be made immediately profitable by opening it as a hotel, but I believe the great interests of the North Side of the river, can be saved, and the house itself be made eventually valuable, by opening it and sustaining it. But if it is not opened, and that soon, the house itself becomes a useless pile of brick and mortar and great injury is done to the property on that side of the river. Whatever is done to sustain that side of river will mainly have to be done by you and myself . . . .[49]

Despite his substantial property interest in the Chicago region, Bronson refused to contribute additional capital to improvements like the Lake House Hotel; instead, he sold the hotel in 1844.[50] Unlike the Chicagoans, Bronson accepted the direction of the city's growth to the south and preferred to reduce his liabilities rather than to throw "good money after bad." Although Bronson's decision was a sound business policy, it stranded many Chicago businessmen less willing or able to scale down their business interests. As a result, Bronson was often no more popular in Chicago than he was in Michigan.

Bronson made equally difficult decisions in regard to the failing townsite at Cassville in southwestern Wisconsin. Cassville was originally intended as the territory's capital city, but that prospect vanished with

Madison's selection. The town then experienced a rapid decline. Garrett V. Denniston, the Albany lawyer and friend of Thomas Olcott who shared in the town's promotion, was twice challenged to duels and once threatened with a pistol by local residents frustrated in their attempts to obtain the designation as the territorial capital. These irritations must have been compounded when Cassville lost the race to become the county seat in 1837. Added to these setbacks, the eastern promoters realized that the local agent, Lyman J. Daniels, was not only inept but also dishonest.[51]

Conscious that he had remained too long connected with the Cassville project and unwilling to compound his errors, Arthur Bronson and his principal partner, John Ward, sold their interest to Garrett Denniston and Lucius Lyon in April 1837.[52] Lyon and Denniston mistakenly believed that Cassville still could be elevated to the status of a thriving river port. Lyon was sufficiently sure of his judgment that he borrowed the purchase money from Arthur Bronson and mortgaged the city's lots as security for the loan.[53] Indeed, in 1837, Denniston and Lyon had grandiose plans to build steam mills (requiring the purchase of expensive engines), to pay for the printing of a newspaper, and to encourage the territory to build a road from Cassville to the new capital at Madison.[54]

But Denniston and Lyon had overestimated Cassville's potential and their capital resources, a miscalculation which forced Arthur Bronson back into the project. In the summer of 1837, Lyon was unable to raise his share of the capital for improvements. Suddenly, Bronson was in an impossible situation: if Lyon no longer advanced money for improvements, the town would further decline, thereby affecting the value of the property which secured Lyon's mortgage. At Lyon's request and after a personal inspection of Cassville in July 1838, Bronson advanced Lyon's share of the capital for the town's improvement. This sum was then added to Lyon's total indebtedness.[55]

Although it would have abruptly ended Cassville's development, Bronson should never have signed this agreement, for it only complicated the situation. In 1838, Garrett Denniston, who was supervising the expenditure of funds for improvements, requested an additional $6,000 from Lyon. When Denniston refused to let Bronson see the accounts, Bronson suspected that the promoters were bilking him for the cost of improvements, and at this point the New Yorker had the good business sense to withdraw. He negotiated a new contract with Lyon in which he erased half of Lyon's indebtedness at Cassville for the westerner's declaration of his remaining obligations. Lyon also assumed the responsibility for any future costs at Cassville, even though Bronson continued to hold mortgages on the property.[56]

In the 1840s, Cassville's fortunes steadily declined not only because geographic and political factors reduced it to the status of a small farming village, but also because of the unresolved financial difficulties of its promoters. Lyon's financial collapse prevented him from either contributing to Cassville or paying the interest on his bonds to Bronson. Consequently, most of the Cassville property was deeded back to Arthur Bronson and his executors. Denniston and the Bronson family subsequently argued over their responsibility for the debts due on the property. In 1842, Arthur Bronson filed suit against Denniston in order to recover money unfairly charged to Lyon's share. The suit was dropped in 1844, but the two men were unable to agree on a division of the property. In 1845 and 1846, Denniston was still requesting that the Bronson family advance the capital for their share of improvements completed in the 1830s. In 1847, Denniston filed suit to obtain the money, and as late as 1857 his heirs were still fighting in the Wisconsin courts.[57] With suits and countersuits over the complicated partnership arrangements and a score of outstanding mortgages, the Cassville property was trapped in a morass of title disputes that seemed impossible to unravel. Its population declined from a high of perhaps 300 in the spring of 1837, to 105 in 1840, 67 in 1841, and approximately 50 in 1842. In its similarity to other projects, Cassville provided strong testimony to the effects of declining land values and the lack of credit. Bronson's decision to pull out was not surprising; it was only surprising that he had waited so long.[58]

Bronson's numerous court suits against former business associates would, at first glance, seem to suggest that he was a harsh creditor during a time of economic upheaval, yet several considerations challenge such an interpretation. First, the agents' experiences were atypical. Since they had greater access to capital in 1835 and 1836, most agents were far more overextended than the normal western debtor. Second, Bronson's agents clearly were responsible for their own mistakes. They had exercised no restraint during the boom years of 1835 and 1836, despite Bronson's advice and example; therefore, they should have expected to suffer the consequences of their bad judgment. Third, it must be remembered that changing financial conditions also affected Bronson. He owned land and held morgages in at least six states. These business interests required constant supervision and the expenditure of capital for improvements and taxes and therefore limited Bronson's options in dealing with individual debtors. In drawing outlines of a utopian world, a scenario might find Bronson unilaterally freeing all his debtors and leasing land to them at minimal fees, but such action was neither sensible nor expected by farmers and city residents. Instead, Bronson introduced policies which would soften the depression's certain impact on his land and mortgage business.

Despite the constraints of Bronson's business situation, his western policies often had a positive effect on western communities. Bronson did not seek to foreclose the outstanding mortgages of farmers and city residents. In fact, only a small minority of Bronson's debtors ever ended up in the courts, a step which Bronson took only as a last resort. Most often, he extended the debtor's period for payment because such action was beneficial to both parties, tending to stabilize property values and to keep the land under cultivation. Bronson wrote to one debtor in 1840 that "the times are very difficult, and it is my pleasure as well as my duty to give indulgence, and I would not order you to sell at a sacrifice to pay me now. I prefer you should keep the property and I will make the payments easy."[59] To another debtor, he made the principle more explicit: "If you pay the interest punctually, you may, and you must rely on my indulgence as to the installment of principal, so long as the security continued sufficient all I want is, interest punctually, and to feel that the principal is secure . . . ."[60]

Besides his willingness to extend the time for repayment, the New Yorker also provided other services to western communities. He continued to lend money, although on a highly selective basis, to farmers and city residents. Interest rates reflected the troubled times and ran to twelve percent; similarly he required that the collateral should be triple the face value of the note.[61] Bronson also made efforts to maintain his relationships with important businessmen. He extended Charles Butler's notes and accepted the bonds of Detroit and Chicago entrepreneurs. For a good part of the depression, therefore, Bronson buttressed the fragile credit structure between East and West.

Yet Bronson also had a breaking point. He could not, in his mind, continue investments or the support of debtors beyond the point where their recovery was impossible. Thus Bronson decided to reduce some of his commitments to Cassville, Chicago, and Detroit citizens. He did not hesitate, moreover, to defend his financial interests when it appeared that westerners sought to escape their obligations. Bronson, therefore, responded to the depression in the expected role of the creditor, but that role was not that of the ogre as described by western agents. The New Yorker was certainly not a philanthropist, and he sometimes required an overly strict accounting from his debtors; yet, on balance, his business policies exhibited a more tolerant approach to the depression than historians typically have ascribed to absentee investors.

10. Arthur Bronson and the Defense of Property Rights

As demonstrated in the preceding two chapters, the depression of 1837 fostered an antagonistic relationship between the creditor and the debtor as each tried to inflict the depresssion's hardships on the other. Throughout the depression, therefore, Arthur Bronson's concern for the security of his western real estate and the sanctity of his contractual agreements with western citizens necessitated his vigilance over state laws, administrative practices, and court decisions. In protecting his interests, Bronson concentrated on two general areas. First, he monitored state laws relating to the assessment and the collection of taxes. Given the hostility of western citizens toward absentee ownership and the quantity of Bronson's holdings, slight alterations in the tax laws, which shifted the burden onto the absentee owner, could mean a substantial increase in taxes. Second, Bronson held hundreds of mortgages and therefore watched changes in mortgage law. Western legislatures often tried to ameliorate the depression's impact on their citizens by extending payment periods or by reducing the debt's face value. When the New Yorker decided that a western legislature had unfairly modified either tax or mortgage laws, he lobbied against such laws, drafted new legislation, or protested in the courts. Bronson's efforts generally helped to shape a favorable legal environment for capitalists. In one instance, Bronson's objections to an Illinois state law led to the United States Supreme Court case of *Bronson* v. *Kinzie* which set a precedent in contract law that lasted until 1934.

The tax systems of western states were often a source of difficulty for absentee landholders like Bronson. Although there were substantial variations from state to state, the typical tax system began with the local assessor who valued, or accepted the owner's valuation, of each tract.

After the completion of the assessment, citizens could object, in person, to the assessor. When the period for objections had passed, the tax list was considered final, and local officials—sheriff or township treasurer—collected the tax. The local official notified the taxpayer either through the newspaper or by posting public notices of the time and date for collection. If the taxes were not paid by a certain date, penalties were affixed ranging from 10 to 20 percent of the assessment. Usually after a year, each county compiled a list of lands on which taxes were delinquent, and then within three years the county auctioned the delinquent lands giving the purchaser a tax deed. After the sale, the original owner might still redeem his property for specified periods that ranged from six months to three years by paying the interest, penalty charge, and the original tax. In general, the laws favored the original property holder over the purchaser of a tax deed.[1]

At every step in this process there were dangers for the nonresident landholder. Taxes were collected in local districts—county, township, and city. If an eastern capitalist held land in more than one county, not to mention in several states, he had the arduous task of acquiring adequate information on tax levies. Each state differed as to the time of payment and the manner of collection. The easterner, thus, had to peruse many local newspapers in order to obtain notification of assessments. It was also difficult for an easterner to protest his taxes because laws required a personal appearance; this may explain why local assessors might have been tempted to place a higher value on nonresidents' lands. If the absentee owner missed the tax deadline,he then entered the even more confusing field of interest and penalty charges, tax sales, and redemption periods.

Besides the confusion inherent in the tax laws, the absentee landholder occasionally faced western officials who intended to defraud him. Arthur Bronson felt that the tax laws were unnecessarily biased against nonresidents, and warnings from his agents that local officials overassessed his lands reinforced these attitudes. In 1842 Edward Macy, a Michigan agent, alerted the New Yorker to the fact that "There is a set of sharpers about Marshall who live by extorting from nonresidents, and I have heard that they often remark that they would give much to get hold of Arthur Bronson's land, for they would fleece him without feeling."[2] William Thompson, who rode from county to county in Michigan paying the taxes of eastern capitalists, related the following conversation: "At one place I inquired of a man how the settlers got on, he said they had not raised anything much. I asked how they lived, 'o on nonresident taxes' he said."[3]

It would be misleading to leave the impression that absentee owners correctly perceived the intent of all western tax laws. Certainly there were laws and local officials that placed an unfair tax burden on out-of-state landowners, yet they were the exception rather than the rule. The western states needed capital during the depression, and it was to their advantage to develop an equitable tax system which produced revenue and encouraged continued investment. Indeed, Robert Swierenga's recent study of Iowa's tax policy in the mid-nineteenth century indicated that absentee lands were taxed higher, but only a "little higher." Swierenga thus questioned the common assumptions of absentee owners at the time and of later historians that western states routinely subjected nonresidents to unfair tax levies.[4]

Whatever the intent of the western states might have been, the variety of tax laws from state to state, the confusion inherent in such laws, and the fear that states were hostile to nonresidents forced most absentee capitalists to depend on the increasing number of land agencies to care for their tax obligations in the late 1830s. After 1837, Bronson terminated agreements with his independent agents and concentrated his business in a few centrally–located land agencies. In Michigan, he worked with Edward Macy's Michigan Land Agency at Kalamazoo and with George Bates of the Detroit law firm of Bates and Talbot. William B. Ogden's Chicago firm handled the majority of the New Yorker's land business in Illinois and in the Wisconsin Territory. These land agencies provided specialized services such as monitoring local and state tax assessments, paying taxes in individual counties, protesting unfair levies, and redeeming lands which might have been mistakenly sold for back taxes. Throughout the late 1830s and early 1840s, Bronson's correspondence with these agencies was primarily concerned with taxes.[5]

Bronson, though, never lapsed in his personal vigilance of state laws. The New Yorker meticulously read local papers because they carried news of recent legislation and local assessments. He inundated his agents with instructions on how to pay taxes and when to protest unfair levies. If required by circumstances, the New Yorker wrote to state legislative committees or state officials to protect his interests. Bronson's active role was particularly obvious in Michigan where tax laws changed almost every year. In 1837, Bronson worked through members of the state legislature and Governor Stephen T. Mason to obtain a provision in the Michigan tax law which required that the assessment rolls distinguish between resident and nonresident lands and that the names of owners, whenever possible, accompany the land's description. This clause simplified the absentee landholder's identification of his tax obligation.[6]

In 1842, Bronson balked when Michigan changed its laws and required taxes to be paid in each township and county promptly after the assessment, instead of the earlier practice which had allowed taxes to be paid at the Auditor General's Office in Detroit any time within the tax year. The new law also increased the penalties for delinquent taxes; if the tax were not paid promptly at the township level, the taxpayer was penalized 10 percent of the assessment. If the tax were not paid after approximately six months, interest on the tax liability accumulated at an annual rate of 50 percent.[7] Such a drastic alteration, which increased the penalties for nonpayment while complicating the collection procedure, naturally struck the New Yorker as anti-capitalist. Indeed, Bronson's agents had to spend considerable time traveling from county to county checking on assessments and paying taxes. Bronson wasted no time, therefore, in alerting state lawmakers to the unnecessary hardships which the law imposed on absentee owners. Charles Butler personally presented Bronson's case to the Michigan legislature in early 1843. These efforts produced several changes. In 1843, new legislation reduced the penalty for non-payment at the local level to 5 percent while the annual interest rate on delinquent taxes was set at 15 percent. Nonresident capitalists could again pay their taxes at the Auditor General's Office in Detroit, although they still faced the 5 percent penalty. Even though Bronson did not obtain all the desired changes, his attention to detail had succeeded in softening the law's harshest provisions.[8]

Bronson was also concerned with tax laws in Illinois. Illinois taxes were collected in each county, requiring the absentee landholder or his agent to watch the newspapers and public announcements in every county and to travel there to pay the tax. Bronson complained that local officials overvalued nonresidents' lands, maintained poor records, and spent taxes for frivolous items. He maintained a steady correspondence with members of the Illinois legislature concerning these laws. In 1841, for example, he presented the nonresidents' viewpoint to the Illinois legislature's committee on finance:

> . . . The interest of the nonresident land holders should be as fairly and fully respected, as those of resident proprietors, and also that facilities should be furnished to enable them to ascertain the amount of their taxes, and the place of payment, which, I think, should be at one place, instead of compelling the nonresident to apply to the officers of the counties, whose inattention and inaptitude to business, almost always causes great delays and mistakes, by which the interests of the nonresident who pays, and the State who receives, are both, not infrequently, the innocent sufferers.[9]

In Wisconsin, Arthur and Frederic Bronson wrote to James Duane Doty, the territorial governor, asking him to urge the territorial legislature to draft tax laws friendly to eastern capitalists. Again the Bronsons attacked the existing system where taxes were collected in each county because ". . . the receipts of the county offices are so vague and indefinite and their contracts so slovenly kept that very imperfect records of the payments of taxes are . . . furnished."[10] The Bronsons were also disturbed by the territory's practice of taxing land before the purchaser had received a final patent from the federal government. Arthur Bronson suggested legislation, but he acknowledged that further effort was senseless because of ". . . the prejudices of 'the people' against nonresident landholders . . . ."[11] Bronson's frustration was unwarranted because Doty and other western citizens were sensitive to grossly unfair tax laws. In December 1841, for example, Doty urged the legislature to act on tax reforms because ". . . the system of taxation throughout the Territory is considered unequal, illegal and highly oppressive."[12] Doty specifically mentioned the need to change the laws which brought about unequal taxation of nonresident lands.[13]

Bronson also affected western laws relating to tax sales. Such sales were common throughout the Old Northwest as the depression dragged on and farmers, speculators, and merchants were unable to pay their yearly tax bills.[14] The tax sale was the state's ultimate recourse. Typically sales were conducted a year or more after the land was publicly listed as delinquent, and usually there was an auction in which the highest bidder acquired a tax title.[15]

Frontier historians have disagreed about the purpose and effect of tax sales. One view has maintained that speculators used tax sales as a means of acquiring lands at low prices—the amount of the delinquent tax. A Chicago merchant in 1838 described the advantages of these purchases:

> If a man had the cash and I was disposed to speculate in that way he might make many excellent bargains at sheriff's sale—and the fact is at private sales also . . . . I should deem it a very safe kind of speculation for in most instances I do not believe that the lands so sold will be redeemed because the owner will not have the means of raising the money when all their property is sold and encumbered, unless they should have *mighty, mighty* good friends.[16]

Tax sales also attracted many other purchasers besides speculators. Some farmers and town residents took advantage of the opportunity to acquire additional acreage, particularly the lands of absentee owners unaware of the tax or unable to maintain the title. Moreover, Robert Swierenga's recent study of tax sales in Iowa indicated that such sales became elaborate money-lending systems in which the tax buyer paid the taxes on land to protect a farmers title for two or three years until the original owner could redeem the acreage and repay the tax purchaser. Swierenga discovered that quite frequently the tax buyer was not interested in obtaining the land but rather in lending money at interest.[17]

Arthur Bronson, however, generally avoided tax sales. In the early 1840s, he was reducing his holdings in western real estate. Moreover, the New Yorker did not like "speculative" investments in which he gambled on gaining title. He knew that the courts protected the land's original owner and routinely abrogated tax titles for minor errors in administrative procedure.[18]

Bronson actually considered tax sales a threat to his existing land titles. He often discovered that his lands had been advertised as tax delinquent or had even been sold as a result of the confusing tax systems of the western states.[19] In order to redeem land before or after these sales, Bronson usually incurred many additonal expenses, especially for agents' and lawyers' fees. Consequently, he maintained a close watch on each state's legislation. In 1840, he wrote to Michigan's auditor general arguing that the tax sale procedure was unjust because county officials who listed and sold delinquent properties could benefit directly from the sale. In some cases, Bronson claimed that county officials were in collusion with the tax buyers or purchased the land for their own use. Thus he suggested that the state auditor should advertise all delinquent lands through a central source and conduct all sales at Detroit to reduce the opportunity for fraud and to protect the interest of outside capitalists. Although it would be impossible to assess Bronson's influence on the change, Michigan's tax law in 1842 stipulated that the auditor general should compile the list of all tax delinquent properties in the state.[20]

Arthur Bronson and his brother Frederic corresponded with Governor James Doty concerning similar problems in the Wisconsin Territory. They told the Governor that county officials often conducted tax sales without giving adequate notification to nonresidents. Arthur Bronson was especially upset by a territorial law which allowed only two years to redeem land sold for taxes. In a petition which asked Congress to set aside the territorial law, Bronson and other eastern financiers pointed out that the statute of limitations on most other deeds ran for twenty years. The New Yorkers argued that the law was unjust to both absentee property owners and to small farmers who, through their own neglect, the mistakes of county officials, or the fraudulent design of tax speculators, might lose their land titles.[21] Bronson's protest typified his efforts to present the easterner's viewpoint at state and national levels.

Although Bronson's influence on western laws related to tax sales is difficult to evaluate, his efforts in protecting the mortgagees legal rights had verifiable results. Under most state laws, taxes were levied on land, but no effort was made to identify the property's real owner. It was possible for land to be sold for taxes even when that land previously had been mortgaged to a nonresident either as security for payment on the land or as security for another debt. The state was under no obligation and had no way of knowing or notifying the mortgagee. If a local farmer did not pay his taxes, he might very well be risking the title of the mortgagee. To prevent this occurrence, Bronson supported two pieces of legislation at the state level. In the first, he drafted a bill providing that mortgages or title changes executed out of state would be recognized and recorded in the state in which the land was located. This law covered the innumerable cases in which Bronson sold Illinois and Michigan lands or executed a mortgage in New York State with Michigan and Illinois lands as security. With the transaction formally recorded in the appropriate western jurisdiction and Bronson clearly listed as the mortgagee, he would have an easier task of presenting his claim before or after a tax sale. Bronson sent the proposed bill to his contacts in the Illinois, Wisconsin, and Michigan legislatures. Michigan adopted Bronson's law in 1840; Illinois passed a law with almost verbatim wording of Bronson's original proposal in 1841; and the Wisconsin Territory enacted similar legislation in 1842.[22]

Bronson also wanted states to recognize their responsibility for protecting the mortgagee's rights by passing a law requiring the purchaser of a tax title to notify the holder of a mortgage on that property. New York State had passed such a law in 1840, and when it was threatened with repeal a year later, Bronson lobbied against the repeal. His arguments in this case were cogent and illustrative of his concern with state legislation. Bronson contended first that "any law which increases the security of the money lender facilitates the borrower in obtaining credit, and diminishes the rate of interest which he is obligated to pay."[23] With equal conviction, Bronson warned that "If the law affords no security to the lender—instead of lending he will hoard his capital or expend it for actual necessaries & withold it from the aid of the enterprising or necessitous borrower."[24] To support his argument, Bronson presented a horror story of debtor frauds in the absence of such laws. In one case, Bronson explained, a New York capitalist loaned $8,000 taking land as security and later learned that the land had been sold for $25 to cover a tax debt. In many instances, Bronson claimed, debtors and tax purchasers were in collusion to defraud the creditors.[25] In addition to his concern with the New York law, Bronson drafted similar legislation and sent it to his political contacts in Michigan, Illinois, and Wisconsin. In this case, however, he was unable to convince western legislators that the law was appropriate.[26]

Bronson's involvement in the tax and mortgage laws of western states, then, demonstrated several important themes. First, Bronson was always the advocate of the large absentee landholder, and his position understandably restricted his perception of the problems peculiar to local farmers and debtors. For example, Bronson's request that the states designate a central location for tax collection and tax sales eased his administrative tasks of supervising thousands of acres, yet this procedure would have complicated tax payment and collection for local citizens. Second, despite the limitations of his viewpoint, Bronson presented an important perspective to western legislators who were naturally more conversant with local needs. Without capitalists like Bronson who constantly suggested improvements in the tax laws, western lawmakers might well have prevented the movement of eastern and foreign capital into the agricultural sector. Third, this investigation of tax and mortgage laws indicated that Bronson had substantial influence, but little real control, over the western laws and lawmakers. He wrote letters, drafted legislation, and lobbied with legislative members and executive officials, but he only occasionally obtained new laws or changed existing ones. More often than not, Bronson's influence was subtle because it forced westerners to at least consider the impact of their actions on absentee landholders.

Bronson also watched western states closely as they considered legislation to alter the terms of existing mortgages among creditors and debtors. State and federal governments had to explore methods for lowering, delaying, or extinguishing debts because farmers, merchants, speculators—and even state governments—had so extended their credit that full payment was impossible. If no relaxation of these obligations occurred, then the depression's effects might last for generations. Yet if the state or federal government abolished or reduced debts without regard for the creditors' rights, it might destroy the business environment that would stimulate investment and recovery.

State and federal governments considered several alternatives in responding to the debt problem. In 1837, the federal government began discussion on a national bankruptcy statute, but the political and economic opposition delayed passage for years, and although a law was finally approved in 1841, it was subsequently repealed.[27] Without federal bankruptcy laws, it was not surprising that individuals discussed the option of repudiation, that is, simply refusing to pay an existing debt. Often angry farmers and town residents held mass meetings to demand the closing of courts, debt reductions, or repudiation. One such meeting in Chicago in 1837 was defused by William B. Ogden who argued for public and personal honesty in acknowledging debts.[28] Responding to popular pressure, state governments did pass stay and relief laws. These laws, which had been used in the 1819 depression, gave debtors extra time to pay, delayed court sessions thereby preventing foreclosure sales, and lengthened the redemption time for a debtor to regain property lost through a forced sale. The laws hurt the creditor by altering the terms of existing contracts, and thus their constitutionality was the subject of endless discussion and litigation.[29]

Bronson sought to protect his property and mortgage contracts from stay and relief laws. He lobbied against an 1840 Michigan law which allowed two years for debtors to redeem land already foreclosed as payment for a bond or mortgage.[30] Although Bronson was not adverse to granting extended periods for payment, he believed that a foreclosure should be the irrevocable last step in the process of clearing a debt. If the debtor could still redeem his land after the foreclosure, Bronson argued, then the creditor lost the use of the property plus interest. Bronson's view respresented the capitalist's standard definition of a contract. If A agreed to pay B, then he must pay. If unable to do so, then he must allow the creditor to seek his remedy under the contract, that is, to recover the property offered as security. The creditor, at his discretion, could extend the grace period, but individuals still had to fulfill the bargain. Bronson believed that the developing economic system of nineteenth–century America rested on the fulfillment of these simple principles of the contract.[31]

Bronson's insistence on defending creditor rights was most evident in his challenge of the constitutionality of state appraisal laws. Western states routinely passed such laws to meet the needs of farmers and town residents who had purchased property on time or borrowed money using land as security. Because of the depression, westerners were unable to pay these obligations, and creditors thus foreclosed taking the propety or selling it for cash to cancel the debt. Because of the deflated specie and property values, land and personal possessions often returned a paltry sum when sold at auction. A Michigan legislator recounted in 1841 that a yoke of oxen sold for just nine dollars.[32] Consequently, low prices forced farmers to sacrifice more and more property to pay their debts. Western legislators understandably searched for a way to prevent property sales at low prices. Appraisal laws required that property sold at auction must reach a price representing two-thirds of the property's value as determined by local citizens. In theory, local citizens would tend to disregard the land's deflated value and appraise it very high, thereby protecting their fellow citizens from the auctioneer's block. Bronson's Michigan agent explained the rationale for such legislation by observing that "when there is not some mode of relief, the debtor states whenever in trouble will resort to special legislation for the benefit of their own people."[33]

Appraisal laws were passed in Michigan and Illinois in 1841. The Illinois law provided that no real or personal property could be sold to pay overdue debts unless it was sold for two-thirds of its "cash value" as judged by three householders of the county. Moreover, the statute was applied retroactively to all contracts signed before May 1841. Another law, passed at the same time and also retroactive, allowed debtors fifteen months to regain property sold at auction, even though mortgages generally had no provisions for redemption.[34] Michigan's law required an appraisal of foreclosed property by "disinterested freeholders" at "the actual cash value" at the time of the appraisal. If the property did not receive a bid of at least two-thirds of the appraisal, then it could not be sold. The debt still existed, but the creditor had no way to collect, that is, to obtain the remedy of the contract. A year later, Michigan amended the law so that the appraised value was "the true value" rather than the "actual cash value" thereby avoiding any misunderstanding about the law's intent to prevent auction sales at low prices. If the creditor refused to accept the appraisal, he still had to pay local officials for the cost of the appraisal.[35] This provision was probably intended to discourage the creditor from pressing the courts to take action.

The laws worked to the debtor's advantage in two ways. First, the appraisal provision of the law altered existing contracts between the creditor and the debtor. The creditor was forced to accept an appraisal primarily conducted by local citizens and presumably favorable to the debtor. If the appraisal was set too high, the land would not be sold, thereby delaying the foreclosure and, more than likely, frustrating the creditor's efforts to gain title. This was not an unlikely possiblity during the depression since money was scarce throughout the West. The debtor, of course, maintained the title and possession of the land if no bid equalled the appraised value. Thus the appraisal laws delayed the contract's execution and gave the debtor additional time to raise the money.

The laws also worked to the debtor's advantage by opening the possibility that the creditor would have to take lands, arbitrarily valued high, to cancel a specie debt. A creditor, for example, might foreclose on a debtor who owed $10,000 in specie and attach all his available property intending to sell whatever amount necessary to regain his $10,000. Yet the appraisals set on the property might bear little relation to the land's market value and thus prevent any sale. At this point, the creditor would be forced to take the land as settlement for the specie debt even though that land might represent no more than $1,000 in real market value. In this case, debtors would flock to the courts to exchange their worthless lands for cancellation of their specie debts.[36]

Arthur Bronson believed that the appraisal laws tipped the legal balance too heavily in the debtor's favor. According to Bronson, capitalists would either charge very high interest rates or simply not lend money in states where such laws existed. The Illinois law, which made the legislation retroactive, particularly angered Bronson. (Of course, the laws made little sense if applied other than retroactively, because they were intended to relieve the existing burden of debt.)[37] It was one thing, Bronson reasoned, to draft legislation of which all persons concerned were aware when they entered a contract, but it was quite another law which altered the terms of existing contracts. I suspect that Bronson would have reacted with less anger to a simple moratorium on all debts for five years knowing that, at the end of the period, his rights would still exist. But retroactive laws meant that his rights might be abrogated.

Bronson decided to challenge Illinois' appraisal law, partly on the advice of Roger M. Sherman, the family's long-time friend and lawyer. Sherman instructed the New Yorker that states could alter the contract's remedy, that is, the contract's provisions regulating the method of fore-closure or the length of time available for redemption, but Sherman also said that the legal precedents were unclear as to how far the state might go in such actions. Yet Sherman left little doubt that the appraisal laws were unconstitutional when applied to existing contracts, for they violated the contract clause of the Constitution which forbade states from impairing the obligation of a contract. The contract's obligation, Sherman ex-plained, "consists in the legal power of enforcing it, which existed at the time of its formation."[38] He therefore advised Bronson to seek redress through the federal courts, a recommendation which Bronson followed.

Bronson's decision to go to court was also the result of personal chal-lenges from his own debtors who sought to use the appraisal laws against him. In particular, Bronson proceeded against Chicagoan John Kinzie who earlier had cooperated with Bronson and Charles Butler in the promotion of the city's North Side. In 1838, Bronson lent Kinzie four thousand dollars so that Kinzie could save property from another creditor who threatened to foreclose. Bronson required two lots in Chicago plus Kinzie's half interest in a failing hotel as collateral. Kinzie was also to pay an annual interest of 12 percent and repay the principal by January 1842. If he defaulted, Kinzie agreed that Bronson could sell the collateral at a strict foreclosure—an auction sale to the highest bidder without any possibility of redemption.[39] One loan proved insufficient, and Kinzie again borrowed from Bronson in 1839. By 1840, the Chicagoan was unable to make his interest payments. With his business interests on Chicago's North Side in trouble and land values declining, Kinzie re-quested extensions of time, which Bronson granted on pledges of addi-tional security. Kinzie also sought additional employment as the Register of the Chicago Land Office. Yet the Chicagoan was never an impov-erished debtor, one step away from penury, as suggested by more than one legal historian; he was instead an important Chicago businessman who possessed substantial financial resources searching for any available means to delay or postpone his creditors.[40]

The conflict between Bronson and Kinzie began in February 1841. At that time, Kinzie knew that he could not repay the four-thousand-dollar note, and he requested Bronson to foreclose. In March, Bronson asked for a bill of foreclosure from the United States Circuit Court at Springfield, Illinois. Since Kinzie did not contest the action, the Court ordered him immediately to pay the outstanding debt or allow the security to be sold at a public auction. Shortly thereafter, Kinzie learned of the Illinois legislature's passage of an appraisal law and a law extending the time a debtor might redeem property after a foreclosure sale. In December 1841, Kinzie reapplied to the Circuit Court asking that the former order be set aside and that his property be sold under the terms of the recently passed appraisal laws. After Bronson's attorney opposed Kinzie's request, the court split over whether to sell the property under the terms of the original contract or under the provisions of the Illinois laws. Consequently, the case was referred to the United States Supreme court for adjudication.[41]

Although Kinzie and Bronson had remained friends throughout most of 1840 and 1841, their relationship changed after Kinzie used the appraisal laws. Bronson, I believe, was genuinely nonplussed and delayed the legal proceedings in order to discuss the issue with Kinzie. Bronson argued that his contract was fair since he had lent specie when it was in short supply, taking land in return even though it was decreasing in value. Moreover, he had submitted the bill of foreclosure upon Kinzie's request as a means of clearing part of his debts and of avoiding any further interest charges. To demonstrate his good faith, Bronson offered to further extend Kinzie's note, but the Chicagoan refused, preferring instead a foreclosure under the new Illinois laws.[42]

Kinzie stood to benefit from the new law in several ways. Since the law required three residents of the county to appraise the security, Kinzie was gambling that the appraisal would reflect pre-1842 values. If the appraisal were set high, it would more than likely delay any sale and force Bronson to wait indefinitely for settlement of the contract. If, on the other hand, Bronson accepted a high appraisal and took the land to wipe out Kinzie's debt, he would have cancelled a specie debt for a fraction of its real value. If, in the unlikely case that someone else purchased the property, then the money went first to satisfy Bronson's claim and the remainder to Kinzie.[43] In any of the possible results, Kinzie stood to suffer the least damage. The appraisal law, then, had transferred the onus of the depression from Kinzie to Bronson. Both men understood this fact. In 1842, Bronson expressed his disgust with Kinzie's tactics in the following manner:

As I have frequently declared, so do I now repeat . . . that my wish, is not to possess myself of any portion of the property mortgaged to me—far from it—but the restitution of my money—my own property—which in reliance on your solemn promise, and pledge to restore to me, I let go out of my possession, and into your own, for a definite period fixed by yourself, and which has long since expired. If it is your design, to endeavor to compel me to take that which I did not lend, I do not want, instead of money, I mean *Real Estate*, and at a valuation to be *made by others*, you will find yourself signally defeated . . . .[44]

The case of *Bronson* v. *Kinzie* came before the Supreme Court in January 1843, but, despite its importance, it was curiously handled. There were no oral arguments by either lawyer and only one brief, that from Bronson's attorney, Isaac Arnold of Chicago. Bronson's selection of Arnold as his lawyer was a bit surprising since he was only thirty years old and only a resident of Chicago since 1836. Yet Arnold already had represented William B. Ogden and the American Land Company, and he had presented Bronson's case against the appraisal laws before the Circuit Court. In the early 1840s, moreover, Arnold was known as a staunch defender of creditor rights.[45]

In his brief presented to the Supreme Court, Arnold fashioned a classic argument defending the rights of creditors under the law. He first argued that the Illinois laws were a violation of Article 1, Section 10, of the Constitution which forbade any state to impair the obligation of a contract. Since Bronson and Kinzie had signed their contract prior to 1841, Arnold claimed that they were bound only by laws in effect at that time. The power to sell the mortgaged premises, Arnold further explained, was an essential part of the contract even though the action represented only its remedy, that is, the method of payment or the means of fulfilling the contract. Bronson considered it so important, according to Arnold, that he had specifically written it into the contract. Thus Arnold summarized the point by claiming that "The contract gave to the mortgagee a right to sell, and the statute cut down that power and crippled it. The obligation of the contract was a right of payment, and *to the then established means to enforce payment,* and all this the mortgagor had himself granted to the mortgagee, and the statute intervenes and enfeebles that right, and consequently greatly impairs it."[46]

Moving beyond the question of constitutionality, Arnold asked the Court to consider the effects of such valuation laws on the whole economic system. Financiers would simply refuse to invest their capital, Arnold explained, if such laws could be legislated whenever there were fluctuations in the economy. Thus Arnold petitioned the Court not only to reject retroactive legislation, but also to prohibit all laws which unnecessarily interfered with contracts between individuals. He sketched a gloomy picture of the economic world if the justices supported Kinzie:

> By sustaining appraisal laws, as well as any other law impairing the obligation of contracts, trade is crippled, and credit is destroyed, and all commercial intercourse suspended. The eastern creditor, although abundantly able to meet his own obligations, may be sacrificed by this unjust and unconstitutional legislation, and bankrupted, and ruined, though in point of fact he may be himself a debtor with abundant resources, suspended, and rendered unavailable, if not annihilated by the operation of these laws.[47]

Bronson v. *Kinzie* was not the first time that the Supreme Court had debated the issues of a state's right to alter a contract. In *Fletcher* v. *Peck* and in the Dartmouth College case, the Marshall Court had strictly prohibited the state from altering any contract whether between individuals or between the state and a corporation. But later the Court assumed the responsibility for erecting the legal framework of a market system, and it slowly delineated the rights of both the creditor and the debtor before the law. In 1819, for example, Chief Justice John Marshall had invalidated a New York law which granted citizens relief from debts contracted before the law's passage. Although Marshall ruled that the law was unconstitutional because it was retroactive, he acknowledged that the state could enact some laws to assist debtors. Yet Marshall so narrowly defined the scope of such laws that merely extending a contract's date of payment appeared to be illegal. In 1827, however, the Court went further in the *Ogden* v. *Saunders* decision and allowed a state to make several alterations in a contract, such as extending the time for payment, so long as the law applied to future contracts and did not affect the contract's essential obligation.[48]

Roger B. Taney carried on the Supreme Court's slow and conservative elaboration of creditor-debtor relationships after his appointment as chief justice by Andrew Jackson.[49] In *Bronson* v. *Kinzie,* Taney followed the Court's tendency to strike what it considered a proper balance between the rights of creditors and debtors. Taney pointed out that the obligation of the contract between Bronson and Kinzie depended upon the Illinois laws at the time of the contract's signing. If the Illinois statutes subsequently passed did not seriously alter the contract's obligation, Taney argued, then the laws were constitutional. If they impaired the contract's obligation, then they were unconstitutional. Taney thus reiterated and strengthened previous Court decisions which recognized that a "state may regulate at pleasure the modes of proceeding in its courts in relation to past contracts as well as future."[50] Such action, Taney said, might include an extension of time for the debt to be paid or the exclusion of certain personal items from a creditor's remedy. Taney, then, summarized the Court's view of the state's role in balancing the interests of creditors and debtors:

> Regulations of this description have always been considered, in every civilized community, as properly belonging to the remedy, to be exercised or not by every sovereignty according to its own views of policy and humanity. It must reside in every State to enable it to secure its citizens from unjust and harassing litigation, and to protect them in these pursuits which are necessary to the existence and well-being of every community. And, although a new remedy may be deemed less convenient than the old one, and may in some degree render the recovery of debts more tardy and difficult, yet it will not follow that the law is unconstitutional.[51]

But having given the state a wide field in which to maneuver and protect its citizens, Taney contended that certain laws affected both the contract's obligation and its remedy, thereby denying the rights of the creditor. Taney set out a rule of reason that "whatever belongs merely to the remedy may be altered according the the will of the State, provided the alteration does not impair the obligation of the contract."[52] Accepting in general the reasoning of Arnold's brief, Taney held that the Illinois laws impaired Bronson's rights and therefore were unconstitutional. The first law, which added a redemption period of twelve months after a foreclosure sale, was unconstitutional because it attached new conditions to the *existing* mortgage and extended Kinzie's interest in the property. Taney nullified the second law, which prohibited foreclosure sales at less than two–thirds of the property's value, because it so affected the contract's remedy that Bronson was unable to recover his property. Yet Taney also stated that the Illinois laws were binding on future contracts because the parties would be aware of the law's restrictions.[53]

Justice McLean, in whose circuit the case had originated, issued the lone dissenting opinion. His argument was not convincing, for he believed that the state could alter a contract almost without restriction. He thus refused to accept either the concept of the creditor's rights or the idea that state legislation could affect the value of existing contracts. Perhaps, as one historian suggested, McLean was thinking less about legal issues and more about his presidential aspirations.[54]

The decision drew predictable responses from the involved individuals and the public. Debtors were appalled while financiers approved of the Court's action. The Whig press, in particular the *Washington Daily National*

Intelligencer, praised the sagacity of Taney's opinion. Bronson, of course, was overjoyed because he had won a very personal fight and also had established a valuable rule for the business community. After the decision, the New Yorker paid Arnold's fee of $150, adding a bonus of $500. Moreover, he financed the publication of Arnold's brief and sent him a personal copy bound in leather with elaborate ornamentation.[55]

The *Bronson* v. *Kinzie* case, therefore, enlarges our perspective both on creditor-debtor relations and on the interplay of law and economic development in the antebellum period. Neither Bronson's actions nor the Supreme Court's decision was a victory of rich over poor or creditor over debtor. Bronson, of course, had used the Court to protect his own financial interests, yet he also believed that appraisal laws endangered the sanctity of all contracts between individuals. In fact, Kinzie had attempted to use the appraisal laws to avoid his obligations to Bronson, and thus the Court's decision in this case was unquestionably just. More important, though, this case represented the Court's effort to adjust the legal mechanisms of a developing business sytem so that it could function. State laws protecting debtors had reached beyond what the Court considered a safe limit and threatened to disrupt and to stifle the investment of capital. Eastern financiers, as well as western entrepreneurs, would have hesitated to invest in Illinois if such laws continued to exist. In fact, Bronson placed very little capital in Illinois, the Wisconsin Territory, and Michigan after 1843 because he distrusted the laws regulating mortgages.[56] Even though the Court clearly favored the business viewpoint in this instance, it did not accept Bronson's unlimited definition of creditor rights—that the state could not regulate any private contracts. Taney allowed states to adjust contracts within reason, and he put the burden on the states to draft legislation which ensured the debtor's access to temporary relief while simultaneously protecting the financier's incentives for capital investment.[57] Taney's decision stood essentially unchanged until 1934 when the demands of an industrialized society and altered concepts of social justice impelled the Court to allow the states more latitude in altering contracts.[58]

Throughout the depression, therefore, Bronson had devoted considerable energies to supervising the actions of several states in laws relating to property. He lobbied with politicians, suggested legislation, and eventually challenged the constitutionality of certain laws. His performance again supports the contention that eastern capitalists exerted a substantial, if not always direct, influence on the West's economic growth.

11. Eastern Capitalists and State Debts

The depression not only produced thousands of individual financial failures, but it also threatened to bankrupt many American states over-committed to the building of railroads and canals. In their scramble to escape from debt, states often reacted like individuals and sought to postpone, reduce, or repudiate their obligations. Throughout this period, Arthur Bronson and Charles Butler represented the interests of creditors particularly the American and foreign bondholders, in attempting to influence, bargain with, and force American states to respect their contracts. Arthur Bronson was the principal intermediary in the early discussions between the English bondholders and the state of Illinois, while in Indiana and Michigan, Charles Butler served as the bondholders' agent. Butler and Bronson, of course, assisted the bondholders in order to protect their own financial interests, yet their efforts substantially affected the course of economic development in several western states.

State debts resulted from the speculative boom which spawned grandiose internal improvements in most states of the Old Northwest. Because western states lacked private capital for the building of railroads and canals, each state government borrowed the funds by issuing bonds and by pledging the state's credit to their repayment. The bonds were sold either to eastern and foreign investors directly or, more often, to financial institutions such as the Morris Canal and Banking Company, the United States Bank in Philadelphia, and the North American Trust and Banking Company. These companies, in turn, resold the bonds to eastern and foreign capitalists.

These arrangements were inherently unstable because state legislatures had approved many projects which were impractical and wasteful. Such actions resulted from the naive but pervasive feeling that the success

202

of the proposed projects was assured. The state of Michigan, for example, launched an internal improvements program in 1837 which called for several canals and three railroads. One railroad, the northern route, was projected to traverse the state from Port Huron through an area of little population and no trade to a point on Lake Michigan near Grand Rapids. When the depression struck, each state lost the tax revenues needed to support continued construction and to pay the interest on the bonds. States also had pledged railroad and canal revenues for repayment of the bond's principal. When construction stopped, there was no possibility of acquiring sufficient funds to pay these immense debts. Indiana was responsible for $15 million, Illinois for nearly the same amount, and Michigan owed $5 million. With interest on the bonds accumulating every year, each state confronted a problem not unlike that faced by individual debtors: whom to pay, when, and how much?[1]

States considered several alternatives in an effort to meet their obligations. Even though state governments realized that the Constitution prevented foreign bondholders from suing for their money in American courts, most states rejected repudiation as an acceptable alternative. The rationale was simple: repudiation, like bankruptcy, would have destroyed a state's credit and would have made the obtaining of new loans impossible.[2] On the other hand, none of the state's concerned—Indiana, Illinois, and Michigan—seriously considered a full, on-time payment to the bondholders. Instead, each state sought either to reduce the principal and interest, to delay payment, or to change the terms of the contract. For a brief period, states even hoped that the federal government would assume their debts on the model of Alexander Hamilton's assumption plan in the 1790s. A committee of the House of Representatives actually recommended this action in the early 1840s, but states which had no outstanding debts quashed the proposal.[3] Each state was thus left to bargain with its creditors. Similar to the negotiations between western citizens and eastern capitalists, the states sought to force the bondholders to assume part of the financial burden caused by the depression.

Neither contemporaries nor later historians were neutral in their analysis of state actions. Most interpretations have argued the pro-creditor position—that each state owed to the bondholders exactly the sum borrowed. Any attempts to reduce the amount or delay its payment was interpreted as repudiation and an indication of bad faith.[4]

Yet any analysis totally blaming the states for attempting to escape their debts fails to reflect a full understanding of the dynamics of the period. In fact, all of the parties to the contracts were at fault, and each should have expected to bear part of the hardship. Entrepreneurs within the states, such as Charles Trowbridge and Elon Farnsworth in Michigan, were responsible for pushing the state into an impossible program of economic development. State legislators, who bowed to promotional sentiment and to the desire of every section within the state for improvement, shared the blame. Highly speculative eastern capitalists and foreign bondholders, such as the Morris Canal and Banking Company and the North American Trust and Banking Company, were also culpable. The North American Trust and Banking Company, for example, reflected the intersts of its board of directors, a board which included many entrepreneurs involved in banks, canals and railroads. Among these directors were Thomas W. Olcott, Gould Hoyt, Joseph Beers, and James B. Murray. These firms, however, did not dupe the leading financiers in England and on the Continent; Europeans purchased the stocks and bonds of American states fully aware that they carried the risk of failure.[5] The bondholders should have expected to suffer some ill effects from the depression since their capital had fueled the overzealous state projects of the 1830s. The struggle between the bondholders and the American states, then, should not be cast in moral terms; rather, it should be viewed as a necessary step in ameliorating the depression's impact on both creditors and debtors.

As a result of their financial alliances both East and West, Arthur Bronson and Charles Butler were principal actors in the negotiations between the bondholders and the western states. Bronson naturally was concerned with the debt question since western property values were related to state solvency; therefore, he wanted to influence both sides toward a settlement and consequently acted as a mediator between Illinois and its creditors. Moreover, he had close ties to the American firms which sold the bonds since his brother-in-law, James B. Murray, had been president of the Morris Canal and Banking Company at the time of the Michigan loan and an agent of the North American Trust and Banking Company in London from 1839 to 1841.[6] Butler, on the other hand, was a direct representative of the foreign bondholders. He first met important European capitalists during his trip to England and the Continent in 1838. Although the trip was primarily for his health, Butler also sold bonds for the state of Michigan.[7] In the 1840s, he was a logical choice to represent the bondholders since he possessed excellent contacts with western politicians and a reputation as a successful lobbyist stemming from his earlier work for the New York and Ohio trust companies.

Throughout the negotiations, Bronson and Butler represented the creditors' viewpoint: states should pay their whole debt, they reasoned, because strict observance of contractual obligations formed the basic underpinning of the entire economic system. If either party reneged on a contract, then economic exchanges would come to a standstill. Bronson also maintained that the state had a special responsibility to set an example and to preserve the public's faith in the state's credit. If the state refused to recognize its legal debts, Bronson said, then citizens might follow a similar course. "A government without integrity and good faith," Bronson wrote, "will create among the people, a disregard to law and justice, and propagate extravagance, discord, idleness and poverty."[8]

Arthur Bronson followed his economic principles in attempting to unravel Illinois' complex financial tangle. Illinois' problems began in 1835 when the legislature authorized the borrowing of a half-million dollars for the construction of the Illinois and Michigan Canal. The state issued bonds secured by canal revenues and the state's credit. In 1837, the legislature increased the state's financial liabilities when it passed an omnibus internal improvements bill for the construction of seven railroads and the navigational improvement of several rivers. The price tag was set at $8 million, a sum to be raised through bonds issued by the state.

Although New York banks had suspended specie payments in the spring of 1837, Illinois did not heed the warning and went ahead with its gargantuan program. It borrowed money in Europe and inaugurated the construction of several railroads. When the state ran short of funds in 1839, the legislature suspended work on most projects; yet few wished to stop work on the Illinois and Michigan Canal since it had been the first state improvement and had the greatest potential for producing revenue. By 1840, however, the state reached the breaking point. In that year, it borrowed funds in order to pay the interest on outstanding internal improvement bonds, and it sold state lands to pay the interest on the canal debt. Annual interest on the combined debts amounted to over a half-million dollars. The state then faced a financial crisis which posed two immediate questions: first, whether and how to pay the next year's interest; and second, whether to continue all the projected improvements.[9]

Bronson was well informed on Illinois' plight since his agents and friends were in key positions. William Ogden, for example, was a principal contractor on the Illinois and Michigan Canal, so he naturally lobbied for its continued construction. Throughout the early 1840s, Ogden continually alerted Bronson to the connection between Chicago land values and the canal, and on more than one occasion, he requested the New Yorker's aid in securing favorable legislation.[10] In 1841, for example, Ogden organized the canal contractors and requested that the state legislature provide funds, through a direct tax, to complete the canal. Bronson assisted this effort by writing a letter to the Illinois legislature's committee on finance, recommending a tax to avoid default on canal and internal improvement bonds. These lobbying efforts contributed to the passage of a law setting a tax of ten cents on each one hundred dollars of property in order to pay the state's indebtedness. But this law only guaranteed the payment of the existing debt and failed to provide money for the completion of the Illinois and Michigan Canal. Ogden attributed the failure to gain additional money for construction to "bad men and bad legislation."[11]

Despite the state's efforts in the 1841 legislative session, it was unable to prevent economic collapse. The state failed to meet its interest payments after July 1841, and shortly thereafter work stopped on the canal. Ogden attempted to enlist Bronson's aid in selling more bonds for construction, but no investors were interested in a bankrupt state government.[12] As of late 1841 then, Illinois had defaulted on its debts, thus halting work on all improvements and threatening property values throughout the state.

To protect his own economic interests, Bronson exerted considerable energy toward reestablishing Illinois' credit. In the summer of 1842, Arthur Bronson met with Chicagoans William B. Ogden, Justin Butterfield, and Isaac N. Arnold at the Lake House Hotel in Chicago in order to discuss plans for saving the Illinois and Michigan Canal.[13] They worked out a tentative proposal for the consideration of the Illinois legislature which they hoped would convince the canal's bondholders to supply additional capital for its completion. Bronson and his allies gambled that the bondholders would be receptive since they knew that their bonds would never be redeemed unless the canal was completed. In return for a loan of $1.6 million, the state was to entrust the canal and its adjacent lands to the bondholders as security. This plan also required the state to levy a tax if canal and state revenues were not sufficient to pay the bondholders. At the Chicago meeting, Bronson was selected to draft the final proposal and to gain the approval of the American and foreign bondholders. At the same time, Butterfield and Arnold, the two Chicago lawyers, were responsible for securing the support of key state legislators. They were joined in this endeavor by Michael Ryan, state senator from LaSalle County and chairman of an important committee on canals in the state legislature.[14]

Bronson assiduously worked on the preparation of the formal proposal and on securing the cooperation of domestic and foreign capitalists. He corresponded with Charles Macalester of Macalester and Stebbins of New York, a firm which had sold Illinois bonds to English investors. Writing from London, Macalester informed Bronson that "there appears to be a strong disposition here among some who are deeply interested in Illinois to assist her if it can be done safely."[15] Bronson also contacted John Horsley Palmer of the London banking house of Palmer, MacKillop, Dent and Company who strongly supported the move to save Illinois' credit. Yet Palmer refused to support any plan until Illinois took the first step. He suggested that the Governor of Illinois should open the legislature with a public statement indicating that the state intended to pay its debts. Palmer also stated that the foreign bondholders would insist that Illinois levy a tax in order to guarantee payment.[16]

After negotiating with the bondholders, Bronson finalized his plan and sent it to Michael Ryan, Justin Butterfield, and Isaac Arnold for their comments. In this draft, Bronson incorporated the suggestions of the bondholders. He urged that the governor should recommend to the state legislature that it adopt a solemn resolution acknowledging its debt. Bronson said that "this would seem to be an indispensable step preliminary to any effort at negotiation for further aid."[17] Bronson also called for a state property tax, independent of any existing taxes for operating expenses, for payment of the state's whole debt (estimated at $15 million) with a promise that the tax would not be reduced or repealed for several years.[18] Not all of Bronson's western associates agreed with these ideas. Justin Butterfield, who had been traveling throughout the northern and western parts of Illinois, doubted that citizens would consent to additional taxes even though they favored the canal's completion. But through further correspondence, Bronson, Butterfield and Arnold worked out minor differences, and by November 1842, the bill was ready for submission to the legislature.[19]

Bronson, Butterfield and Arnold had carefully prepared for the legislature's meeting in December. On November 28, Arnold delivered an address to the Mechanics Institute in Chicago on "The Legal and Moral Obligations of the State to Pay Her Debts" in which he described the bill and the state's moral responsibility to honor its obligations. The *Chicago Democrat* supported Arnold's position and confirmed that this plan had the support of influential easterners such as Arthur Bronson. Arnold, Ogden, and Bronson also had coached the state's new governor, Thomas Ford, for his opening address to the legislature in which he stressed the need for the canal's completion as a first step in restoring the state's credit. Moreover, Ford acknowledged the state's responsibility for its debts. In due course, Isaac Arnold, a member of the Illinois House of Representatives, introduced the bill into the legislature, and it was promptly referred to Michael Ryan's committee on canals.[20]

The legislature moved quickly to settle its debt problems. First, it passed emergency measures such as selling state land in order to obtain needed funds. Bondholders were allowed to cash in existing bonds and receive lands in return. The legislature also passed an act to guarantee the completion of the Illinois and Michigan Canal. This act incorporated most of Bronson's ideas: it authorized the governor to negotiate a loan for $1.6 million with the canal property and revenues offered as security; it ordered the canal to be placed in a trusteeship to be composed of two representatives of the bondholders and one appointed by the governor;

and it stipulated that the canal was to remain under this arrangement until the debts were paid. But the bill lacked a provision for a state tax in the event that money for repayment of the loan could not be raised in other ways.[21] When Bronson learned of the bill, he warned Governor Ford that it was "essentially defective" and predicted that the bondholders would refuse to lend the additional funds.[22]

Despite Bronson's warning, Governor Ford went ahead with the act's implementation. He appointed two Illinois residents, Michael Ryan and Charles Oakley, to bargain with the bondholders. Some disagreed with Oakley's appointment, feeling that the state should have selected Bronson because of his connections with the bondholders. Yet Oakley and Ryan at least consulted with Bronson in New York City. Bronson told them that the foreign capitalists would never accept the proposition, and he instructed the Illinois representatives to work for changes in the law. Even though Bronson preferred that the state levy a tax, he suggested a compromise whereby the state would assure that the subscribers to the second canal loan would receive their payments before anyone else. Bronson also insisted that the bondholders should be able to appoint agents to ascertain the real cost of completing the canal, to appraise the value of lands offered as security, and to appraise the value of canal sections already completed. When he could not get assurances that such changes would be considered, Bronson apparently refused to assist Illinois' agents in negotiating with the bondholders.[23]

Oakley and Ryan, therefore, bypassed Arthur Bronson; instead, they consulted first with David Leavitt, president of the American Exchange Bank of New York, and then directly with the foreign financiers. Leavitt's bank, which had marketed many state bonds, accepted the state's proposal and pledged to raise $600,000 from the American bondholders.[24] Oakley and Ryan next set out for England to secure the remaining $1,000,000. As Bronson had predicted, the bondholders refused to advance the full amount without additional security. Baring Brothers and Company and Magniac, Jardine and Company, however, agreed to at least investigate the Illinois proposals. They appointed American agents to examine the canal and its property, and the agents subsequently supported the state's original estimate of the canal's value and the capital needed to complete it. Despite this information, though, the European bondholders still refused to advance additional money without a guaranty from the Illinois legislature that a tax would be pledged to the loan's repayment.[25]

Although Bronson had little direct contact with the Illinois negotiations after his refusal to aid Oakley and Ryan in 1843, he maintained an active interest. His position that no further monies should be advanced to

Illinois without a pledge of taxation was exactly that adopted by the European bondholders. Even though Illinois newspapers attacked Bronson for having undermined the state's bargaining position, he denied any contact with the European financiers. With negotiations at a standstill, he now wrote a public letter to Governor Ford which was published in the *Journal of Commerce*. It detailed the long debate over the bond issue and urged the Governor to support a direct tax. Bronson stressed that the state must adopt the "honorable" course or it would be guilty of moral offenses similar to the stay and relief laws which altered private contracts. Bronson further wrote that the " . . . imposition of a moderate tax, as had been before suggested, the proceeds of which should be kept and held independent and distinct from all other revenues, is an act of simple justice to the public creditor—a measure due to the honor of the State—to the memory of our common ancestors—to the present generation—and absolutely necessary to screen us from the merited indignation and contempt of posterity."[26]

Bronson's letter represented only a small part of the pressure which now surfaced within the state in favor of a tax. By March 1845, the legislature finally passed an acceptable tax measure and, at the same time, a bill to deed the canal in trust to the bondholders. Of course, the state had made only a beginning in solving its debt problems, for it still was responsible for the internal improvement bonds. Nevertheless, the Illinois and Michigan Canal settlement proved that the state intended to respect its contracts.[27]

The whole episode, then, demonstrated the substantial influence of the eastern capitalist on western polities. Although not always the principal actor, Arthur Bronson had initiated action through his western agents and employed moral suasion and political pressures where he felt necessary. Even though Bronson did not live to see the completion of the final bill in 1845, it reflected his conviction that creditors and debtors must strictly adhere to their contractual obligations.

Charles Butler was even more directly involved in the settlement of Michigan's internal improvement debt. Michigan's problems began in 1837 when the legislature passed a bill which authorized the construction of several railroads and canals and which gave the young governor, Stephen T. Mason, the responsibility for obtaining a loan not to exceed $5 million. Mason's inexperience in the financial world and the necessity of selling the bonds during the financial contraction of 1837 complicated his task. He opened discussions with John Delafield of the Phoenix Bank of New York City and with Prime, Ward and King, but neither firm was satisfied with the loan's terms or with Michigan's growth potential. Mason soon grew impatient with those conservative bankers, and he unwisely signed a contract with the more speculative Morris Canal and Banking Company of New Jersey in June 1838.[28]

The contract reflected the haste with which it had been arranged, and it later became the source of many disagreements between the state and its creditors. Because the Morris Canal and Banking Company refused to purchase Michigan's bonds at par as required by state law, Mason avoided the law by designating the New Jersey firm as the state's agent to sell the bonds for a commission of 2½ percent. Mason was to deliver the bonds in installments, and the company promised an initial payment of $250,000 and periodic payments thereafter.[29] In the first several months, the Morris Canal and Banking Company sent the state $1,187,000 from its bond sales. Understandably encouraged, Mason was unconcerned when the Morris Canal and Banking Company suggested an alteration in their contract. The New Jersey company wanted to send the remaining three-quarters of the bonds to the United States Bank in Philadelphia, which was prepared to assume responsibility for their sale. The state agreed to the proposition, and in 1839 Mason delivered bonds worth $3.7 million to the Philadelphia Bank without any additional security for the state or any advanced payment required. The United States Bank in Philadelphia was to pay for the bonds whenver the state called for funds.

No sooner had the state completed this contract than its financial condition deteriorated. Its railroad and canal projects were short of funds because in April 1840, the Morris Canal and Banking Company defaulted on its remaining payments. The state sent commissioners to the East in an unsuccessful attempt to retrieve any unsold bonds and to curtail the state's indebtedness. In late 1841 and early 1842, the United States Bank at Philadelphia also failed to make payments to the state. Without incoming funds, Michigan was unable to meet its interest payments to the bond-holders in January 1842, to say nothing of its failure to provide for the construction of railroads and canals. But there was little the state could do. The United States Bank at Philadelphia had sold the state's bonds to foreign investors and received the capital, but it had utilized that capital in other ventures and now stood close to bankruptcy.[30] The state had no hope of obtaining further capital from the eastern banks and it could not expect revenues from canals and railroads on which work had stopped.

Governor John Barry encouraged the Michigan legislature to take immediate action to maintain the state's credit by providing for the payment of outstanding bonds. After a brief debate over whether to acknowledge the state's debts, the legislature overwhelmingly defeated a move toward repudiation. The legislature instructed the state treasurer to prepare a statement of the money actually received on the $5,000,000 loan. After determining that amount, the state subtracted 25 percent for damages incurred because the state had not received the full capital. Governor Barry subsequently issued a proclamation in April 1842, calling for the return of all Michigan bonds in exchange for new bonds totaling $2,342,960—the amount the state was actually paid. The legislature, then, intended to sell its railroads and canals and to accept the bonds as payment.[31]

Michigan's action, though, created a number of perplexing problems. Most capitalists considered Michigan's plan as a repudiation of part of its debt. Michigan had sold its $5 million in bonds, many to foreign capitalists, the critics charged, and it was immaterial to the bondholders whether Michigan had received the money from its agents, the Morris Canal and Banking Company and the United States Bank at Philadelphia, since Michigan was ultimately responsible for the bonds. Creditors also viewed Michigan's decision to subtract a damage charge as an attempt to unilaterally reduce its indebtedness. Even though some critics understood Michigan's reluctance to pay when the state had never received the funds, they were also aware that Michigan's action hurt some bondholders from whom the state had received full payment. Michigan's law actually was unclear on the question of whether the state intended to treat all the bondholders alike or whether it proposed to discriminate between two major classes—those from whom the state had received full payment and those from whom the state had received partial payment.[32]

It was at this point, in 1842, that Charles Butler entered the dispute as the representative of the bondholders from whom the state had received full payment. These bonds were easily identified because they had been numbered and purchased from the Morris Canal and Banking Company prior to the transfer of the remaining bonds to the United States Bank in Philadelphia. These bondholders included the Farmers Loan and Trust Company of New York City, $907,000; George Griswold, $200,000; James Buchanan, $30,000; and various other banks and individuals totaling $1,362,000. George Griswold, a partner in the commercial house of Nathaniel and George Griswold and a director of the Morris Canal and Banking Company was the principal spokesman for the bondholders. Griswold and his associates wanted Charles Butler to use his substantial influence in Michigan in order to obtain Michigan's pledge to repay them in full.[33] Butler had to accept the position since his brother, Benjamin, was heavily indebted to the Farmers Loan and Trust Company, a debt incurred in efforts to aid Charles. If he gained a favorable settlement, Charles Butler hoped that the bank might reduce his brother's debt.[34]

Butler first wrote to Elon Farnsworth, an important Michigan Whig politician and former land agent, describing for him the desires of the bondholders and enlisting his aid in speaking to members of the legisla-

Fig. 10. Photograph of Charles Butler (Courtesy of the New York Historical Society)

ture. Although Farnsworth agreed to help, he warned Butler that it would be difficult to influence the upcoming legislature. He, therefore, recommended that Butler come to Detroit.[35] Butler accordingly left New York in January 1843, but his lack of optimism is reflected in his statement: "I have no heart for this journey tho I have entered on it—I do not think that the advantage to my brother or myself will compensate for it and it may make things worse and protract settlements—but I will go."[36]

Although Butler in his reminiscences exaggerated his role in securing Michigan's debt payment, he did influence the course of events which resulted in an eventual settlement.[37] When the New Yorker arrived in Michigan, the legislature had weakened in its resolve to pay the bondholders. Part of the problem was that eastern and foreign capitalists had not surrendered any bonds, fearing the partial payment and the 25 percent penalty in the 1842 law. Governor Barry earnestly desired a solution to the problem, but he was handicapped by popular pressure for a reduction of the debt, political threats to his tenure in office, and widespread fear of any additional taxes.[38] Butler, therefore, took the initiative. He met with Governor Barry and then spoke to Farnsworth and other politicians who were friendly to his cause and anxious to prevent the state's repudiation. Utilizing some of the information gained in these conversations, Butler wrote a public letter to the Governor, which he subsequently read to the Michigan Senate, describing his position as an agent of the eastern bondholders and presenting a program which he felt resolved the state's dilemma.[39]

Butler's letter exhibited his substantial political and diplomatic skills. He assured the state that he represented only those creditors from whom the state had received full capital, and thus he avoided the more complex issue of the partially paid bonds. Next, Butler asserted in strong language that his clients were in no way responsible for the "fraud" committed by the state's banking agents; consequently, they should be excluded from any plan for partial payment. The original contract, Butler further pointed out, guaranteed the revenues of the projected railroads for interest payments, and yet the state had diverted that money into other uses, such as the extension of the existing railroad lines. On that basis, Butler scolded the state for abandoning its original contract. If the state ". . . can in no other way provide the means," Butler argued, "it should be done by direct taxation, and no man in the state, but should under such circumstances be willing cheerfully to meet his share of the liability."[40]

Having expended his heaviest ammunition in the first part of the letter, Butler then softened his appeal for a direct tax. He proposed that the state use the railroads' proceeds to extend existing lines for another year; that the bondholders accept new bonds for back interest; that the state apply the proceeds of the railroads after January 1, 1844, to the payment of the interest; and that the state, if necessary, levy a tax. Butler accompanied these proposals with an exaggerated description of the effects of Michigan's nonpayment on the livelihood of artisans, retired workers, widows and orphans who had purchased state bonds from eastern banks.[41]

After Butler personally read his letter to the Michigan Senate, it was referred to a Joint Committee of the Senate and House for discussion and recommendation. Butler looked forward to the political challenge although he also recognized the inherent difficulties. He described his feelings as he awaited the report of the Joint Committee in a letter to his wife, Eliza:

> It has excited a great deal of interest, and I bid fair to be quite a lion, or rather a stribling bearding the lion in his den. It is queer business all around, and a Legislature here is a queer body, and they have queer notions . . . . I have really laid myself out to bring about something, and they give me credit for urging sound doctrine and insisting on reasonable terms. Still, the idea of any one coming here and insisting on Michigan fulfilling her obligations is *monstrous* in the estimation of some . . . it involves the honor and the dignity of a Sovereign State . . . .[42]

The Joint Committee's report indicated that Butler faced an uphill struggle. The committee first reproached the New Yorker for the censorious tone of his letter. It insisted that the state always intended to compensate the holders of fully paid bonds and had only discounted the partially paid bonds. Despite the fact that the Joint Committee reaffirmed Michigan's responsibility for the fully paid bonds, it challenged Butler's view that the state should use the railroads' revenues to pay interest on the bonds. In a somewhat convoluted argument, the state claimed that the law only obliged the use of the railroads' proceeds for payment after the full loan had been received and the railroads had been completed. When the full loan was not received through the default and fraud of the contracting agencies, the committee claimed that "the faith of the state was no longer pledged for the fulfillment on their part, under that contract."[43] The Joint Committee therefore recommended that the state should complete the two major railroads, the Central and Southern, before paying either the principal or interest on the bonds. They specifically rejected the idea of a state tax to pay the outstanding debt.[44] In essence, then, the Joint Committee only marginally admitted the justice of the bondholders' case, refused to support a tax bill, and implied that the bondholders would be compensated after the completion of the railroads.

Butler vociferously objected to the Joint Committee's report, and in less than a month, between mid-February and late March 1843, he succeeded in convincing a slim majority of the legislature that his approach, rather than that of the Joint Committee, protected the state's interest. Butler introduced two amendments into the Senate to be attached to an existing bill: the first amendment specified that the state should use the earnings of the railroads to make interest payments, and the second required the legislature to impose a tax if sufficient funds were not available to pay the bondholders. Butler's bill sailed through the Senate on a vote of 14 to 1. With such an impressive victory in the Senate and having gained the *Detroit Daily Free Press's* support, Butler felt certain of success in the lower house.[45] Nevertheless, he met privately with different factions of Michigan's House of Representatives to explain the legislation's purpose and to acquire the necessary political support. In his usual moralistic and bombastic prose, Butler described one such meeting in a letter to his wife:

> You should have seen me this evening in a room with half a dozen members seated around a table, laying down sound principles of democracy in relation to the *payment of the public debt* and the maintenance of the public credit; telling them that whereas a good citizen should be ready always to lay down his life in defense of his country against an invading foe, so he should always be ready to give up his property to preserve and defend the honor of his country and pay its debts.[46]

But despite his previous success, Butler faced a serious challenge in Michigan's lower house. When the bill entered the House of Representatives on March 6, it faced substantial opposition from representatives opposed to a tax and from those in favor of repudiation of the entire debt. Opponents of the bill suggested one amendment after another in an attempt to delay and eventually to defeat the law. One such amendment proposed that the tax provision should be submitted to the voters. Although defeated by a 30 to 17 vote, the motion came up again, but in this subsequent round, it included a requirement that the ballot should be labeled "repudiation" or "no repudiation." This motion was defeated by a single vote. Butler lobbied continually with both the dissidents and his supporters, and he successfully repelled each challenge to the legislation. The House of Representatives eventually passed the "Butler Bill" and returned it to the Senate for final agreement.[47] After the Senate quickly passed the bill and then forwarded it to the Governor for his signature, Butler felt his work was completed.

Those opposed to the taxation provision, however, made one last stand. They alerted Governor Barry to the political implications of signing a tax bill before the next election, and their strategy was successful: Governor Barry intimated that he might veto the legislation. A representative of

Governor Barry asked Butler to approve the removal of the tax provision from the bill in order to save the Democratic party in the upcoming elections. Butler refused, however, ". . . because this was the only feature of the bill worth saving; the Governor must take responsibility, and I had rather have the bill vetoed than signed without the tax clause."[48] Butler immediately sought out the bill's strongest supporters and asked them to assure the governor of the law's benefits. In a few tense days, the governor consulted again and again with his advisors and finally decided to sign the bill after balancing its political liabilities against its favorable effects on the state's credit.[49]

The Act of 1843, also called the Butler Bill, temporarily resolved the issue of Michigan's public debt. It provided that the state would issue new bonds in order to fund the principal and past due interest on the fully paid bonds. The state also promised to pay the interest on bonds after 1845 by pledging the revenues derived from the operating railroads. The act specifically authorized a tax in the event the state could not meet its payments. Finally, the legislation provided that when the partially paid bonds were surrendered, the state would issue new bonds that reflected the money actually received minus a damage charge.[50] In sum, the state pledged to completely repay the holders of fully paid bonds, those represented by Butler, but it maintained its original position on the partially paid bonds.

Michigan's struggle over its public debt, then, exemplified Butler's powerful influence on Michigan's economic policies. As a landholder and urban promoter, Butler would gain from the stabilization of the state's credit. Moreover, his role determined, in some measure, the actual course of events. Although the state would never have repudiated all its bonds, neither would it have agreed to prompt payment and the tax law without Butler's pressure. Finally, and most important, the bondholders that Butler represented were satisfied with the bargain; consequently they maintained a substantial capital investment in Michigan. In 1846, many of these bondholders shared in the purchase of the Michigan Central Railroad, using their state bonds as payment, when the state opted to raise funds through the sale of its public works. Butler again was the principal intermediary as eastern financiers acquired control of Michigan's Central Railroad.[51]

Neither contemporaries nor later historians endorsed Michigan's action. Benjamin Curtis, in an influential article in the *North American Review* in 1844, asserted that Michigan had repudiated a part of her debt, the partially paid bonds, and later historians accepted that interpretation.[52] Curtis and most historians, though, simply accepted the creditor position without viewing the 1843 solution as a product of the creditor-debtor struggle. In Michigan's view, there was no compelling reason for the state to suffer the total loss on the bonds on which the capital had never been received. In essence, the Michigan law arranged a compromise that allowed the bondholders to recover a part of their capital. The compromise was not unlike those typically struck between individual creditors and debtors.

Charles Butler was also a key figure in the liquidation of Indiana's state debt. As a result of his successful negotiations in Michigan, Butler wrote to English and European investors offering to represent them in discussions with other state governments that threatened repudiation. In 1844, London financier John Horsley Palmer, who chaired a committee of bondholders that included the Rothschilds and Hope and Company of Amsterdam, asked Butler to aid in securing Indiana's payment of its outstanding obligations.[53]

Indiana had acquired hundreds of foreign and domestic creditors during the economic boom of the 1830s. Its internal improvements program began in 1832 when the legislature approved the borrowing of $200,000 to begin construction of the Wabash and Erie Canal, a canal projected to link Lake Erie with the Ohio River. No sooner had the state begun work on the canal than pressure surfaced to construct other canals and railroads throughout the state. In 1836, Indiana passed the Mammoth Bill which established a board of internal improvements to plan and to build a network of railroads, canals, and roads which would please every conceivable political and regional group. The price tag was set at $10,000,000, a sum which the board was to borrow by pledging the state's credit and the future revenues generated by the improvements as security. The legislature also stipulated that work was to begin immediately on all the approved projects.

Three years later, Indiana was bankrupt, and all work on the railroads and canals stopped. Of course, the depression was the principal cause of the work stoppages, but poor planning and inefficient and fraudulent financing exacerbated the situation. Like Michigan, Indiana had allowed the Morris Canal and Banking Company to market its securities in the United States and in Europe, receiving from the company periodic payments in order to construct the public works. In 1839, the Morris Canal and Banking Company was unable to meet its installments, and consequently Indiana ceased construction. Of a total of $15 million worth of bonds issued by the state and sold by the New Jersey firm, the state had received only $8.5 million, and a part of that sum was in worthless securities.[54] As the issuing agency, the state of Indiana was responsible for the principal and interest due on the bonds. That Indiana had been defrauded by its own commissioners and victimized by the failure of the

Morris Canal and Banking Company was not of legal or practical concern to the bondholders.

Indiana took several steps to reduce its liabilities. It first decided to pay the canal and railroad contractors—domestic creditors—yet this program so strained the state's resources that it was unable to remit the 1841 interest due on its bonds. The state also rethought the entire internal improvements scheme and established a list of priorities. Because of its trade potential, the Wabash and Erie Canal was considered essential to the state's economic development. Governor James Whitcomb sent an agent to assure the creditors that the state had not repudiated its debts but had defaulted only on a single payment. Indiana would pay its just debts, according to Governor Whitcomb, whenever economic conditions permitted the state to obtain the needed revenues.[55]

Despite Indiana's rhetoric of good intentions, the bondholders grew impatient and understandably suspicious because the state repeatedly failed to pay its interest and lacked a plan to do so in the future. The bondholders accordingly hired Charles Butler to persuade Indiana to convert rhetoric into reality. Butler made his first trip to Indiana in the spring of 1845 in order to begin discussion of the issues before the legislature's meeting in December 1845. The New Yorker delivered an address in Terre Haute suggesting a general plan for stabilizing the state's credit. Butler's proposal required that the state pass a tax guaranteeing repayment of a part of the interest on the bonds. The bondholders, in turn, would assent to take the Wabash and Erie Canal's revenues for the other part. Initial reaction to the proposal was favorable. A few months later, a convention which assembled to discuss methods of finishing the Wabash and Erie Canal also endorsed Butler's plan.[56] There was, therefore, a favorable climate for the settlement of the debt throughout the spring and summer of 1845.

Butler arrived in Indianapolis several weeks before the December 1845, meeting of the Indiana legislature is order to contact local officials and to lobby for his program. There were substantial problems to be overcome within the short space of six weeks, the legislature's normal meeting period. With statewide elections scheduled for the following year, Butler worried that political officials would hesitate to support a tax program. Yet Governor Whitcomb and other Democratic legislators backed his efforts. Butler and Whitcomb jointly prepared a series of recommendations for the legislature and a strategy for their presentation. Butler also wrote a letter outlining this basic program which the Governor agreed to submit to the legislature with his endorsement.[57] As Butler prepared this letter, he once again cast the struggle in moral and economic terms: "I am fully persuaded that it is only by addressing myself to the conscience of the people, stirring that up, and bringing that to bear, that I stand the slightest chance of success; and this cannot be done in a day. A revolution, a reformation, is required to be wrought. The whole population has got to be . . . made over again, before justice can or will be done to the holders of the pledged faith of the state."[58]

To open his campaign, Butler read his letter before the Indiana House of Representatives. The New Yorker scolded the state for its failure to secure its debts. Pointing out that the state's landed wealth had increased and that the state had paid its own contractors, Butler contended that the foreign bondholders had a prior claim on the state's resources. He reminded the lawmakers that both Pennsylvania and Illinois had subordinated purely local interests to satisfy foreign creditors. He also appealed to their sense of morality with an overly dramatic description of the hardships suffered by widows and orphans who held Indiana bonds and depended on regular interest payments. The greater part of Butler's letter, though, outlined specific proposals. So that his position was unmistakable, Butler informed the legislature that he was not authorized to negotiate any reduction of the debt and that all discussions must concentrate on the full payment of principal and interest. To soften this inflexible statement, Butler then assured the delegates that the bondholders would accept a program of gradual payment that included sufficient security. Such security required a tax law which would be used only if the state could not pay its interest in any other way. Butler tried to make the tax provision more palatable by presenting evidence that the state possessed the necessary landed wealth to increase taxes. Butler also inferred that if the legislature approved a tax, the bondholders would make additional loans sufficient to complete the Wabash and Erie Canal. However, the canal would then be placed in a trust controlled by the bondholders.[59]

After listening to Butler's presentation, the legislature immediately appointed a joint committee composed of twenty-four members selected equally from the House and the Senate to negotiate with Butler and to formulate a recommendation for the legislature. Butler met with this committee six times between December 18 and December 26 in sessions lasting from one and one-half to four and one-half hours. Butler needed all the political skills he could muster because the discussions did not proceed smoothly. On December 25, 1845, the Joint Committee refused Butler's plan and invited him to submit another proposal. Butler faced a difficult decision. If he failed to reply to the committee, the debt question was dead for that session. If he submitted another proposition, he could easily exceed his instructions from the bondholders and lose their support. Yet Butler was convinced that the current legislative session was the best chance for a settlement. Thus, he submitted another plan which included substantial concessions and which presented an ultimatum to the committee—this proposition or nothing.[60]

Although refusing to bargain for less than the *full payment* of the principal and interest, Butler's new offer again reduced the bondholders' security. In his original statement, Butler had stipulated that the state might delay remitting overdue interest (1841 to 1846) until 1851. He had also proposed that the state levy a tax to guarantee the payment of 60 percent of the interest, yet he allowed the remaining 40 percent of the interest to depend on canal revenues. In his new presentation, Butler proposed that interest would be paid on an equal basis—50 percent from taxes and 50 percent from the canal's revenues. He also allowed the state until 1853 to settle the unpaid interest. These proposed changes swayed the committee, and it recommmended the plan to the legislature.[61]

Since both political parties had agreed to delay discussion until after the party conventions scheduled for the first week in January 1846, Butler had over a week to prepare for the great debate that was sure to occur in the House of Representatives and in the Senate. During this period, the New Yorker worked on amendments to an increasingly complex bill of thirty clauses. At the same time, he lobbied with members of the legislature. His most influential allies were Governor Whitcomb and Michael Bright, a former agent of the state who had originally worked with the bondholders. Whitcomb, a Democrat, was an especially important ally because opposition to the bill centered in the Democratic party. Whereas the Whig party convention had expressed general approval for Butler's plan, the Democrats could not reach a consensus.[62] As a result, Whitcomb, Butler, and Bright held last minute discussions with leading Democratic senators and representatives, in an attempt to prevent a floor fight in the legislature.[63]

The debate opened in the House of Representatives on January 13, only six days before the scheduled end of the session. During this week, Butler lobbied incessantly and altered his position on a number of occasions to insure the bill's passage. The bill's enemies predictably attacked Butler as a representative of outside capital and the legislation as a sell out of the people. The first serious challenge came when a member moved to submit the bill to the voters. Although the motion was defeated 49 to 41, it was reconsidered the following day. By Wednesday noon, Butler realized that the whole program was in trouble. There were too many factions to whom this amendment appealed. The enemies of the bill saw a referendum as a means of killing the whole debt question while other members perceived it as a means of avoiding the political repercussions of a tax measure. Butler knew that he could not agree to the motion, for if such a question were submitted to the people and it lost, then the debts would never be paid. Consequently, Butler and Bright drew up a compromise and discussed it with key members of the opposition. They agreed to a new clause which made the bond's principal as well as its interest payable half through state taxation and half through canal revenues. Until that moment, Butler had always insisted that the debt's principal had to be fully paid and not left to the uncertainties of the canal's revenues. With this considerable strengthening of the state's position, the bill acquired sufficient support to pass the House of Representatives.[64]

Butler then faced an equally arduous fight in the Senate. The bill's enemies used every available parliamentary tactic to delay action, including absenting themselves from the meetings to effect the loss of a quorum. Opposing senators suggested amendments to soften the law's impact. One senator wanted to require that all outstanding bonds be surrendered before new bonds funding the interest could be issued. Such a procedure would have prevented the law from ever taking effect since all the bonds would never be returned. To forestall that amendment, Butler consented to a requirement that half of the bonds had to be surrendered before the state placed the Wabash and Erie Canal under the bondholders' trusteeship. In Section 35, inserted at the last moment to secure additional votes, Butler agreed to allow the state some control over the canal's trustees, including the power to set their salaries. This section was designed to prevent outside capitalists from totally controlling the canal. Finally, the legislature passed the bill. So intense was the struggle that Governor Whitcomb fell seriously ill at the week's end and signed the bill from his bed.[65]

After such a long and confused debate, what exactly were the bill's terms? Butler had consented to a program of debt payment considerably less certain than the bondholders originally had envisioned. The state basically agreed to pay a half of the interest and principal on the debt out of taxation while forcing the bondholders to accept the revenues from the Wabash and Erie Canal as payment for the remainder. The bondholders also were asked to contribute an additional $2,250,000 to complete the canal. As security for their investment, the bondholders were to control the canal under a trust arrangement, but the state still maintained certain powers over the canal such as determining salaries for the trustees and setting tolls.[66]

As the legislators hurried home, Butler remained in Indianapolis for several weeks to prepare two reports on the settlement, one for the people of Indiana and one for the bondholders. The first report was a lengthy pamphlet of over 100 pages which included Butler's original letter to the legislature, memorials from the bondholders, and Butler's explanations of the bill. All this information was calculated to help the Democratic politicians secure reelection by convincing the people that the legislature had taken the proper action. Butler stressed the fact that the state had met its moral obligations on very favorable terms. "The state, not having the ability to give a whole loaf, to a suffering bondholder," Butler said, "does offer to him half a loaf certain, and makes a provisional arrangement for the other half."[67]

The New Yorker's report to the bondholders conveyed a much different tone because the whole package depended on their acquiescence. In justifying the compromises in the bill, Butler asked the bondholders to understand that the Indiana legislature believed that the state had been defrauded in the sale of the bonds. In particular, Butler urged the bondholders to accept Section 32 which guaranteed state taxation to pay only 50 percent of the principal and interest. The legislature's pledge of taxation for any amount, Butler explained, was a major concession given the depression and the state's disappointment with the internal improvements program. "It is an indisputable fact," Butler reported, "that in no other form could the bill have passed the House of Representatives . . . ."[68] Because the canal was the principal element of security for 50 percent of the debt, Butler included a lengthly analysis of its trade potential. Accompanying the report were testaments from canal engineers and state legislators on the probable tolls for the next fifteen years. Butler tried to leave no doubt that the Wabash and Erie Canal was ample security, and he asserted that it was "second only to the New York and Erie Canal."[69]

In the report's conclusion, Butler warned the bondholders that the 1845-1846 legislative session had been the optimal time for achieving their goals. Next year, Indiana would be preoccupied with presidential year politics, Butler explained, and the political climate would be unfavorable.[70] The London bondholders, however, were not pleased with the agreement, and they refused to accept it even after Butler's visit to London in the fall of 1846. The creditors were disturbed by their dependence on the Wabash and Erie Canal and reluctant to throw another $2,250,000 into its completion. Consequently, they sent Butler back to Indiana to obtain more security and to reduce the amount of the new loan.[71] The bondholders were gambling that they could secure slight alterations in the bill despite Butler's warnings that reopening negotiations might threaten the entire bill.

When Butler returned to Indiana in December 1846, an organized opposition to the settlement had developed. Many Whigs wanted to defeat any new bill, Butler reported, in order to embarrass the Democratic governor. Butler was attacked in a more personal fashion than during the previous session. Those opposed to the measure made liberal use of epithets describing Butler as a "stock jobber," "Wall Street speculator." and "British agent."[72] During a particularly acrimonious debate in the Senate, a member read from a recently published book which slandered Benjamin F. Butler and which included an 1819 letter of Benjamin F. Butler describing Charles Butler as ". . . rather overlayed with false pride, squeamish sensibility and ill guided ambition. I have been obliged to tell him very plainly what I thought of his style of writing and modes of thought—the first, like the latter, is frothy and bombastic— indeed, precisely like a boy of 18 of some genius, but that untutored, and misdirected."[73]

The debate on amendments to the new bill dragged on through December and into January 1847, but it finally passed both houses. After months of work on Butler's part, the bondholders had only secured a reduction in the capital required to support the canal's construction. Nevertheless, the bondholders now reluctantly accepted the settlement. Shortly thereafter, the parties organized the board of trustees for the Wabash and Erie Canal, and Charles Butler was chosen as the board's first president.[74]

Butler's effectiveness in Indiana is difficult to evaluate. His presence certainly assured that the bondholders would receive at least 50 percent of their principal and interest, yet it also seems reasonable to assume that Indiana would never have repudiated the whole debt. As it turned out, moreover, the canal was not sound security for the remaining 50 percent of the debt. Railroads later challenged the canal for business, and the state consistently undercut the canal by funding the railroads. Butler struggled for thirty years as a canal trustee to secure equitable treatment by the state, but to no avail. By the early 1870s the canal was totally bankrupt, and in 1876 its fixed assets were sold and the proceeds given to the bond-holders.[75] In a sense, Indiana won the struggle between the debtor and creditor by forcing the bondholders to accept a substantial part of the state's bad debts. Yet the settlement was perhaps no better or worse than that in the other states of the Old Northwest. Whereas Michigan partially repudiated bonds for which it never received full payment, Indiana effectively accomplished the same thing. Butler secured as equitable a settlement as was possible under the circumstances. It should be recalled that there were other states in the 1840s that simply refused to acknowledge their debts.[76]

Butler's and Bronson's efforts to establish state responsibility for internal improvements debts demonstrated several important themes. First, their participation in the struggle illustrated the pervasiveness of the eastern capitalists' involvement with the politics and economies of western states. Second, Bronson's and Butler's insistence on the sanctity of contracts and on the equitable treatment of foreign and eastern financiers was an important step in protecting the political and legal environment for future capital investment. Finally, this struggle, along with the *Bronson* v. *Kinzie* case, suggests that Arthur Bronson and Charles Butler were themselves extremely influential, if little known, elements in some of the most important economic and political decisions of the 1840s.

Conclusion

Even though eastern financiers continued to influence midwestern economic development after the mid-1840s, this date marks a logical termination point for this study. The depression had ended in the Old Northwest by 1845. Agricultural regions were producing numerous products for outside markets, and the volume of trade and the number of retail businesses were increasing daily in the major urban centers. A case in point was Chicago. It was again a thriving commercial center with populations of 12,088 in 1845 and 29,963 in 1850, and it possessed a lively business class actively competing with other midwestern cities for commercial hegemony. The establishment of new banks, the renewed construction of railroads, and the organization of schools, churches and voluntary associations signaled the end of the settlement period.[1] By 1850, the frontier was located west of the Mississippi River.

Despite the fact that Arthur Bronson had been at the center of the region's economic development during the boom and bust period, he did not live to see its renaissance in the late 1840s. In the summer of 1844, Bronson was stricken with a violent attack of a chronic lung disease on a steamboat trip from Chicago to Detroit. He hovered precariously close to death in a Detroit hotel for several days. Charles Butler, who was also in Detroit at this time, wrote to his wife that "Mr. Bronson, who with me visited this place first in 1833 and who is associated with all my thoughts and business here, is in all human probability on the verge of the eternal world."[2] Although still seriously ill, Bronson eventually was able to return to his home in New York City. In November 1844, Butler visited Bronson at his home, and shortly thereafter he wrote the following melodramatic description of their last meeting: "I went into his chamber and found him lying in the bed . . . . I was shocked and overwhelmed with the great and

solemn change which had taken place in his appearance . . . . He pressed
my hand and spoke distinctly and said 'goodbye Mr. Butler.' My feelings
were too much excited to speak, I could whisper 'farewell' . . . ."[3] Arthur
Bronson died that same night.

Neither the Bronson family nor Charles Butler curtailed their western
investments after Arthur Bronson's death. Frederic Bronson maintained
the family's mortgage loan business and its ownership of city lots and farm
lands. After the depression's worst days had passed, he renewed land
purchases and assisted in the promotion of western improvement, such as
the Chicago, Burlington, and Quincy Railroad.[4] Charles Butler lived on
for over a half century, building a remarkable career as an independent
businessman who invested for foreign capitalists and promoted midwestern railroads often in conjunction with his brother-in-law, William B.
Ogden. During his lifetime, Butler was known for his many philanthro-
pies, his long presidency of the Union Theological Seminary and his brief
term as president of New York University. He died in 1897 after a life
which spanned nearly the entire period of the nineteenth–century frontier experience.[5]

In summary, then, what was the significance of the Bronsons' and
Charles Butler's business careers? To answer this question, one first must
determine whether their investment activities were common among eastern financiers of the Jacksonian period. Obviously I cannot hypothesize
with certainty since this study is deliberately limited in scope and since
definitive statements would require many additional business biographies
and intensive analyses of interregional capital flows. Nevertheless, there is
sufficient evidence to suggest that the Bronsons and Butler, while perhaps more energetic and influential than most financiers, still reflected a
common investment pattern among New York State capitalists.

It should be remembered that the Bronsons and Butler rarely embarked alone on business ventures; rather they cooperated with other
eastern businessmen who shared in partnership agreements, purchased
stock in land companies and financial institutions, and, to varying extents,
participated in investment decisions. Gould Hoyt, a New York City retail
merchant; Thomas B. Olcott, president of the Mechanics and Farmers
Bank of Albany; and John Ward of the investment firm of Prime, Ward
and King were only a few of the New Yorkers who helped in the planning
and subscribed over $1,500,000 for the stock of the Ohio Life Insurance
and Trust Company (OLTC). The Bronsons regularly purchased city lots
and agricultural lands in association with Hoyt, Ward, Olcott, and with
their brother-in-law, James B. Murray, who was also president of the
Morris Canal and Banking Company.[6] Similarly Charles Butler's investments at Chicago, Huron, and Toledo were joint ventures which included

businessmen such as Erastus Corning of the Albany City Bank; Joseph Beers, a wealthy New York City merchant and private banker; and Edward Nicoll and William Bard, secretary and president of the New York Life Insurance and Trust Company (NYLTC).[7]

These New York financiers also had business investments separate from their relationships with the Bronsons and Butler. Thomas Olcott, for example, was not only president of the Mechanics and Farmers Bank of Albany but also owned land in Ohio, Michigan, and Illinois and held stock in the Michigan State Bank. Erastus Corning surely surpassed most of his contemporaries in juggling an assortment of business enterprises that included manufacturing firms, bank stock, town promotions, agricultural lands, and canal and railroad stock in New York State, Michigan, Illinois, and Wisconsin.[8]

The names of Olcott, Corning, Bronson, and Butler in no way exhaust the list of easterners who were involved in the economic affairs of the Old Northwest. John Astor, for example, spent thousands of dollars in promoting Green Bay, Wisconsin, a townsite which was then called Astor. He formed a stock company in order to pool the capital of eastern businessmen from New York City and from smaller towns such as Utica and Watertown. John Martin, a banker in Martinsburgh, New York, was also a conspicuous figure in the Green Bay region. His land and business investments at Green Bay were superintended by his brother, Morgan L. Martin, an influential Wisconsin political and economic figure. Levi Beardsley, a banker from Cherry Valley, New York, later a director of the Farmers Loan and Trust Company of New York City and a member of the New York State Senate, associated with friends in the New York and Western Land Company in order to purchase lots at Huron, Toledo, Milwaukee and many other cities along the shores of Lakes Michigan and Huron. Jacob Barker, a Buffalo commission merchant, acquired Chicago lots as early as 1833 and then dispatched his brother, Benjamin, to oversee the property's improvement and sale. Jacob Barker later owned a one-third interest and shared in the development of Racine in the Wisconsin Territory. He obviously intended to use both Chicago and Racine as sites for expanding his Great Lakes' commission business.[9]

New Yorkers were not the only eastern businessmen with investments in the Old Northwest. Boston entrepreneurs, for instance, were prominent shareholders both in the American Land Company and in the Boston and Western Land Company. The latter firm possessed a capital stock of $100,000 and purchased Illinois and Wisconsin town lots as well as mineral lands. Edward and Samuel Russell of Middletown, Connecticut, bought and improved lots in Chicago and acquired agricultural lands throughout Illinois. Perhaps John Rockwell, a Norwalk, Connecticut, lawyer, banker, railroad entrepreneur, and politician most clearly reflected the investment pattern of the New Yorkers. Through his agent, Dixwell Lathrop, he and his brother, Charles, purchased farm land in Ohio, Michigan, and Illinois and town lots in Cleveland, Toledo, and Chicago. In 1835, they formed the Rockwell Land Company to build the town of Rockwell on the Illinois River in the hope that it would become the southern terminus of the Illinois and Michigan Canal. When LaSalle, located a short distance away, acquired the canal terminus, the Rockwell family shifted their money into a coal mining company and a bank in the same region.[10] Alongside the Rockwells, the Bronsons, and Corning, there were also countless European capitalists who bought stock in canal and railroad companies in the 1830s. It seems highly unlikely, therefore, that any substantial economic endeavor in the Old Northwest, such as the establishment of a large bank or townsite, could have developed without the support of outside capitalists.

Even though the list of individuals could be expanded, such examples are still an imprecise indication of capital movements from East to West. Occasional records of western banks, though, further confirm the easterners' influence over local economies. In 1834, eastern capitalists owned 70.9 percent of Ohio's total bank stock of $4,730,000. As Ohio's economy matured in the 1830s, the state's own citizens gradually acquired surplus capital and invested in bank stock. Nevertheless, Ohio's need for outside capital remained. In 1840, nonresidents still possessed 49.9 percent of the state's bank capital of $11,921,579 and held an absolute majority of the stock in the four leading banks: the Ohio Life Insurance and Trust Company, the Franklin Bank of Cincinnati, the Commercial Bank of Cincinnati, and the Lafayette Bank of Cincinnati.[11]

Eastern financiers also owned stock and often controlled the operation of leading banks during the settlement period in Michigan. In the 1830s, the Dwight family from Geneva, New York, and Springfield, Massachusetts, held a stock majority and appointed the cashier of the Bank of Michigan, the territory's oldest and most influential institution. They had the same power over the Commercial Bank of Lake Erie at Cleveland and the Bank of Geneva, New York. As late as 1840, the Dwights still held 46 percent of the Bank of Michigan's stock while other easterners owned an additional 29 percent leaving only 23 percent of the stock in the hands of Michigan residents.[12] New York State capitalists, like Erastus Corning, also dominated the Farmers and Mechanics Bank of Detroit. Corning, Thomas Olcott, and other Albany businessmen later gained stock control of the Michigan State Bank after its establishment in 1835.[13]

In Illinois and the Wisconsin Territory, similar patterns prevailed. When Illinois chartered its second state bank in 1835 (the first Illinois

State Bank had failed in 1831), several syndicates of eastern financiers vied for control of the available stock. Stockholder lists in 1840 revealed that Illinois residents held but a slender majority of the bank's stock. The largest stockholders included the New York Life Insurance and Trust Company and the New York City brokerage firm of Nevins, Townsend and Company.[14] In the Wisconsin Territory, the first effort to establish a bank, the Bank of Wisconsin, brought a rush of potential subscribers from the East. The Bronsons and Thomas Olcott competed for stock control against John Jacob Astor and New York State resident John Martin.[15]

The relatively free movement of eastern capital into western banks benefited businessmen both East and West. Western banks provided credit for local merchants, issued bank notes to facilitate trade, and invested capital in agricultural mortgages. Larger institutions such as the OLTC, also purchased state internal improvement bonds which were then resold to European investors. While frontier economies obtained capital and credit for commercial and agricultural expansion, eastern capitalists received a 7 to 9 percent annual dividend on what then seemed a sound investment.[16] Adding the evidence of bank ownership to the numerous individual examples, then, it seems safe to assert that the Bronsons and Butler reflected a general pattern of eastern involvement in the Old Northwest's economic expansion.

Although historians know little about the careers of Thomas Olcott and John Rockwell or of the histories of individual banks, this intensive study of the Bronsons and Butler can suggest several broad themes. The New Yorkers certainly demonstrated that eastern financiers were crucial—although not the only—factors in the economic development of the West. Historians must abandon the notion that frontier regions grew in isolation from the East and that farmers and urban pioneers alone created a complex economic society out of the wilderness. In the 1830s, the Old Northwest was a colony into which eastern financiers poured their surplus capital and utilized their financial expertise in order to make profits and to build an integrated national economy. Despite the problems caused by distance, rudimentary transportation facilities, and the lack of financial institutions, the Bronsons and Butler moved their capital with surprising ease onto the frontier by establishing banks and trust companies, by employing local citizens as agents to purchase and improve lands, and by acquiring stock interests in canal and railroad companies.[17]

This study also has shown that the relationship between East and West changed dramatically during the frontier period since the influence of eastern capitalists declined as the West developed its own business leadership and generated its own capital resources. The history of the OLTC exemplified this process. In its first years, the Bronsons wrote the charter, controlled over three-fourths of the stock, and selected the officers. Even though the Bronsons designed the company to operate on conservative banking principles, the demands of the western economy for risk capital and the growing independence of the company's western leaders eventually broke the easterners' hold. This same pattern was evident in Arthur Bronson's and Charles Butler's relationships with their western agents. From 1833 to 1836, Bronson and Butler supplied the capital and made the major investment decision. With the growth of trade and retail businesses, westerners like William Ogden and Charles Trowbridge, were less dependent for capital and, in due course, asserted their economic independence. The ties to eastern financiers, however, were never severed completely. William Ogden later became the Midwest's leading railroad promoter precisely because of his continuing links to eastern capital markets. Yet by 1845, western businessmen commonly stood as financial equals alongside their eastern counterparts.[18]

The business career of Arthur Bronson and Charles Butler also illustrated their sophisticated approach to western economic development and their perception of the West as an integral part of the nation's economy. If the Bronsons and Butler had purchased land only for quick resale at higher prices, they would have contributed little capital and no business leadership to the West. Instead the New Yorkers were simultaneously land speculators, urban promoters, banking entrepreneurs, and canal advocates. Arthur Bronson, for example, developed the North Side of Chicago while, at the same time, assisting in the promotion of the Illinois and Michigan Canal and speculating in surrounding agricultural properties. His mortgage loan business in Illinois, Indiana, and the Wisconsin Territory and his association with the NYLTC and the OLTC similarly manifested his belief that the cultivation of the soil, in harmony with the growth of towns and the building of transportation improvements, would eventually modernize the nation's economic structure. Arthur Bronson and his father, Isaac, also realized that such developments could not take place without a supporting financial structure in the East which controlled the flow of credit and capital. They accordingly expended as much time and effort on the national bank issue as they did on supervising their western real estate.

Charles Butler's western investments exhibited the same comprehensive view of economic development. Butler not only promoted three principal urban locations—Chicago, Huron and Toledo—but also purchased agricultural lands for quick resale, assisted in the establishment of western financial institutions, and encouraged the construction of railroads and canals. In addition, Butler's business arrangements illustrated the financial linkages which united East and West. He participated in and often directed a constantly shifting assemblage of eastern capitalists whose interests, at various times, included the NYLTC; the OLTC; the American Land Company; the promotion of Chicago, Toledo, and Huron; the Illinois and Michigan Canal; the Erie and Kalamazoo Railroad; and the internal improvement bonds of Illinois, Michigan, and Indiana.

Despite the similarity of their economic goals and investment portfolios, the Bronsons and Charles Butler followed different business strategies. The Bronsons were conservative investors who believed in gradual economic change. They opposed efforts to increase the nation's credit resources through the unrestricted chartering of new banks and warned against the building of cities and internal improvements which were far in advance of the economy's needs. While never rejecting the windfall profits that accrued from land investments in 1835 and 1836, they were, nevertheless, fundamentally opposed to the expansionism that characterized so many nineteenth–century capitalists. Charles Butler, on the other hand, personified the risk-taker who pushed his urban developments far ahead of market demands and population pressures. The nation adopted this booster mentality, and it undoubtedly contributed to a phenomenal rate of growth from 1832 to 1837. One cannot help but wonder, nevertheless, whether the economic dislocation and personal suffering caused by the depression might have been tempered under the more cautious and planned approach to western expansion advocated by the Bronsons. The Bronsons' conservative policies certainly accounted for their own financial stability during the depression while the boosters, like Butler and Lyon, struggled for nearly a decade to avoid financial ruin.

Contrary to popular impressions of absentee investors, neither Charles Butler nor Arthur Bronson abandoned their western investments or automatically forced their debtors into bankruptcy during the depression. It was to their advantage to sustain as best they could the existing economic framework so that it could support the economy's eventual recovery. During these years, Bronson continued to lend money to farmers and to extend the contracts of his urban debtors on the guarantee of regular interest payments or the presentation of additional security. Meanwhile, Butler oversaw the difficult task of reducing the scope of his investments at Huron, Toledo, and Chicago. The process of economic contraction inevitably generated hostilities between eastern creditors and western debtors and financial losses for all concerned, yet most western businessmen outlasted the depression and revived their financial careers as the economy began its recovery in the 1840s.

At the same time, both New Yorkers helped to maintain the viability of the nation's business system by protecting the rights of nonresident investors in the Old Northwest. Arthur Bronson frequently presented the absentee landholders' viewpoint to western legislatures, which occasionally overtaxed nonresidents and reduced or delayed the payment of debts. Bronson's persistence led to the Supreme Court case of *Bronson* v. *Kinzie* which set limits on state legislation for the benefit of debtors. Equally important, Arthur Bronson and Charles Butler assisted western states in negotiating agreements with the holders of internal improvement bonds which assured their partial repayment and provided for the completion of some canals and railroads. These settlements also preserved the investors' faith in the willingness of western citizens and their legislative bodies to honor existing contracts. Without such guarantees, eastern and foreign capitalists would have been reluctant to invest in America's future westward expansion.

Finally, this work affirms the importance of individual businessmen in the development of the American economy. The Bronsons and Butler, though, were not unique nor were they the crucial elements in the resolution of national economic issues, the establishment of financial institutions, or the growth of western communities. Instead they typified many eastern investors whose individual economic decisions often collectively resulted in new business enterprises, institutional innovations, and urban and agricultural expansion. Surrounded by the more statistically–oriented studies of the "New Economic History," this book, with its emphasis on the individual, aptly might be subtitled "An Essay in the Old Economic History"—an approach which, I believe, is still necessary in order to understand the process of American economic growth.

Notes

Preface

1. The importance of eastern and foreign money to the West's expansion is not an unknown theme in historical literature. Allan Bogue and Robert Swierenga have demonstrated the impact of eastern capital on midwestern farming in the nineteenth century while Arthur Johnson, Barry Supple, and Paul Gates have explored the role of outside financiers in extending midwestern railroad connections. Gene Gressley has led historians of the Trans-Mississippi West in elaborating the migration of foreign capital into the mining and cattle industries. See Allan Bogue, *From Prairie to Cornbelt* (Chicago: University of Chicago Press, 1963) and *Money at Interest* (Ithaca, New York: Cornell University Press, 1955); Arthur M. Johnson and Barry Supple, *Boston Capitalists and Western Railroads* (Cambridge: Harvard University Press, 1967); Paul Gates, *The Illinois Central Railroad and Its Colonization Work* (Cambridge: Harvard University Press, 1934); and Gene Gressley, *Bankers and Cattlemen* (New York: Alfred Knopf, 1968). Other important studies include: Dorothy Adler, *British Investments in American Railways, 1834-1898* (Charlottesville, Virginia: The University Press of Virginia, 1970); Harry N. Scheiber, *Ohio Canal Era: A Case Study of Government and the Economy, 1820-1861* (Athens, Ohio: The Ohio University Press, 1961) and "The Commercial Bank of Lake Erie, 1831-1843," *Business History Review* 30(Spring 1966): 47-65; W.G. Kerr, *Scottish Capital on the American Credit Frontier* (Austin, Texas: Texas State Historical Association, 1976); and H. Peers Brewer, "Eastern Money and Western Mortgages in the 1870s," *Business History Review* 50(Autumn 1976): 356-380.

2. Bessie L. Pierce, *A History of Chicago*, vol. I: *The Beginning of a City* (New York: Alfred A. Knopf, 1937), p. 44.

3. There are already several good biographies of antebellum businessmen. See Henry Cohen, *Business and Politics in America from the Age of Jackson to the Civil War: The Career Biography of W.W. Corcoran* (Westport, Connecticut: Greenwood Publishing Company, 1971); Daniel Hodas, *The Business Career of Moses Taylor* (New York: New York University Press, 1976); Kenneth W. Porter, *John Jacob Astor, Businessman*, 2 vols. (Cambridge: Harvard University Press, 1931); and Francis Gregory, *Nathan Appleton: Merchant and Entrepreneur, 1779-1861* (Charlottesville: University Press of Virginia, 1975).

4. See Harry Scheiber, "Entrepreneurship and Western Development: The Case of Micajah T. Williams," *Business History Review* 37(Winter 1963):345-368; Patrick McClear, "William Butler Ogden: A Chicago Promoter in the Speculative Era and the Panic of 1837," *Journal of the Illinois State Historical Society* 70 (November 1977):283-291; Jack Kilfoil, "C.C. Trowbridge, Detroit Banker and Michigan Land Speculator, 1820-1845" (Ph.D. dissertation, Claremont Graduate School, 1969); and John Shirigian, "Lucius Lyon: His Place in Michigan History" (Ph.D. dissertation, University of Michigan, 1961).

5. Paul Gates, "Frontier Land Business in Wisconsin," *Wisconsin Magazine of History* 52 (Summer 1969):309.

6. See Frederick Jackson Turner, "The Significance of the Frontier in American History," in *The Early Writings of Frederick Jackson Turner,* ed. Edward Everett (Madison: University of Wisconsin Press, 1938), pp. 185-229. Also see Richard Jensen, "On Modernizing Frederick Jackson Turner: The Historiography of Regionalism," *Western Historical Quarterly* 11 (July 1980):307-322. A convenient summary of frontier historiography is Ray A. Billington, *America's Frontier Heritage* (New York: Holt, Rinehart and Winston, 1966). Also see the articles by Jackson C. Putnam, "The Turner Thesis and the Westward Movement: A Reappraisal," *Western Historical Quarterly* 7 (October 1976):377-404; and Bradford Luckingham, "The City in the Westward Movement—A Biographical Note," *Western Historical Quarterly* 5 (July 1974):295-306.

7. Paul Gates is the best known historian of American land policy. His works have criticized the speculator's effect on the disposal of the public domain. See Paul Wallace Gates, *Landlords and Tenants on the Prairie Frontier, Studies in American Land Policy* (Ithaca: Cornell University Press, 1973); *History of Public Land Law Development* (Washington: Government Printing Office, 1968); and "Frontier Land Business in Wisconsin," passim. An excellent review of the revisionist literature on American land policy can be found in Robert P. Swierenga, "Land Speculation and Its Impact on American Economic Growth and Welfare: A Historiographical Review," *Western Historical Quarterly* 8 (July 1977):283-302; and the same author's *Pioneers and Profits: Land Speculation on the Iowa Frontier* (Ames, Iowa: Iowa State University Press, 1968), pp. xix-xxviii.

8. Swierenga, "Land Speculation and Its Impact on American Economic Growth," p. 302.

9. Richard C. Wade, *The Urban Frontier: The Rise of Western Cities, 1790-1830* (Cambridge: Harvard University Press, 1959), passim.

10. Daniel Boorstin identified the western promoter as a peculiarly American type. See Daniel Boorstin, *The Americans, The National Experience* (New York: Random House, 1965), pp. 113-123. Also see Thomas C. Cochran, "The History of a Business Society," *Journal of American History* 54 (June 1967):9; and Luckingham, "The City in the Westward Movement," pp. 295-306.

11. See John Haeger, "Eastern Money and the Urban Frontier: Chicago, 1833-1842," *Journal of the Illinois State Historical Society* 64 (Autumn 1971):267-284 and "Capital Mobilization and the Urban Center: The Wisconsin Lakeports," *Mid-America* 60 (April-July 1978):75-93.

12. See Boorstin, *The Americans,* pp. 116-119; McClear, "William Butler Ogden," pp. 284-285; and Luckingham, "The City in the Westward Movement," p. 297.

13. Douglas C. North, *The Economic Growth of the United States, 1790-1860* (New York: The Norton Library, 1966); David C. Klingaman and Richard K. Vedder,

eds., *Essays on Nineteenth Century Economic History, The Old Northwest* (Athens, Ohio: Ohio University Press, 1975); Jeffrey G. Williamson and Joseph A. Swanson, "A Model of Urban Capital Formation and the Growth of Cities in History," *Explorations in Economic History* 8 (Winter 1970-71):213-222; Oliver Knight, "Toward an Understanding of the Western Town," *The Western Historical Quarterly*, 4 (January 1973):27-42; Allan Pred, *The Spatial Dynamics of U.S. Urban-Industrial Growth, 1800-1914: Interpretation and Theoretical Essays* (Cambridge: The M.I.T. Press, 1966), pp. 177-196; David Ward, *Cities and Immigrants: A Geography of Change in Nineteenth Century America* (New York: Oxford University Press, 1971), pp. 11-12, 20-21; Allan Pred, *Urban Growth and the Circulation of Information: The United States System of Cities, 1790-1840* (Cambridge: Harvard University Press, 1973); Roberta Miller, *City and Hinterland: A Case Study of Urban Growth and Regional Development* (Westport, Connecticut: Greenwood Press, 1979); and Dianne Lindstrom, *Economic Development in the Philadelphia Region, 1810-1850* (New York: Columbia University Press, 1978).

14. Robert R. Dykstra, *The Cattle Towns* (New York: Atheneum, 1970); Stuart Blumin, *The Urban Threshold* (Chicago: University of Chicago Press, 1976); and Don H. Doyle, *The Social Order of a Frontier Community, Jacksonville, Illinois, 1825-1870* (Urbana, Illinois: University of Illinois Press, 1978).

15. Of course, the concept of entrepreneurial history has a long tradition in the writing of American economic history. Recently there has been renewed interest in evaluating the individual's role, although today historians speak of the role of elites. See particularly Frederic Cople Jaher, "Old and New Elites and Entrepreneurial Activity in New York City from 1780 to 1850," *Working Papers from the Regional Economic History Research Center*, 2 (1978):55-78.

Chapter 1

1. Henry Bronson, *The History of Waterbury, Connecticut, The Original Township Embracing Present Watertown and Parts of Oxford, Wolcott, Middlebury, Prospect and Naugutuck* (Waterbury: Published by the Bronson Brothers, 1858), pp. 137-140; 372-374. Also see the extended description of the early history of the Bronson family in Grant Morrison, "Isaac Bronson and the Search for System in American Capitalism, 1789-1838" (Ph.D. dissertation, City University of New York, 1974), pp. 1-10.

2. Bronson, *History of Waterbury*, pp. 372-373; Morrison, "Isaac Bronson," pp. 18-20; and Elizabeth R. MacRury, *More About the Hill-Greenfield Hill* (North Haven, Connecticut: City Printing Company, 1968), p. 82. Information on economic conditions after the war and the techniques of stock trading appears in E. James Ferguson, *The Power of the Purse* (Chaple Hill: University of North Carolina Press, 1961), pp. 282-283; and Robert A. East, *Business Enterprise in the American Revolutionary Era* (New York: Columbia University Press, 1938), pp. 250-256, 273-275.

3. Edward Pessen, "The Wealthiest New Yorkers of the Jacksonian Era: A New List," *New York Historical Society Quarterly* 54 (April 1970):155. Also see Edward Pessen, *Riches, Class and Power Before the Civil War* (Lexington, Massachusetts: D.C. Heath & Company, 1973), pp. 320-323; and Henry W. Lanier, *A Century of Banking in New York, 1822-1922* (New York: The Gillis Press, 1922). Lanier reprints Moses Beach, *Wealth and Wealthy Citizens of New York* for 1845. However, see Edward Pessen's critique of the Beach pamphlets: Edward Pessen, "Moses Beach Revisited: A Critical Examination of His Wealthy Citizens Pamphlets," *Journal of American*

History 58 (September 1971):415-426. Also see Pessen's more general essay on wealth and mobility in the nineteenth century in Pessen, *Riches, Class, and Power,* pp. 77-91, 130-150.

4. Morrison, "Isaac Bronson," p. 135; "Autobiography of James B. Murray," Murray Family Papers, New York Historical Society, New York, New York, Box IV. On the lifestyle of the nineteenth-century aristocracy see Douglas T. Miller, *Jacksonian Aristocracy: Class and Democracy in New York, 1830-1860* (New York: Oxford University Press, 1967), pp. 56-80; 155-189; and Pessen, *Riches, Class and Power,* pp. 205-247.

5. Oliver Bronson to Mrs. Isaac Bronson, 12 April 1828, Bronson Papers, Box 204; Oliver Bronson to Isaac Bronson, 12 June 1828, Bronson Papers, Box 200; Maria Murray to Arthur Bronson, 23 August 1839, Bronson Papers, Box 215; and MacRury, *More About the Hill,* p. 100. There are several collections of Bronson Papers. The principal collection is housed in the New York Public Library and includes 200 manuscript boxes. A smaller collection is held by the Clarke Historical Library at Central Michigan University, Mt. Pleasant, Michigan. The boxes are numbered consecutively between the New York Public Library [Boxes 1-199] and the Clarke Historical Library [Boxes 200-215]. Hereafter, references will be BP [Bronson Papers] and box number. Isaac Bronson, Arthur Bronson and Frederic Bronson will be abbreviated IB, AB, and FB.

6. "Autobiography of James B. Murray," Muray Papers, IV; James B. Murray to Maria Bronson, 23 May 1814, Murray Papers, I.

7. Ibid. On the Morris Canal and Banking Company, see Carter Goodrich, ed., *Canals and American Economic Development* (New York: Columbia University Press, 1961), pp. 145-146.

8. Bronson, *History of Waterbury,* p. 374; Pessen, *Riches, Class and Power,* pp. 83, 98, 212; Lanier, *A Century of Banking,* p. 97; R.B. Lacey, "Sketches and Personal Reminiscences," in Scrapbook of Frederic Bronson, BP, 215; Carroll Storrs Alden, "Theodorus Bailey," *Dictionary of American Biography,* ed. by Alice Johnson (New York: Charles Scribner, 1927), 1:501-502; and John G. VanDeusen, "Roger Troup: Agent of the Pulteney Estate," *New York History* 28 (April 1942):166-171.

9. C.C. Cambreleng to IB, 13 June 1833, BP, 200; James B. Murray to IB, 30 November 1818, BP, 215; and John Hamilton to IB, 25 February 1829, BP, 79; Bronson, *History of Waterbury,* p. 374; and Mechanics and Farmers Bank, *Span of a Century, 1811-1911, Mechanics and Farmers Bank of Albany, New York* (Albany, New York: Quayle and Son, 1911), p. 9.

10. A. Gorham to AB, 24 October 1842, BP, 205; John Vorhees to AB, 5 April 1835, BP, 203; and N. Freeman to IB, 1 April and 7 February 1834; BP, 200. Also see the "Autobiography of James B. Murray," Murray Papers, IV; Morrison, "Isaac Bronson," pp. 38-41; and MacRury, *More About the Hill,* p. 12.

11. Pessen, *Wealth, Class and Power,* p. 174. Pessen cites the fact that 23 percent of the city's wealthy lived on Broadway and that the entire street came to be known as an "aristocratic thoroughfare." Also see AB to Charles Butler, 11 January 1833, Charles Butler Papers, Library of Congress, Washington, D.C., III; Rental agreement of Frederic Bronson, 7 November 1834, BP, 211; and AB to Gerrit Smith, 1 June 1833, BP, 203.

12. J.B. Murray to IB, 24 September 1819, BP, 215; AB to Lucius Lyon, 24 June 1834, Lucius Lyon Papers, William L. Clements Library, Ann Arbor, Michigan; "Diary of Arthur Bronson, 1835," BP, 119; and MacRury, *More About the Hill,* pp. 87-101.

13. General background on the wealthy and their social concerns can be found in Pessen, *Wealth, Class and Power*, pp. 251-280. On Frederic's involvement with the Union Club, see Pessen, *Wealth, Class and Power*, p. 228 and Robert Ray, Treasurer, Union Club House to Frederic Bronson, 20 September 1837, BP, 208. On social concerns, see Gorham Abbot, Secretary of American Society for Useful Knowledge, to AB, 25 March 1837, BP, 204; Peter Schermerhorn to AB, 20 January 1843, BP, 207; R.S. Cook, Secretary of American Tract Society, to AB, 21 March 1844, BP, 205; and Francis Olmstead to AB, 30 July 1842, BP, 203.

14. My description of early American banking is indebted to the following: Bray Hammond, *Banks and Politics in America* (Princeton, New Jersey: Princeton University Press, 1957), pp. 7, 24-39; Fritz Redlich, *The Molding of American Banking, Part I: 1781-1840* (New York: Hafner Publishing Company, 1951), pp. 6-10; Morrison, "Isaac Bronson," pp. 111-112.

15. Redlich, *The Molding of American Banking, Part I*, p. 10; Thomas C. Cochran, *Business in American Life: A History* (New York: McGraw-Hill Book Company, 1972), p. 63; Morrison, "Isaac Bronson," pp. 112-113; Hammond, *Banks and Politics*, pp. 40-55; Bray Hammond, "Long and Short Term Credit in Early American Banking," *The Quarterly Journal of Economics* 49 (November 1934):80-83.

16. Isaac's basic theory of banking appears in a number of places: IB to C. C. Cambreleng, 17 October 1831, BP, 200; [Isaac Bronson], "Propositions Illustrative of the Principles of Banking," BP, 14; and A Citizen [Isaac Bronson], *An Appeal to the Public on the Conduct of the Banks in the City of New York* (New York: Office of the *New York Courier*, 1815). The best current descriptions of the "soundness" tradition are Richard Sylla, "American Banking and Growth in the Nineteenth Century, A Partial View of the Terrain," *Explorations in Economic History* 9 (Winter 1971-1972): 197-227, and Donald R. Adams, Jr., *Finance and Enterprise in Early America* (Philadelphia: University of Pennsylvania Press, 1978), pp. 1-3, 90-111. Sylla has criticized Bray Hammond and Fritz Redlich for adopting the soundness tradition in their writings, but the reader should look at Bray Hammond's "Banking in the Early West: Monopoly, Prohibition and Laissez Faire," *Journal of Economic History* 14 (May 1948):1-24. Hammond recognized the role of western banks and loose credit in stimulating expansion. Also see Carter Golembe, "State Banks and the Economic Development of the West, 1830-1844" (Ph.D. dissertation, Columbia University 1942). A more recent work on banking that breaks away from the soundness tradition is George D. Green, *Finance and Economic Development in the Old South, Louisiana Banking, 1804-1861* (Stanford, California: Stanford University Press, 1972).

17. Both contemporary and present-day historians have recognized Isaac's influence on commercial banking. See Morrison, "Isaac Bronson," p. 117; and Redlich, *The Molding of American Banking, Part I*, pp. 45-47.

18. Redlich, *The Molding of American Banking, Part I*, p. 11; Morrison, "Isaac Bronson," pp. 120-121; and Sylla, "American Banking," pp. 202-203. Historians are now debating the very issues which divided nineteenth-century financiers. Many historians today believe that inflationary banking was, in the long run, an absolute necessity to facilitate economic growth. The best summary of this debate is Sylla, "American Banking," pp. 197-227.

19. The most reliable account of the Bridgeport Bank was written by Arthur Bronson after his father's death and was published in William Gouge's *Journal of Banking*. Although Arthur did not sign the article, it can be definitely ascribed to him through letters found in the Bronson Papers. See especially William Gouge to

AB, 27 December 1841, BP, 204. The correct citation to the article by Arthur Bronson is: An Old Fashioned Man [Arthur Bronson], "History of the Bank of————," in *The Journal of Banking from July, 1841 to July, 1842: Containing Essays on Various Questions Relating to Banking and Currency* . . . , ed. William Gouge (Philadelphia: J. Van Court, 1842), pp. 209-211, 225-226.

20. AB, "The History of the Bank of————," pp. 207-211; Minutes of Directors of the Bridgeport Bank, 19 February 1815, BP, 202; Redlich, *The Molding of American Banking, Part I,* pp. 19, 45-47, 56; Morrison, "Isaac Bronson," p. 128; and Abraham Venit, "Isaac Bronson: His Banking Theory and the Financial Controversies of the Jacksonian Period," *Journal of Economic History* 5 (November 1945):201-214.

21. AB, The "History of the Bank of————," pp. 210-211.

22. Ibid.; and IB, "Propositions Illustrative of the Principles of Banking," BP, 14.

23. Ibid.

24. Redlich, *The Molding of American Banking, Part I,* pp. 70, 67-95; Hammond, *Banks and Politics,* pp. 549-550. Also see J. Van Fenstermaker, *The Development of American Commercial Banking: 1782-1837* (Kent, Ohio: Kent State University Bureau of Economic and Business Research, 1965), p. 42.

25. A Citizen [Isaac Bronson], *An Appeal to the Public;* Redlich, *The Molding of American Banking, Part I,* p. 70; and Morrison, "Isaac Bronson," p. 133.

26. Hammond, *Banks and Politics,* pp. 551-554.

27. The basic monograph on the Safety Fund is Robert Chaddock, *The Safety-Fund Banking System in New York State, 1829-1866* (Washington: United States Government Printing Office, 1910). Also see Hammond, *Banks and Politics,* p. 559; and Redlich, *The Molding of American Banking, Part I,* pp. 90-91.

28. James A. Hamilton to Governor Van Buren, 1828, in James A. Hamilton, *Reminiscences of James A. Hamilton; or Men and Events at Home and Abroad During Three Quarters of a Century* (New York: Charles Scribner's and Company, 1869), pp. 82-86.

29. Joshua Forman to IB, 17 January, 26 January, and 6 February 1829, BP, 200. Forman accepted the post as agent for the North Carolina lands in 1829. See the Contract between Forman and Bronson, 28 August 1829, BP, 68.

30. John Bolton to IB, 26 January, 5 February, and 29 February 1829, BP, 200.

31. [Isaac Bronson], Letter to the editor of the *Albany Argus,* [1829], BP, 14; Morrison, "Isaac Bronson," pp. 286-288.

32. Morrison, "Isaac Bronson," p. 288.

33. On the land speculation activities of the Albany Regency politicians see Irene Neu, *Erastus Corning: Merchant and Financier* (Ithaca, New York: Cornell University Press, 1960), pp. 129-131. The extent to which regency politicians were involved in land speculation can be discerned in the Thomas W. Olcott Papers, Columbia University Library, New York, New York.

34. AB, "History of the Bank of————," pp. 209-211, 225-226; and William M. Gouge, "Commercial Banking, " *Hunt's Merchant Magazine* 8 (January 1843):315-321.

35. AB, "History of the Bank of————," p. 226.

36. Ibid., pp. 225-226.

37. Ibid; E. Jesup and Jesup Wakeman to IB, 22 September 1832, BP, 200; and E. Jesup to AB, 19 November 1832, BP, 203. Isaac Bronson did hold stock in trust companies, but they were not strictly commercial banks.

38. Bronson's general policies in regard to land investment are best obtained from a perusal of his letters to and from agents. See particularly the BP, 33-64,

78-79, 200-201. Also see AB to Andrew Frank, 21 July 1830, BP, 18; George Griffin to IB, 2 October 1821, BP, 78; N. Howell to IB, 14 June 1829, BP, 79; Thomas R. Gold to IB, 24 September 1814; C. F. Mercer to AB, 20 September 1820; James W. Glass to IB, 19 July 1821, BP, 200.

39. Isaac Bronson's Tenants Book, 1823-1828, BP, 10; Frederick Whittelsey to IB, 10 February 1836, BP, 87; and De Labad to Isaac Bronson, 15 July 1818, BP, 200.

40. Morrison, "Isaac Bronson," p. 217; and BP, 39-64. Grant Morrison recently completed an excellent article on Bronson's moneylending in selected counties. See Grant Morrison, "A New York City Creditor and His Upstate Debtor: Isaac Bronson's Moneylending, 1819-1836," *New York History,* 61(July 1980): 255-276. The elder Bronson also had interests in other states, such as Connecticut and Ohio. See Thomas P. Gold to IB, 12 May 1815 and 19 August 1815, BP, 200.

41. Legal contracts between Ethel Bronson and Isaac Bronson, 1 March 1815, BP, 13. Also see the remainder of Box 13 containing documents relating to Jefferson County. Information on Ethel Bronson obtained from Franklin B. Hough, *A History of Jefferson County in the State of New York* (Albany: Joel Munsell, 1854), p. 420.

The reputation of land investors in western New York has been subjected to considerable revision over the years. See, for example, Raymond Walters and Philip Walters, "David Parish: New York State Land Promoter," *New York History* 26 (April 1945):146-61; Sung-Bok Kim, "A New Look at the Great Landlords of Eighteenth Century New York," *William & Mary Quarterly* 27 (October 1970): 581-614; Robert Silsby, "Credit and Creditors in the Phelps-Gorham Purchase," (Ph.D. dissertation, Cornell University, 1958); Sung-Bok Kim, *Landlord and Tenant in Colonial New York* (Chapel Hill, North Carolina: University of North Carolina Press, 1978).

42. Frederic Bronson to IB, 8 June 1827 and 9 April 1829, BP, 200; Le Ray de Chaumont to AB, 1 January 1825, BP, 203; Alex Le Ray to AB, 29 April 1824 and 19 November 1824, BP, 203; and IB to Andrew Frank, 21 July 1830, BP, 18.

43. James Pompelly to AB, 8 April 1823, 19 May 1823, 16 April 1824, BP, 16; and Agreement of AB and James Pompelly, 1 February 1823, BP, 22.

44. Statement of Shares held by Directors of the Peru Iron Company, 15 September 1826, BP, 207; U.S., Treasury Department, *Documents Relative to the Manufacturers in the United States . . .,* H.R. 308, 22d. Cong., 1st sess., 1833, Vol. II:134. (This is the famous Louis McLane, *Report on Manufacturers,* which appears under several titles. Hereinafter cited as *Report on Manufacturers.*)Also see several letters of Eleazar Lord to AB, 28 August and 7 November 1823, BP, 203. Lord is identified in Redlich, *The Molding of American Banking, Part I*, p. 215; and Morrison, "Isaac Bronson," p. 226. Also see Harry J. Carman and August Baer Gold, "The Rise of the Factory System," in *History of the State of New York,* Vol. II: *The Age of Reform,* ed. Alexander Flick (New York: Columbia University Press, 1934), pp. 205, 209; Duane Hamilton Hurd, *History of Clinton and Franklin Counties, New York* (Philadelphia: J. W. Lewis & Company, 1890), II, p. 139.

45. AB to Francis Saltus, Peru Iron Company, 29 October 1827, BP, 203; Statement of Shares held by Directors of the Peru Iron Company, 15 September 1826, BP, 206. Francis Saltus was identified by Lanier, *A Century of Banking,* p. 130. Also see "Autobiography of James B. Murray," pp. 40-41, Murray Papers, IV.

46. *Report on Manufacturers,* II: 134; "Autobiography of James B. Murray," pp. 40-42, Murray Family Papers, IV; and James B. Murray to Maria Murray, 2 September 1826, Murray Papers, IV.

47. James B. Murray to Maria Murray, 6 May and 3 July 1827, Murray Papers, IV. Francis Welch to J. B. Murray, 3 November 1826, BP, 200. Also see AB to Francis Saltus, 29 October 1827, BP, 203. For information on Murray and Bronson withdrawing from the Peru Iron Company, see "Autobiography of James B. Murray," Murray Papers, IV; Contracts between John Hone and AB, 18 October 1826, BP, 207; H. B. Lloyd to AB, 20 March 1827, BP, 203.

48. Legal documents between Henry Sewall and AB, 26 October 1826, BP, 207; Henry Sedgwick to AB, 15 July 1825, BP, 203; AB to Henry Sedgwick, 5 July 1826, BP, 203; AB to Henry Sedgwick, 3 May 1828, BP, 203; and AB to Robert Schuyler, 2 May 1828, BP, 200.

49. This pattern can be seen in Arthur Bronson's operations in the Peru Iron Company. See AB to Francis Saltus, 29 October 1827, BP, 203; Statement of Shares held by Directors of the Peru Iron Company, 1826; and Legal contracts between John Hone and AB, 18 October 1826, BP, 207.

50. Le Ray de Chaumont to IB, 10 August 1829, BP, 200; Articles of Agreement among James Thomson, Gould Hoyt, Arthur Bronson, James B. Murray and Luther Bingham, 16 August 1825, BP, 68. Boxes 65-67 contain many deeds, contracts and letters on the North Carolina projects. A letter of Arthur Bronson to Frederic Bronson, 9 March 1825, BP, 203, provides the best explanation of the essentials of the purchase. Also see Jacob Cooke, *Tench Coxe and the Early Republic* (Chapel Hill, North Carolina: University of North Carolina Press, 1978), pp. 316-324, 408-409, and 509-510. Information on Augustus Sackett and J. Le Ray de Chaumont can be found in Hough, *Jefferson County*, pp. 444-452.

51. Memorandum of Agreement of Arthur Bronson, Gould Hoyt, James Thompson, James B. Murray, and Jacob Hyatt, 12 March 1835, BP, 68; Agreement of AB and Oliver Bronson, 14 May 1825, BP, 206; AB to Robert Burton, 24 February 1825, BP, 16; AB to James B. Murray, 3 and 4 March 1825, BP, 16.

52. Agreement between AB and Oliver Bronson, 14 May 1825, BP, 206; Agreement between Gould Hoyt, Isaac Bronson, and Charles Julet, 24 January 1829, BP, 68; *Act of the North Carolina Legislature, 1840-41*, BP, 69; and AB to G. Hoyt and J. B. Murray, 11 January 1828, BP, 16.

53. *Washington Globe*, 7 April 1826; James B. Murray to AB, 29 April 1840, BP, 215; Murray to Arthur Bronson, 2 June 1840 and 24 February 1845, BP, 215; "Frederic Bronson's Account Sheet, 1868," BP, 71.

54. On the difference between traditional and modern financiers see Walt W. Rostow, *The Stages of Economic Growth: A Non-Communist Manifesto*, 2nd ed. (Cambridge, England: Cambridge University Press, 1971), pp. 17-28; Richard D. Brown, *Modernization: The Transformation of American Life, 1600-1865* (New York: Hill and Wang, 1976), pp. 94-121; and Frederic C. Jaher, "Old and New Elites and Entrepreneurial Activity in New York City from 1780 to 1850," *Working Papers from the Regional Economic History Research Center* 2 (1978):55-78.

Chapter 2

1. There is surprisingly very little of a substantive nature written on the early history of the trust company in the United States. Gerald T. White, *A History of the Massachusetts Hospital Life Insurance Company* (Cambridge: Harvard University Press, 1955) is the only monograph of modern scholarship on an early institution performing trust functions. Several authors earlier traced the history of the contemporary industrial trust. See Edward Ten Broek Perine, *The History of the Trust Company* (New York: G.

P. Putnam's Sons, 1916); James G. Smith, *The Development of Trust Companies in the United States* (New York: Henry Holt and Company, 1927); Clay Herrick, *Trust Companies, Their Organization, Growth and Management* (New York: Bankers Publishing Company, 1915).

2. The evolution of banks, trust, and savings institutions performing investment functions has only been given limited attention. See Lance Davis, "Capital Immobilities and Finance Capitalism: A Study of Economic Evolution in the United States, 1820-1920," *Explorations in Entrepreneurial History* I (Fall 1963):88-105; Peter L. Payne and Lance E. Davis, *The Savings Bank of Baltimore, 1818-1866: A Historical and Analytical Study* (Baltimore: The Johns Hopkins University Studies in Historical and Political Science, Series LXXII, 1956); Alan L. Olmstead, *New York City Mutual Savings Bank, 1819-1861* (Chapel Hill, North Carolina: University of North Carolina Press, 1976); Richard Sylla, "Forgotten Men of Money: Private Bankers in Early United States History," *Journal of Economic History* 36 (March 1976):173-188; J. Van Fenstermaker, *The Development of American Commercial Banking: 1782-1837* (Kent, Ohio: Kent State University, Bureau of Economic and Business Research, 1965); and George Green, *Finance and Economic Development in the Old South: Louisiana Banking, 1804-1861* (Stanford: Stanford University Press, 1972).

3. White, *A History of the Massachusetts Hospital Life Insurance Company*, pp. 2-38; Perine, *Story of the Trust Company*, pp. 2, 11; Herrick, *Trust Companies*, p. 3 and Smith, *The Development of Trust Companies*, pp. 238-282.

4. White, *A History of the Massachusetts Hospital Life Insurance Company*, pp. 2-3, 17-18.

5. Ibid., pp. 38, 42-54. The history of the Massachusetts Hospital Life Insurance Company is available in a large manuscript collection of its papers at the Baker Library, Harvard University.

6. Allan Nevins, *History of the Bank of New York and Trust Company, 1784-1934* (New York: Printed privately, 1934), p. 49; Perine, *Story of the Trust Company*, pp. 21-22. A list of the original incorporators can be found in *New York Life Insurance and Trust Company, Act of Incorporation, Passed March 9, 1830, Amended May 2, 1834,* (New York: Bowne & Co., Printers, 1850), p. 1. Hereafter cited as *NYLTC Charter.*

7. Isaac Bronson's role in chartering the company was evident in his personal correspondence. See especially William Bard to IB, 26 February 1830, BP, 80; Roger Sherman to IB, 25 May 1830, BP, 80; William Bard to IB, [1830], BP, 200; Horatio Kingsland to IB, 8 March 1830, BP, 200; Roger Sherman to IB, 7 May 1830, BP, 202; and Legal Agreement transferring power of attorney to Isaac Bronson, 4 May 1830, BP, 202.

Bard is identified by Gerald White as having played a prominent role in setting up the New York Life Insurance and Trust Company. See White, *Massachusetts Hospital Life*, p. 55. This is also evident in Bard's own correspondence. He lobbied in Albany for the company's original charter. See William Bard to Susan Bard, 20 February 1833, Bard Family Papers, Columbia University, New York, New York, Box II. In addition, see Hon. James Lloyd to William Bard, 7 September 1829, in New York State, Assembly, *Report of the Committee on the Incorporation and Alteration of the Charters, of Banking and Insurance Companies*, Assembly Document 84, 53rd Session, 1830, II:9-13.

8. New York State, Assembly Doc. 84, 1830, II:4-5; New York State, Assembly, *Report of the Bank Committee, on the Resolution Relating to the Life Insurance and Trust Company*, Assembly Doc. 331, 54th Session, 1831, II: 20-26; and Roger Sherman to IB, 5 March 1830, BP, 80.

9. *NYLTC Charter*, pp. 3-4.

10. Edward Pessen, *Riches, Class, and Power Before the Civil War* (Lexington, Massachusetts: D. C. Heath & Company, 1973), pp. 320-326; and Henry W. Lanier, *A Century of Banking in New York, 1822-1922* (New York: The Gillis Press, 1922). Lanier reprints the Moses Beach lists from 1819 and 1845. Also see Frederic Cople Jaher, "Old and New Elites and Entrepreneurial Activity in New York City from 1780 to 1850," *Working Papers from the Regional Economic History Research Center* 2 (1978):55-78.

11. New York State, Assembly Doc. 84, 1830, II:5-6. See also Smith, *The Development of Trust Companies*, pp. 250-254.

12. New York State, Assembly Doc. 84, 1830, pp. 2-7; Perine, *The Story of the Trust Company*, pp. 22-24. Bronson was involved in the distribution of stock, and it may be that he possessed sufficient clout to acquire stock for his friends. See Roger Sherman to William Bard, 7 May 1830, and Power of Attorney Granted to Isaac Bronson by stockholder applicants, 4 May 1830, BP, 202. A complete list of the company's stockholders can be found in New York State, Assembly, *Communication from William Bard . . .*, Assembly Doc. 279, 57th Session, 1834, IV:1-4.

13. Figures on the breakdown of the amount of stock held by the trustees was calculated from the company's annual reports found in the following documents: New York State, Senate, *Communication from the Chancellor, Relative to the New York Life Insurance and Trust Company*, Senate Doc. 112, 55th Session, 1832, II:14; New York State, Assembly, *Communication from the Chancellor Relative to the New York Life Insurance and Trust Company*, Assembly Doc. 143, 59th Session, 1836, III:14; and New York State, Assembly, *Communication from the Chancellor Relative to the New York Life Insurance and Trust Company*, Assembly Doc. 353, 61st Session, 1838, VI:18-19.

14. *NYLTC Charter*, pp. 3-7. The company later withdrew the requirement that all stock had to be paid for. It allowed stockholders to obtain loans from the company using land as security. See New York State, Assembly Doc. 331, IV:13.

15. Roger Sherman to IB, 5 March 1830, BP, 80; and William Bard to J. W. Woodsworth, 28 September 1830, New York Life Insurance and Trust Company Papers, Baker Library, Harvard University, Letterbooks, Vol. I. Hereafter this collection will be cited as NYLT, LB (Letterbooks), Vol. No.

16. Nevins, *Bank of New York*, p. 50; William Bard to Nathaniel Bowditch, 17 May 1830, NYLT, LB, I; New York State, Assembly Doc. 331, 1831, IV:34-35; and William Bard to IB, 15 June 1837, BP, 88.

17. *NYLTC Charter*, p. 2. Bard, however, later devoted attention to the business and wrote a pamphlet on the subject.

18. New York State, Assembly Doc. 331, IV:16-17; New York Life Insurance and Trust Company Papers, Certificates of Trust, 1832-1837; Perine, *Story of the Trust Company*, pp. 16-17; and William Bard to Thomas Olcott, 14 December 1830, NYLT, LB, I. Also see New York State, Assembly, *Communication from the Chancellor Relative to the New York Life Insurance and Trust Company*, Assembly Doc. 284, 58th Session, 1835, IV:54.

19. Bard to J.Woodsworth, 28 September 1830, NYLT, LB, I; and New York State, Assembly Doc. 143, 1836, III:4-11.

20. *NYLTC Charter*, p. 3.

21. The NYLTC's pattern of investment did fluctuate over time. In 1835 and 1836, it reacted to inflationary trends and extended more personal loans. Bard discussed his own theory of investment in New York State, Assembly Doc. 331, 1831, IV:20-26.

22. New York State, Assembly Doc. 331, 1831, IV:24-25.

23. Bard to Charles Butler, 23 December 1830, NYLT, LB, I; Bard to N. Randall, 25 October 1830, LB, I; and Bard to Edward Knowell, 31 May 1832, NYLT Papers,

LB, II. Also see Neil A. McNall, *An Agricultural History of the Genesee Valley* (Philadelphia: University of Pennsylvania Press, 1953), p. 213.

24. List of New York Life Insurance and Trust Company Agents, (1834), NYLT, LB, IV; W. Bard to Lot Clark, 22 February 1832, NYLT, LB, II; and Nathan Miller, *The Enterprise of a Free People: Aspects of Economic Development in New York State During the Canal Period, 1792-1838* (Ithaca: Cornell University Press, 1962), pp. 144-145. Figures on Clark's bank investments can be found in New York State, Assembly, *Report of the Bank Commissioners. . . .*, Assembly Doc. 89, 56th Session, 1833, II:38.

25. The agents of the NYLTC are listed in New York State, Assembly, "Communication from William Bard," Assembly Doc. 279, 57th Session, IV:1-4. Also see Bard to Frederick Whittlesey, 25 July 1832, NYLT, LB, II; Blake McKelvey, *Rochester, The Water Power City, 1812-1854* (Cambridge: Harvard University Press, 1945), pp. 262-263; McNall, *Agricultural History,* p. 213; Dixon Ryan Fox, *The Decline of Aristocracy in the Politics of New York* (New York: Columbia University Press, 1919), p. 379; and Clark Waggoner, ed., *History of the City of Toledo and Lucas County, Ohio* (Toledo: Munsell and Co., 1888), p. 400. Fuller's Michigan career will be discussed in Chapter 6.

26. There is surprisingly nothing of a scholarly nature written on Charles Butler despite a small but valuable collection of manuscripts at the Library of Congress. There are two early laudatory biographies which reprint many of his letters: G. L. Prentiss, *The Union Theological Seminary in the City of New York: Its Design and Another Decade of Its History, With a Sketch of the Life and Public Services of Charles Butler, L. L. D.* (Asbury Park, New Jersey: M. W. & C. Pennypacker, 1899) and Francis H. Stoddard, *The Life and Letters of Charles Butler* (N. Y.: Charles Scribner's Sons, 1913). W. L. Jenks, "Charles Butler," *Michigan History* 29 (April-June 1945):319-326, has reviewed Butler's career but he failed to acknowledge sources.

The material on Butler's early career is taken from Stoddard, *Life and Letters,* pp. 3, 42 and Prentiss, *Charles Butler,* pp. 427-429. Also valuable is a recent article by Arthur Ekirch, Jr., "Benjamin Franklin Butler of New York: A Personal Portrait," *New York History* 58 (January 1977):47-68, and William A. Butler, *A Retrospect of Forty Years* (New York: Charles Scribner's Sons, 1911), pp. 17-20.

27. Stoddard, *Life and Letters,* pp. 12-13, 18, 58-59; Prentiss, *Charles Butler,* pp. 427-429; Edward A. Collier, *A History of Old Kinderhook* (New York: G. P. Putnam's Sons, 1914), p. 428; Charles Butler to Eliza Ogden, 16 March 1824, Charles Butler Papers, Box III, Library of Congress, Washington, D.C. (Hereafter cited as Butler Papers, Box No.); also see Ekirch, "Benjamin Franklin Butler," pp. 52-55.

28. Charles Butler to Eliza Ogden, 23 January 1824; 8 August 1824; and 6 November 1824; Butler Papers, III. Also see Stoddard, *Life and Letters,* pp. 79-80, 106-107. The backgrounds of the anti-masonic movement can be studied in Alice Felt Tyler, *Freedom's Ferment* (New York: Harper and Row Publishers, 1962), pp. 351-358; and Whitney R. Cross, *The Burned-Over District: The Social and Intellectual History of Enthusiastic Religion in Western New York, 1800-1850* (Ithaca: Cornell University Press, 1950), pp. 114-120; Edward Pessen, *Jacksonian America,* 2nd ed. (Homewood, Illinois: The Dorsey Press, 1978), pp. 261-269; and Ronald P. Formisano and Kathleen Kutolowski, "Antimasonry and Masonry: The Genesis of Protest, 1826-1827," *American Quarterly* 29(Summer 1977):139-165.

29. On the Albany Regency see Robert V. Remini, *Martin Van Buren and the Making of the Democratic Party* (New York: Columbia University Press, 1959), pp. 7-10; and Robert V. Remini, "The Albany Regency," *New York History* 39 (October 1958):341-355.

Butler's involvement in the Regency is documented in Box 3 of his correspondence which contains many letters from Regency politicians. See Lot Clark to Butler, November 1828; Martin Van Buren to Butler, 29 July 1828; Edwin Croswell to Butler, 27 November 1827; Thomas W. Olcott to Butler, 18 December 1828; Butler Papers, III.

On Butler's political appointments see W. T. Barry, Postmaster, to Butler, 2 June 1829; Butler to Citizens of Geneva, 10 June 1828, Butler Papers, III. Also see Stoddard, *Life and Letters*, pp. 86, 111-112.

30. Walter Hubbell to Butler, 16 September 1825 and 22 December 1825, Butler Papers, III; Stoddard, *Life and Letters*, p. 99. Also see Lewis C. Aldrich, *History of Ontario County, New York* (Syracuse, New York: D. Mason & Co., 1893), p. 288 and Charles Milliken, *A History of Ontario County, New York and Its People* (New York: Lewis Historical Publishing Co., 1911), 1:364. The connection between religion and business in the Jacksonian period has attracted substantial attention in recent years. See the excellent brief discussion in Thomas C. Cochran, *Business in American Life: A History* (New York: McGraw Hill, 1972), pp. 102-109. Also see Ronald G. Walters, *American Reformers, 1815-1860* (New York: Hill and Wang, 1978); and Paul E. Johnson, *A Shopkeeper's Millenium* (New York: Hill and Wang, 1978).

31. IB to Butler, 20 July 1831, Butler Papers, III; Butler to AB, 15 August 1831, BP, 98; Stoddard, *Life and Letters*, p. 87; and William Bard to Butler, 6 July 1830, Butler Papers, IV.

32. Bard to Butler, 1 July 1830, Butler Papers, IV; Bard to Butler, 30 September 1833, NYLT, LB, III; Bard to Butler, 23 December 1830, NYLT, LB, I; Bard to Butler, 12 November 1830, Butler Papers, III; Bard to Butler, 12 October 1830, Butler Papers, III; Stoddard, *Life and Letters*, p. 127. Butler's role during the early years of the NYLTC is described in two documents: "Notes on Charles Butler's Role in the New York Life Insurance and Trust Company," [1880s], Butler Papers, II; and "Reminiscences of Charles Butler," [1880s], Butler Papers, IV.

33. Bard to Butler, 20 July 1831, Butler Papers, III; Bard to George Clinton, 7 October 1834, NYLT, LB, IV; Stoddard, *Life and Letters*, p. 124; and AB to Butler, 19 December 1834, Butler Papers, III.

34. Charles Butler, "Copy of a Communication to the New York Life Insurance and Trust Company," [1830s], Butler Papers, III. A published version of this letter can be found in New York State, Assembly Doc. 112, 1832, II:54-57. Also see McNall, *An Agricultural History of the Genesee Valley*, p. 210.

35. Paul D. Evans, *The Holland Land Company*, Buffalo Historical Society Publications (Buffalo: Buffalo Historical Society, 1924), 28:380-386; Stoddard, *Life and Letters*, pp. 115-122; John G. Van Deusen, "Roger Troup: Agent of the Pulteney Estates," *New York History* 23 (April 1942):176-177; and McNall, *Agricultural History*, pp. 35-36, 51.

36. Butler, "Copy of a Communication," pp. 2-3; Bard to J. Vanderkamp, 10 October 1833, NYLT, LB, I; Bard to L. Clark and other agents, 17 October 1833, NYLT, LB, III; McNall, *Agricultural History*, p. 211; and Evans, *Holland Land Company*, pp. 388-393. The trust company purchased only part of the Holland Land Company's contracts. Later the Farmers Loan and Trust Company entered this business.

37. Charles Butler, "Copy of a Communication," pp. 1-6; "Reminiscences of Charles Butler on the New York Life Insurance and Trust Company," Butler Papers, IV; McNall, *Agricultural History*, p. 215.

38. Ibid. Also see Bard to N. Randall, 25 October 1830, NYLT, LB, I. The quote

is taken from "Reminiscences of Charles Butler on the New York Life Insurance and Trust Company," Butler Papers, IV.

39. Bard to W. Randall, 25 October 1830, NYLT, LB, I.

40. "Reminiscences of Charles Butler on the New York Life Insurance and Trust Company," Butler Papers, IV; Charles Butler, "Copy of a Communication," pp. 6-7; Charles Butler, Letter to New York Life Insurance and Trust Company, [1830s], Butler Papers, II.

41. Bard to Edward Knowell, 31 May 1832, NYLT, LB, II.

42. Bard to Lot Clark, 28 November 1832, NYLT, LB, II; and Charles Butler, "Copy of a Communication," pp. 1-3.

43. Charles Butler, "Copy of a Communication," pp. 6-7; *NYLTC Charter*, p. 3.

44. Bard to Lot Clark, 14 November 1832, NYLT, LB, II.

45. Bard to Lot Clark, 8 August 1832, NYLT, LB, II. There are scores of letters from Bard to various agents in New York State describing the company's policies in granting loans on land and buildings. See, for example, Bard to Edward Howell, 11 September 1832, NYLT, LB, II; Bard to C. Butler, E. Whittlesey, Lot Clark, E. Mack, 4 October 1832, NYLT, LB, II; Bard to A. Yates, 5 December 1832, NYLT, LB, II.

46. Bard to Edward Knowell, 31 May 1832, NYLT, LB, II; Bard to Edward Howell, 11 September 1832, NYLT, LB, II.

47. New York State, Assembly, *Report of the Committee on banks and insurance companies. . . ,* Assembly Doc. 209, 56th Session, 1833, III:27-29. Also see Bard to Butler, 6 August 1831, Butler Papers, III; Bard to Butler, 19 April 1832, NYLT, LB, II; Bard to E. Mack, 3 November 1832, NYLT, LB, II.

48. McNall, *Agricultural History,* pp. 214-219. See also the NYLT *Annual Reports* previously cited but especially New York State, Assembly Doc. 284, 1835, IV:3 and New York State, Assembly Doc. 257, 1837, III:10. Added support is given to these observations by Allan Bogue, "Land Credit for Northern Farmers," *Agricultural History* 50 (January 1976):73.

49. Figures on dividends were compiled from several reports. See New York State, Senate, Doc. 59, 1834, II:15-16; New York State, Assembly Doc. 3, 1836, III:18; New York State, Assembly Doc. 267, 1837, III:17; and New York State, Assembly Doc. 353, 1838, VI:17.

50. Butler, "Copy of a Communication," p. 7. Also see Bard to E. Mack, 5 November 1832, NYLT, LB, II; and Bard to Lot Clark, 14 November 1832, NYLT, LB, II.

51. Bard to Lot Clark, 21 April 1831; Bard to W. James, 11 February 1831, NYLT, LB, I. Also see Bard to Lot Clark, 28 November 1832, NYLT, LB, II.

52. Bard to Charles Butler, 1 December 1832, NYLT, LB, II.

53. New York State, Senate, Doc. 112, 1832, II:51; New York State, Senate Doc. 59, 1833, III:25; New York State, Assembly Doc. 284, 1835, IV:24, 56-58; Bard to Butler, 1 December 1832, NYLT, LB, II; Butler to Whiting, 21 March 1833, Butler Papers, III.

54. Report of Legislative Hearing in New York State Assembly, *Albany Argus,* 12 January 1834. Several companies were applying for charters. The Farmers Fire Insurance and Loan Company was actually requesting a change in name to put "Trust" in its title. Descriptions of the various charters can be found in Perine, *The Story of Trust Companies,* pp. 38-40; Smith, *Development of the Trust Company,* p. 260. Also see New York State, Assembly Doc. 209, 1833, III:7-9.

55. *Albany Argus,* 22 and 24 January 1834; Bard to George Atkinson, 13 May

1834, NYLT, LB, IV; Bard to Thomas Olcott, 26 January 1834, NYLT, LB, IV.

56. Bard to E. Corning, 24 December 1832, NYLT, LB, II; Bard to F. Whittlesey, 27 February 1833, NYLT, LB, II; William Bard to NYLTC Agents, 22 July 1833, NYLT, LB, III; Bard to Lot Clark, 10 September 1833, NYLT, LB, III; Bard to Thomas Olcott, 26 January 1834, NYLT, LB, IV; and Butler to B. Whiting, 21 March 1833, Butler Papers, III.

57. Butler to Whiting, 21 March 1833, Butler Papers, III; Bard to Thomas Olcott, 26 January 1834; Bard to J. N. Edwards, 5 February 1834; and Bard to George Atkinson, 13 May 1834, NYLT, LB, IV.

58. *Albany Argus*, 1 May 1834; AB to Buter, 28 May 1833, Butler Papers, III. Also see the discussion of the trust company charter in Chapter III.

59. Smith, *The Development of the Trust Company*, pp. 279-280; White, *A History of the Massachusetts Hospital Life Insurance Company*, p. 54.

60. Frederic Bronson to Thomas Olcott, 15 March 1835, Thomas W. Olcott Papers, Columbia University, New York, New York; Perine, *The Story of Trust Companies*, p. 61; J. B. Gallagher to AB, 2 June 1835, BP, 100; Julius D. Dovell, *History of Banking in Florida, 1838-1954* (Orlando, Florida: Florida Bankers Association, 1955), pp. 19-20; and David Y. Thomas, *A History of Banking in Florida* (N.P., 1930), pp. 26-30.

61. Roger M. Sherman to IB, 22 June 1835, BP, 86; Smith, *Development of Trust Company*, p. 271. There were many other companies mentioned in the correspondence of Bronson and Butler. There were plans for a New Haven Trust Company and a similar company at Hartford. Whether control was ever exercised or any investment took place cannot be determined without access to subscription lists. See Olcott to IB, 23 September 1833, BP, 84; Olcott to AB, 3 October 1833, BP, 99; AB to Thomas Olcott, 1 October 1833, Olcott Papers; and Olcott to FB, 13 March 1835, BP, 208.

Chapter 3

1. See, for example, Lance E. Davis, "Capital Immobilities and Finance Capitalism: A Study of Economic Evolution in the United States, 1820-1920," *Explorations in Entrepreneurial History* 1 (Fall 1963):88-105; Lance Davis, "Capital Mobility and American Growth," in *The Reinterpretation of American Economic History*, eds. Robert W. Fogel and Stanley Engerman (New York: Harper & Row, 1971), pp. 285-300; and Lance Davis, Richard Easterlin, William Parker et. al., *American Economic Growth* (New York: Harper & Row, 1972), pp. 285, 327-328.

2. New York State, Assembly Doc. 143, 1836, III: 18; Harry N. Scheiber, "The Commercial Bank of Lake Erie, 1831-1843," *Business History Review* 40 (Spring 1966):47-65; Carter Golembe, "State Banks and the Economic Development of the West, 1830-1844" (Ph.D. dissertation, Columbia University, 1952), pp. 225-226; Thomas W. Olcott to Micajah T. Williams, 23 May 1833, Micajah T. Williams Papers, Ohio State Library, Columbus, Ohio, Card 28. [I have used a micro-card copy of these papers. Hereafter this collection will be referred to as Williams Papers, card number.]

3. AB to Williams, 30 September 1837, Elisha Whittlesey Papers, Container 5, Western Reserve Historical Society, Cleveland, Ohio. [Hereafter cited as Whittlesey Papers, Container Number.]

4. Few works discuss the development of interstate regulation of corporations. A good discussion of the problem of conducting business across state boundaries is

Tony Allan Freyer, *Forums for Order: The Federal Courts and Business in American History* (Greenwich, Connecticut: JAI Press, 1979), pp. 1-30; and Tony Allan Freyer, "The Federal Courts, Localism, and the National Economy, 1865-1900," *Business History Review* 53(Autumn 1979):344-363. My information on Ohio came from the following: Golembe, "State Banking," pp. 54-55; Nelson W. Evans, *A History of Taxation in Ohio* (Cincinnati: The Robert Clarke Company, 1906), pp. 13-17; Ernest L. Bogart, *Financial History of Ohio*, University of Illinois Studies in the Social Sciences (Champaign: University of Illinois Press, 1912), pp. 336-337; James G. Smith, *The Development of Trust Companies in the United States* (New York: Henry Holt & Co., 1927), pp. 248-250; C. C. Huntington, "A History of Banking and Currency in Ohio Before the Civil War," *Ohio Archaeological and Historical Quarterly* 24 (1915):360-361.

Recent authors have investigated the relationship between law and economic growth. See especially Harry N. Scheiber, "Federalism and the American Economic Order, 1789-1810," *Law and Society Review* 10 (Fall 1975):77-98; and James Willard Hurst, *The Legitimacy of the Business Corporation in the Laws of the United States, 1780-1970* (Charlottesville: The University Press of Virginia, 1970), p. 64.

5. On Ohio's economic development see Harry N. Scheiber, *Ohio Canal Era: A Case Study of Government and the Economy, 1820-1861* (Athens, Ohio: Ohio University Press, 1969), pp. 187-206; Harold E. Davis, "Economic Basis of Ohio Politics, 1820-1840," *Ohio State Archaeological and Historical Quarterly* 47 (October 1938):288-309; Richard C. Wade, *The Urban Frontier: Pioneer Life in Early Pittsburgh, Cincinnati, Lexington, Louisville, and St. Louis* (Chicago: University of Chicago Press, Phoenix Books, 1964), pp. 161-202; U.S. Bureau of the Census, *The Statistical History of the United States from Colonial Times to the Present* (Stamford, Connecticut: Fairfield Publishers, 1965), pp. 7, 12-13; and Huntington, "Banking and Currency," p. 353.

6. Davis, "Economic Basis," pp. 289, 308, 313; Huntington, "Banking and Currency," pp. 342, 359-360; R. Carlyle Buley, *The Old Northwest, 1815-1840*, 2 vols. (Bloomington: Indiana University Press, 1951), 1:607; and William G. Shade, *Banks or No Banks, The Money Issue in Western Politics, 1832-1865* (Detroit: Wayne State University Press, 1972), p. 23.

7. *Niles Weekly Register*, 43 (18 August 1832), p. 436, as cited in Buley, *The Old Northwest*, 1:608; and Huntington, "Banking and Currency, pp. 355-56.

8. Francis P. Weisenberger, *The Passing of the Frontier, 1825-50* (Columbus: Ohio State Archaeological and Historical Society, 1941), pp. 277-285; Huntington, "Banking and Currency," pp. 363-365.

9. Weisenberger, *Passing of the Frontier*, p. 279; Huntington, "Banking and Currency," pp. 363-365; and Shade, *Banks or No Banks*, pp. 25-26.

10. Weisenberger, *Passing of the Frontier*, pp. 279-283; Huntington, "Banking and Currency," pp. 365-366; and Davis, "Economic Basis," p. 313.

11. *Ohio Monitor*, 12 December 1833, as cited in Huntington, "Banking and Currency," pp. 366-367.

12. Huntington, "Banking and Currency," pp. 367-368; and Weisenberger, *Passing of the Frontier*, p. 283.

13. Butler to AB, 8 February 1833, BP, 88.

14. Ibid. Butler commented in the letter that he had only spoken with three people in detail, but he apparently informed others in a general way.

15. Ibid. The original "associates" connected with the Ohio Life Insurance and Trust Co. included the following:

Isaac Bronson	E. T. Throop	A. McIntyre
Arthur Bronson	Goodhue and Co.	Stephen Whitney
Frederic Bronson	John Ward	Rufus Lord
Charles Butler	J. Rathbone	James King
Lot Clark	W. B. Lawrence	John Barr
G. Hoyt	T. Ludlow	B. F. Butler
Prime, Ward and King	J. D. Beers	James Murray

These names are contained in a letter of AB to M T. Williams, 18 October 1833, Williams Papers, 28.

16. Butler to AB, 16 March and 14 April 1833, BP, 99. Also see AB to Butler, 28 May 1833, Butler Papers, III.

17. Butler to AB, 24 April 1833, BP, 99; Arthur Bronson to Butler, 28 May 1833, Butler Papers, III.

18. On Whittlesey's early career see Kenneth Davison, "Forgotten Ohioan: Elisha Whittlesey, 1783-1863" (Ph.D. dissertation, Case Western Reserve University, 1953), pp. 8-12; 35-41; 50-112. Simon Perkins is the subject of a biography by M. L. Conlin. See Mary Lou Conlin, *Simon Perkins of the Western Reserve* (Cleveland: The Western Reserve Historical Society, 1968).

19. Davison, "Elisha Whittlesey," pp. 111-112, 124-127; Harold E. Davis, "Elisha Whittlesey and Maumee Land Speculation, 1834-1840," *Northwest Ohio Quarterly* 15 (July 1943):139-158; and Whittlesey to Mr. Lawrence, 5 March 1836, Whittlesey Papers, 41.

20. Harry N. Scheiber, "Entrepreneurship and Western Development: The Case of Micajah T. Williams," *Business History Review* 37 (Winter 1963):345-368. Also see Samuel Williams, "Micajah Terrell Williams—A Sketch," *Wisconsin Magazine of History* 6 (1922-23):307-310.

21. Scheiber, "Entrepreneurship," pp. 355, 364-366; Williams, "Micajah Terrell Williams," pp. 308-310; Letter of M. T. Williams, 20 February 1833, Williams Papers, 27; Byron Kilbourn to Williams, 20 September 1836, 16 September 1835, and 6 October 1835, Williams Papers, 32.

22. Williams to AB, 4 May 1833, Williams Papers, 28; Scheiber, "Entrepreneurship," p. 356; *Cincinnati Advertiser*, 8 May 1833, contains a list of the directors of the Franklin Bank of Cincinnati. Also see S. Reynolds to Williams, 21 May 1833, Williams Papers, 28; and Alfred Kelley to Williams, 29 April 1833, Williams Papers, 28.

23. Scheiber, "Entrepreneurship," pp. 346, 365-66.

24. Williams to AB, 4 May 1833, Williams Papers, 28; and Lot Clark to AB, 31 May 1833, BP, 99.

25. Williams to AB, 4 May 1833, Williams Papers, 28.

26. AB to Williams, 4 June 1833, Williams Papers, 28; and AB to Butler, 28 May 1833, Butler Papers, III.

27. Thomas W. Olcott to Williams, 22 May 1833, Williams Papers, 26.

28. Ibid.

29. Lot Clark to Williams, 6 June 1833, Williams Papers, 28.

30. Ibid.

31. Olcott to Williams, 23 May 1833, Williams Papers, 28.

32. Butler to AB, 10 June 1833, BP, 99.

33. AB to Williams, 3 July and 24 July 1833, Williams Papers, 28; Butler to Williams, 20 August 1833, Williams Papers, 28.

34. Butler to AB, 10 June 1833, BP, 99; Olcott to Williams, 19 June 1833,

Williams Papers, 19; Charles Butler, "Diary of a Journey," October-November 1833, Butler Papers, IV; Butler to his wife, 14 and 25 October 1833, Butler Papers, III; and Francis H. Stoddard, *The Life and Letters of Charles Butler* (New York: Charles Scribners' Sons, 1913), pp. 150-161.

35. Butler, "Diary of a Journey"; Butler to his wife, 14, 16, 20, and 27 October 1833 and 6 November 1833, Butler Papers, III. David T. Disney and Jacob Burnet are described in the *Biographical Directory of the American Congress, 1774-1961* (Washington, D.C.: U.S. Printing Office, 1961), p. 631 and p. 814. The list of the first trustees can be found in *The First Annual Report of the Ohio Life Insurance and Trust Company* (Columbus, Ohio: Jacob Medary, Jr. & Co., 1835), pp. 25-26.

36. Butler, "Diary of a Journey."

37. Ibid.; Butler to AB, 6 November 1833, BP, 19; Butler to his wife, 17 and 21 November 1833, Butler Papers, III.

38. Roger M. Sherman to IB, 16 April 1833, BP, 84. Roger M. Sherman was a close friend of IB, who often wrote on banking matters and advised the Bronsons on legal issues relating to banks and land speculation. There is a brief sketch of Sherman in Franklin B. Dexter, *Biographical Sketches of the Graduates of Yale College, 1792-1805* (New York: Henry Holt & Co., 1911), 5:41-45. There are small collections of Sherman Papers revealing his connection with the Bronsons at the Bridgeport Public Library, Bridgeport, Connecticut, and at the Connecticut State Library, Hartford, Connecticut.

39. Butler to AB, 14 April 1833, BP, 99.

40. Olcott to Williams, 23 May 1833, Williams Papers, 28; Butler to AB, 18 May 1833, BP, 99.

41. AB to Williams, 4 June 1833, Williams Papers, 28; AB to Butler, 18 May 1833, Butler Papers, III; and IB to Lucius Lyon, 22 May 1835, Lucius Lyon Papers, William L. Clements Library, Ann Arbor, Michigan.

42. AB to Williams, 4 June 1833, Williams Papers, 28; AB to Butler, 28 May 1833, Butler Papers, III; and *An Act to Incorporate the Ohio Life Insurance and Trust Company* (New York: E. B. Clayton, 1834), passim. Hereafter referred to as *OLTC Charter*. Most state legislatures ensured their control over a corporation by including a reserve clause in the charter which gave the state a general right to amend or repeal the charter. See James Willard Hurst, *The Legitimacy of the Business Corporation in the Law of the United States, 1780-1970* (Charlottesville: The University Press of Virginia, 1970), pp. 62-63.

43. AB to Williams, 4 June 1833, Williams Papers, 28; *OLTC Charter*; and *New York Life Insurance and Trust Company, Act of Incorporation, 9 March 1830* (New York: Bowne and Company Printers, 1850), pp. 1-2.

44. Williams to AB, 4 May 1833, Williams Papers, 28, and Williams to Benjamin Tappan, 3 October 1833, Benjamin Tappan Papers, Ohio Historical Society, Columbus, Ohio, Microfilm Copy, Reel 1.

45. *Ohio State Journal*, 29 January 1834; AB to Williams, 31 December 1833, Williams Papers, 29.

46. Ibid. Also Ohio General Assembly, House, *Journal of the House of Representatives of the State of Ohio* (Columbus: David Smith, 1833), p. 506; and *OLTC Charter*, passim.

47. AB to Williams, 11 March 1834, Williams Papers, 24. Also see Scheiber who contends that the OLTC Charter had little connection with the bank issue. See Scheiber, "Entrepreneurship," p. 357.

48. The reference to the right kind of men is in AB to Williams, 11 March 1834,

Williams Papers, 24.

49. AB to Willams, 18 February 1834, Williams Papers, 29; Williams to AB, 8 February 1834, Williams Papers, 29; and *OLTC Charter*, pp. 5-6. Also see AB to Williams, 11 March 1834, Williams Papers, 29; AB to Thomas Olcott, 4 March 1834, Thomas W. Olcott Papers, Columbia University Library, New York, New York; AB to Williams, 9 April 1834, Williams Papers, 29.

50. FB to Judge Burnet, 29 May 1834, BP, 208; FB to Williams, 23 May 1834, BP, 215; Butler to AB, 23 September 1834, BP, 100; and AB to Thomas Olcott, 2 June 1834, BP, 213.

51. Frederic Bronson letter of 23 May 1834, BP, 208; AB to Lewis Cass, 1 June 1834, BP, 203; and AB to N. Tallmadge, 2 June 1834, BP, 203.

52. AB to Williams, 2 June 1834, BP, 203; Butler to AB, 23 September 1834, BP, 100; Butler to AB, 9 Ocotber 1834, BP, 100.

53. List of the stockholders of the Ohio Life Insurance and Trust Company, 23 July 1834, BP, 203. There is an incomplete list of the stockholders in the *Ohio Monitor*, 14 March 1836.

54. There is no complete list of Ohio stockholders, although a partial list was published in the *Ohio Monitor,* 14 March 1836. Also see FB to Williams, 28 May 1834, BP, 208; AB to Williams, 1 June 1834, BP, 203; Alfred Kelley to Williams, 28 July 1834, Williams Papers, 29; and Scheiber, "Entrepreneurship," pp. 358-359.

55. AB to Williams, 12 and 14 June 1834, BP, 200; Elisha Whittlesey to Jesup Wakeman, 2 September 1834, Whittlesey Papers, 41; Davison, "Forgotten Ohioan," pp. 113-115.

56. The complicated financial and legal arrangements prior to the actual opening of the Ohio Life Insurance and Trust Company are difficult to reconstruct. See, however, FB to Williams, 25 July 1834, BP, 208; William Bard to Messers Williams and Burnet, 23 July 1834, BP, 203; AB to Roger Sherman, 14 June 1834, BP, 203; AB's draft of letter to Williams, 20 June 1834, BP, 207; Contract between John Groesbeck of the Franklin Bank of Cincinnati and M. T. Williams and J. Burnet, 28 June 1834, BP, 207.

57. *Cincinnati Advertiser,* 17 February 1836.

58. *OLTC Charter*, pp. 5-8; List of stockholders to the OLTC, 23 July 1834, BP, 203. This list contains a memo indicating which financiers had transferred their powers of attorney. Also see FB to Williams, 25 July 1834, BP, 208.

59. IB to EW, 4 October 1835, Whittlesey Papers, 5; and *The First Annual Report of the Ohio Life Insurance and Trust Company* (Columbus: Jacob Medary, Jr. & Co., 1835), p. 25. James G. King was the son of Rufus King, an old New York Federalist. Also he was a partner in Prime, Ward and King. Gould Hoyt and Isaac Carrow were prominent New York merchants and listed among the city's wealthiest men. See Henry W. Lanier, *A Century of Banking in New York, 1822-1922* (New York: The Gillis Press, 1922), pp. 99, 113. Walter Bowne was a Democrat, merchant and former mayor of the city. See James Grant Wilson, ed., *The Memorial History of the City of New York,* 5 vols. (New York: New York History Co., 1893), 3:338. The character of the Ohio trustees is described in Scheiber, "Entrepreneurship," pp. 358-359; and Davis, "Economic Basis,"p. 313. Also see Harry N. Scheiber, "Alfred Kelley and the Ohio Business Elite, 1822-1859," *Ohio History* 87 (Autumn 1978): 381-383. The first board of trustees also included the following Ohio citizens: George Luckey, William Green, Vachel Worthington, Jeptha Garrard, Samuel Fosdick, Samuel Wiggins, Noah Swayne, Daniel Kilgore, and Samuel Forrer.

60. There is a long correspondence on the company's presidency. See for

example, EW to J. Wright, 5 October 1834; EW to Zalmon Fitch, 8 October 1834; EW to John Wright, 8 October 1834; EW to Simon Perkins, 8 October 1834; and 11 November 1834; EW to S. Perkins, 20 October 1834, Whittlesey Papers, 41. Also see AB to Olcott, 27 October 1834, Olcott Papers and AB to Olcott, 8 November 1834, Olcott Papers.

61. Williams to B. Tappan, 6 May 1834, Tappan Papers, Reel 1; AB to Olcott, 8 November 1834, Olcott Papers; and Davison, "Forgotten Ohioan," pp. 115-116.

62. AB to Olcott, 27 October 1834, and 8 November 1834, Olcott Papers, and Mortimer Spiegelman, "The Failure of the Ohio Life Insurance and Trust Company," *Ohio Archaeological and Historical Quarterly* 57 (July 1948):247.

63. *Report of the Special Master Commissioner in the Matter of the Ohio Life Insurance and Trust Company* (Cincinnati: Cincinnati Journal Office, 1836), pp. 5-13; *OLTC First Annual Report*, pp. 12, 26; *The Second Annual Report of the Ohio Life Insurance and Trust Company* (Cincinnati: Looker, Ramsay & Co., 1836), p. 5; and *OLTC Charter*, p. 5.

64. *Report of the Special Master Commissioner*, 1836, pp. 12-13, 22-23; *OLTC First Annual Report*, pp. 10-12, i-xxxvi; and *Fifth Report of the Master Commissioner in the Matter of the Ohio LIfe Insurance and Trust Company, 1840* (Columbus: C. Scott, 1840), pp. 11.

65. Frederick Whittlesey to Micajah Williams, 16 December 1835, *OLTC First Annual Report*, p. xxi.

66. *OLTC First Annual Report*, p. 35; *OLTC Charter*, pp. 11-12; and *Report of the Special Master Commissioner, 1836*, pp. 7-8, 33-34.

67. *OLTC First Annual Report*, pp. 20, 38; *OLTC Second Annual Report*, pp. 15, 20; *Report of the Special Master Commissioner, 1836*, pp. 22-23; and Simon Perkins to IB, 30 April 1835, BP, 86.

68. *OLTC First Annual Report*, pp. 25, 29. See Chapter 7 for additional discussion of the Ohio Life Insurance and Trust Company.

Chapter 4

1. Floyd Russell Dain, *Every House a Frontier, Detroit's Economic Progress, 1815-1825* (Detroit: Wayne State University Press, 1956), pp. 1-15.

2. John D. Haeger, "A Time of Change: Green Bay, 1815-1834," *Wisconsin Magazine of History* 54 (Summer 1971):285-298; Augustin Grignon, "Seventy-Two Years' Recollections of Wisconsin," in *Wisconsin Historical Collections*, ed. Reuben G. Thwaites (Madison: Published by the Society, 1904),3:242. The *Wisconsin Historical Collections* consist of 30 volumes published from 1855 to 1929. Hereafter documents cited from the *Collections* will be cited as *WHC*. For the early history of Green Bay, see Alice Smith, *James Duane Doty, Frontier Promoter* (Madison: State Historical Society of Wisconsin, 1954), pp. 63-70. On Milwaukee's early history, see Bayrd Still, *Milwaukee: The History of a City* (Madison: The State Historical Society of Wisconsin, 1948), p. 4. Other Wisconsin locations are described in Alice E. Smith, *From Exploration to Statehood*, Vol. I of *The History of Wisconsin* ed. William F. Thompson (Madison: The State Historical Society of Wisconsin, 1973): pp. 104-105. On early Chicago, see John D. Haeger, "The American Fur Company and the Chicago of 1812-1835," *Journal of the Illinois State Historical Society* 61 (Summer 1968):117-139.

3. Francis Paul Prucha, *The Sword of the Republic: The United States Army on the Frontier, 1783-1846* (New York: The MacMillan Company, 1969), pp. 119-137; Francis Paul Prucha, *Broadax and Bayonet: The Role of the United States Army in the Development of the Northwest, 1815-1860* (Lincoln: University of Nebraska Press,

1967), pp. 200-222.

4. Francis Paul Prucha, *American Indian Policy in the Formative Years* (Cambridge: Harvard University Press, 1962), pp. 66-101; Ronald Satz, "Indian Policy in the Jacksonian Era: The Old Northwest as a Test Case," *Michigan History* 60 (Spring 1976):76-81; and Ronald Satz, *American Indian Policy in the Jacksonian Era* (Lincoln, Nebraska: University of Nebraska Press, 1975).

5. There are many works on the fur trade. For the older view that the trade was linked to the frontier's economic expansion, see Frederick Jackson Turner,"The Character and Influence of the Indian Trade in Wisconsin," in *The Early Writings of Frederick Jackson Turner*, ed. Everett Edwards (Madison: The University of Wisconsin Press, 1938), pp. 87-181; Paul Phillips, *The Fur Trade*, 2 vols. (Norman: University of Oklahoma Press, 1961), 2:575. A different view is James L. Clayton, "The Growth and Economic Significance of the American Fur Trade, 1790-1860," in *Aspects of the Fur Trade*, ed. Russell Fridley (St. Paul: Minnesota Historical Society, 1967), pp. 62-72. Also see Haeger, "A Time of Change," passim. Information on the fur trade's operation in the Old Northwest can be found in Kenneth W. Porter, *John Jacob Astor: Business Man*, 2 vols. (Cambridge: Harvard University Press, 1931), 2:686-851; and David Lavender, *The Fist in the Wilderness* (Garden City, New York: Doubleday and Co., 1964).

6. Clayton, "Growth and Economic Significance," pp. 71-72; Haeger, "A Time of Change," pp. 295-298; and Haeger, "The American Fur Company," pp. 135-139.

7. See Haeger, "A Time of Change," pp. 295-298 and "The American Fur Company," pp. 138-139. Population figures on Chicago can be found in Bessie L. Pierce, *A History of Chicago*, vol. 1: *The Beginning of a City, 1673-1848* (New York: Alfred A. Knopf, 1937), p. 46. Also see Jacqueline Peterson, "Wild Chicago: the Formation and Destruction of a Multiracial Community on the Midwestern Frontier, 1816-1837," in *The Ethnic Frontier*, ed. Melvin G. Holli and Peter d'A. Jones (Grand Rapids: Eerdmans Publishing Company, 1977), pp. 26-71; and Rhoda Gilman, "Last Days of the Upper Mississippi Fur Trade," in *People and Pelts*, ed. Malvina Bolus (Winnipeg, Manitoba: Peguis Publishers, 1972), p. 13.

8. *Fifth Census of the United States on Enumeration of the Inhabitants of the United States, 1830* (Washington: Duff Green, 1832), pp. 152-153.

9. Charles Royce, comp., *Indian Land Cessions in the United States, Eighteenth Annual Report of the Bureau of American Ethnology*, Part I (Washington: U.S. Government Printing Office, 1899), Plates 17, 18, 19, 29, 30, 31, 32, 49, 50, 64, 65. Also see the series of maps in R. Carlyle Buley, *The Old Northwest*, 2 vols. (Bloomington, Indiana: Indiana University Press, 1951), 1:111.

10. Charles Butler, "Account of a Trip to the West, 1881," Butler Papers, III:1-2. This manuscript is signed by Charles Butler and dated 1881. I have titled it since it was untitled in the papers. Another copy can be found in the Charles Butler Papers, Chicago Historical Society, Chicago, Illinois.

There are several sources for studying Butler's and Bronson's trip to Chicago. 1. Charles Butler, Diary of a Journey, 1833, Butler Papers, IV. 2. Letters of Charles Butler to Eliza Butler, July-August 1833. These are excellent sources, but Butler occasionally embellished the letters for his wife. 3. [Charles Butler] "The Far West—Internal Improvement—Trade and Intercourse in the State of New York," *Daily Albany Argus*, 18 September 1833. 4. A. T. Andreas, *History of Cook County, Illinois* (Chicago: A. T. Andreas, Publisher, 1884), pp. 129-131. Andreas reprints portions of Butler's 1881 address. 5. Francis H. Stoddard, *The Life and Letters of Charles Butler* (N.Y.: Charles Scribner's Sons, 1903), pp. 129-155. He reprints excerpts from Butler's letters and Diary.

11. Butler, "Account of a Trip," p. 2, Andreas, *Cook County*, p. 98.

12. Memorandum of an Agreement between Robert A. Kinzie and Arthur Bronson, 27 April 1833, Arthur Bronson Papers, Chicago Historical Society, Chicago, Illinois, Letter Folder, 44. Also see Butler, "Account of a Trip," pp. 2-3.

The Bronson Papers in Chicago are much smaller than the New York collection, but they are very important for tracing Arthur's western investments. They are arranged into letter folders each dealing with a separate correspondent. Hereafter cited as BP, CHS, Letter Folder Number.

13. John Farmer, *The Emigrant's Guide or Pocket Gazetteer of the Surveyed Part of Michigan* (Albany: B. D. Packard, & Co., 1831). There were several editions of Farmer's *Guide* after 1833. See AB to Lucius Lyon, 6 August 1833, Lucius Lyon Papers, William L. Clements Library, Ann Arbor, Michigan.

14. Diary, pp. 1-2; Charles Butler to Eliza Butler, 5 July 1833, Butler Papers, III. Hereafter letters from Butler to his wife will be cited as Butler to EB.

15. Diary, p. 2; Butler to EB, 5 July 1833, and 8 July 1833, Butler Papers, III. Blackhawk's movements can be traced in Donald Jackson, ed., *Black Hawk, An Autobiography* (Urbana: University of Illinois Press, 1964), pp. 4-15, 149.

16. Butler to EB, 5 July and 8 July 1833, Butler Papers, III. On the condition of Detroit in the early 1830s, see Buley, *The Old Northwest*, 2:80-81. Also see Jack Kilfoil, "C. C. Trowbridge, Detroit Banker and Michigan Land Speculator, 1820-1845" (Ph.D. dissertation, Claremont Graduate School, 1962), pp. 8-9.

17. Butler to EB, 5 July 1833, Butler Papers, III.

18. Butler to EB, 11 July and 5 July 1833; Diary, pp. 2-3.

19. Diary, pp. 2-5.

20. Diary, p. 7; Butler to EB, 8 July 1833, Butler Papers, III.

21. Robert J. Parks, *Democracy's Railroads, Public Enterprise in Jacksonian Michigan* (Port Washington, New York: Kennikat Press, 1972), p. 33; George N. Fuller, *Economic and Social Beginnings of Michigan* (Lansing, Michigan: Wynkoop Hallenbeck Crawford Co., 1916), pp. 160-166; and Diary, pp. 7-9.

22. Butler to EB, 17 July 1833, Butler Papers, III; Diary, pp. 9-10.

23. Ibid.

24. Diary, pp. 9-12.

25. There is surprisingly little written on Lucius Lyon despite the presence of a large collection of Lyon Papers at the William L. Clements Library. Information on Lyon can be gathered from a dissertation by John Shirigian, "Lucius Lyon: His Place in Michigan History" (Ph.D. dissertation, University of Michigan, 1969), pp. 1-23; and George W. Thayer, "Life of Senator Lucius Lyon," *Michigan Pioneer and Historical Collections*, 27:404-408. The *Michigan Pioneer and Historical Collections* consist of forty volumes published from 1874 to 1929 with varied titles and publishers. Hereafter cited as *MPHC*.

26. Butler to Bowen Whiting, 19 July 1833, Butler Papers, III.

27. Ibid.; Butler to EB, 5 July 1833, Butler Papers, III.

28. Ibid.

29. Butler to EB, 23 July 1833, Butler Papers, III.

30. Butler to EB, 8 July 1833, Butler Papers, III.

31. Butler to EB, 11 July 1833, Butler Papers, III.

32. Buley, *The Old Northwest*, 2:83-84; Fuller, *Economic and Social Beginnings*, p. lxv; and Ray Allen Billington, *Westward Expansion*, 4th ed. (New York: MacMillan Publishing Co., 1974), p. 212.

33. Diary, pp. 12-15; and Andreas, *Cook County,* p. 91.

Two excellent sources for more detailed descriptions of land and towns along the route are Fuller, *Economic and Social Beginnings,* pp. 186-363 and Bernard C. Peters, "Early American Impressions and Evaluations of the Landscape of Inner Michigan With Emphasis on Kalamazoo County" (Ph.D. dissertation, Michigan State University, 1969). See the same author's, "Early Town-site Speculation in Kalamazoo County," *Michigan History* 56 (Fall 1972):200-215.

34. Diary, pp. 19-22, and Butler to EB, 28 July 1833, Butler Papers, III. Prairies can be identified through a map in Fuller, *Economic and Social Beginnings,* lxiii, and in Peters, "Early American Impressions," pp. 80, 87, 89.

35. Fuller, *Economic and Social Beginnings,* p. 272; Butler to EB, 28 July 1833, Butler Papers, III; and Parks, *Democracy's Railroads,* p. 242.

36. Diary, pp. 28-29; Butler, "Account of a Trip," p. 4; Shirigian, "Lucius Lyon," pp. 50-54; Peters, "Early Impressions," pp. 203-204; and Fuller, *Economic and Social Beginnings,* pp. 194-196. On the identity of Lyman J. Daniels see E. Lakin Brown, "Autobiographical Notes," *MPHC,* 30:455-457.

37. Butler to EB, 28 July 1833; "The Far West," *Albany Argus,* 18 September 1833; Diary, pp. 29-35; and Butler, "Account of a Trip," p. 4. There are a number of sources to be consulted on the settlement of Indiana. A good survey is found in Buley, *The Old Northwest,* II:43-53; Billington, *Westward Expansion,* pp. 292-293; and Paul W. Gates, "Land Policy and Tenancy in the Prairie Counties of Indiana," *Indiana Magazine of History* 35 (March 1939):1-26.

38. Diary, pp. 33-35, and "The Far West," *Albany Argus,* 18 September 1833.

39. Diary, pp. 33-34.

40. Butler to EB, 4 August 1833, Butler Papers, III; Diary, pp. 33-35; Butler, "Account of a Trip," p. 4.

41. Diary, pp. 36-37; Butler, "Account of a Trip," pp. 5-6; and Butler to EB, 4 August 1833, Butler Papers, III.

42. Pierce, *History of Chicago,* 1:44-46.

43. Diary, p. 36.

44. Diary, pp. 36-37; and Butler to EB, 4 August 1833, Butler Papers, III.

45. Diary, pp. 38-46; Andreas, *Cook County,* p. 91; and Butler, "Account of a Trip," pp. 6-10.

46. Butler to EB, 4 August 1833, Butler Papers, III; Diary, p. 41; Butler, "Account of a Trip," pp. 9-12; and Butler to Bowen Whiting, 7 August 1833, Butler Papers, III.

47. Diary, pp. 49-59; Butler to EB, 13 August 1833; and Butler to Bowen Whiting, 19 August 1833, Butler Papers, III.

48. Butler to Whiting, 19 August 1833, Butler Papers, III; Diary, pp. 55-59; and Butler to AB, 23 August 1833, BP, 203.

49. Diary, pp. 29-35; and Butler to EB, 4 August 1833, Butler Papers, III.

50. Butler to AB, 10 and 11 December 1833, BP, 32; and Contract of Charles Butler and Isaac Bronson, 25 November 1833, BP, 32. Also see Butler to EB, 7 August 1833, Butler Papers, III; Butler to Bowen Whiting, 19 July 1833, Butler Papers, III; and AB and Butler to Governor Lewis Cass, 20 August 1833, BP, 203.

51. Paul Wallace Gates, *History of Public Land Law Development* (Washington: U. S. Government Printing Office, 1968), p. 165.

52. The literature on land speculation is voluminous, but the basic starting point for a description of speculation is Paul Wallace Gates, "The Role of the Land Speculator in Western Development," *Pennsylvania Magazine of History and Biography*

66 (July 1942):314-33; Paul Wallace Gates, "Frontier Land Business in Wisconsin," *Wisconsin Magazine of History* 52 (Summer 1969):306-327; and Malcolm Rohrbough, *The Land Office Business* (New York: Oxford University Press, 1968), pp. 240-241.

53. Contract between Thomas Olcott, Benjamin Knower, James Thompson, and William Thompson, 25 November 1835, Thomas W. Olcott Papers, Columbia University Library, New York, New York; and Dixwell Lathrop to John Rockwell, 11 June 1835, Dixwell Lathrop Papers, Chicago Historical Society, Chicago, Illinois.

54. Levi Beardsley, *Reminiscences; Personal and Other Incidents; Early Settlement of Otsego County; Notices and Anecdotes of Public Men: Judicial, Legal and Legislative Matters; Field Sports; Dissertations and Discussions* (New York: Printed by Charles Vinten, 1852), pp. 250-252; and James B. Murray to his wife, 18 July 1835, Murray Papers, Box I, New York Historical Society, New York, New York.

55. Robert Swierenga has written two excellent reviews of the literature on land speculation. See Robert Swierenga, *Pioneers and Profits: Land Speculation on the Iowa Frontier* (Ames, Iowa: The Iowa State University Press, 1968), pp. xix-xxviii and "Land Speculation and Its Impact on American Economic Growth and Welfare: A Historiographical Review," *Western Historical Quarterly* 8 (July 1977):283-302. Also see Douglas C. North, *Growth and Welfare in the American Past*, 2nd ed. (Englewood Cliffs, New Jersey: Prentice Hall, 1974), pp. 118-129.

Chapter 5

1. See, for example, Malcolm J. Rohrbough, *The Land Office Business* (New York: Oxford University Press, 1968), pp. 221-224; Paul W. Gates, "Frontier Land Business in Wisconsin," *Wisconsin Magazine of History* 52 (Summer 1969):306-311. For a review of the literature on the land business, see Robert P. Swierenga, "Land Speculation and Its Impact on American Economic Growth and Welfare: A Historiographical Review," *Western Historical Quarterly* 8 (July 1977):283-302.

2. Douglas C. North, *Growth and Welfare in the American Past*, 2nd ed. (Englewood Cliffs, New Jersey: Prentice-Hall, Inc. 1974), p. 125.

3. Charles Butler was a frequent partner in many of these ventures.

4. George McIntosh to AB, 18 December 1835, BP, 204; AB to James B. Murray, 11 March 1840, BP, 20; Contract of AB and Philo Andrews, March 1834, BP, 206; Albert Harrison to IB, 25 April 1836, BP, 200.

5. Bronson's land business in New York State can be traced in the Bronson Papers, Boxes 18, 19, 39-64. Also see "Articles of Association of the Olean Land and Hydraulic Company, 24 June 1836, BP, 211; *Description of New Brighton on Staten Island . . . ,* April 1836, BP, 211; and IB to K. Pritchette, 7 January 1835, BP, 200.

6. Examples of Arthur Bronson's different agencies can be seen in the *Land Book of Arthur and Frederic Bronson*, BP, CHS. This account book is divided by state and by contracts with agents in various states. Hereafter cited as *Bronson Land Book*, then the particular state.

7. Butler to Bowen Whiting, 19 July 1833, Butler Papers, III.

8. Jack Kilfoil, "C. C. Trowbridge, Detroit Banker and Michigan Land Speculator, 1820-1845," (Ph.D. dissertation, Claremont Graduate School, 1969), pp. 1-28.

9. Charles C. Trowbridge, *Personal Memoirs of Charles C. Trowbridge* (Detroit: n.p., 1893), pp. 27-28, 33; Kilfoil, "Trowbridge," p. 114.

10. Clark F. Norton, "Appointments to the Michigan Supreme and Chancery Courts, 1836-1850," *Michigan History* 30 (Spring 1945):331-334; Scrapbook of Elon Farnsworth, Elon Farnsworth Papers, Bentley Historical Library, Ann Arbor, Michigan; Clarence Burton, ed., *The City of Detroit, Michigan,* 7 vols. (Detroit: S. J. Clarke Publishing Company, 1922), 2:1136; and William Potter, "The Michigan Judiciary Since 1805," *Michigan History* 27 (Winter 1943):656.

11. The terms of the contract are derived from several sources. See Trowbridge, *Memoirs,* p. 33; Butler to Bowen Whiting, 19 July 1833, Butler Papers, III; AB to Trowbridge, 2 September 1833, Charles C. Trowbridge Papers, Box II, Burton Historical Collections, Detroit Public Library, Detroit, Michigan. Hereafter cited as Trowbridge Papers. All the cited letters come from Box II. Also see Kilfoil, "Trowbridge," pp. 84-85.

12. Trowbridge, *Memoirs,* p. 33; Butler to Whiting, 19 July 1833, Butler Papers, III; Farnsworth to AB, 11 September 1833, BP, 203; Trowbridge and Farnsworth to AB, 15 December 1834 and 29 September 1833, Trowbridge Papers.

13. Bronson, however, was never successful in enforcing this provision of the contract. See Farnsworth to AB, 11 November 1833, BP, 203.

14. AB to Trowbridge, 31 January 1834; AB to Trowbridge, 30 November 1833; Trowbridge to AB, 29 November 1833, Trowbridge Papers. Also see Farnsworth to AB, 11 November 1833 and 17 October 1834, BP, 203.

15. Silas Farmer, *The History of Detroit and Michigan* (Detroit: Silas Farmer and Company, 1884), p. 336. Bronson's purchase of farm lands is evident in Farnsworth to AB, 29 August 1833, BP, 99; Farnsworth to AB, 11 September 1833, BP, 203; and Farnsworth to AB, 20 November 1833, BP, 203.

16. Trowbridge and Farnsworth to Butler, 21 March 1835; Trowbridge to AB and Butler, 29 November 1835; Trowbridge and Farnsworth to AB and Butler, 22 March 1834, Trowbridge Papers. The best contemporary description of Detroit's business district is Thomas W. Palmer, "Detroit Sixty Years Ago," in the *Michigan Pioneer and Historical Collections* (Lansing: Wynkoop and Hallenbeck, 1902), 31:491-492. The Michigan Pioneer and Historical Collections will hereafter be abbreviated as *MPHC.*

17. Trowbridge to AB and Butler, 22 March 1834; Trowbridge and Farnsworth to AB and Butler, 15 December 1834; Trowbridge to Jonathan Chapman, 24 April 1841, Trowbridge Papers.

18. Kilfoil, "Trowbridge," pp. 144-145; Charles Butler, Diary of a Journey, 1833, Butler Papers, IV; and Butler to B. Whiting, 19 July 1833, Butler Papers, III.

19. AB to Governor Cass, 20 August 1833, BP, 203; Butler to Trowbridge and Farnsworth, 8 April 1835, Trowbridge Papers; Trowbridge, *Memoirs,* pp. 35-37.

20. Butler to Trowbridge, 2 December 1833, Trowbridge Papers; Farnsworth to AB, 30 November 1833, BP, 203; Butler to AB, 22 May 1834, BP, 100; Kilfoil, "Trowbridge," pp. 84-94; and Robert J. Parks, *Democracy's Railroads, Public Enterprise in Jacksonian Michigan* (Port Washington, New York: Kennikat Press, 1972), pp. 46-47.

21. Farnsworth to AB, 22 June 1835, BP, 100; FB to Lucius Lyon, 26 August 1835, Lucius Lyon Papers, William L. Clements Library, Ann Arbor, Michigan; Butler to Trowbridge and Farnsworth, 19 December 1836, Trowbridge Papers; and Butler to Trowbridge and Farnsworth, 19 April 1836, Butler Papers, IV.

22. Farnsworth to AB, 23 May 1834, BP, 203.

23. Butler to AB, 23 September 1833, BP, 203.

24. Trowbridge to James Polk, 20 September 1836, Trowbridge Papers; and Butler to AB, 7 August 1834, BP, 100.

25. Farnsworth to AB, 8 October 1834, BP, 203; Trowbridge and Farnsworth to AB and Butler, 15 December 1834; Trowbridge and Farnsworth to Butler, 16 February 1835; Butler to Trowbridge and Farnsworth, 14 January 1835; and Butler to Trowbridge and Farnsworth, 9 November 1835, Trowbridge Papers.

26. AB and IB to Lucius Lyon, 30 June 1836, Lyon Papers.

27. John Shirigian, "Lucius Lyon: His Place in Michigan History" (Ph.D. dissertation, University of Michigan, 1961), pp. 1-2, 36-80; George W. Thayer, "Life of Senator Lucius Lyon," *MPHC*, 27:404-414; M.T. Williams to Lyon, 8 August 1833; Lyon to Thomas Sheldon, 6 September 1832; and Trowbridge to Lyon, 3 December 1833, Lyon Papers.

28. AB to Lyon, 15 July 1834; Contract of Lyon and IB, 24 October 1834; and IB to Lyon, 10 March 1836, Lyon Papers.

29. AB to Lyon, 24 August 1833; and AB to Lyon, 24 June 1834, Lyon Papers.

30. Albert Baxter, *History of the City of Grand Rapids, Michigan* (New York: Munsell & Co., 1891), pp. 19-21; William J. Etten, *A Citizen's History of Grand Rapids, Michigan* (Grand Rapids, Michigan: A. P. Johnson Co., 1926), pp. 10-15; Shirigian, "Lyon," pp. 42-43. Also see Lyon to Thomas Sheldon, 6 September 1832, Lyon Papers; and Lyon to George Macy, 12 December 1844, BP, 23.

31. Etten, *Grand Rapids*, pp. 9-14; Map of the City of Grand Rapids, 1832, and Map of the Town of Kent, c. 1834, Clarke Historical Library, Central Michigan University, Mt. Pleasant, Michigan.

32. AB to Lyon, 24 August 1833, Lyon Papers; Lyon to G. Macy, 12 December, 1844, BP, 23; and Etten, *Grand Rapids*, pp. 9-14.

33. AB to Lyon, 17 June 1835, Lyon Papers; Lyon to AB, 12 October 1835, in L. G. Stuart, "Letters of Lucius Lyon," *MPHC*, 27:459-460.

34. AB to Lyon, 17 June 1835, Lyon Papers.

35. AB to Lyon, 27 August 1835, Lyon Papers; Agreement of AB and Lyon, 5 December 1835, Lyon Papers; and Lyon to George Bates, 12 December 1844, BP,23.

36. AB to Lyon, 27 August 1835; 30 June 1836; and 25 February 1839, Lyon Papers.

37. AB to Lyon, 24 August and 22 October 1833; 12 August 1834; 6 August and 31 October 1835, Lyon Papers. Also see Agreement of AB and Lyman J. Daniels, June 1835, BP, CHS, 24; E. Hayward to Lyon, 18 January 1834, Lyon Papers; Contract of AB and Lyon, 9 December 1835, Lyon Papers; and Shirigian, "Lyon," pp. 46-59.

38. AB to Lyon, 30 June 1836; and AB to Lyon, 17 October 1836, Lyon Papers.

39. Almy to Lyon, 4 December 1836; Almy to Lyon, 29 November 1836, Lyon Papers. Also see Shirigian, "Lyon," p. 43; Douglas H. Gordon and George S. May, eds., "The Michigan Land Rush in 1836," *Michigan History* 43 (March 1959):465; Charles Carrol to Lyon, 1 October 1838, Lyon Papers; and Neil A. McNall, "The Landed Gentry of the Genesee," *New York History* 26 (April 1945):164-167.

40. C. K. Green to AB, 8 October 1835, 30 June 1835, and 18 September 1835, BP, 204; and James Grant to AB, 8 March 1836, BP, CHS; and *Bronson Land Book*, passim.

41. Jacob Walker to AB, 30 May 1835, BP, 204; and Contract of Jacob Walker and AB, 17 February 1836, BP, 206.

42. Butler to Eliza Butler, 4 and 5 August, 1833, Butler Papers, III; Butler, Diary of a Journey, 1833, Butler Papers, IV; Bessie L. Pierce, *A History of Chicago*, vol. 1: *The Beginning of a City, 1673-1848* (New York: Alfred A. Knopf, 1937), pp. 45-56.

43. Agreement of Robert Kinzie and Arthur Bronson, 27 April 1833, BP, CHS,

48; Charles Butler, "Account of a Trip to the West," (1881), Butler Papers, pp. 1-15; Butler to his wife, 19 July 1833, Butler Papers, III; A. T. Andreas, *History of Cook County, Illinois* (Chicago: A. T. Andreas, 1884), p. 98; and J. Young Scammon, *Chicago Historical Society, Introductory Address* (Chicago: Fergus Printing Co., 1877), p. 11.

44. Butler, "Account of a Trip," p. 14; and AB to Lyon, 24 August 1833, Lyon Papers.

45. AB to David Hunter, 19 September 1833, Lyon Papers. Descriptions of the Hunter property can be found in a Deed of Sale between AB and David Hunter, 1 November 1834, BP, CHS, I; and Butler, "Account of a Trip," pp. 14-15.

46. Deed of AB and David Hunter, 1 November 1834, BP, CHS, I; Contract of FB and Lyon, 1 November 1834, Lyon Papers; Lot Clark to FB, 18 August 1835, BP, 124; AB to Micajah Williams, 24 May 1834, Micajah T. Williams Papers, Ohio State Library, Microcard, 29. Also see Trowbridge, *Personal Memoirs of Charles C. Trowbridge,* pp. 33-34.

47. John Temple Memo, August 1833, BP, CHS, 63; Contract of Bronson and Temple, 9 October 1833, BP, CHS, 63; Andreas, *Cook County,* p. 287; A. T. Andreas, *History of Chicago,* 3 vols. (Chicago: A. T. Andreas, 1884), 1:132.

48. George B. Utley, "Walter Newberry," *Dictionary of American Biography,* 7:447-448; Butler to AB, 9 October 1834, BP, 100; Walter Newberry to Lyon, 13 December 1833, Walter L. Newberry Letters, Newberry Library, Chicago, Illinois. Also see Contract of Gould Hoyt, Charles Hoyt, AB, and Newberry, 1 October 1834, BP, 211.

49. A good, concise description of early Chicago can be found in Homer Hoyt, *One Hundred Years of Land Values in Chicago: The Relationship of the Growth of Chicago to the Rise of Its Land Values, 1830-1933* (Chicago: University of Chicago Press, 1933), pp. 10-23. Also see Gurdon Hubbard to Edward A. Russell, 5 July 1835, Gurdon Hubbard Papers, Chicago Historical Society, Chicago, Illinois, Letter Folder II.

50. AB to John Kinzie, 2 May 1834; 26 May 1834; 18 June 1834; BP, CHS, 14. Also see R. J. Hamilton to AB, 26 August and 16 October 1833, BP, 203; and Pierce, *History of Chicago,* 1:296.

51. *Chicago Democrat,* 9 July 1834 and 25 March 1835; and R. J. Hamilton to AB, 11 February 1834, BP, 203.

52. Butler, "Account of a Trip," pp. 11-13; and *Illinois Advocate and State Register,* 28 September 1833. Gurdon Hubbard of Chicago had tried to interest the Illinois legislature in 1832 but without success. See Pierce, *History of Chicago,* 1:46-47; and John Krenkel, *Illinois Internal Improvements 1818-1848* (Cedar Rapids, Iowa: The Torch Press, 1958), p. 52.

53. Butler and AB to Lyon, 21 August 1833, Butler Papers, III; AB to Lyon, 24 August 1833, Lyon Papers; Butler and AB to Lyon, 17 August 1833, Lyon Papers; and Butler and AB to Lyon, 27 August 1833, BP, 203.

54. Ibid.

55. Ibid.; "Charter of the Illinois and Michigan Railroad Company," 8 December 1833, Business Folders, Lyon Papers; AB to Lyon, 1 March 1834; AB to Lyon, 7 September 1833, 22 October 1833, and 6 June 1834, Lyon Papers; and Temple to AB, 27 February 1834, BP, CHS, 63; Hamilton to AB, 26 August 1833, BP, 203; and Hamilton to AB, 28 November 1833, BP, 203.

56. Temple to AB, 12 June 1834 and 21 May 1834, BP, CHS, 63; Hamilton, Owen, Kinzie, and Hubbard to AB, 9 August 1834, BP, 203; Hamilton and Kinzie

to AB, 11 January 1835, BP, 203; and Gurdon Hubbard to Edward Russell, 12 August 1834, Gurdon Hubbard Papers, Letter Folder I, CHS.

57. *Chicago Democrat,* 19 November 1834.

58. Hamilton and Kinzie to AB, 11 January 1835, BP, 203.

59. AB to Lyon, 13 December 1834, Lyon Papers; and Temple to AB, 14 January 1835, BP, CHS, 63.

60. James William Putnam, *The Illinois and Michigan Canal* (Chicago: University of Chicago Press, 1918), p. 56, n. 1.

61. Lyon to AB, 5 September 1833, Butler Papers, III; AB to Temple, 17 April 1834, BP, CHS, 63; and Temple to AB, 27 February 1834, BP, 64.

62. Hoyt, *One Hundred Years of Land Values,* pp. 26-27; *Chicago Democrat,* 7 October 1835; Butler, "Account of a Trip," pp. 15-17; and FB to Lyon, 7 February 1835, Lyon Papers.

63. AB to Lyon, 18 and 23 May 1835, Lyon Papers; Butler, "Account of a Trip," pp. 15-16. It is unclear, however, whether Bronson himself maintained an interest in the Hunter purchase. See AB to Lyon, 18 and 23 May 1835, Lyon Papers. The American Land Company will be discussed in Chapter 6.

64. Walter L. Newberry to Lyon, 14 June 1835, Lyon Papers.

65. James B. Murray to Albert G. Ellis, 1 February 1836, BP, CHS, 29; Ellis to Murray, 10 May 1836, BP, CHS, 29; and Ellis to Murray, 20 February 1837, BP, CHS, 30.

66. Lyman J. Daniels to Lyon, John Ward, AB, and G. Denniston, 4 April 1836, Lyon Papers; FB, Agreements Relating to Cassville, (c. 1850), BP, CHS, 26; AB to the President, 25 May 1836, BP, CHS, 69. Also see Daniels to Lyon, 24 December 1834, Lyon Papers. There were earlier attempts to promote Cassville. For background, see Alice Smith, *From Exploration to Statehood,* vol. 1: *History of Wisconsin* (Madison: State Historical Society of Wisconsin, 1973), pp. 226-227.

67. AB to Denniston, 8 August 1836, BP, CHS, 25; AB to the President, 25 May 1836, BP, CHS, 29; AB to Lyon, 29 April and 5 February 1836, Lyon Papers; FB to Lyon, 3 February 1836, Lyon Papers. The struggle to obtain a bank charter is a long and complex story. For example, see AB to Morgan L. Martin, 4 June 1835, Morgan L. Martin Papers, Box III, State Historical Society of Wisconsin, Madison, Wisconsin; J. W. Martin to M. L. Martin, 5 and 12 October 1835, Martin Papers, IV. Also see Smith, *From Exploration to Statehood,* pp. 278-279.

68. Daniels to Lyon, John Ward, AB, and Denniston, 4 April 1836, Lyon Papers; *History of Grant County, Wisconsin* (Chicago: Western Historical Company, 1881), p. 841; Copy of a letter of Ethan Brown, Commissioner of the General Land Office to the President, c. 1836, BP, CHS, 69; Benjamin F. Butler to Levi Woodbury, 18 April 1836, BP, CHS, 69; and AB to Ethan Brown, 29 April 1836 and 23 May 1836, BP, CHS, 69.

69. Benjamin F. Butler to Levi Woodbury, 18 April 1836, BP, CHS, 69; and AB to Denniston, 8 August 1836, BP, CHS, 25.

70. AB to Lyon, 5 August 1834 and 26 March 1836, Lyon Papers. Also see AB to Denniston, 11 March 1836 and 2 May 1836, BP, CHS, 25; Contract between Nelson Dewey and Denniston, 14 September 1837, Nelson Dewey Papers, State Historical Society of Wisconsin, Madison, Wisconsin, Box III; and the *Milwaukee Sentinel,* 22 July 1889.

71. Smith, *From Exploration to Statehood,* pp. 233-238; Newberry to Lyon, 10 February 1836, Newberry Letters; AB to Lyon, 5 February 1836, Lyon Papers; and Newberry to Lyon, 13 March 1836, Newberry Letters.

72. John Horner to Lyon, 17 April 1836; 16 and 30 May 1836, Lyon Papers.

73. Smith, *From Exploration to Statehood*, pp. 251-259; and John Horner to Lyon, 5 and 23 November 1836, 29 December 1836, Lyon Papers.

74. *Bronson Land Book*, "Wisconsin,"; John Sheldon to Lyon, 17 December 1835, John P. Sheldon Papers, State Historical Society of Wisconsin, Madison, Wisconsin; Andrew Palmer to Lyon, 2 and 24 November 1836, Lyon Papers.

75. See, for example, Bronson's contracts with Illinois agents. Contract of FB and Clybourne, 22 June 1835, BP, 182; FB and Stephen Forbes, 23 June 1835, BP, 182. The estimation of average price was obtained from the figures in the *Bronson Land Book*. Also see AB and FB to S. V. Wilder, 9 July 1836, BP, 101; AB and FB to A. Burnham, 13 February 1836, Williams Papers, 33.

76. AB and FB to A. Burnham, 13 February 1836, Williams Papers, 33. Also see James Bryant to AB, 28 April 1836, BP, 19; and James Bryant to AB, 16 April 1836, BP, 19.

77. Paul Gates, of course, has been the most consistent critic of the deleterious effects of land speculation in America. See especially Paul Gates, "The Role of the Land Speculator in Western Development," *Pennsylvania Magazine of History and Biography* 66 (July 1942):314-333, and the excellent collection of his articles, *Landlords and Tenants on the Prairie Frontier* (Ithaca: Cornell University Press, 1973). Gates mentions the Bronsons in several places. See Gates, *Landlords and Tenants*, pp. 5 and 128; and Gates, "Frontier Land Business in Wisconsin," p. 309.

78. Bronson's policies regarding the sale of land can be seen in his correspondence with agents such as Trowbridge. See, for example, Trowbridge and Farnsworth to Bronson, 15 December 1834 and 12 March 1835, Trowbridge Papers; and *Bronson Land Book*, "Michigan." The one exception to Bronson's policies was his purchase of 5,000 acres in southwestern Wisconsin to start a stock farm where he planned to retire. Gates mistakenly cites this purchase as an example of Bronson's general policies. See AB to Charles Bracken and A. Van Zandt, 4 April 1836, Sheldon Papers; AB to Lyon, 6 August 1835, Lyon Papers; AB to Leander Judson, 22 July 1838, BP, CHS, 39; and Gates, "Frontier Land Business in Wisconsin," pp. 316-317.

79. AB to Farnsworth, 17 November 1834, BP, 203; AB to J. Wells, 17 November 1834, BP, 203.

80. Ibid. Bronson's fears and reactions to national banking policy are discussed in Chapter 7.

81. Charter of the Michigan Life Insurance and Trust Company, c. 1834, BP, 203.

82. There is an extensive correspondence in the Bronson Papers relating to the projected trust company in box 203. Specific citations would include: AB to Lyon, 15, 17, and 22 November 1834; AB to Farnsworth, 21 and 22 November 1834, BP, 203.

83. Hamilton to AB, 11 and 18 February 1834, BP, 203; FB to Thomas Olcott, 2 March 1835, BP, 208; T. Smith to AB, 19 May 1835, BP, 100. Also see George Dowrie, *The Development of Banking in Illinois, 1817-1867*, University of Illinois Studies in the Social Sciences, II (Urbana: University of Illinois Press, 1913), pp. 60-71. Bronson also considered a trust company in Indiana. See Calvin Fletcher to AB, 14 November 1835, BP, 100; and James Bryant to AB, 26 August 1836, BP, 19.

84. Contract of Gould Hoyt, Charles Hoyt, AB, and Walter Newberry, 1 October 1834, BP, 211; AB and FB to S. V. Wilder, 9 February and 9 July 1836, BP, 101; *Bronson Land Book*, "Wisconsin" and "Indiana"; Contract of FB and John

Ward, 4 May 1835, BP, 182; and A. Clybourne to FB, 22 August 1835, BP, 182.

85. Terms of Mortgage Contracts are listed in the *Bronson Land Book.* In addition, consult Bryant to AB, 24 May and 18 June 1836, BP, 19; and Grant Goodrich to AB, 7 April 1836, BP, 204. Also see Lawrence Friedman, "The Usury Laws of Wisconsin: A Study in Legal and Social History," *Wisconsin Law Review* (July 1963):515-565.

86. Gates, "Frontier Land Business," p. 309; *Bronson Land Book,* passim.

87. Paul Gates, *History of Public Land Law Development* (Washington: U.S. Government Printing Office, 1968), p. 171.

88. AB and FB to S. V. Wilder, 9 July 1836, BP, 101.

89. Paul Gates, of course, best represents the older view which stresses the western agent's crucial importance. See his most recent statement in "Frontier Land Business in Wisconsin," p. 309. Studies attributing a more important role to the eastern capitalist include Robert P. Swierenga, *Pioneers and Profits: Land Speculation on the Iowa Frontier* (Ames, Iowa: Iowa State University Press, 1968), pp. 158-185. Also see Allan G. Bogue, *Money At Interest* (Ithaca, New York: Cornell University Press, 1955).

Chapter 6

1. Butler to Martin Van Buren, 6 August 1839, Butler Papers, III. Butler also invested with his brother Benjamin. See Butler to Benjamin F. Butler, 10 November 1836, Butler Papers, III. Also see Francis H. Stoddard, *The Life and Letters of Charles Butler* (New York: Charles Scribner's Sons, 1903), p. 165.

2. Butler to Lucius Lyon, 15 August 1834, Lyon Papers; and William Bard to Butler, 19 September 1836, Butler Papers, III.

3. Daniel Boorstin, *The Americans, The National Experience* (New York: Random House, 1965), pp. 115-121; Charles Butler, Diary of a Journey, Summer, 1833, Butler Papers, IV. Also See Butler's letters home in the early 1840s when he traveled extensively in the West. Of particular interest are the letters that he wrote while in Indiana negotiating with the state legislature over its bonded indebtedness. Many of these letters are reprinted in George L. Prentiss, *The Union Theological Seminary in the City of New York: Its Design and Another Decade of Its History* (Asbury Park, New Jersey: M. W. & C. Pennypacker, 1899), pp. 427-499.

4. See Letter of Absalom Peters, 19 June 1833, Butler Papers, III; Butler to AB, 23 September 1833, BP, 203; and Diary, pp. 23-26.

5. Diary, pp. 44-45.

6. William L. Jenks, "Charles Butler," *Michigan History* 29 (April-June 1945): 321; Stoddard, *Life of Charles Butler,* pp. 166, 306-309; and Prentiss, *The Life and Letters of Charles Butler,* p. 433.

7. *First Annual Report of the American Land Company* (New York: E. B. Clayton, 1836), p. 3; American Land Company, *Articles of Agreement, 1835* (New York: n.p., 1835), pp. 1-3; Paul Wallace Gates, *History of Public Land Law Development* (Washington: U.S. Government Printing Office, 1968), pp. 171-174; Irene Neu, *Erastus Corning: Merchant and Financier, 1794-1872* (New York: Cornell University Press, 1960), pp. 129-136. Also see letter of W. Kent to Thomas W. Olcott, 6 November 1835, Thomas W. Olcott Papers, Columbia University, New York, New York. American Land Company is hereafter referred to as ALC.

8. *ALC Annual Report,* pp. 27-31. On occasion, Paul Gates has identified the Bronsons as co-founders of the ALC, but he has little proof for this assertion. More

than likely, the Bronsons were merely stockholders since their correspondence carries no letters on this subject. See Gates, *Public Land Law*, p. 171; and Contract of Frederic Bronson, John B. James, Edward Nicoll, and Erastus Corning, 1 September 1837, BP, 182.

The identity of the Boston stockholders has never been explored. Some, such as Franklin Dexter, Samuel Walley, and Franklin Haven were also railroad promoters. See Arthur M. Johnson and Barry Supple, *Boston Capitalists and Western Railroads* (Cambridge: Harvard University Press, 1967), pp. 18, 83.

9. Account sheet of the Corning Proprietors, 1 July 1837, Olcott Papers; Articles of Association of the Irving Land Company, 17 August 1836, Olcott Papers. Also see Thomas Clark to Thomas Olcott, 30 October 1841; 21 March 1843; and 24 August 1842; William Thompson to Governor Marcy, 12 October 1835 and 4 November 1835; Contract of Olcott, Benjamin Knower, and James Thompson, 19 November 1835, Olcott Papers. Olcott's bank investments are mentioned in Chapters 2 and 3. Also see William G. Shade, *Banks or No Banks, The Money Issue in Western Politics, 1832-1865* (Detroit: Wayne State University Press, 1966), p. 35.

10. *ALC Annual Report*, p. 27; and Mary Young, *Redskins, Ruffleshirts and Rednecks* (Norman: University of Oklahoma Press, 1961), pp. 138-139.

11. *ALC Annual Report*, pp. 5, 23, and 27.

12. *ALC Annual Report*, pp. 4-7, 9-16; Butler to Henry Anderson, 24 January 1837, and 2 July 1838, Butler Papers, IV; Neu, *Corning*, pp. 129-130; Young, *Redskins, Ruffleshirts and Rednecks*, pp. 117-118, 138-139; Stoddard, *The Life and Letters of Charles Butler*, p. 209; and Gates, *Public Land Law*, pp. 169-173.

13. Butler to Lyon, 14 May 1835, 2 July 1835, 24 August 1835, Lyon Papers. Also see Neu, *Corning*, pp. 129-130; American Land Company, *Catalogue of Lands Belonging to the American Land Company to be Sold at Public Auction . . . 1844* (New York: American Land Company, 1844), pp. 9-59; American Land Company, *Supplement to Catalogue Valuation of Town Property, and of Land in Wisconsin . . .* (New York: American Land Company, 1844), p. 1; and *ALC Annual Report*, pp. 16-21.

14. ALC, *Catalogue 1844*, pp. 60-87; ALC, *Catalogue, Supplement*, pp. 2-3; *ALC Annual Report*, pp. 16-21; Neu, *Corning*, pp. 2-3; and H. S. Knapp, *History of the Maumee Valley* (Toledo: H. S. Knapp, 1877), p. 422. The American Land Company invested in many other states, including Indiana and New York.

15. The American Land Company trustees often entered the company's lands under their own names. Gates found examples of this when Charles Butler and Frederic Bronson entered lands for the company. Mary Young discovered the same practice in the South. See Gates, *Landlords and Tenants*, p. 150, and Young, *Redskins*, p. 132 n.

The ALC entered lands in the names of individual trustees because land office certificates were not set up to handle the entering of lands by joint-tenants or corporations. See the *ALC Annual Report*, p. 24.

Gates incorrectly lumps together the private and corporate investments of F. Bronson and Butler. It might be that many of Bronson's and Butler's promotions at Chicago, Port Huron, and Toledo were actually owned by the ALC. A more likely explanation is that the ALC invested in areas attractive to private investors as well.

16. *Chicago American*, 3 September 1836, and 12 August 1836. Also see Neu, *Corning*, pp. 130-131; Gates *Public Land Law*, pp. 172-173; and *ALC Annual Report*, p. 27.

17. William L. Mackenzie, *The Lives and Opinions of Benj'n Franklin Butler and Jesse Hoyt* (Boston: Cook & Co., 1845), pp. 122-123; and Arthur Ekirch, Jr., "Benjamin F. Butler of New York: A Personal Portrait," *New York History* 58 (January 1977):61-63.

18. Gates, *Public Land Law*, p. 173.

19. Neu, *Corning*, pp. 129-130; *ALC Annual Report*, pp. 27-28.

20. Charles Butler to T. O. Davis, 17 August 1836, Butler Papers, IV; and *Chicago American*, 3 September 1836.

21. *ALC Annual Report*, pp. 25-26; Douglas C. North, *Growth and Welfare in the American Past* (Englewood Cliffs, New Jersey: Prentice-Hall, Inc., 1974), pp. 124-126; and ALC, *Articles of Agreement*, pp. 9.

22. *ALC Annual Report*, pp. 22-23; Butler and Franklin Dexter to AB, July 1842, BP, 205; Butler to Oliver Bronson, 20 March 1844, BP, 202; and Neu, *Corning*, pp. 134-136.

23. Clark Waggoner, ed., *History of the City of Toledo and Lucus County, Ohio* (Toledo: Muncell and Co., 1888), pp. 370-371; Harry N. Scheiber, "Entrepreneurship and Western Development: The Case of Micajah T. Williams," *Business History Review* 37 (Winter 1963):355; H. S. Knapp, *History of the Maumee Valley* (Toledo: H.S. Knapp Co., 1877), pp. 536-537; and Harvey Scribner, *Memoirs of Lucas County and the City of Toledo*, 2 vols. (Madison, Wisconsin: Western Historical Association, 1910), 1:77-78.

24. Waggoner, *Toledo*, pp. 375-376; Knapp, *History of the Maumee Valley*, p. 555; and Ted Ligibel, "Toledo Minus Port Lawrence Equal Vistula: A Retrospective Look at Toledo's Oldest Remaining Neighborhood," *North West Ohio Quarterly* 46 (Fall 1974):123-124. On Bissell and the Lockport connection, see William Pool, ed., *Landmarks of Niagara County* (n.p.: D. Mason and Brothers, 1897), p. 164. Bissell's role is documented in the Port Lawrence Proprietor's Collection, Account Books, Toledo—Lucas County Public Library, Toledo, Ohio.

25. Scribner, *Memoirs of Lucas County*, 1:82; Kenneth Davison, "Forgotten Ohioan: Elisha Whittlesey, 1783-1863" (Ph.D. dissertation, Case Western Reserve University, 1953), pp. 122-123; Harry N. Scheiber, "State Policy and Public Domain: The Ohio Canal Lands," *Journal of Economic History* 25 (March 1965):86-95; Waggoner, *Toledo*, pp. 373-375; Harold E. Davis, "Elisha Whittlesey and Maumee Land Speculation, 1834-1840," *Northwest Ohio Quarterly* 15 (July 1943):139-158; and John Weatherford, "The Short Life of Manhattan, Ohio," *The Ohio Historical Quarterly* 65 (October 1965):376-398.

26. Ligibel, "Toledo Minus Port Lawrence," pp. 123-124; and Waggoner, *Toledo*, pp. 372-375.

27. AB to Lyon, 22 October 1833, Lyon Papers; E. Farnsworth to AB, 15 April 1834, BP, 203; Farnsworth to AB, 23 May 1834, BP, 203; Farnsworth to AB, 12 July 1834, BP, 203; and Farnsworth to AB, 8 October 1834, BP, 203.

28. ALC, *Catalogue 1844*, pp. 60-87, 115, 9-59; ALC, *Supplement*, pp. 1-2. On Butler's private interest, see Butler to John Berdam, 12 March 1836, Butler Papers, IV; William Jones to Henry Anderson, 21 January 1839, Butler Papers, IV; Butler to Edward Bissell, 23 June 1836, Butler Papers, IV; and *ALC Annual Report*, pp. 17, 20.

29. "An Act to Incorporate the Erie and Kalamazoo Railroad Company, 22 April 1833," in Michigan, *Laws of the Territory of Michigan*, 3 vols. (Lansing: W. S. George & Co., 1874), 3:1125-1126. The best, brief description of the local stockholders is Willis F. Dunbar, *All Aboard! A History of Railroads in Michigan* (Grand

Rapids, Michigan: William B. Eerdmans Publishing Company, 1969), pp. 13-19.

30. Erie and Kalamazoo Railroad Company, Minute Book, 20 May 1834-9 October 1919, pp. 1-10, in Erie and Kalamazoo Railroad Papers, Bentley Historical Library, Michigan Historical Collections, Ann Arbor, Michigan. Hereafter cited as E & K Minute Book, E & K Papers. Waggoner, *Toledo*, pp. 400-402, reprints many of the original minutes but mistakes were made in the copying. Also see Dunbar, *All Aboard*, pp. 20-21.

31. E & K Minute Book, 24 June 1835, pp. 17-19; A. L. Comstock to Jacob Barker, 18 April 1836, Jacob Barker Papers, Ohio Historical Society, Columbus, Ohio; William Jones to Henry Anderson, 21 January, 1839, Butler Papers, IV; "Names of Stockholders, Their Respective Holdings, 1839," E & K Papers, Box VII. For an identification of McCollum, see Pool, *Landmarks of Niagara County*, pp. 108-109.

32. "An Act to Amend an Act to Incorporate the Erie and Kalamazoo Railroad Company, 26 March 1835," in Michigan, *Laws of the Territory*, 3:1393-1397. Also see Robert J. Parks, *Democracy's Railroads, Public Enterprise in Jacksonian Michigan* (Port Washington, New York: Kennikat Press, 1972), pp. 53-55; Dunbar, *All Aboard*, pp. 24-25; and Waggoner, *Toledo*, pp. 400-401.

33. Butler to Edward Bissell, 23 June 1836; Butler to Bissell, 1 October 1836, 29 August 1836, and 14 October 1836; Butler to Watts Sherman, 5 December 1836, Butler Papers, IV. Also see Butler to Levi Woodbury, Secretary of the Treasury, 15 September 1836, Butler Papers, IV; and E & K Minute Book, 24 June 1835, pp. 17-19.

34. E & K Minute Book, 24 June 1835 - July 1836, pp. 17-36; New York State, Assembly, "Communication from William Bard," Assembly Doc. 279, 57th session, IV:1-4; and U.S. Congress, Senate, *Biographical Dictionary of the American Congress 1774-1971* (Washington: U.S. Government Printing Office, 1971), p. 976. It is important to note that Fuller later entered Michigan politics as a state representative, then Speaker of the House, and finally ran for governor on the Whig ticket in 1841. It appears that the bank and the railroad were never legally separated.

35. Dunbar, *All Aboard*, pp. 24-25; Parks, *Democracy's Railroads*, pp. 54-55; and E & K Minute Books, pp. 42-50.

36. Butler to Bissell, 23 June 1836, Butler Papers, IV; Butler to Levi Woodbury, 29 August 1836 and 15 September 1836, Butler Papers, IV.

37. William Lee Jenks, *St. Clair County, Michigan, Its History and People*, 2 vols. (Chicago: The Lewis Publishing Company, 1912), 1:95, 142-144, 255; Alta M. Lloyd, "Nineteenth Century Economic Development of the Port Huron Area" (M.A. thesis, Wayne State University Press, 1945), pp. 11-31; Parks, *Democracy's Railroads*, p. 33.

38. Butler to Henry Hubbard, 30 May 1836, and Butler to Nicholas Ayrault, 30 September 1837, Butler Papers, IV; Jenks, *St. Clair County*, 1:255-263; *ALC Annual Report*, p. 19. The exact boundaries of Butler's lands are not clear. Two separate maps were published each showing a slightly different plat. See Plan of the Land and Town of Huron in Michigan, 1836, Map Collection, Clarke Historical Library, Mt. Pleasant, Michigan, and Plan of the Canal and Town of Huron, 1837, in William R. Hopkins, *Report on the New Town at the Foot of Lake Huron* (Geneva, N.Y.: Matteson and Haskell, 1837).

39. Butler to Simeon Cumming, 13 July 1836; Butler to Eliza Butler, 19 July 1833; Butler to Nicholas Ayrault, 17 August 1836 and 6 May 1837, Butler Papers, IV.

40. Butler to Simeon Cumming, 14 February 1837, Butler Papers, IV; "Map of

the Plan of the Canal and Town of Huron, 1836, Clarke Historical Library, Mt. Pleasant, Michigan; *The Town of Huron at the Foot of Lake Huron, St. Clair County, Michigan* (New York: E. B. Clayton, 1837), pp. 1-8, 19-31; and Hopkins, *Report on the New Town,* pp. 4-6. Although it cannot be absolutely ascertained that Butler wrote the whole pamphlet, it reflected his style. Without question, it represented his ideas.

41. *Town of Huron,* pp. 1-8, 19-31; Hopkins, *Report on the New Town,* pp. 9-14.

42. *Town of Huron,* pp. 7-9.

43. Ibid., pp. 11-12, 14-19; and Hopkins, *Report on the New Town,* pp. 16-19.

44. *Town of Huron,* pp. 11-13.

45. Butler to Lyon, 17 December 1836; Butler to Lyon, 28 January 1837, Lyon Papers.

46. "Report of the Committee on Internal Improvements of the Legislative Council of Upper Canada, 17 February 1837," in *Town of Huron,* p. 25; *Town of Huron,* pp. 19-33; Fred C. Hamil, *The Valley of the Lower Thames, 1640-1850* (Toronto: University of Toronto Press, 1951), p. 316; Elisha Johnson, *Report of the Engineer upon Preliminary Surveys for the London and Gore Rail Road* (Toronto: G. H. Hackenstaff, 1836), passim; *Some Obsevations Respecting a Great Western Rail Road* (Toronto: G. H. Hackenstaff, [1836]), pp. 3-5; and G. P. det Glazebrook, *A History of Transportation in Canada,* Vol. 1: *Continental Strategy to 1867* (Toronto: Ryerson Press, 1934), pp. 143-159.

47. Park, *Democracy's Railroads,* pp. 76-84; Michigan, *Acts of the Legislature of the State of Michigan: Passed at the Annual Session of 1837* (Detroit: John Bagg, 1837), p. 130.

48. Butler to Farnsworth, 23 February 1837, Butler Papers, IV; Butler to Lyon, 28 January 1837, Lyon Papers; and Parks, *Democracy's Railroads,* p. 85.

49. Michigan, House of Representatives, *Annual Report of the Board of Commissioners of Internal Improvements,* 1838, H.R. 9, 1838, pp. 14-16; and Tracy McCracken to Board of Internal Improvements, H.R., 9, 1838, pp. 46-56. Also see Jenks, *St. Clair County,* 1:387-388.

50. Michigan, *Board of Internal Improvements,* H.R., 9, p. 46.

51. Contract of John Kinzie, Hiram Pearson, and Charles Butler, 20 April 1835; Schedule of Lands Purchased by Kinzie and Pearson, May and June 1835; Olcott Papers. Also see Butler to John Kinzie and Hiram Pearson, 23 June 1836, Butler Papers, IV.

52. AB to Lyon, 18 May 1835 and 23 May 1835, Lyon Papers; Butler, "Reminiscences of a Trip to the West," [1881], Butler Papers, IV, pp. 15-16; *ALC Annual Report,* p. 20; and Stoddard, *Life and Letters,* pp. 149-150.

53. Butler, "Reminiscences," pp. 15-16; Stoddard, *Life and Letters,* pp. 91, 149; Thomas W. Goodspeed, *The University of Chicago Biographical Sketches* (Chicago: University of Chicago Press, 1922), 1:36-38, 85; Isaac N. Arnold, *William B. Ogden,* Fergus Historical Series, no. 17 (Chicago: Fergus Printing Company, 1882), pp. 9-10. The early friendship of Butler and Ogden is evident in Charles Butler to William B. Ogden, 30 September 1823, Butler Papers, III. Also see Patrick McClear, "William Butler Ogden: A Chicago Promoter in the Speculative Era and the Panic of 1837," *Journal of the Illinois State Historical Society* 70 (November 1977):283-284.

54. Butler to FB, 30 May 1835, BP, 208; Butler to Lyon, 24 May 1835, Lyon Papers; FB to Lyon, 14 September 1835, Lyon Papers; Butler, "Reminiscences," pp. 16-18; and Ogden to John Sullivan, 10 June 1836, William B. Ogden Papers, Letterbook, I, Chicago Historical Society, Chicago, Illinois.

55. Butler to FB, 2 June 1835, BP, 208. Also see Butler to FB, 30 May 1835, BP, 208; Butler, "Reminiscences," pp. 17-18.

56. *Chicago American*, 20 June 1835 and 10 October 1835; *Chicago Democrat*, 7 October 1835; Gurdon Hubbard to Edward A. Russell, 22 May 1835, Gurdon Hubbard Papers, Letter Folder, I, CHS; and Bill of Receipt from Franklin and Jenkins Auctioneers, 1835, Edward A. Russell Papers, Letter Folder, I, CHS.

57. James B. Murray to Maria Murray, 19 June 1835, Murray Papers, Box IV, New York Historical Society, New York, New York.

58. Walter Newberry to Lucius Lyon, 22 January 1836 and 13 March 1836, Walter L. Newberry Papers, Newberry Library, Chicago, Illinois; and Butler, "Reminiscences," pp. 18-19.

59. On Butler's participation at Green Bay, see John Haeger, "Capital Mobilization and the Urban Center: The Wisconsin Lakeports," *Mid-America* 60 (April-July 1978):80-81. On the Detroit speculation, see Butler to E. Farnsworth, 23 February 1837, Butler Papers, IV.

Chapter 7

1. These themes are elaborated in Chapter 1. Bronson's theories are succinctly stated in Isaac Bronson, "Propositions Illustrative of the Principles of Banking," BP, 14.

2. There is no agreement among historians on the precise role of the BUS in controlling other banks or the economy. For example, see J. Van Fenstermaker, *The Development of American Commercial Banking: 1782-1837*, Bureau of Economic and Business Research (Kent, Ohio: Kent State University, 1965), 5:69-76; and Peter Temin, *The Jacksonian Economy* (New York: W. W. Norton and Company, 1969), pp. 44-58. There is also a voluminous literature on the bank controversy. I will suggest only a few works. For the older view which sees a struggle of political and financial interests, see Bray Hammond, *Banks and Politics in America* (Princeton, New Jersey: Princeton University Press, 1957), pp. 369-450. A good critique of the Hammond view plus additional perspectives on politics see Frank Otto Gatell, "Sober Second Thoughts on Van Buren, the Albany Regency, and the Wall Street Conspiracy," *Journal of American History* 53 (June 1966):19-40; John McFaul, *The Politics of Jacksonian Finance* (Ithaca: Cornell University Press, 1972); and Richard B. Latner, *The Presidency of Andrew Jackson* (Athens, Georgia: The University of Georgia Press, 1979), pp. 107-123, 164-192. On the bank's economic effect see Temin, *The Jacksonian Economy*, and Richard Timberlake, *The Origins of Central Banking in the United States* (Cambridge: Harvard University Press, 1978), pp. 27-41.

3. Bronson's basic plan and the reasoning behind it remained unchanged for many years. The rationale is seen in IB to C. C. Cambreleng, 17 October 1831, BP, 200; IB, "Propositions Illustrative of the Principles of Banking," BP, 14; New York City Citizens, *Outline of a Plan for a National Bank, With Incidental Remarks on the Bank of the United States* (New York: Newcomb and Cropsey, 1833), pp. 13-14. A copy of Bronson's 1832 plan with comments by Roger Sherman can be found in the *New York Evening Post*, 9 June 1832. Bronson's plan is described in Abraham Venit, "Isaac Bronson and the Financial Controversies of the Jacksonian Period," *Journal of Economic History* 5 (November 1945):201-214, and in the excellent dissertation by Grant Morrison, "Isaac Bronson and the Search for System in American Capitalism" (Ph.D. dissertation, City University of New York, 1974), pp. 289-295.

4. G. Tomlinson to Isaac Bronson, 9 February 1832, BP, 215; J. B. Murray to Isaac Bronson, 11 February 1832 and 17 February 1832, BP, 215; C. C. Cambreleng to Isaac Bronson, 24 April 1832, 28 March 1832, 18 February 1832 and 25 May 1832, BP, 200. Also see Morrison, "Isaac Bronson," pp. 316-321.

5. C. C. Cambreleng to Isaac Bronson, 6 September 1832, BP, 200; and Morrison, "Isaac Bronson," pp. 316-321.

6. Isaac Bronson to Roger M. Sherman, 25 December 1832, Roger M. Sherman Papers, Bridgeport Public Library, Bridgeport, Connecticut.

7. New York City Citizens, *Outline of a Plan for a National Bank*, p. 14.

8. Morrison, "Isaac Bronson," p. 323.

9. James A. Hamilton, *Reminiscences of James A. Hamilton; or Men and Events at Home and Abroad, During Three Quarters of a Century* (New York: Charles Scribner's and Company, 1869), pp. 253-258.

10. Robert V. Remini, *Andrew Jackson and the Bank War* (New York: W. W. Norton, 1967), pp. 125-129.

11. IB to G. Tomilson, 27 January 1834, BP, 201; and Morrison, "Isaac Bronson," p. 337.

12. Thomas Suffern to Martin Van Buren, 12 January 1834, and Martin Van Buren to Thomas Suffern, 15 January 1834, Vol. 19, Martin Van Buren Papers, Library of Congress, Microfilm Edition, Washington, D.C. Also see Morrison, "Isaac Bronson," p. 307.

13. Butler to Silas Wright, 10 February 1834, Butler Papers, III.

14. Ibid.

15. Letter of Charles Butler, 12 March 1834, Butler Papers, III; Butler to Bowen Whiting, 20 March 1834, Butler Papers, III; and Francis H. Stoddard, *The Life and Letters of Charles Butler* (New York: Charles Scribner's Sons, 1903), p. 165. Butler's proposal is interesting because it questions older interpretations of the bank war which argued that New Yorkers wished to transfer the nation's financial center from Philadelphia to New York City. Butler and Bronson would have been part of any such conspiracy, and yet here they were willing to place the bank's headquarters in the District of Columbia. The New Yorkers certainly intended to advance the fortunes of their city, but that goal seemed secondary in the overall effort to achieve financial stability. For a review of the older interpretations, see Gatell, "Sober Second Thoughts," pp. 19-20.

16. Butler to Bowen Whiting, 20 March 1834, Butler Papers, III; and Butler to his wife, 22 March 1834, Butler Papers, III. Also see Remini, *Andrew Jackson and the Bank War*, pp. 132-134.

17. Butler to AB, 21 March 1834, BP, 100; Butler to Whiting, 20 March 1834, Butler Papers, III; and Butler to his wife, 22 March 1834, Butler Papers, III.

18. See Chapter III. Bronson made specific references to the relationship of the Ohio firm and the national bank issue in AB to M. T. Williams, 30 September 1837, Elisha Whittlesey Papers, Western Reserve Historical Society, Cleveland, Ohio, Container 5. Hereafter cited as WP, container no.

19. Temin, *The Jacksonian Economy*, pp. 69-91; Timberlake, *The Origins of Central Banking*, pp. 42-62; and Hugh Rockoff, "Money, Prices, and Banks in Jacksonian America," in *The Reinterpretation of American Economic History*, eds. Robert Fogel and Stanley Engerman (New York: Harper and Row Publishers, 1971), pp. 448-458.

20. IB to EW (Elisha Whittlesey), 23 February 1836, WP, 5. Also see IB to EW, 26 February 1836, WP, 6; IB to Roger Sherman, 10 March 1836, Sherman Papers, Bridgeport Public Library; and IB to Cambreleng, 10 May 1836, BP, 200.

21. Ibid.; IB to EW, 1 April 1836, WP, 5. IB mentioned the relationship between the trust company and the fiscal agent plan in IB to Roger Sherman, 10 March 1836, Sherman Papers, Bridgeport Public Library.

22. EW to IB, 28 February 1836, BP, 6; and IB to EW, 26 March 1836, WP, 5; and IB to EW, 6 March 1836, WP, 6.

23. [Elisha Whittlesey], "Memorandum on the Position of Parties and Things Upon the Plan of Adopting the Fiscal Bank So Far as I Can Judge . . . ." [1836], BP, 87. Although unsigned and undated, the manuscript can be identified by internal criticism and handwriting comparisons. There is also a note on the manuscript indicating that its author had spent fourteen years in Congress: a fact which was true of Whittlesey.

24. AB to Lyon, 28 March 1836, Lyon Papers; and James B. Murray to Henry Toland, 29 March 1836, BP, 215.

25. Benjamin F. Butler to Charles Butler, 18 March 1836, Butler Papers, III; Hammond, *Banks and Politics*, p. 439.

26. IB to EW, 1, 16, 22 April 1836, WP, 5.

27. IB to Cambreleng, 10 and 17 May 1836; and Cambreleng to IB, 12 May 1836, BP, 200.

28. IB to Cambreleng, 17 May 1836, BP, 200.

29. IB to EW, 16 April 1836, WP, 5; IB to EW, 5 and 17 March 1836, WP, 5.

30. Lucius Lyon, "Report of the Committee on Banking," in *The Michigan Constitutional Convention of 1835-1836*, ed. Harold Dorr (Ann Arbor: The University of Michigan Press, 1940), pp. 524, 520-523; AB to Lyon, 22 May 1834; IB to Lyon, 22 May 1835; and AB to Lyon, 25 May 1835, Lyon Papers.

31. Dorr, *Constitutional Convention*, pp. 390-392.

32. My discussion of free banking depends on a number of works. See Hammond, *Banks and Politics in America*, pp. 572-583; Fritz Redlich, *The Molding of American Banking, Part I: 1781-1840* (New York: Hafner Publishing Company, 1951), pp. 187-204; Walter Hugins, *Jacksonian Democracy and the Working Class* (Stanford, California: Stanford University Press, 1960), pp. 172-174, 187-190; Morrison, "Isaac Bronson," pp. 350-366; Leo Hershkowitz, "The Loco-Foco Party of New York: Its Origins and Career," *New York Historical Society Quarterly* 46 (October 1962):309-310; Carl Degler, "The Locofocos: Urban 'Agrarians,'" *Journal of Economic History* 16 (September 1956):322-326; and Harold Reinholds, "The Free Banking Law: The Michigan Experience," (Ph.D. dissertation, Michigan State University, 1975), pp. 22-25.

33. IB to Lucius Lyon, 7 December 1835, Lyon Papers; IB to EW, 16 and 22 April and 1 May 1836, WP, 5; *Daily Albany Argus*, 28 April 1836. Also see Leo Hershkowitz, "New York City, 1834-1840, A Study in Local Politics," (Ph.D. dissertation, New York University, 1960), pp. 191-197.

34. IB to EW, 1 May 1836, WP, 5; and Hammond, *Banks and Politics*, p. 580.

35. "Minutes of the Proceedings in Relation to the Organization of a Joint Stock Banking Company," February 1837, BP, 27; and Morrison, "Isaac Bronson," pp. 356-359.

36. New York Free Banking Act, 18 May 1838, in Herman E. Krooss, ed., *Documentary History of Banking and Currency in the United States* (New York: Chelsea House Publishers, 1969), 1:1183-1192. Redlich, *Molding of American Banking*, pp. 187-204 has a good discussion of the New York law. It is interesting that Arthur Bronson's draft charter for the Michigan Trust Company contained a clause calling for the state auditor to issue the bank's notes based on its capital stock. See

the charter of the Michigan Trust Company, BP, 203.

37. On Michigan's free banking law, see IB to Lyon, 7 December 1835, Lyon Papers; Reinholds, "The Free Banking Law," pp. 103-104; and William G. Shade, "The Background of Michigan's Free Banking Law," *Michigan History* 52 (Fall 1968):233-237.

38. Economic historians are currently reevaluting the free banking movement. See Hugh Rockhoff, "The Free Banking Era, A Reexamination," *Journal of Money, Credit and Banking,* 6 (May 1974):141-167, and the same author's "Varieties of Banking and Regional Economic Development, 1840-1860," *Journal of Economic History* 35 (March 1975):160-181.

39. *Cincinnati Advertiser,* 20 February 1836. There are several accounts of Lytle's hostility to the OLTC. Historians see it primarily as an intra-party fight and only secondarily as a real ideological struggle. See Francis P. Weisenberger, *The Passing of the Frontier, 1825-1850* (Columbus, Ohio: Ohio State Archeological and Historical Society, 1941), pp. 309-312; Harry N. Scheiber, "Entrepreneurship and Western Development: The Case of Micajah T. Williams," *Business History Review* 37 (Winter 1968):360-361.

40. *Cincinnati Advertiser,* 1 October 1834, 2 May 1835, 17 February 1836; and the *Cincinnati Daily Republican,* 2 March 1836, 24 February 1836, and 19 February 1836. Also see EW to Williams, 3 August 1835, WP, 41.

41. *Ohio Monitor,* 14 March 1836.

42. *Niles Weekly Register,* 12 September 1835.

43. IB to EW, 4 October 1835, WP, 5; EW to IB, 9 November 1835, BP, 6; IB to EW, 23 February 1836, WP, 5; and Simon Perkins to IB, 30 April 1835, BP, 86. David T. Disney, A Democrat and a member of the OLTC's board of trustees, also tried unsuccessfully to drag Charles Butler and the national Democratic Party into this dispute. See David T. Disney to Charles Butler, 27 February 1836, and Benjamin F. Butler to Charles Butler, 18 March 1836, Butler Papers, III.

44. *Report of the Special Master Commissioner in the Matter of the Ohio Life Insurance and Trust Company* (Cincinnati: Cincinnati Journal Office, 1836), pp. 38, 45-46; Samuel R. Miller to AB, 25 August 1835, Micajah T. Williams Papers, Ohio State Library, Card 32. Hereafter cited as Williams Papers, Card Number.

45. IB to EW, 1 May 1836, WP, 5; Williams to IB, 7 July and 7 May 1836, BP, 87.

46. *The First Annual Report of the Ohio Life Insurance and Trust Company* (Columbus: Jacob Medary & Co., 1835), pp. 24-29. On the economic activities of the Ohio trustees, see Scheiber, "Entrepreneurship and Western Development," pp. 362-365; and Harry Scheiber, "Alfred Kelley and the Ohio Business Elite, 1822-1859," *Ohio History* 87 (Autumn 1978):377-388; and Harold E. Davis, "Elisha Whittlesey and Maumee Land Speculation, 1834-1840," *Northwest Ohio Quarterly* 15 (July 1943):139-158.

47. *Report of the Special Master Commissioner in the Matter of the Ohio Life Insurance and Trust Company* (Cincinnati: Cincinnati Journal Office, 1836), pp. 37-38; *Second Report of the Master Commissioner in the Matter of the Ohio Life Insurance and Trust Company* (Cincinnati: Looker, Ramsay and Company, 1837), pp. 11, 17-18; *The Second Annual Report of the Ohio Life Insurance and Trust Company* (Cincinnati: Looker Ramsay & Co., 1836), p. 20; and *The Third Annual Report of the Ohio Life Insurance and Trust Company* (Cincinnati: Looker, Ramsay & Co., 1837), p. 22. For a retrospective view on the company's performance see *Fifth Report of the Master Commissioner in the Matter of the Ohio Life Insurance and Trust Company* (Columbus: C. Scott, 1840). On the value of the company's stock see Edmund C. Stedman, *The*

New York Stock Exchange (New York: New York Stock Exchange, 1905; Reprint ed., New York: Greenwood Press, 1969), pp. 97-98.

48. Williams to FB, 13 April 1836, BP, 23; IB to EW, 18 September 1836, WP, 5; EW to IB, 28 April 1836, BP, 6; IB to EW, 1 May 1836, WP, 5; EW to Simon Perkins, 14 November 1836, WP, 41; EW to Roger Sherman, 15 November 1836, WP, 41; EW to IB, 11 November 1836, BP, 6; Simon Perkins to EW, 17 November 1836, WP, 23; EW to IB, 5 December 1836, BP, 6.

49. IB to Williams, 14 November 1836, WP, 5; and Williams to IB, 18 November 1836, BP, 87.

50. Williams to IB, 3 October 1836, BP, 87.

51. Williams to IB, 18 November 1836, BP, 87; IB to EW, 24 November 1836, WP, 5.

52. Jacob Burnet to IB, 14 November 1836, BP, 87; Burnet to IB, 23 January 1837, BP, 88.

53. *Second Report of the Master Commissioner,* p. 15. Also see IB to EW, 25 March 1837, WP, 5; EW to IB, 31 March 1837, BP, 6; and Jacob Burnet to IB, 10 May 1837, BP, 88.

54. C. C. Huntington, "A History of Banking and Currency in Ohio Before the Civil War," *Ohio Archaeological and Historical Quarterly* 24 (1915):388; and Scheiber, "Entrepreneurship and Western Development," p. 361.

55. Letter of Isaac Bronson, 4 May 1837, BP, 6. Arthur Bronson's sentiments were the same: "Indeed, the lesson it teaches me, is to disconnect myself in the future, with all monied corporations." See letter of Arthur Bronson, 30 May 1837, BP, 19.

56. AB to Williams, 30 September 1837, WP, 5; *First Annual Report of the OLTC,* p. 35.

57. Ibid.

58. Butler to his wife, 4 and 30 March 1837, Butler Papers, III; and Butler to Edwin Croswell, 22 March 1837, Erastus Corning Papers, Albany Institute of History and Art, Albany, New York.

59. Charles Butler to B. F. Butler, 29 March 1837, Butler Papers, III.

60. Butler's financial situation in the late 1830s is discussed in Chapter 8.

61. IB to EW, 18 April 1837, WP, 5; and EW to IB, 17 March 1837, BP, 6.

62. [Isaac Bronson] to Secretary of the Treasury, 20 April 1837, BP, 6.

63. Ibid.

64. Ibid.; IB to EW, 5 January 1837 and 2 March 1837, WP, 4. Historians have offered many conflicting explanations for the depression. Reginald C. McGrane, *The Panic of 1837* (Chicago: The University of Chicago Press, 1924) stresses the role of Jacksonian financial policies in causing the depression. More recent historians have rejected the notion that Jackson's policies were directly related; and instead they argue that international factors, such as the movement of specie, were more important. Temin, *The Jacksonian Economy,* pp. 76-78, 137-149 is the most provocative of the new economic historians. Timberlake, *Origins of Central Banking,* pp. 54-62 further refines Temin's analysis. Also see the criticism of Temin by Marie Elizabeth Sushka, "The Antebellum Money Market and the Economic Impact of the Bank War," *Journal of Economic History* 36 (December 1976):809-835. A balanced view is presented by Edward Pessen, *Jacksonian America: Society, Personality and Politics,* 2nd ed. (Homewood, Illinois: The Dorsey Press, 1978), pp. 146-148.

65. IB to EW, 18 April 1837, WP, 5; and IB to the Secretary of the Treasury, 20 April 1837, BP, 6.

66. IB to Roger Sherman, 21 April 1837, Sherman Papers, Bridgeport Public Library; "Franklin" [Roger Sherman], *Letters to the Honourable Levi Woodbury, Secretary of the Treasury* (New York: E. B. Clayton, 1837), passim.

67. IB to Lucius Lyon, 10 September 1837, Lyon Papers. Good descriptions of Van Buren's plan are in James C. Curtis, *The Fox at Bay, Martin Van Buren and the Presidency, 1837-1841* (Lexington: The University of Kentucky Press, 1970), pp. 94-136; McFaul, *The Politics of Jacksonian Finance*, pp. 184-209; Timberlake, *Origins of Central Banking*, pp. 63-66; and Hammond, *Banks and Politics*, pp. 542-545.

68. Curtis, *Van Buren*, pp. 126-151; Isaac Bronson, Arthur Bronson, *et al.* "Memorial to the House of Representatives, 1838," BP, 37; Hershkowitz, "New York City," pp. 275-276.

69. "Old Fashioned Man," [Arthur Bronson], "History of the Bank of _____," in *The Journal of Banking From July, 1841 to July, 1842: Containing Essays on Various Questions Relating to Banking and Currency. . . .*, ed. William Gouge (Philadelphia: J. Van Court, 1842), pp. 209-211, 225-227.

70. William R. Brock, *Parties and Political Conscience: American Dilemmas, 1840-1850* (Millwood, New York: KTO Press, 1979), pp. 90-99. Brock is very critical of Tyler's leadership throughout this period. For a more favorable but less convincing view see Oliver Chitwood, *John Tyler* (New York: Russell & Russell, 1964), pp. 212-249. Other sources would include Hammond, *Banks and Politics*, pp. 542-543; and Robert Seager, *And Tyler Too: A Biography of John and Julia Gardiner Tyler* (New York: McGraw-Hill Book Company, 1963), pp. 151-158, 163-164. The various plans for bank projects and presidential messages can be followed in Thomas C. Cochran, *The New American State Papers*, Vol. 26: *Public Finance* (Wilmington, Delaware: Scholarly Resources, Inc. 1973), pp. 429-484.

71. Ibid.; The President's plan was presented as "Report from the Secretary of the Treasury Communicating. . . . A Plan for a Fiscal Agent of the Government, December 21, 1841," in *ASP, Public Finance*, 26:447-464. Also see Timberlake, *Origins of Central Banking*, pp. 66-69.

72. AB to Roger Sherman, 13 December 1841, Roger Sherman Papers, Connecticut State Library, Hartford, Connecticut; N. P. Tallmadge to AB, 10 December 1841, BP, 204; Silas Wright to AB, 10 December 1841, Sherman Papers, Connecticut State Library. Tallmadge is identified in Curtis, *Van Buren*, pp. 68, 74, 87, and in McFaul, *Jacksonian Finance*, pp. 190-191. Bronson and Sherman's plan was printed under the pseudonym of "Franklin" in the *New York Commercial Advertiser*, 29 November 1842.

73. Silas Wright to AB, 10 December 1841, Sherman Papers, Connecticut State Library.

74. N. P. Tallmadge to AB, 10 December 1841, BP, 204; Richard Davis to AB, 23 January 1842, BP, 108; AB to Roger Sherman, 21 January 1842, Sherman Papers, Connecticut State Library.

75. Silas Wright to AB, 28 February 1842, BP, 108; N. P. Tallmadge to AB, 14 December 1842, and 20 December 1842, BP, 109; N. P. Tallmadge to R. M. Sherman, 20 December 1842, Sherman Papers, Connecticut State Library. The bill is in U.S. Congress, Senate, "Report of the Select Committee to whom was referred the report from the Secretary of the Treasury, 21 February 1842," 27th Congress, 2nd session, 1842, in *ASP Public Finance*, 26:465-485.

76. On the trust company see Chapter 2. On the adoption of conservative banking practices, see the descriptions of the system in Louisiana in Hammond, *Banks and Politics*, pp. 679-685; and George Green, *Finance and Economic Develop-*

ment in the Old South, Louisiana Banking, 1804-1861 (Stanford, California: Stanford University Press, 1972), pp. 118-122.

77. Of course, the larger question is whether Bronson's conservative theories would have more effectively promoted economic development throughout the whole country. I will leave that counterfactual proposition to the economists, but one should consult Green, *Finance and Development*, pp. 37-69; and Richard Sylla, "American Banking and Growth in the Nineteenth Century: A Partial View of the Terrain," *Explorations in Economic History* 9 (Winter 1971-1972):197-211.

Chapter 8

1. Historical studies have rarely examined the history of western communities or of individual businessmen as they struggled to cope with the 1837 depression. General works on the depression include, however, Reginald C. McGrane, *The Panic of 1837: Some Financial Problems of the Jacksonian Era* (Chicago: University of Chicago Press, 1924) and Peter Temin, *The Jacksonian Economy* (New York: W. W. Norton and Company, 1969), pp. 113-171. Paul Gates, of course, has studied the depression's effect on farmers, yet his studies do not acknowledge that speculators were also trapped by the depression. See Paul Gates, "Land Policy and Tenancy in the Prairie Counties of Indiana," *Indiana Magazine of History* 35 (March 1939):1-26; and "Frontier Land Business in Wisconsin," *Wisconsin Magazine of History* 52 (Summer 1969):311. For the comments of contemporaries, see George C. Bates, "By-Gones of Detroit," *MPHC*, 22:379-380; Charles C. Trowbridge, *Personal Memoirs of Charles Christopher Trowbridge* (Detroit: n.p., 1893), pp. 31-33; and *Chicago American*, 27 May 1837.

2. James Fenimore Cooper, *Home As Found* (New York: Capricorn Books, 1961), pp. 100-103; and Charles Dickens, *Martin Chuzzlewit* (New York: New American Library, 1965), pp. 383-412. Dickens' story of Eden was similar to an account published in 1839. See Major Walter Wilkey, *Western Emigration, Narrative of a Tour to and One Year's Residence in "Edensburgh"* (New York: G. Clairborne Publishers, 1839).

3. Levi Beardsley, *Reminiscences; Personal and Other Incidents; Early Settlement of Otsego County; Notices and Anecdotes of Public Men: Judicial, Legal, and Legislative Matters; Field Sports; Dissertations and Discussions* (New York: Printed by Charles Vinten, 1852), p. 250.

4. Charles Butler to Benjamin F. Butler, 31 October 1836, Butler Papers, III.

5. Butler to Trowbridge and Farnsworth, 19 December and 15 August 1836, Trowbridge Papers.

6. Butler to E. Croswell, 22 March 1837, Erastus Corning Papers, Albany Institute of History and Art, Albany, New York. Also see Butler to Bowen Whiting, 8 May 1837, Butler Papers, III.

7. Butler to Philo Fuller, 11 May 1837, Butler Papers, IV; Butler to Trowbridge and Farnsworth, 28 May 1836, Trowbridge Papers; Butler to William Ogden, 12 May 1837, Butler Papers, IV; and Ogden to Butler, 18 May 1837, William B. Ogden Papers, CHS, LB, I.

8. Butler to Corning, 7 April 1837, Corning Papers; Butler to Ogden, 3 November 1837, and Butler to Thomas Olcott, 10 November 1837, Butler Papers, IV; AB to Alex Fullerton, Grant Goodrich, R. S. Stewart, and Truman Wright, 4 May 1837, BP, 6; and Trowbridge to AB, 6 June 1842, Trowbridge Papers.

9. Charles Butler to Benjamin Butler, 31 July and 26 November 1838, Benja-

min Franklin Butler Papers, Box 3, Folder 4, New York State Library, Albany, New York; C. Bushnell to Henry Anderson, 8 June 1839, Butler Papers, IV; William A. Butler, *A Retrospect of Forty Years* (New York: Charles Scribner's Sons, 1911); and Francis H. Stoddard, *The Life and Letters of Charles Butler* (New York: Charles Scribner's Sons, 1903), pp. 167-168, 182-183.

10. Charles Butler's statement of indebtedness to AB, 27 January 1840, BP, CHS, 20; Bond of Charles Butler and Benjamin F. Butler, 31 January 1840, BP, 30; Contract of Butler and Joseph Beers, 20 December 1844, Butler Papers, I; and Benjamin F. Butler to Thomas W. Olcott, 11 November 1839, Thomas W. Olcott Papers, Columbia University, New York, New York.

11. Martin Van Buren to Butler, 25 April 1836, Butler Papers, III; Butler to Ogden, 3 November 1837, Butler Papers, IV; Butler to Olcott, 10 November 1837, Butler Papers, IV; Butler to Olcott, 18 June 1838, Olcott Papers; and Butler to Van Buren, 22 January 1841, Butler Papers, IV.

12. AB to Justin Butterfield and James Collins, 29 February 1840, BP, 30. Also see AB to Ogden, 27 January 1840, BP, 30; AB to Butterfield and Collins, 6 February 1840, BP, 30.

13. Bond of Charles and Benjamin F. Butler, 31 January 1840, BP, 30; and Roger Sherman to AB, 26 April 1841, BP, 30.

14. Butterfield and Collins to AB, 16 March 1840, BP, 204; AB to Butterfield and Collins, 4 March 1840, BP, 30; Butler to Eliza Butler, 16 January 1843, Butler Papers, I; William Bard to FB, 17 May 1841, BP, 208; Butler to Alexander Fullerton, 25 June 1840, BP, CHS, 23; and Contract of AB and A. Steele, Sheriff of Cook County, 30 September 1840, BP, CHS, 33.

15. Butler to Henry Anderson, 24 January 1837, Butler Papers, IV; AB to Corning, 3 September 1840, Corning Papers; and Butler to Henry Anderson, 2 July 1838, Butler Papers, IV.

16. Butler to Franklin Dexter, 4 March 1844, Corning Papers; Butler to Franklin Dexter and Oliver Bronson, 20 March 1844, BP, 202; Butler to Corning, 10 and 12 October 1844, Corning Papers; Butler to Franklin Dexter and Erastus Corning, 28 December 1844, Corning Papers; and American Land Company, *Catalogue of Lands Belonging to the American Land Company to be Sold at Public Auction . . . 1844* (New York: American Land Company, 1844), passim.

17. Butler to Corning, 24 June 1846, Corning Papers; Butler to Elisha Whittlesey, 22 November 1846, Elisha Whittlesey Papers, Container 5, Western Reserve Historical Society, Cleveland, Ohio; and Irene Neu, *Erastus Corning: Merchant and Financier* (Ithaca: Cornell University Press, 1960), pp. 135-136.

18. Minute Book, Erie and Kalamazoo Railroad Company, 20 May 1834, to 9 October 1919, pp. 42-47, Erie and Kalamazoo Railroad Papers, Michigan Historical Collections, Bentley Historical Library, Ann Arbor, Michigan. Hereafter cited as E & K Minute Book, page no. Also see Clark Waggoner, *History of the City of Toledo and Lucas County, Ohio* (New York: Munsell & Co., 1888), pp. 40-41; and List of the Stockholders of the Erie and Kalamazoo Railroad, October 1837, E & K Papers, Box IV.

19. On the Michigan and Ohio boundary dispute, see Sister Mary Karl George, *The Rise and Fall of Toledo, Michigan . . .* (Lansing: The Michigan Historical Commission, 1971), p. 18; Anna May Soule, "The Southern and Western Boundaries of Michigan," *MPHC*, 27:376-377; and Carl Wittke, "The Ohio-Michigan Boundary Dispute Re-Examined," *Ohio State Archaeological & Historical Quarterly*, 45 (1936): 18-19.

20. Willis F. Dunbar, *All Aboard! A History of Railroads in Michigan* (Grand Rapids, Michigan: William B. Eerdmans Publishing Company, 1961), p. 29; Robert J. Parks, *Democracy's Railroads, Public Enterprise in Jacksonian Michigan* (Port Washington, New York: Kennikat Press, 1972), pp. 54-55; Michigan House of Representatives, *Annual Report of the Board of Commissioners of Internal Improvements, 1838*, H. R. Doc. 9, 1838, p. 4; and *Report of the Erie and Kalamazoo Railroad Company for 1840*, H. R. Doc. 40, 1840, in *Documents Accompanying the Journal of the House of Representatives* (Detroit: George Dawson Printer, 1841), pp. 149-150.

21. E & K Minute Book, pp. 57-84. Also see Philo Fuller to Erastus Corning, 16 June 1837, Corning Papers; Butler to Bissell, 1 October 1836 and 14 October 1836, Butler Papers, IV; Butler to Watts Sherman, 5 December 1836, Butler Papers, IV.

22. Butler to Fuller, 11 May 1837, Butler Papers, IV.

23. Butler to Fuller, 11 May and 2 August 1837, Butler Papers, IV.

24. Butler to Corning, 23 February 1838, Corning Papers; Ogden to Corning, 16 and 17 February 1839, Corning Papers; Ogden to Fuller, 21 March 1839, Ogden Papers, LB, II; and E & K Minute Book, 15 May 1838, p. 55. Also see Michigan, *Laws of the Territory of Michigan*, 3 vols. (Lansing: W. S. George & Co., 1874), 3:1392-1393.

25. Ogden to Jones, 20 March 1839; Ogden to Fuller, 21 March 1838; Ogden to Bates, Walker, and Douglas, 14 March 1839; and Ogden to Fuller, 26 March and 30 March 1839, Ogden Papers, LB, II. Also see E & K Minute Books, 15 April 1839, pp. 68-69.

26. Ogden to Butler, 17 June 1839, Ogden Papers, LB, II.

27. Butler to Ogden, 8 July 1839; Butler to J. Stringham, 6 July 1839; and Butler to John Fitch, 8 July 1839, Butler Papers, IV.

28. E & K Minute Book, 7 August 1839 and 6 September 1839, pp. 76-84.

29. E & K Minute Book, October 1839, p. 93; and 16 January 1840, pp. 96-97. Also see Butler to John Fitch, 8 June 1840, Butler Papers, IV; Butler to Corning, 12 March 1842, Corning Papers; Ogden to Corning, 22 May 1843, Corning Papers; and Butler to Eliza Butler, 12 February 1843, Butler Papers, I.

30. List of the Directors of the Erie and Kalamazoo Railroad Company Elected in 1848 and Subsequent Years, E & K Papers, VII; Names of Stockholders of the E & K Railroad, Their Respective Holdings in 1839, 1849, 1857, 1865 . . . , E & K Papers, VII.

31. E & K Minute Books, pp. 100-202, passim. Also see the selected minutes in Waggoner, *Toledo*, p. 402.

32. Butler outlined the whole plan to Elisha Whittlesey in 1845. See Butler to Whittlesey, 22 November 1845, Whittlesey Papers, 5. On the proposed sale and the accompanying politics see Parks, *Democracy's Railroads*, pp. 130-131; Arthur Johnson and Barry Supple, *Boston Capitalists and Western Railroads* (Cambridge: Harvard University Press, 1967), pp. 90-94; and Marian Sears, "A Michigan Bureaucrat Promotes the State's Economic Growth: George F. Porter Sells Michigan's Central Railroad to Eastern Capitalists," *Explorations in Entrepreneurial History* 5 (Spring-Summer 1966):200-219.

33. Parks, *Democracy's Railroads*, pp. 130-131; Michigan, House of Representatives, "Proposition for the Purchase of the Southern Railroad," H. R. Doc. 10, and "Proposal to Purchase the Southern Railroad," H. R. Doc. 11, Michigan, *Documents Accompanying the Journal of the House of Representatives* (Detroit: Bagg & Harmon, 1846), pp. 1-5.

34. Butler to John Fitch, 27 June 1846, E & K Papers, IV; Dunbar, *All Aboard,* pp. 68-69, 27; Bissell to W. Hunt, 26 November 1847, E & K Papers, IV; and E & K Minute Book, pp. 180-200.

35. *Chicago Herald,* 8 June 1893, Butler Papers, IV; and Bessie L. Pierce, *A History of Chicago,* vol. 2: *From Town to City* (New York: Alfred Knopf, 1940), p. 57, n. 74.

36. Butler to Trowbridge, 14 August 1837; and Butler to Ayrault, 26 July 1837 and 30 September 1837, Butler Papers, IV.

37. Butler to Corning, 19 February 1838 and 27 February 1838, Corning Papers.

38. Jones to Corning, 16 August 1838, Corning Papers; Jones to John MacNeil, 19 November 1838, Butler Papers, IV; Fred C. Hamil, *The Valley of the Lower Thames, 1640-1850* (Toronto: University of Toronto Press, 1951), p. 316; Jones to N. Ayrault, 13 September 1838, Butler Papers, IV; and Butler to Ayrault, 10 January 1840, Butler Papers, IV.

39. Memorandum on the Property of the Huron Land Association, 1 October 1840, Lyon Papers; W. L. Jenks, "Charles Butler," *Michigan History* 29 (April-June 1945):322; and W. L. Jenks, *St. Clair County, Michigan,* 2 vols. (Chicago: The Lewis Publishing Company, 1912), 1:263.

40. Butler to Corning, 20 April 1842 and 12 October 1844, Corning Papers.

41. See Map of the Plan of the Canal and Town of Huron in Michigan at the Head of and Around the Rapids of the River St. Clair, 1836, Clarke Historical Library, Central Michigan University, Mt. Pleasant, Michigan. This map can be compared with plats of the later city. See George Ogle, ed., *Standard Atlas of St. Clair County, Michigan* (Chicago: George Ogle & Co., 1916), pp. 18-19 and plates 10 and 11.

42. Ogden to Walter Butler, 30 May 1840, Ogden Papers, LB, II, and Ogden to H. Moore, 25 January 1841, Ogden Papers, LB, II. Also see AB to Alex Fullerton, Grant Goodrich, R. Stewart and Truman Wright, 4 May 1837, BP, 6.

43. Butler, "Reminiscences," pp. 18-20; Ogden to Butler, 23 June 1836, Ogden Papers, LB, I; Butler to Henry Anderson, 24 January 1837, Butler Papers, IV; and Butler to Ogden, 8 July 1839, Butler Papers, IV.

44. *Chicago American,* 29 April and 6 May 1837.

45. See the circular issued by Ogden, December 1838, BP, 204. Similar agencies include the Wisconsin Land Agency of Albert G. Ellis and Morgan L. Martin, 23 May 1836, BP, 204, and the General Land Agency of Wisconsin under Byron Kilbourn, 1836, Lyon Papers. Also see American Land Company, *Catalogue of Lands Belonging to the American Land Company to be Sold at Public Auction . . . 1844* (New York: American Land Company, 1844), p. 114.

46. Ogden's importance has been noted in several places. See Daniel Boorstin, *The Americans: The National Experience* (New York: Random House, 1965), pp. 116-119; Patrick McLear, "Speculation, Promotion, and the Panic of 1837 in Chicago," *Journal of the Illinois State Historical Society* 62 (Summer 1969):137; Patrick McLear, "William Butler Ogden: A Chicago Promoter in the Speculative Era and the Panic of 1837," *Journal of the Illinois State Historical Society* 70 (November 1977):283-291; and John D. Haeger, "Eastern Money and the Urban Frontier, Chicago, 1833-1842," *Journal of the Illinois State Historical Society* 64 (Autumn 1971):272-275.

47. Ogden to J.H. Foster, 8 December 1838; Ogden to Lt. March, 5 March 1839; Ogden to FB, 26 May 1837; and Ogden to AB, 5 March 1839, Ogden Papers, LB, I.

48. Ogden to Butler, 21 July 1836, and Ogden to R. Stewart, 7 February 1839, Ogden Papers, LB, I; and Pierce, *A History of Chicago,* Vol. 1: *The Beginning of a City* (New York: Alfred Knopf, 1937), p. 146.

49. A. T. Andreas, *History of Chicago,* 3 vols. (Chicago: A. T. Andreas, 1884), 1:198-199; Pierce, *History of Chicago,* 1:54, 340-341; Ogden to AB, 22 November 1839, Ogden Papers, LB, II.

50. Ogden to AB, 22 November 1839 and 18 December 1839, Ogden Papers, LB, II; Ogden to A. Wright, 26 December 1840, Ogden Papers, LB, III.

51. *Chicago American,* 19 March 1836; Pierce, *History of Chicago,* 1:114-115; Ogden to AB, 22 November 1839, and 25 January 1840, Ogden Papers, LB, II; and Walter Newberry to AB, 4 September 1840, BP, CHS, 67. Also see Patrick McLear, "The Galena and Chicago Union Railroad: A Symbol of Chicago's Economic Maturity," *Journal of the Illinois State Historical Society* 73(Spring 1980): 17-26.

52. Alexander Fullerton to AB, 15 November 1840, BP, CHS.

53. John Wentworth, *Early Chicago,* Fergus Historical Series, No. 7 (Chicago: Fergus Printing Co., 1876), p. 35.

Chapter 9

1. George Bates, "By-Gones of Detroit," *MPHC,* 22:379.

2. George Macy to AB, 13 January 1843, BP, 22. Paul Gates was the most important historian to argue that nonresident investors delayed western settlement particularly during the depression. He felt that eastern speculators often neglected their lands either by refusing to pay taxes or by charging excessive rates of interest. See especially Paul W. Gates, "The Role of the Land Speculator in Western Development," *Pennsylvania Magazine of History and Biography* 46 (July 1942):314-333 and the same author's collection of essays *Landlords and Tenants on the Prairie Frontier, Studies in American Land Policy* (Ithaca: Cornell University Press, 1973). Also see Henry Cohen, "Vicissitudes of an Absentee Landlord: A Case Study," in *The Frontier in American Development,* ed. by David Ellis (Ithaca: Cornell University Press, 1969), pp. 192-216. A recent examination of the principal work on land speculation stressing the revisionist approach is Robert P. Swierenga, "Land Speculation and Its Impact on American Economic Growth and Welfare: A Historiographical Review," *Western Historical Quarterly* 8 (July 1977):283-302.

3. For example, see the New Yorker's particularly revealing letter to Lucius Lyon. AB and IB to Lyon, 30 June 1836 and 17 October 1836, Lyon Papers. Also see FB to Lyon, 5 June 1837, Lyon Papers.

4. Memorandum of Accounts of Charles Butler, Elon Farnsworth, and Charles Trowbridge, 22 June 1833, Trowbridge Papers; Trowbridge to AB, 26 June 1842, Trowbridge Papers; Charles Trowbridge, *Personal Memoirs of Charles C. Trowbridge* (Detroit: n.p., 1893), pp. 28, 35-36; and Jack Kilfoil, "C. C. Trowbridge, Detroit Banker and Michigan Land Speculator, 1820-1845" (Ph.D. dissertation, Claremont Graduate School, 1969), pp. 99-113, 142-155.

5. Kilfoil, "Trowbridge," pp. 158, 161-162.

6. AB to Trowbridge and Farnsworth, 8 September 1841; Butler to Trowbridge and Farnsworth, 28 May 1836; AB to Trowbridge, 12 May 1841; and Trowbridge to James F. Joy, 2 December 1842, Trowbridge Papers.

7. Trowbridge to Joy, 2 December 1842; Trowbridge to Thomas W. Olcott, 2 December 1840; and Trowbridge to Jonathan Chapman, 24 April 1841, Trowbridge Papers.

8. The course of the negotiations over this debt can be followed in a series of letters. See AB to Trowbridge and Farnsworth, 8 September 1841;-AB to Butler, 1 September 1841; AB to Trowbridge, 3 March 1842; Thomas Olcott to Trowbridge, August 1842; Trowbridge to Olcott, 2 December 1840; Trowbridge to J. Chapman, 24 April 1841; and AB to C. Butler, B. F. Butler, and Bowen Whiting, 1 September 1841, Trowbridge Papers.

9. Olcott to Trowbridge, 1 August 1842; Trowbridge to Joy, 2 December 1842; Butler to Olcott, 10 March 1843; Trowbridge to AB, 12 March 1843, Trowbridge Papers.

10. Trowbridge to Olcott, 22 August 1842, Trowbridge Papers.

11. Trowbridge to AB, 1 February 1844, BP, 32.

12. Kilfoil, "Trowbridge," pp. 167, 178-179, and 248-254. Also see Silas Farmer, *The History of Detroit and Michigan* (Detroit: Silas Farmer & Company, 1884), p. 859.

13. William Potter, "The Michigan Judiciary Since 1804," *Michigan History Magazine* 27 (October-December 1943):656; and Clark F. Norton, "Appointments to the Michigan Supreme and Chancery Courts, 1836-1850," *Michigan History Magazine* 30 (Spring 1946):331-334.

14. Trowbridge to Butler, 13 November 1843; Olcott to Trowbridge, 1 August 1842; Trowbridge to Joy, 2 December 1842; Butler to Trowbridge, 4 December 1843; Butler to Trowbridge, 30 October 1844, Trowbridge Papers. Also see Trowbridge to AB, 1 February 1844, BP, 32.

15. John Shirigian, "Lucius Lyon: His Place in Michigan History" (Ph.D. dissertation, University of Michigan, 1961), p. 63.

16. Agreement between AB and Lyon, 5 December 1833; J. Almy to Lyon, 4 December and 14 December 1836; and J. Almy to Lyon, 14 February 1837, Lyon Papers.

17. AB to Lyon, 30 June 1836, Lyon Papers.

18. Lyon to Henry R. Schoolcraft, 22 October 1844, Henry Rowe Schoolcraft Papers, Microfilm, Reel 34, Clarke Historical Library, Mt. Pleasant, Michigan. Hereafter cited as Schoolcraft Papers, reel no.

19. Statement of Account between Isaac Bronson and Lucius Lyon, 7 April 1837, Lyon Papers.

20. Statement of Account between AB and Lyon, 23 January 1839, Lyon Papers. Also see Lyon Papers, 1838-1839, passim.

21. AB to Lyon, 25 February 1839; AB to Lyon, 10 October 1838; AB to Lyon, 5 December and 12 December 1839, Lyon Papers. Also see Shirigian, "Lyon," pp. 156-157.

22. AB to Lyon, 19 February 1839, and 31 May 1839, Lyon Papers; Contract between AB and Lyon, 12 May 1840, in *Bronson Land Book*, BP, CHS; Copy of Decision of Circuit Court, Michigan District, 17 July 1841, in case of *Arthur Bronson* vs. *Thomas Sheldon, Lucius Lyon* and *Justin Burdick*, Lyon Papers; and E. Macy to AB, 4 September 1842, BP, 2.

23. Lyon to William Woodbridge, 6 June 1842, in L. G. Stuart, ed., "Letters of Lucius Lyon," *MPHC*, 27:549. Hereafter cited as Stuart, vol. no.

24. Ibid; Lyon to General Fitzgerald, 26 September 1843, Stuart, "Letters of Lucius Lyon," *MPHC*, 27:562-563. Also see Lyon to Schoolcraft, 23 October 1844, Schoolcraft Papers, Reel 34.

25. AB to Lyon, 12 June 1843; AB to Henry Taylor, 14 July 1843; and George Macy to Lyon, 20 December 1844, Lyon Papers.

26. Frederic Bronson to Lyon, 18 December 1844, Lyon Papers; and Lyon to George Macy, 12 December 1844, BP, 23.

27. C. H. Carroll to Lyon, 1 October 1845; FB to Lyon, 13 March 1847; Carroll to Lyon, 23 August 1849, Lyon Papers; and Legal agreement of FB and Michigan residents, 1 May 1857, BP, 211. On Lyon's later career see Shirigian, "Lyon," pp. 198-209.

28. Green to AB, 20 January 1836, BP, 101; Green to AB, 2 October 1837, BP, 102; George Bates to AB, 31 January 1841, BP, 107; Copy of AB's legal brief in the case of *Green v. Bronson*, BP, 206; Copy of C. K. Green's charges against Arthur Bronson, 1842, BP, 132; and George Bates to AB, 2 January 1844, BP, 112.

29. Ibid.

30. George Bates to AB, 2 January 1844, BP, 112; Joy and Porter to FB, 28 February 1845, BP, 127; and Orville Coolidge, *A Twentieth Century History of Berrien County, Michigan* (Chicago: The Lewis Publishing Company, 1906), pp. 143, 164-165.

31. Bronson's agent in central Indiana, James R. Bryant, also went bankrupt during the depression. Bryant ended up in court disputing the ownership of land with the Bronsons. There were charges of bad faith on both sides. See Bryant to FB, 6 April 1838, BP, 23; Bryant to AB, 29 December 1838, BP, 19; and Bryant to AB, 22 July 1839, BP, 20.

32. See, for example, A. Garrett to AB, 2 November 1842, BP, 205; William Jeunes to IB, 31 March 1838, and John Reynolds to IB, 12 January 1837, BP, 181; and Bond of John Tillson and Frederic Bronson, 2 September 1841, BP, CHS, 65.

33. Contract of Stephen Forbes and FB, 23 June 1840, and 18 May 1840, BP, CHS, 32; FB to Forbes, 22 December 1838, BP, 124; William B. Ogden to FB, 7 January 1843, BP, 126; and Map of Land Belonging to Stephen Forbes, 3 February 1846, BP, CHS, 32.

34. Grant and Peyton to AB, 1 August 1837, BP, 102; Account of AB and Archibald Clybourne, 1 June 1841, BP, CHS, 23; and Contract of AB and Clybourne, 25 June 1840, BP, CHS, 23. Also see Clybourne to AB, 14 January 1839, 5 October 1841; and 31 January 1842, BP, CHS, 23.

35. Contract of Charles Butler and Arthur Bronson, 6 June 1838, Gurdon Hubbard Papers, Chicago Historical Society, Chicago, Illinois, LF, IV; and Arthur Bronson to Alexander Fullerton, Grant Goodrich, R. Stewart, and Truman Wright, 4 May 1837, BP, 6.

36. Bronson's relationship with Ogden can be seen in the following: Ogden to AB, 24 January 1838; 15 January 1838; 1 February 1838; and 9 February 1838, William B. Ogden Papers, CHS, LB, 1. Also see AB to Ogden, 6 August 1840, Ogden Papers, LF, 2; Arnold and Ogden to Oliver Bronson, 15 February 1839, BP, 30; Memorandum of AB, 15 June 1839, BP, CHS, 56.

37. Walter L. Newberry to AB, 4 September 1840; 26 January 1841; and 6 November 1842, BP, CHS, 47.

38. On Butler's financial problems see Chapter 8. An excellent description of the South Side's growth is found in a letter of Alexander Fullerton to AB, 15 November 1840, BP, CHS, 33.

39. Contract of Gurdon Hubbard, Henry G. Hubbard, and Daniel Griswold, 23 September 1837, Gurdon Hubbard Papers, CHS, II; Contract of Hubbard and AB, 8 June 1835, Hubbard Papers, LF, IV; Hubbard to John Wallace, 3 April 1837, Hubbard Papers, LF, II; Hubbard to Edward Russell, 5 July 1835, Hubbard Papers, LF, II. On Hubbard's early career, see my two articles: "Eastern Money and the Urban Frontier: Chicago, 1833-1842," *Journal of the Illinois State Historical Society* 44 (Autumn 1971):227; and "Capital Mobilization and the Urban Center:

The Wisconsin Lakeports," *Mid-America* 60 (April-July 1978):91-92.

40. Hubbard to AB, 27 December 1838, Hubbard Papers, LF, II; Contract of Butler and AB, 6 June 1838, Hubbard Papers, LF, V; Contract of Hubbard and AB, 11 July 1838, Hubbard Papers, LF, V.

41. Ogden to AB, 18 December 1839, Ogden Papers, LB, II; and Hubbard to AB, 26 June 1839, Hubbard Papers, LF, II.

42. Letter of Gurdon Hubbard, 10 February 1840; Hubbard to AB, 6 February 1840, Hubbard Papers, LF, II. See also AB to Mr. Smith and Webster, 19 June 1840, BP, CHS, 36; Copy of a Court Decision in *Bronson* v. *Hubbard*, 1 June 1840, Hubbard Papers, LF, VI; and Contract of Hubbard and AB, 19 June 1840, Hubbard Papers, LF, VI.

43. Ogden to AB, 28 December 1840 and 15 April 1841, Ogden Papers, LB, III. Also see Levi C. Turner to AB, 16 April 1843 and 1 March 1843, BP, CHS, 9.

44. Draft of Gurdon Hubbard Reminiscences, [1870s], Hubbard Papers, LF, X.

45. Bessie L. Pierce, *A History of Chicago,* vol. 1: *The Beginning of a City* (New York: Alfred Knopf, 1937), pp. 95, 139, 193.

46. Contract of John Kinzie and Hiram Pearson with Charles Butler, 20 April 1835, Thomas W. Olcott Papers, Columbia University Library, New York, New York; Contract of John Kinzie, James Campbell, and George Walker, 4 July 1838, BP, CHS, 43; and A. T. Andreas, *History of Chicago,* 3 vols. (Chicago: A. T. Andreas, 1884), 1:634.

47. James S. Buckingham, *The Eastern and Western States of America,* 3 vols. (London: Fisher, Son, and Co., 1842), 3:262-263.

48. Contract of Daniel Griswold and John Kinzie, 12 February 1840, BP, CHS, 42; Kinzie to AB, 16 February 1840, BP, CHS, 42; Kinzie to AB, 20 January 1841, BP, CHS, 43; AB to Kinzie, 7 February 1842, BP, CHS, 43; and AB, "Description of Certain Real Estate in the City of Chicago and the State of Illinois," December 1843, BP, 182.

49. Walter L. Newberry to AB, 30 March 1843, BP, CHS, 47.

50. James Hildreth to AB, 1 May 1844, BP, 205; Sanford Robinson to AB, 15 March 1843, BP, CHS, 9; Newberry to AB, 30 March 1843 and 29 January 1844, BP, CHS, 47; and James W. Norris, *Business Directory and Statistics of the City of Chicago for 1846* (Chicago: Eastman & Davis, 1846), p. 44.

51. Walter Newberry to Lyon, 1 January 1837, Walter Newberry Papers, Newberry Library, Chicago, Illinois; Castello N. Holford, *History of Grant County, Wisconsin* (Lancaster, Wisconsin: The Teller Press, 1900), p. 38.

52. Contract between AB and John Ward and G. Denniston and Lucius Lyon, 4 April 1837, Nelson Dewey Papers, Box III, State Historical Society of Wisconsin, Madison, Wisconsin; and AB to L. J. Daniels, 4 April 1837, BP, 19.

53. Frederic Bronson's notes on the history of Cassville, [1850s], CHS, 26.

54. John Bertram to Denniston, 24 March 1837, Lyon Papers; and Lyon to Denniston, 4 January 1838, in L. G. Stuart, ed., "Letters of Lucius Lyon," *MPHC,* 27:495.

55. Lyon to Denniston, 12 July 1837, Lyon Papers; AB to Lyon, 10 July 1838 and 4 August 1838, Lyon Papers; AB to Denniston, 1 March 1839, BP, CHS, 25; and Contract of Lyon with Oliver, Arthur, and Frederic Bronson, 3 June 1838, Lyon Papers.

56. AB to Denniston, 1 March 1839, BP, CHS, 25; and Frederic Bronson's notes on the history of Cassville, [1850s], CHS, 26.

57. Denniston to AB, 11 February 1840; 25 August 1840; and 27 January 1842;

BP, CHS, 25. Also see Denniston to FB, 15 November 1844, BP, CHS, 25; Denniston to Lyon, 29 September 1845, Lyon Papers; Complaint filed in Wisconsin Circuit Court of John Denniston against FB, 1857, BP, CHS, 26; and FB's notes on the history of Cassville, BP, CHS, 26.

58. Population figures are from Denniston to Lyon, 22 February 1841, Lyon Papers.

59. AB to Emma Beardsley, 29 July 1840, BP, 106. Also see Letter of FB, 26 December 1844, BP, 208.

60. AB to Mark Norris, 13 November 1839, BP, 20.

61. James Bryant to FB, 6 April 1838, BP, 23; Mark Norris to AB, 3 July 1839, BP, 20; and H. G. Wells to AB, 12 March 1842, BP, 108. Bronson lent a great deal more money in New York State. See BP, 107-111. Also see Ogden to AB, 15 June 1838, Ogden Papers, LB, I.

Chapter 10

1. See, for example, laws in Michigan and Illinois: Michigan, "An Act to Provide for the Assessment and Collection of Taxes," *Acts of the Legislature of the State of Michigan* (Detroit: Ellis and Briggs, 1843), pp. 60-87; Illinois, "An Act to Amend an Act entitled 'An Act concerning the public revenue' . . . , Approved February 26, 1839," reprinted in *Chicago Democrat*, 10 May 1843. Also see the excellent description of the whole process in Robert P. Swierenga, *Acres for Cents: Delinquent Tax Auctions in Frontier Iowa* (Westport, Connecticut: Greenwood Press, 1976), pp. 20-24.

2. E. H. Macy to AB, 4 September 1842, BP, 21; George Macy to AB, 20 February 1843, BP, 22. On Bronson's attitude see FB to James Duane Doty, 8 December 1840, James Duane Doty Papers, Box III, State Historical Society of Wisconsin, Madison, Wisconsin; and AB to Doty, 7 February 1839, Doty Papers, WHS, II.

3. William Thompson to Thomas W. Olcott, 2 November 1841, Thomas W. Olcott Papers, Columbia University Library, New York, New York.

4. Older views on the intent and effect of tax policies of western states can be found in Ernest L. Bogart, *Financial History of Ohio*, University of Illinois Studies in the Social Sciences (Urbana: University of Illinois Press, 1912), I:185-186; Howard Jay Graham, "Acres for Cents: The Economics and Constitutional Significance of Frontier Tax Titles, 1800-1890," in *Everyman's Constitution*, ed. Howard Jay Graham (Madison: State Historical Society of Wisconsin, 1968), pp. 500-515. More recent work of a quantitative nature has been done by Robert Swierenga. See Robert P. Swierenga, "Land Speculation and Frontier Tax Assessments," *Agricultural History* 44 (July 1970):253-254.

5. The following are examples of the numerous agencies with which Bronson was connected: Land Agency of Sidney Allcott and James A. Van Horn, Marshall, Michigan, BP, 205; F. W. Hatch Land Agency, 1842, Schoolcraft, Michigan, BP, 211; Edward H. Macy's Michigan Land Agency, 1842, Lyon Papers; and Circular of the William B. Ogden Agency, Ogden Papers, LF, 1, CHS.

6. Stephen Mason to AB, 29 December 1837, BP, 204; and Michigan, *Acts of the Legislature of the State of Michigan* (Detroit: John S. Bagg, 1838), pp. 80-81.

7. Michigan, *Acts of the Legislature*, 1838, p. 92; and Michigan, *Acts of the Legislature of the State of Michigan* (Detroit: Bagg and Herman, 1842), pp. 95-101.

8. E. H. Macy to AB, 5 October 1842, BP, 21; Butler to AB, 6, 16 and 28

February 1843, BP, 110. Also see Butler to Thomas Olcott, 10 March 1843, Trowbridge Papers; and Michigan, *Acts of the Legislature of the State of Michigan* (Detroit: Ellis and Briggs, 1843), pp. 60-87.

9. AB to Chairman, Committee on Finance, 11 January 1841, as printed in the [New York] *Journal of Commerce,* 20 January 1844. On existing Illinois legislation see Robert Murray Haig, *A History of the General Property Tax in Illinois,* University of Illinois Studies in the Social Sciences (Urbana: University of Illinois Press, 1914), III:35-58, 74-92. A copy of the Illinois revenue law can be found in the *Chicago Democrat,* 10 May 1843.

10. FB to James Duane Doty, 8 December 1840, Doty Papers, III.

11. AB to Doty, 7 February 1839, Doty Papers, II.

12. Doty to AB, 8 January 1842, BP, 108; James Duane Doty, "Message to the Legislature," 10 December 1841, in Clarence E. Carter, ed., *The Territorial Papers of the United States,* vol. 27: *The Territory of Wisconsin* (Washington: The National Archives, 1969), pp. 309-311.

13. Ibid.

14. As early as 4 March 1837, the *Chicago American* began to carry lists of tax delinquent lands. A quick check of newspapers in Milwaukee, Detroit and Green Bay revealed the same pattern.

15. See the excellent descriptions in Robert P. Swierenga, "The Tax Buyer as a Frontier Type," *Explorations in Economic History* 7 (Spring 1970):257-292; and Swierenga, "The Odious Tax Title: A Study in Nineteenth Century Legal History," *American Journal of Legal History* 15 (April 1971):124-126; and Swierenga, *Acres for Cents,* pp. 21-57. Sample laws are Michigan, *Acts of the Legislature of the State of Michigan,* 1838, pp. 95-99; and Michigan, *Acts of the Legislature of the State of Michigan,* 1843, pp. 78-83.

16. Solomon Wills to J. B. Campbell, 13 May 1838, James Campbell Papers, Chicago Historical Society, Chicago, Illinois.

17. Swierenga presents an excellent review of the literature on tax sales. See Swierenga, *Acres for Cents,* pp. 4-5, 16-18. The older view that tax sales were a device used against absentee owners is contained in Graham, "Acres for Cents," pp. 505-513.

18. I found only isolated cases of Bronson's purchasing land at tax sales. See, for example, Certificate of tax sale, 10 May 1840, BP, CHS, 6. Also see Swierenga, *Acres for Cents,* pp. 20-23.

19. E. H. Macy to AB, 3 June 1842 and 19 August 1842, BP, 21; James Putnam to AB, 26 September 1843, BP, 22; and George Macy to AB, 29 August 1843, BP, 22.

20. AB to E. Hastings, 15 December 1840, BP, 106; Stephen Preston to AB, 31 July 1840, BP, 106; and Michigan, *Acts of the Legislature,* 1838, pp. 95-101, and *Acts of the Legislature,* 1843, pp. 55-60, 78-79.

21. FB to James Duane Doty, 8 December 1840, Doty Papers, III; Charles Butler, Arthur Bronson, and Aaron Vanderpohl, "Petition to the Senate and House of Representatives, 29 April 1844," BP, 206; and James Doty, "Message to the Legislature," 10 December 1841, in Carter, ed., *The Territorial Papers of the United States,* 27:310-311.

22. [Arthur Bronson], Copy of "An act relating to the recording and registering of conveyances and other instruments in writing, executed out of this state and within the United States," BP, 206; E. Peck to AB, 7 February 1841, BP, 107; Illinois, "An Act relating to the recording and registering of conveyances . . . ," *Laws of the State of Illinois Passed by the Twelfth General Assembly* (Springfield: Wm.

Walters, 1841), pp. 166-167; and Wisconsin, *Laws of the Territory of Wisconsin 1842-1843* (Madison: Printed by Sheldon and Hyer, 1843), pp. 42-43; George Bates to AB, 31 January 1841, BP, 107; and Michigan, *Acts of the Legislature,* 1840, pp. 166-167.

23. AB to William Murray, 13 March 1841, Gulian C. Verplanck Papers, New York Historical Society, New York, New York.

24. Ibid.

25. Ibid. Also see "Memorial to the Senate and House of Representatives of the State of New York, 1840," BP, 206. Many New Yorkers signed this memorial and its arguments resembled those of Bronson's letter above.

26. Draft of "An Act Entitled an Act to Amend the Law for the Collection of Taxes." This draft is signed by Arthur Bronson and Lot Clark. Also see E. Peck to AB, 7 February 1841, BP, 107.

27. On bankruptcy legislation see Peter J. Coleman, *Debtors and Creditors in America: Insolvency, Imprisonment for Debt, and Bankruptcy, 1607-1900* (Madison: The State Historical Society of Wisconsin, 1974), p. 23; David Beesley, "The Politics of Bankruptcy in the United States 1837-1845" (Ph.D. dissertation, University of Utah, 1968), pp. 7-31; and the earlier work by Charles Warren, *Bankruptcy in United States History* (Cambridge: Harvard University Press, 1935).

28. Bessie L. Pierce, *A History of Chicago,* vol. 1: *The Beginning of a City, 1673-1848* (New York: Alfred A. Knopf, 1937), p. 67; Thomas W. Goodspeed, *The University of Chicago Biographical Sketches* (Chicago: University of Chicago Press, 1922), pp. 42-43; and Thomas Hoyne, *The Lawyer as Pioneer,* Fergus Historical Series, No. 22 (Chicago: Fergus Printing Company, 1882), p. 88.

29. Robert H. Skilton, "Developments in Mortgage Law and Practice," *Temple University Law Quarterly* 16 (August 1943):315-326 and 357-367; A. H. Feller, "Moratory Legislation: A Comparative Study," *Harvard Law Review* 46 (May 1933): 1068-1085; and Lawrence M. Friedman, *A History of American Law* (New York: Simon and Schuster, 1973), pp. 215-218.

30. AB to E. Hastings, 15 December 1840, BP, 106.

31. Bronson most clearly articulated his philosophy to Governor Ford of Illinois. See AB to Governor Ford, 15 January 1844, in *Journal of Commerce,* 20 January 1844. Also see the article "State Debts," *Journal of Commerce,* 17 February 1841, for additional contemporary opinion. A recent discussion of the meaning of the contract in the nineteenth century is Morton J. Horwitz, "The Historical Foundations of Modern Contract Law," *Harvard Law Review* 87 (March 1974):917-949.

32. *Detroit Advertiser,* 13 March 1841.

33. George Bates to AB, 20 April 1841, BP, 107.

34. Illinois, *Laws,* 1841, pp. 168-172. Also see the extended discussion of these laws in Skilton, "Mortgage Law," pp. 331-333; and George L. Priest, "Law and Economic Distress: Sangamon County, Illinois, 1837-1844," *The Journal of Legal Studies* 2 (June 1973):473-474.

35. Michigan, *Acts of the Legislature,* 1841, pp. 45-47; and Michigan, *Acts of the Legislature,* 1842, pp. 135-138.

36. Priest, "Law and Economic Distress," pp. 484-485 argues that the appraisal laws were not effective in preventing forced sales, yet his analysis was based on a limited sample. The effect of the Illinois laws, moreover, would have been blunted since Bronson immediately challenged them. Bronson's reaction to these laws was evident in the following: AB to John Kinzie, 21 August 1841, BP, CHS, 42; AB to John Kinzie, 7 February 1842, BP, CHS, 43; and AB to Hiram Pearson, 27

February 1843, BP, CHS, 58.

37. Ibid. Also see Priest, "Law and Economic Distress," p. 491.

38. Roger Sherman to AB, 4 May 1841, BP, 30; AB to Roger Sherman, 31 January 1842, Roger Sherman Papers, Connecticut State Library, Hartford, Connecticut; and Sherman to AB, 2 February 1842, BP, 108.

39. Bill to Foreclose Mortgage, Circuit Court of Illinois, 27 March 1841, *Bronson* v. *Kinzie*, Supreme Court Appellate Case File, Number 2271, National Archives, Washington, D.C. Also see Kinzie to AB, 2 April 1838, BP, CHS, 41; and Contract of Kinzie and Bronson, 12 March 1838, BP, CHS, 41. There were co-defendants in this case consisting of Kinzie's partners and other creditors in the Lake House Hotel.

40. John Kinzie to AB, 17 December 1838, BP, CHS, 41; Kinzie to AB, 30 October 1839, BP, CHS, 42; Kinzie to AB, 30 January 1841, BP, CHS, 43; and AB to Honorable Thomas Ewing, 14 July 1841, BP, CHS, 43.

41. AB to John Kinzie, 27 August 1841, BP, CHS, 42; Kinzie to Walter Forward, 1 December 1841, BP, CHS, 43; AB to Kinzie, 7 February 1842, BP, CHS, 43; and *Bronson* v. *Kinzie*, Supreme Court Appellate Case File, No. 2271.

42. Ibid. Also see AB to Walter Forward, 24 January 1842, BP, CHS, 43.

43. This reasoning was primarily that of Bronson and his lawyer, Isaac Arnold. See AB to Kinzie, 7 February 1842, BP, CHS, 43; AB to Hiram Pearson, 27 February 1843, BP, CHS, 58; and Isaac N. Arnold, *Argument before the United States Supreme Court in the Case of Arthur Bronson . . . and John Kinzie . . .* (n.p., 1843), pp. 5-9. A copy of this publication was found at the Widener Library, Harvard University.

44. AB to John Kinzie, 7 February 1842, BP, CHS, 43.

45. *Bronson* v. *Kinzie*, 1 Howard 311 (1843); Isaac N. Arnold, *William B. Ogden,* Fergus Historical Series, no. 18 (Chicago: Fergus Printing Company, 1882), pp. 9-10; Isaac N. Arnold, *Reminiscences of the Illinois Bar Forty Years Ago: Lincoln and Douglas as Orators and Lawyers* (Chicago: Fergus Printing Company, 1881), pp. 16-17; and A. T. Andreas, *History of Chicago,* 3 vols. (Chicago: A. T. Andreas, 1884), 1:435-436; and *Chicago Daily American,* 23 June 1841. This issue carried a notice of Arnold's argument before the Circuit Court. A copy is available in BP, 214.

46. Arnold, *Argument before the United States Supreme Court,* pp. 10-11, passim.

47. Ibid., pp. 7-8.

48. The background of court action on the contract clause can be obtained in a number of excellent works. I have depended on the following: Lawrence Friedman, *A History of American Law* (New York: Simon and Schuster, 1973), pp. 217-218; Lawrence Friedman, *Contract Law in America* (Madison: University of Wisconsin Press, 1965), pp. 132-134; Coleman, *Debtors and Creditors,* p. 34; Horwitz, "The Historical Foundations of Modern Contract Law," p. 953; Benjamin F. Wright, *The Contract Clause of the Constitution* (Cambridge: Harvard University Press, 1938), pp. 254-256; and R. Kent Newmeyer, *The Supreme Court Under Marshall and Taney* (New York: Thomas Y. Crowell Co., 1968), pp. 56-101. Also see Robert L. Hale, "The Supreme Court and the Contract Clause," *Harvard Law Review* 57 (April 1944): 512-588; and Morton J. Horwitz, *The Transformation of American Law, 1790-1860* (Boston: Harvard University Press, 1976), pp. 104-139.

49. Taney's most important decision had been in the Charles River Bridge case. In this instance, he abrogated an existing monopoly of a toll bridge company so that a second company might also build a bridge in the same area. Although Taney appeared to attack the sanctity of the contract and the rights of capital, he actually

balanced the rights of the community to have competing enterprises against those of entrenched capital. See Newmeyer, *The Supreme Court,* pp. 109-113; Stanley J. Kutler, *Privilege and Creative Destruction: the Charles River Bridge Case* (Philadelphia: J. B. Lippincott Company, 1971), p. 134; and Marvin L. Winitsky, "The Jurisprudence of Roger B. Taney" (Ph.D. dissertation, University of California, Los Angeles, 1973), pp. 139-144.

50. *Bronson* v. *Kinzie,* 1 Howard 311 (1843).

51. Ibid.

52. Ibid.

53. Ibid. Taney thus ordered that the property should be sold at auction without reference to the two Illinois laws. Also see Hale, "Supreme Court and the Contract Clause," pp. 539-541.

54. *Bronson* v. *Kinzie,* 1 Howard 311 (1843); also see Charles G. Haines and Foster H. Sherwood, *The Role of the Supreme Court in American Government and Politics, 1835-1864* (Los Angeles: University of California Press, 1957), pp. 340-341.

55. *Chicago Democrat,* 11 March 1843; Paul Freund, gen. ed., *History of the Supreme Court,* vol. 5: *The Taney Period, 1836-64,* by Carl B. Swisher (N.Y.: MacMillan Co., 1974), pp. 149-153; Kutler, *Privilege and Creative Destruction,* p. 135; Arnold, "Forty Years," pp. 17-18; and AB to Hiram Pearson, 27 February 1843, BP, CHS, 58.

56. Bronson lent small amounts of capital in Illinois and Michigan compared to his operations in New York State. See BP. 107-111, for a comparison of his correspondence with New York and western agents.

57. The problem of adjusting laws to the needs of an expanding business system was common in antebellum America. Tony Allan Freyer has explored this theme in "The Federal Courts, Localism, and the National Economy, 1865-1900," *Business History Review* 53 (Autumn 1979): 344-363; and *Forums for Order: The Federal Courts and Business in American History* (Greenwich, Connecticut: JAI Press, 1979), pp. 11-30. Also see the classic study by James Willard Hurst, *Law and the Conditions of Freedom in the Nineteenth Century United States* (Madison: University of Wisconsin Press, 1956), pp. 28-29.

Not all historians would agree with my view of the case. See Priest, "Law and Economic Distress," p. 493; Swisher, *History of the Supreme Court,* pp. 148-149, and Carl B. Swisher, *Roger B. Taney* (New York: The MacMillan Co., 1935), pp. 388-389.

58. See Kutler, *Privilege and Creative Destruction,* pp. 134-135; Wright, *Contract Clause,* pp. 70-71, 109; Hale, "Supreme Court and the Contract Clause," pp. 543-557.

Chapter 11

1. The two best studies on American state debts are Benjamin Curtis, "Debts of the States," *North American Review* 58 (January-April 1844): 109-157; and Reginald C. McGrane, *Foreign Bondholders and American State Debts* (New York: The MacMillan Co., 1935), pp. 1-20 and passim. Also see Leland H. Jenks, *The Migration of British Capital to 1875* (1927; reprint ed., New York: Harper and Row, 1973), pp. 65-108.

2. William A. Scott, *The Repudiation of State Debts* (New York: Thomas Y. Crowell & Co., 1893), pp. 4-30.

3. McGrane, *Foreign Bondholders,* pp. 21-40.

4. See, for example, McGrane, *Foreign Bondholders,* pp. 382-383, and Curtis,

"Debts of the States," pp. 115-117. Also see Thomas P. Kettel, "Debts and Finances of the States of the Union: With Reference to Their General Condition and Prosperity. Chapter VIII: The Western States—Michigan," *The Merchants' Magazine* 22 (February 1850): 131-145; and Thomas P. Kettel, "Debts and Finances of the States . . . : Chapter VI: The Western States—Indiana," *The Merchants' Magazine* 21 (August 1849): 147-163.

5. The complicity of foreign banking houses can be studied in Joseph Dorfman, "A Note on the Interpenetration of Anglo-American Finance, 1837-44," *Journal of Economic History* 11 (Spring 1951): 140-147. On the role of the North American Trust and Banking Company see Henry Cohen, *Business and Politics in America from the Age of Jackson to the Civil War: the Career Biography of W. W. Corcoran* (Westport, Connecticut: Greenwood Publishing Company, 1971), p. 10; William Mackenzie, *The Lives and Opinions of Benj'n Franklin Butler and Jesse Hoyt . . .* (Boston: Cooke &Co., 1845), pp. 147-148; and *New York Evening Post,* 13 February 1844, BP, 30.

6. Mackenzie, *Lives and Opinions,* p. 148; "Autobiography of James B. Murray," Box IV, Murray Papers, New York Historical Society, New York, New York; and James B. Murray to AB, 14 November 1839, 4 July 1839 and 14 April 1840, BP, 215.

7. Lyon to Butler, 27 January 1838, Butler Papers, III; and Butler to Lyon, 21 June 1838, Lyon Papers.

8. AB to Governor Thomas Ford, 15 January 1844, in the *Journal of Commerce,* 20 January 1844.

9. A general background on Illinois internal improvements can be found in McGrane, *Foreign Bondholders,* pp. 102-115; John H. Krenkel, *Illinois Internal Improvements, 1818-1848* (Cedar Rapids, Iowa: The Torch Press, 1958), pp. 110-125; Clarence V. Alvord, ed., *The Centennial History of Illinois,* volume 2: *The Frontier State, 1818-1848* by Theodore C. Pease (Chicago: A. C. McClurg & Co., 1919), pp. 316-325; and James W. Putnam, *The Illinois and Michigan Canal* (Chicago: University of Chicago Press, 1918), passim. On the canal's importance to Chicago, see Bessie L. Pierce, *A History of Chicago,* vol. 1: *The Beginning of a City, 1673-1848* (New York: Alfred A. Knopf, 1937), pp. 70-71.

10. Pierce, *A History of Chicago,* 1:68-73, 151, 377. Also see Ogden to Butler, 19 January 1841; and Ogden to AB, 19 January 1841, Ogden Papers, LB, III.

11. Ogden to William Haas, 16 March 1841; Ogden to AB, 19 January 1841; Ogden to H. Norton, 5 January 1841; and Ogden to Butler, 27 March 1841, Ogden Papers, LB, III. Also see AB to Chairman, Committee on Finance, 11 January 1841, *Journal of Commerce,* 20 January 1844.

12. Ogden to AB, 28 August 1841, Ogden Papers, LB, III.

13. Butterfield, a lawyer came west in 1835 from New York State. In 1841, he was the prosecutor for the United States Judicial District of Illinois. He also served in the Illinois legislature. See A. T. Andreas, *A History of Chicago,* 3 vols. (Chicago: A. T. Andreas, 1884), 1:433.

14. Almost all historians of Illinois' internal improvements have discussed this episode; and, depending on whom you read, the original ideas have been attributed to Butterfield, Arnold, and occasionally to Bronson. The clearest proof that Bronson was the "idea" man comes from his later domination of the whole enterprise. For the various descriptions, see Andreas, *History of Chicago,* 1:169-170; Thomas Ford, *A History of Illinois* (Chicago: S. C. Griggs & Co., 1854), pp. 295-297; Krenkel, *Illinois Improvements,* pp. 18, 180-181, 188; and Putnam, *Illinois-Michigan Canal,* p. 56. Charles Butler was also involved in the plan. See Charles Butler,

"Account of a Trip to the West, 1881," Butler Papers, III.

15. C. Macalester to AB, 3 August 1842, BP, 205; and Krenkel, *Illinois Improvements*, p. 144.

16. John Horsley Palmer to AB, 22 September 1842, BP, 109. Palmer was also a director of the Bank of England in 1811 and on the board of governors from 1830-32. For information on Palmer, see "John Horsley Palmer, " *The Dictionary of National Biography*, ed. Leslie Stephen and Sidney Lee (London: Oxford University Press, 1950), 15:144.

17. AB to Governor Thomas Ford, 15 January 1844, in *Journal of Commerce*, 20 January 1844. Also see Krenkel, *Illinois Improvements*, pp. 180-181.

18. Ibid.

19. Justin Butterfield to AB, 3 October 1842, 2 November 1842 and 17 November 1842, BP, 109.

20. Isaac N. Arnold, "A Lecture on the Legal and Moral Obligations of the State to Pay Her Debts . . ."*Chicago Democrat*, 30 November 1842; Editorial on "Our Canal—a Project for Its Completion," *Chicago Democrat*, 30 November 1842; Illinois, House of Representatives, *Journal of the House of Representatives of the Thirteenth General Assembly* (Springfield: William Walters, 1842), p. 3; Andreas, *History of Chicago*, 1:436, 169-170; and Krenkel, *Illinois Improvements*, pp. 180-181. Also see McGrane, *Foreign Bondholders*, pp. 115-116.

21. Pease, *Frontier State*, p. 321; Krenkel, *Illinois Improvements*, pp. 181-182; and McGrane, *Foreign Bondholders*, pp. 117-119.

22. AB to Governor Ford, 15 January 1844, in *Journal of Commerce*, 20 January 1844.

23. Ibid.; Krenkel, *Illinois Improvements*, pp. 182-183; McGrane, *Foreign Bondholders*, p. 119; and Justin Butterfield to AB, 27 March 1843, BP, 110.

24. AB to Governor Ford, 15 January 1844, in *Journal of Commerce*, 20 January 1844; Krenkel, *Illinois Improvements*, pp. 182-183; and McGrane, *Foreign Bondholders*, pp. 119-120.

25. Ibid. The negotiations can be followed in Illinois, General Assembly, *Report in relation to the Illinois and Michigan Canal to Messrs. Baring Brothers & Co., and Messrs. Magniac, Jardine & Co., 1 March 1844. Illinois Reports*, 1844-46, pp. 163-172. (The *Illinois Reports* consist of reports to the Senate and House of Representatives.) Also see Andreas, *History of Chicago*, 1:170-173 and Pease, *Frontier State*, pp. 316-324.

26. AB to Governor Thomas Ford, 15 January 1844, in the *Journal of Commerce*, 20 January 1844.

27. The final decisions by the Illinois legislature in regard to the canal and its later policy toward the internal improvements bonds can be followed in McGrane, *Foreign Bondholders*, pp. 120-125; and Krenkel, *Illinois Improvements*, pp. 186-217.

28. My description of the Michigan loan depends on McGrane, *Foreign Bondholders*, pp. 145-147; Robert J. Parks, *Democracy's Railroads: Public Enterprise in Jacksonian Michigan* (Port Washington, New York: Kennikat Press, 1972), pp. 187-191; William L. Jenks, "Michigan's Five Million Dollar Loan," *Michigan History Magazine* 15 (Autumn 1931):578-588; and Charles Butler, "Reminiscences on the Michigan and Indiana Loans," [1880s], Butler Papers, IV, pp. 1-2.

29. McGrane, *Foreign Bondholders*, p. 146. The loan was actually $4,800,000 because some bonds had already been sold to Oliver Newberry.

30. McGrane, *Foreign Bondholders*, pp. 148-154; and Jenks, "Five Million Dollar Loan," pp. 589-600.

31. McGrane, *Foreign Bondholders*, pp. 155-159; and Jenks, "Five Million Dollar Loan," pp. 600-609.

32. McGrane, *Foreign Bondholders,* pp. 155-159; Scott, *The Repudiation of State Debts,* p. 164; Butler, "Reminiscences on Michigan and Indiana Loans, pp. 1-3.

33. Butler, "Reminiscences on the Michigan and Indiana Loans, pp. 1-3; Charles Butler to Governor Barry, 1 February 1843, in Michigan, *Documents Communicated to the Senate and House of Representatives of the State of Michigan, 1843* (Detroit: Ellis and Biggs, 1843), pp. 428-429; James Buchanan to Butler, 6 January 1843, Butler Papers, I.

Griswold is identified in Henry W. Lanier, *A Century of Banking in New York, 1822-1922* (New York: The Gillis Press, 1922), p. 109; and in Robert G. Albion, "Commercial Fortunes in New York: A Study in the History of the Port of New York About 1840," *New York History* 16 (April 1935):162.

34. Charles Butler to Benjamin F. Butler, 6 January 1843, Butler Papers, I; and Butler, "Reminiscences on the Michigan and Indiana Loans," p. 1.

35. Butler to Elon Farnsworth, 1 December 1842 and 12 December 1842, Butler Papers, III.

36. Charles Butler to Eliza Butler, 12 January 1843, Butler Papers, I.

37. Parks, *Democracy's Railroads,* pp. 204-206, is critical of Butler's role in the negotiations. He argues that the state was agreeable to the whole idea and that Butler had little effect. Also see McGrane, *Foreign Bondholders,* p. 158.

38. Butler, "Reminiscences of Michigan and Indiana Loans," pp. 1-5; and Butler to his wife, 28 January 1843, Butler Papers, I.

39. Charles Butler to Governor John Barry, 1 February 1843, Michigan, *Documents Communicated to the Senate and House of Representatives, 1843,* pp. 426-430.

40. Charles Butler to Governor Barry, 1 February 1843, in Michigan, *Documents Communicated to the Senate and House of Representatives, 1843,* pp. 425-437.

41. Ibid., pp. 435-436.

42. Charles Butler to Eliza Butler, 4 February 1843, in George L. Prentiss, *The Union Theological Seminary in the City of New York: Its Design and Another Decade of Its History, With a Sketch of the Life and Public Services of Charles Butler, LL.D.* (Asbury Park, New Jersey: M. W. & C. Pennypacker, 1889), p. 438.

43. Michigan, "Report of the Joint Committee of the Senate and House of Representatives, on the subject of the five million dollar loan bonds," in Michigan, *Documents Communicated to the Senate and House of Representatives, 1843,* pp. 411-425.

44. Ibid.

45. Draft of letter of Butler to Digby Bell, Chairman of the Joint Committee, 20 February 1843 Butler Papers, I; Michigan, *Journal of the Senate of the State of Michigan, 1843,* (Detroit: Ellis and Briggs, 1843), pp. 277, 289, 323, 370-371, 405, 408; Charles Butler to Eliza Butler, 24 February 1843, Butler Papers, I; and *Detroit Daily Free Press,* 27 February 1843.

46. Butler to his wife, 27 February 1843, in Prentiss, *Union Theological Seminary,* p. 440. Also see Butler to his wife, 7 March 1843, in Prentiss, *Union Theological Seminary,* pp. 441-442.

47. Ibid.; *Michigan Journal of the House of Representatives, 1843* (Detroit: Ellis and Briggs, 1843), pp. 462-471; and Jenks, "Five Million Dollar Loan," p. 610.

48. Charles Butler to his wife, 14 March 1843, in Prentiss, *Union Theological Seminary,* pp. 443-444.

49. Ibid., pp. 443-449.

50. Michigan, "An Act to Liquidate the Public Debt, and to provide for the payment of interest thereon, and for other purposes," in *Acts of the Legislature of the State of Michigan* (Detroit: Ellis and Briggs, 1843), pp. 150-153; and McGrane, *Foreign Bondholders,* pp. 160-163.

51. Butler, "Reminiscences on the Michigan and Indiana Loans." pp. 4-7; Butler to his wife, 12 March 1846, Butler Papers, I; Marian Sears, "A Michigan Bureaucrat Promotes the State's Economic Growth: George F. Porter Sells the Michigan Central Railroad to Eastern Capitalists, 1846," *Explorations in Entrepreneurial History* 4 (Spring-Summer 1966): 201-210; and Arthur M. Johnson and Barry Supple, *Boston Capitalists and Western Railroads* (Cambridge: Harvard Universtiy Press, 1967), pp. 90-94.

52. Curtis, "Debts of the States," pp. 135-136. Butler disagreed with this article. He jotted down his reactions in "Suggestion to article in the *North American Review*," [1884], Butler Papers, II.

53. Charles Butler to Daniel Meinertzhagen, 29 June 1843, and Meinertzhagen to Butler, 2 September 1843, Butler Papers, I; Butler to Hope and Company, 10 August 1843; Butler Papers, I; Butler, "Reminiscences on the Michigan and Indiana Loans," pp. 8-9; and B. V. Ratchford, *American State Debts* (Durham, North Carolina: Duke University Press, 1941), p. 116.

54. I have depended for general background on Indiana on the following: McGrane, *Foreign Bondholders*, pp. 126-138; Logan Esarey, *History of Indiana from Its Exploration to 1922*, 3 vols. (Dayton, Ohio: Dayton Publishing Company, 1922), 1:408-431; and Elbert Jay Benton, *The Wabash Trade Route in the Development of the Old Northwest*, Johns Hopkins University Studies in Historical and Political Science, Series 21, nos. 1 & 2 (Baltimore: The Johns Hopkins Press, 1903), pp. 45-63.

The story of the fraud accompanying the sale of Indiana bonds can be followed best in a series of documents put together by Butler. See Charles Butler, *Letter of Charles Butler to the Legislature of Indiana in Relation to the Public Debt* (Indianapolis: Morrison & Spann, 1846), pp. 39-57.

55. McGrane, *Foreign Bondholders*, pp. 131-138; and Esarey, *History of Indiana*, 1:424-431.

56. Butler to his wife, 19 May 1845, Butler Papers, I; Esarey, *History of Indiana*, 1:431; Benton, *Wabash Trade Route*, pp. 65-66.

57. Butler to his wife, 29 November 1845, in Prentiss, *Union Theological Seminary*, pp. 454-455; Charles Butler, "Copy of Official Report to the London Committee of Bondholders . . . ," 17 February 1846, pp. 1-3, Butler Papers, I. Hereafter cited as Butler, "Report to the Bondholders."

58. Butler to his wife, 7 December 1845, in Prentiss, *Union Theological Seminary*, p. 456.

59. Charles Butler, *Communication of the Agent of the Foreign Holders of Indiana State Bonds to His Excellency James Whitcomb, December, 1845* (Indianapolis: J. P. Chapman, 1845), pp. 1-23; Butler, "Report to the Bondholders," pp. 1-2; Butler to his wife, 10 and 11 December 1845, in Prentiss, *Union Theological Seminary*, pp. 457-458. The address was reported in the *Indiana State Sentinel*, 16 December 1845. This newspaper also carried a report on the debates in the Senate and House of Representatives throughout the period. Also see Butler, *Letter of Charles Butler to the Indiana Legislature*, pp. 33-36.

60. Butler, "Report to the Bondholders," pp. 2-5; Butler to his wife, 17, 18, 21, 22, and 25 December 1845, in Prentiss, *Union Theological Seminary*, pp. 465-476; and Butler, *Letter to the Indiana Legislature*, pp. 36-39.

61. Butler, *Letter to the Indiana Legislature*, pp. 33-39; Butler, "Report to the Bondholders," pp. 5-6; Benton, *Wabash Trade Route*, p. 69; and Butler, *Communication of the Agent of Foreign Holders*, pp. 8-10.

62. Butler, "Report to the Bondholders," pp. 6-17; Butler to his wife, 1 January

1845 and 10 January 1846, in Prentiss, *Union Theological Seminary*, pp. 479-486; *Indiana State Journal*, 13 January and 15 January 1846. Also see Esarey, *History of Indiana*, 1:433.

63. Butler to his wife, 10, 11, and 12 January 1846, in Prentiss, *Union Theological Seminary*, pp. 485-487.

64. Butler to his wife, 13, 14, and 15 January 1846, in Prentiss, *Union Theological Seminary*, pp. 488-490; Butler, "Report to the Bondholders," pp. 6-11. The debate can be followed in the *Indiana State Sentinel*, January-February 1846, and, of course, in the published Senate and House Journals of Indiana.

65. Butler to his wife, 16, 17, and 19 January 1846, in Prentiss, *Union Theological Seminary*, pp. 490-496; and Butler, "Report to the Bondholders," pp. 11-13. One can discern the differences between Butler's proposal and the final bill in Butler, *Letter to the Indiana Legislature*, pp. 69-86.

66. "An Act to provide for the funded debt of the State of Indiana," in Butler, *Letter to the Indiana Legislature*, pp. 69-86. See particularly Section 1, 18, and 35 of the law. Also see McGrane, *Foreign Bondholders*, p. 139.

67. Butler, *Letter to the Indiana Legislature*, p. 93 and passim. Also see Butler, "Report to the Bondholders," p. 22.

68. Butler, "Report to the Bondholders," pp. 9-10, 18-22.

69. Ibid., pp. 34, 28-39.

70. Ibid., pp. 23-39.

71. Francis H. Stoddard, *The Life and Letters of Charles Butler* (New York: Charles Scribner's Sons, 1903), pp. 279-282; Butler to his wife, 3 September 1846, Butler Papers, I; J. H. Palmer to James King, 18 September 1846, Butler Papers, I; Benton, *Wabash Trade Route*, p. 73; and Esarey, *History of Indiana*, 1:434-435.

72. Butler to his wife, 9, 10, and 23 December 1846, Butler Papers, I.

73. William Mackenzie, *The Life and Times of Martin Van Buren: The Correspondence of his Friends, Family and Pupils . . .* (Boston: Cooke & Co., 1846), p. 154; and Butler to his wife, 25 December 1846, Butler Papers, I.

74. Butler to his wife, 25 December 1846, 17 and 26 January 1847, Butler Papers, I. Also see Kettel, "Debts and Finances of the States—Indiana," pp. 157-158.

75. The later history of the canal can be followed in Benton, *Wabash Trade Route*, pp. 73-85.

76. McGrane, *Foreign Bondholders*, pp. 193-222.

Conclusion

1. Bessie L. Pierce, *A History of Chicago*, vol. 1: *The Beginning of a City* (New York: Alfred Knopf, 1937), pp. 44, 124-128.

2. Butler to his wife, 31 July 1844, Butler Papers, I; and R. Adams to AB, 4 August 1844, BP, 205.

3. Letter of Charles Butler, 17 November 1844, Butler Papers, I.

4. John Wright to FB, 18 November 1847, BP, 208; FB to Samuel Wilson, 11 November 1846, BP, 215; James H. Rees to FB, 10 June 1846, BP, CHS, 52; and Miscellaneous Correspondence, BP, 211.

5. *New York Times*, 14 December 1897, p. 7; and George L. Prentiss, *The Union Theological Seminary in the City of New York: Its Design and Another Decade of Its History* (Asbury Park, New Jersey: M. W. & C. Pennypacker, 1899), pp. 506-524, 530.

6. List of Stockholders of the OLTC, 23 July 1834, BP, 203; Contract of Gould

Hoyt, Charles Hoyt, AB, and Walter Newberry, 1 October 1834, BP, 211; Contract of FB and John Ward, 4 May 1835, BP, 182; FB, Agreements Relating to Cassville, (c. 1850), BP, CHS; and Albert G. Ellis to James B. Murray, 24 February 1836, and Murray to Ellis, 1 February 1836, BP, CHS.

7. See the description of Butler's investments in Chapter 6.

8. Thomas Clark to Thomas Olcott, 30 October 1841, 21 March 1843, and 24 August 1842; Contract of Thomas Olcott, Benjamin Knower and James Thompson, 19 November 1835, Olcott Papers. Also see William G. Shade, *Banks or No Banks, The Money Issue in Western Politics, 1832-1865* (Detroit: Wayne State University Press, 1972), p. 35; and Irene Neu, *Erastus Corning: Merchant and Financier, 1794-1872* (Ithaca: Cornell University Press, 1960), pp. 37-144.

9. See John D. Haeger, "Capital Mobilization and the Urban Center: The Wisconsin Lakeports," *Mid-America* 60 (April-July 1978): 75-93, for a full description of these investors.

10. Larry Gara, *Westernized Yankee* (Madison: State Historical Society of Wisconsin, 1956), pp. 20-41; Edward A. Russell Papers, Chicago Historical Society, Chicago, 1833-1842," *Journal of the Illinois State Historical Society* 64 (Autumn 1971): 275-277; John A. Rockwell Papers, Henry Huntington Library, San Marino, California; U.S. Congress, Senate, *Biographical Directory of the American Congress, 1774-1971* Washington: U.S. Government Printing Office, 1971), p. 1624; and Elmer Baldwin, *History of LaSalle County, Illinois* (Chicago: Rand, McNally and Company, 1877), p. 375.

11. Harold E. Davis, "Economic Basis of Ohio Politics, 1820-1840," *Ohio State Archeological and Historical Quarterly* 47 (October 1938): 313; Ohio, General Assembly, *First Annual Report of the Bank Commissioners of Ohio, Executive Documents* 22, 38th Session, 1839, pp. 78-79; Ohio, General Assembly, *Second Annual Report of the Bank Commissioners of Ohio, Executive Documents* 21, 39th Session, 1840, pp. 52-53.

12. Michigan, House of Representatives, *Report of the Majority and Minority of the Bank Investigating Committee Together with the Minutes of the Committee,* in *Documents Accompanying the Journal of the House of Representatives of the State of Michigan* (Detroit: George Dawson, 1840), House Document 45, 1840, II: 420-422; Jack Kilfoil, "C. C. Trowbridge, Detroit Banker and Michigan Land Speculator, 1820-1845" (Ph.D. dissertation, Claremont Graduate School, 1969), pp. 27-28; Charles C. Trowbridge, *Personal Memoirs of Charles Christopher Trowbridge* (Detroit: n.p., 1893), pp. 24-25; and Harry N. Scheiber, "The Commercial Bank of Lake Erie, 1831-1843," *Business History Review* 30 (Spring 1966): 47-51.

13. Michigan, Senate, *Report of the Select Committee to Investigate the Conduct of the Commissioners Appointed to Settle with the Michigan State Bank,* in *Documents Accompanying the Journal of the Senate* (Detroit: George Dawson, 1841), Senate Document 42, 1841, II:175; Kilfoil, "Trowbridge," pp. 67-68; Neu, *Corning,* p. 147; Frank Otto Gatell, "Spoils of the Bank War: Political Bias in the Selection of Pet Banks," *American Historical Review* 70 (October 1964):56; and Shade, *Banks or No Banks,* p. 35.

14. Illinois, General Assembly, *Reports from the Select Committee to Inquire into the Condition of the State Bank of Illinois, Illinois Reports,* 11th General Assembly, 2nd Session, 1840, pp. 355-359; George Dowrie, *The Development of Banking in Illinois, 1817-1867,* University of Illinois Studies in the Social Sciences, (Urbana: University of Illinois Press, 1913), II: 22-71; Carter Golembe, "State Banks and the Economic Development of the West, 1830-1844" (Ph.D. dissertation, Columbia University, 1952), pp. 40-42; Shade, *Banks or No Banks,* pp. 31-32; and T. Smith to AB, 19 May 1835, BP, 100.

15. Alice Smith, *From Exploration to Statehood,* vol. I: *History of Wisconsin* (Madison: State Historical Society of Wisconsin, 1973), pp. 278-279. Papers Relating to the Organization of the Bank of Wisconsin, 5 August – 2 November 1835, State Historical Society of Wisconsin, Maidson, Wisconsin; AB to Morgan L. Martin, 4 June 1835, Morgan L. Martin Papers, State Historical Society of Wisconsin, Madison, Wisconsin, Box III; John Martin to Morgan L. Martin, 5 October 1835, Martin Papers, Box IV; and Memorandum of Agreement between AB, FB, John Ward, Thomas Olcott, and Daniel Jackson, 3 August 1835, BP, 211.

16. On the later years of the OLTC, see Harry N. Scheiber, *Ohio Canal Era: A Case Study of Government and the Economy, 1820-1861* (Athens, Ohio: Ohio University Press, 1961), pp. 140-158. On the movement of bank capital from East to West, see Michael Conzen, "Capital Flows and the Developing Urban Hierarchy: State Bank Capital in Wisconsin," *Economic Geography* 51 (October 1975):321-338.

17. For a somewhat different view which stresses the difficulty of moving capital into frontier economies, see Lance Davis, "Capital Mobility and American Growth," in *The Reinterpretation of American Economic History,* eds. Robert Fogel and Stanley Engerman (New York: Harper and Row, 1971), pp. 285-287.

18. On Ogden's later career, see Bessie L. Pierce, *A History of Chicago,* vol. 2: *From Town to City, 1848-1871* (New York: Alfred Knopf, 1940), p. 52; and *Chicago Herald,* 5 and 8 June 1893, Butler Papers, IV.

Selected Bibliography

Since the footnotes provide a detailed list of primary sources and discussions of secondary literature wherever appropriate, this bibliography includes only those items on which I relied most heavily.

1. Manuscripts

Albany, New York. Albany Institute of History and Art. Erastus Corning Papers.

Albany, New York. New York State Library. Benjamin F. Butler Papers.

Ann Arbor, Michigan. Bentley Historical Library. University of Michigan. Erie and Kalamazoo Railroad Papers.

Ann Arbor, Michigan. William L. Clements Library. University of Michigan. Lucius Lyon Papers.

Boston, Massachusetts. Baker Library. Harvard University. New York Life Insurance and Trust Company Papers.

Bridgeport, Connecticut. Bridgeport Public Library. Roger M. Sherman Papers.

Chicago, Illinois. Chicago Historical Society. Arthur Bronson Papers.

Chicago, Illinois. Chicago Historical Society. Gurdon S. Hubbard Papers.

Chicago, Illinois. Chicago Historical Society. William B. Ogden Papers.

Chicago, Illinois. Newberry Library. Walter L. Newberry Letters.

Cleveland, Ohio. Western Reserve Historical Society. Elisha Whittlesey Papers.

Cleveland, Ohio. Western Reserve Historical Society. Simon Perkins Papers.

Columbus, Ohio. Ohio State Library. Micajah T. Williams Papers. (This collection is available on microcard.)

Detroit, Michigan. Detroit Public Library. Charles C. Trowbridge Papers.

Fairfield, Connecticut. Farifield Historical Society. Roger M. Sherman Papers.

Hartford, Connecticut. Connecticut State Library. Roger M.Sherman Papers.

Madison, Wisconsin. State Historical Society of Wisconsin. Nelson Dewey Papers.

Madison, Wisconsin. State Historical Society of Wisconsin. John P. Sheldon Papers.

Mt. Pleasant, Michigan. Clarke Historical Library. Central Michigan University. Bronson Family Papers.

New York, New York. Columbia University Library. Thomas B. Olcott Papers.

New York, New York. New York Historical Society. Murray Family Papers.

New York, New York. New York Public Library. Bronson Family Papers.

Washington, D.C. Library of Congress. Charles Butler Papers.

2. Printed Primary Sources

American Land Company. *Catalogue of Lands Belonging to the American Land Company to be Sold at Public Auction . . . 1844.* New York: American Land Company, 1843.

[Bronson, Arthur.] "History of the Bank of ————." In *The Journal of Banking from July, 1841 to July, 1842: Containing Essays on Various Questions Relating to Banking and Currency . . . .* Edited by William Gouge. Philadelphia: J. Van Court, 1842.

Bronson, Isaac. *An Appeal to the Public on the Conduct of the Banks in the City of New York.* New York: Office of the *New York Courier,* 1815.

Beardsley, Levi. *Reminiscences; Personal and Other Incidents; Early Settlement of Otsego County; Notices and Anecdotes of Public Men; Judicial, Legal and Legislative Matters; Field Sports; Dissertations; and Discussions.* New York: Printed by Charles Vinten, 1852.

Butler, Charles. *Communication of the Agent of the Foreign Holders of Indiana State Bonds, to his Excellency James Whitcomb, Governor of Indiana, December, 1845.* Indianapolis: J. P. Chapman Printers, 1845.

————. *Letter of Charles Butler to the Legislature of Indiana in Relation to the Public Debt.* Indianapolis: Morrison and Spann, 1845.

Curtis, Benjamin. "Debts of the States." *North American Review* 58 (January-April 1844):109-157.

First Annual Report of the Trustees of the American Land Company Submitted at a Meeting of the Shareholders, Held in the City of Boston, on the 9th day of June, 1836. New York: E. B. Clayton, 1836.

Ford, Thomas. *A History of Illinois From Its Commencement As a State in 1818 to 1847.* Chicago: S. C. Griggs and Company, 1854.

Hamilton, James A. *Reminiscences of James A. Hamilton; or, Men and Events at Home and Abroad, During Three Quarters of a Century.* New York: Charles Scribners & Co., 1869.

Hopkins, William R. *Report of a New Town at the Foot of Lake Huron.* Geneva, New York: Mattison and Haskell Printer, 1837.

Mackenzie, William L. *The Lives and Opinions of Benj'n Franklin Butler and Jesse Hoyt.* Boston: Cook and Co., 1845.

————. *The Life and Times of Martin Van Buren: The Correspondence of His Friends, Family and Pupils. . . .* Boston: Cook and Co., 1846.

New York City Citizens. *Outline of a Plan for a National Bank, With Incidental Remarks on the Bank of the United States.* New York: Newcomb and Cropsey, 1833.

New York Life Insurance and Trust Company, Act of Incorporation, Passed March 9, 1830. New York: Bowne and Co., 1850.

New York State, Senate. *Communication from the Chancellor Relative to the New York Life Insurance and Trust Company.* Senate Doc. 112, 55th Session, 1832, II.

New York State, Senate. *Communication from the Chancellor Relative to the New York Life Insurance and Trust Company.* Senate Doc. 59, 57th Session, 1834, II.

New York State, Assembly. *Communication from the Chancellor Relative to the New York Life Insurance and Trust Company.* Assembly Doc. 284, 58th Session, 1835, IV.

Ohio Life Insurance and Trust Company. *An Act to Incorporate the Ohio LIfe Insurance and Trust Company.* New York: E. B. Clayton, 1834.

Ohio Life Insurance and Trust Company. *The First Annual Report of the Ohio Life Insurance and Trust Company.* Columbus, Ohio: Jacob Medary, Jr. and Co., 1835.

Ohio Life Insurance and Trust Company. *The Second Annual Report of the Ohio Life Insurance and Trust Company.* Cincinnati: Looker, Ramsay and Co., 1836.

Ohio Life Insurance and Trust Company. *The Third Annual Report of the Ohio Life Insurance and Trust Company.* Cincinnati: Looker, Ramsay and Co., 1837.

Ohio Life Insurance and Trust Company. *The Charter and By-Laws of the Ohio Life Insurance and Trust Company.* Cincinnati: Morgan and Sanxay, 1834.

Sherman, Roger. *Letters to the Honourable Levi Woodbury, Secretary of the Treasury of the United States.* New York: E. B. Clayton, 1837.

Trowbridge, Charles C. *Personal Memoirs of Charles Christopher Trowbridge.* Detroit: n.p., 1893.

3. Books

Adams, Donald. *Finance and Enterprise in Early America.* Philadelphia: University of Pennsylvania Press, 1978.

Albion, Robert G. *The Rise of New York Port.* New York: Charles Scribner's Sons, 1939.

Billington, Ray. *America's Frontier Heritage.* 4th ed. New York: MacMillan Publishing Co., 1974.

Bogue, Allan G. *Money at Interest.* Ithaca: Cornell University Press, 1955.

Boorstin, Daniel J. *The Americans: The National Experience.* New York: Random House, 1965.

Brock, William R. *Parties and Political Conscience: American Dilemmas, 1840-1850.* Millwood, New York: KTO Press, 1979.

Bronson, Henry. *The History of Waterbury, Connecticut.* Waterbury: Published by the Bronson Brothers, 1858.

Brown, Richard D. *Modernization: The Transformation of American Life, 1600-1865.* New York: Hill and Wang, 1976.

Bruchey, Stuart. *The Roots of American Economic Growth, 1607-1861.* New York: Harper and Row, 1968.

Buley, R. Carlyle. *The Old Northwest, 1815-1840.* 2 vols. Bloomington: Indiana University Press, 1951.

Cameron, Rondo, ed. *Banking and Economic Development.* New York: Oxford University Press, 1972.

Chandler, Alfred D. *The Visible Hand.* Cambridge: Harvard University Press, 1977.

Cochran, Thomas C. *Business in American Life: A History.* New York: McGraw-Hill, 1972.

Cohen, Henry. *Business and Politics in America from the Age of Jackson to the Civil War: The Career Biography of W. W. Corcoran.* Westport, Connecticut: Greenwood Publishing Co., 1971.

Davis, Lance, and North, Douglas. *Institutional Change and American Economic Development.* London: Cambridge University Press, 1971.

Davis, Lance; Easterlin, Richard; et. al. *American Economic Growth.* New York: Harper and Row, 1972.

Doyle, Don H. *The Social Order of a Frontier Community, Jacksonville, Illinois, 1825-1870.* Urbana: University of Illinois Press, 1978.

Dykstra, Robert. *The Cattle Towns.* New York: Atheneum, 1970.

Ellis, David, ed. *The Frontier in American Development.* Ithaca: Cornell University Press, 1969.

Everett, Edward, ed. *The Early Writings of Frederick Jackson Turner.* Madison: University of Wisconsin Press, 1938.

Fogel, Robert W., and Engerman, Stanley, eds. *The Reinterpretation of American Economic History.* New York: Harper and Row, 1971.

Formisano, Ronald. *The Birth of Mass Political Parties, Michigan, 1827-1861.* Princeton, New Jersey: Princeton University Press, 1971.

Freyer, Tony Allan. *Forums for Order: The Federal Courts and Business in American History.* Greenwich, Connecticut: JAI Press, 1979.

Friedman, Lawrence. *Contract Law in America.* Madison: University of Wisconsin Press, 1965.

———. *A History of American Law.* New York: Simon and Schuster, 1973.

Gates, Paul. *History of Public Land Law Development.* Washington: U.S. Government Printing Office, 1968.

———. *Landlords and Tenants on the Prairie Fronter, Studies in American Land Policy.* Ithaca: Cornell University Press, 1973.

Graham, Howard J. *Everyman's Constitution*. Madison: State Historical Society of Wisconsin, 1968.

Green, George D. *Finance and Economic Development in the Old South: Louisiana Banking, 1804-1861*. Stanford: Stanford University Press, 1972.

Greesley, Gene. *Bankers and Cattlemen*. New York: Alfred A. Knopf, 1966.

Hammond, Bray. *Banks and Politics in America from the Revolution to the Civil War*. Princeton, New Jersey: Princeton University Press, 1957.

Herrick, Clay. *Trust Companies, Their Organization, Growth and Management*. New York: Bankers Publishing Company, 1915.

Horwitz, Morton J. *The Transformation of American Law, 1790-1860*. Cambridge: Harvard University Press, 1976.

Hoyt, Homer. *One Hundred Years of Land Values in Chicago*. Chicago: University of Chicago Press, 1933.

Hurst, James Willard. *Law and the Conditions of Freedom in the Nineteenth Century United States*. Madison: University of Wisconsin Press, 1956.

Johnson, Arthur M., and Supple, Barry E. *Boston Capitalists and Western Railroads*. Cambridge: Harvard University Press, 1967.

Klingaman, David C., and Vedder, Richard, eds. *Essays in Nineteenth Century Economic History, The Old Northwest*. Athens, Ohio: Ohio University Press, 1975.

Kim, Sung Bok. *Landlord and Tenant in Colonial New York*. Chapel Hill, North Carolina: University of North Carolina Press, 1978.

Lanier, Henry. *A Century of Banking in New York, 1822-1922*. New York: The Gillis Press, 1922.

Latner, Richard B. *The Presidency of Andrew Jackson*. Athens, Georgia: The University of Georgia Press, 1979.

Lindstrom, Diane. *Economic Development in the Philadelphia Region, 1810-1850*. New York: Columbia University Press, 1977.

MacRury, Elizabeth. *More About the Hill—Greenfield Hill*. North Haven, Connecticut: City Printing Company, 1968.

McFaul, John. *The Politics of Jacksonian Finance*. Ithaca: Cornell University Press, 1972.

McGrane, Reginald C. *Foreign Bondholders and American State Debts*. New York: The MacMillan Company, 1935.

McNall, Neil. *An Agricultural History of the Genesee Valley, 1790-1860*. Philadelphia: University of Pennsylvania Press, 1952.

Miller, Douglas T. *Jacksonian Aristocracy: Class and Democracy in New York, 1830-1860*. New York: Oxford University Press, 1967.

Miller, Nathan. *The Enterprise of a Free People: Aspects of Economic Development in New York State During the Canal Period, 1792-1838*. Ithaca: Cornell University Press, 1962.

Neu, Irene. *Erastus Corning: Merchant and Financier, 1794-1872.* Ithaca: Cornell University Press, 1960.

North, Douglas C. *The Economic Growth of the United States, 1790-1860.* New York: W. W. Norton and Co., 1966.

————. *Growth and Welfare in the American Past.* 2nd ed. Englewood Cliffs, New Jersey: Prentice-Hall, Inc., 1974.

Olmstead, Alan L. *New York Savings Banks in the Antebellum Years, 1819-1861.* Chapel Hill, North Carolina: University of North Carolina Press, 1975.

Parks, Robert J. *Democracy's Railroads: Public Enterprise in Jacksonian Michigan.* Port Washington, New York: Kennikat Press, 1972.

Pessen, Edward. *Riches, Class, and Power Before the Civil War.* Lexington, Massachusetts: D. C. Heath and Co., 1973.

————. *Jacksonian America: Society, Personality, and Politics.* 2nd ed. Homewood, Illinois: The Dorsey Press, 1978.

Pierce, Bessie L. *A History of Chicago.* Vol. I: *The Beginning of a City, 1673-1848.* New York: Alfred A. Knopf, 1937.

Porter, Kenneth W. *John Jacob Astor, Businessman.* 2 vols. New York: Harvard University Press, 1931.

Pred, Allan R. *Urban Growth and the Circulation of Information: The United States System of Cities, 1790-1840.* Cambridge: Harvard University Press, 1973.

Prentiss, George L. *The Union Theological Seminary in the City of New York: Its Design and Another Decade in Its History. With a Sketch of the Life and Public Service of Charles Butler.* Asbury Park, New Jersey: M. W. & C. Pennypacker, 1899.

Redlich, Fritz. *The Molding of American Banking: Men and Ideas. Part I: 1781-1840.* New York: Hafner Publishing Co., 1951.

Remini, Robert V. *Andrew Jackson and the Bank War.* New York: W. W. Norton and Co., 1967.

————. *Martin Van Buren and the Making of the Democratic Party.* New York: Columbia University Press, 1959.

Rohrbough, Malcolm. *The Land Office Business.* New York: Oxford University Press, 1968.

————. *The Trans-Appalachian Frontier.* New York: Oxford University Press, 1978.

Scheiber, Harry N. *Ohio Canal Era: A Case Study of Government and the Economy, 1820-1861.* Athens, Ohio: The Ohio University Press, 1961.

Schlesinger, Arthur M. *The Age of Jackson.* Boston: Little, Brown and Company, 1945.

Shade, William G. *Banks or No Banks, The Money Issue in Western Politics, 1832-1865.* Detroit: Wayne State University Press, 1972.

Smith, Alice E. *James Duane Doty, Frontier Promoter.* Madison: State Historical Society of Wisconsin, 1954.

Smith, Alice. *From Exploration to Statehood.* Vol 1. *History of Wisconsin.* Madison: State Historical Society of Wisconsin, 1973.

Smith, James G. *The Development of Trust Companies in the United States.* New York: Henry Holt and Co., 1927.

Stoddard, Francis H. *The Life and Letters of Charles Butler.* New York: Charles Scribner's Sons, 1903.

Swierenga, Robert P. *Acres for Cents: Delinquent Tax Auctions in Frontier Iowa.* Westport, Connecticut: Greenwood Press, 1976.

————. *Pioneers and Profits: Land Speculation on the Iowa Frontier.* Ames, Iowa: Iowa State University Press, 1968.

Temin, Peter. *The Jacksonian Economy.* New York: W. W. Norton and Co., 1969.

Timberlake, Richard. *The Origins of Central Banking in the United States.* Cambridge: Harvard University Press, 1978.

Turner, Frederick Jackson. *The Frontier in American History.* New York: Henry Holt and Company, 1921.

Van Deusen, Glyndon. *The Jacksonian Era, 1828-1848.* New York: Harper Torchbooks, 1959.

Van Fenstermaker, J. *The Development of American Commercial Banking: 1782-1837.* Kent, Ohio: Kent State University, Bureau of Economic and Business Research, 1965.

Wade, Richard. *The Urban Frontier: The Rise of Western Cities, 1790-1830.* Cambridge: Harvard University Press, 1959.

White, Gerald T. *A History of the Massachusetts Hospital Life Insurance Company.* Cambridge: Harvard University Press, 1955.

4. Articles and Dissertations

Abbot, Carl. "The Divergent Development of Cincinnati, Indianapolis, Chicago and Galena, 1840-1960: Economic Thought and Economic Growth." Ph.D. dissertation, University of Chicago, 1971.

Billington, Ray. "The Origins of the Land Speculator as a Frontier Type." *Agricultural History* 19 (October 1945):204-212.

Bogue, Allan G. "Farming in the Prairie Peninsula, 1830-1890." *Journal of Economic History* 33 (March 1963):3-29.

————. "Land Credit for Northern Farmers." *Agricultural History* 50 (January 1976):68-100.

Bogue, Allan G., and Bogue, Margaret. "Profit and the Frontier Land Speculator." *Journal of Economic History* 17 (March 1957):1-24.

Brewer, H. Peers. "Eastern Money and Western Mortgages in the 1870s." *Business History Review* 50 (Autumn 1976):356-380.

Callender, G. S. "The Early Transportation and Banking Enterprises of the States in Relation to the Growth of Corporations." *The Quarterly Journal of Economics* 17 (November 1902):111-162.

Clayton, James. "The Growth and Economic Significance of the American Fur Trade, 1790-1890." In *Aspects of the Fur Trade: Selected Papers of the 1965 North American Fur Trade Conference*, edited by Russell Fridley. St. Paul, Minnesota: Minnesota Historical Society, 1967.

Cochran, Thomas C. "The Business Revolution." *American Historical Review* 79 (December 1974):1449-1466.

————. "The History of a Business Society." *Journal of American History* 54 (June 1967):5-18.

Conzen, Michael. "Capital Flows and the Developing Urban Hierarchy: State Bank Capital in Wisconsin." *Economic Geography* 51 (October 1975):321-338.

Davis, Harold. "Elisha Whittlesey and Maumee Land Speculation, 1834-1840." *Northwest Ohio Quarterly* 15 (July 1943):139-158.

Davis, Lance. "Capital Immobilities and Finance Capitalism: A Study of Economic Evolution in the United States, 1820-1920." *Explorations in Entrepreneurial History* 1 (Fall 1963):88-105.

————. "The New England Textile Mills and the Capital Markets: A Study of Industrial Borrowing, 1840-1860." *Journal of Economic History* 20 (March 1960):1-30.

Davison, Kenneth. "Forgotten Ohioan: Elisha Whittlesey, 1783-1863." Ph.D. dissertation, Case Western Reserve University, 1953.

Dorfman, Joseph. "A Note on the Interpenetration of Anglo-American Finance 1837-1844." *Journal of Economic History 11 (Spring 1951):140-147.*

Ekirch, Arthur Jr. "Benjamin Franklin Butler of New York: A Personal Portrait." *New York History* 58 (January 1977):47-68.

Formisano, Ronald P. "Toward a Reorientation of Jacksonian Politics: A Review of the Literature, 1959-1975." *Journal of American History* 63 (June 1976): 42-65.

Freyer, Tony Allan. "Negotiable Instruments and the Federal Courts in Antebellum American Business." *Business History Review* 50 (Winter 1976):435-455.

————. "The Federal Courts, Localism, and the National Economy, 1865-1900." *Business History Review* 53 (Autumn 1979):344-363.

Gatell, Frank Otto. "Sober Second Thoughts on Van Buren, the Albany Regency, and the Wall Street Conspiracy." *Journal of American History* 53 (June 1966):19-40.

————. "Money and Party in Jacksonian America: A Quantitative Look at New York City's Men of Quality." *Political Science Quarterly* 82 (June 1967):235-252.

Gates, Paul W. "Frontier Land Business in Wisconsin." *Wisconsin Magazine of History* 52 (Summer 1969):306-327.

————. "The Role of the Land Speculator in Western Development." *Pennsylvania Magazine of History and Biography* 66 (July 1942):314-333.

Golembe, Carter. "State Banks and the Economic Development of the West, 1830-1844." Ph.D. dissertation, Columbia University, 1952.

Haeger, John D. "Eastern Money and the Urban Frontier: Chicago, 1833-1842." *Journal of the Illinois State Historical Society* 64 (Autumn 1971):267-284.

———. "Capital Mobilization and the Urban Center: The Wisconsin Lakeports." *Mid-America* 60 (April-July 1978):75-93.

———. "Eastern Financiers and Institutional Change: The Origins of the New York Life Insurance and Trust Company and the Ohio Life Insurance and Trust Company." *Journal of Economic History* 39 (March 1979):259-273.

Hale, Robert. "The Supreme Court and the Contract Clause." *Harvard Law Review* 57 (April 1944):512-892.

Hammond, Bray. "Long and Short Term Credit in Early American Banking." *Quarterly Journal of Economics* 49 (November 1943):79-103.

———. "Banking in the Early West: Monopoly, Prohibition and Laissez Faire." *Journal of Economic History* 14 (May 1948):1-25.

Huntington, C. C. "A History of Banking and Currency in Ohio Before the Civil War." *Ohio Archaeological and Historical Quarterly* 24 (1915):235-539.

Jaher, Frederic Cople. "Old and New Elites and Entrepreneurial Activity in New York City from 1780 to 1850." *Working Papers from the Regional Economic History Research Center* 2 (1978):55-78.

Kilfoil, Jack. "C. C. Trowbridge, Detroit Banker and Michigan Land Speculator, 1820-1845." Ph.D, dissertation, Claremont Graduate School, 1969.

Latner, Richard B. "A New Look at Jacksonian Politics." *Journal of American History* 61 (March 1975):943-969.

Luckingham, Bradford. "The City in the Westward Movement—A Bibliographical Note." *Western Historical Quarterly* 5 (July 1974):295-306.

McLear, Patrick. "William Butler Ogden: A Chicago Promoter in the Speculative Era and the Panic of 1837." *Journal of the Illinois State Historical Society* 70 (November 1977):283-291.

Morrison, Grant. "Isaac Bronson and the Search for System in American Capitalism." Ph.D. dissertation, City University of New York, 1974.

North, Douglas. "International Capital Flows and the Development of the American West." *Journal of Economic History* 16 (December 1956):493-505.

Pessen, Edward. "The Egalitarian Myth and the American Social Reality: Wealth, Mobility, and Equality in the 'Era of the Common Man'." *American Historical Review* 76 (October 1971):989-1034.

———. "The Wealthiest New Yorkers of the Jacksonian Era: A New List." *New York Historical Society Quarterly* 54 (April 1970):145-172.

Priest, George. "Law and Economic Distress: Sangamon County, Illinois, 1837-1844." *The Journal of Legal Studies* 2 (June 1973):469-492.

Putnam, Jackson. "The Turner Thesis and the Westward Movement: A Reappraisal." *Western Historical Quarterly* 7 (October 1969):377-404.

Remini, Robert V. "The Albany Regency." *New York History* 39 (October
1958):341-355.

Rockhoff, Hugh. "The Free Banking Era, A Reexamination." *Journal of Money,
Credit and Banking* 6 (May 1974):141-167.

————. "Varieties of Banking and Regional Economic Development in the United
States, 1840-1860." *Journal of Economic History* 35 (March 1975):160-181.

Scheiber, Harry N. "The Commercial Bank of Lake Erie, 1831-1843." *Business
History Review* 30 (Spring 1966):47-65.

————. "Entrepreneurship and Western Development: The Case of Micajah T.
Williams." *Business History Review* 37 (Winter 1963):345-368.

Shade, William. "The Background of the Michigan Free Banking Law." *Michigan
History* 52 (Fall 1968):229-244.

————. "Banks and Politics in Michigan, 1835-1845: A Reconsideration." *Michigan
History* 57 (Spring 1973):28-52.

Shirigian, John. "Lucius Lyon: His Place in Michigan History." Ph.D. dissertation,
University of Michigan, 1961.

Silsby, Robert. "Mortgage Credit in the Phelps-Gorham Purchase." *New York
History* 41 (January 1960):3-34.

Skilton, Robert H. "Developments in Mortgage Law and Practice." *Temple University Law Quarterly* 17 (August 1943):315-384.

Soltow, James. "The Entrepreneur in Economic History." *American Economic Review* 58 (May 1968):84-92.

Soltow, Lee. "Inequality Amidst Abundance: Land Ownership in Early Nineteenth
Century Ohio." *Ohio History* 88 (Spring 1979):133-147.

Swierenga, Robert P. "Land Speculation and Its Impact on American Economic
Growth and Welfare: A Historiographical Review." *Western Historical Quarterly* 8
(July 1977):283-302.

Sylla, Richard. "American Banking and Growth in the Nineteenth Century: A
Partial View of the Terrain." *Explorations in Economic History* 9 (Winter 1971-
1972):197-227.

————. "Forgotten Men of Money: Private Bankers in Early U.S. History." *Journal
of Economic History* 36 (March 1976):173-188.

Venit, Abraham. "Isaac Bronson: His Banking Theories and the Financial Controversies of the Jacksonian Period." *Journal of Economic History* 5 (November
1945):201-214.

Index